ON BEING A
MISSIONARY

THOMAS HALE

William Carey Library

Pasadena, California

Published by
William Carey Library
P. O. Box 40129
Pasadena, California 91114
(626) 798-0819

Library of Congress Cataloging-in-Publication Data

Hale, Thomas, 1937-
    On being a missionary / by Thomas Hale, Jr.
        p.   cm.
    Includes bibliographical references (p.   )
    ISBN 0-87808-255-7 (pbk.)
    1. Missionaries. 2. Missions--Nepal. I. Title.
    BV2061.H32 1994   94-31473
    255--dc20   CIP

Cover Design by Chi-Gee Wu

Author's Home Mission:
InterServe (International Service Fellowship)
Box 418
Upper Darby, PA 19802

Author's Field Mission:
United Mission to Nepal
Box 126
Kathmandu, Nepal

Other Books by the Author
Don't Let the Goats Eat the Loquat Trees
Living Stones of the Himalayas
On the Far Side of Liglig Mountain

7   6

Printed in the United States of America

iv   *Contents*

Contents

Preface

This book is not designed to be a theoretical textbook. It does not put forward new theses, new approaches to mission. It makes no attempt to break new ground. Instead, I have tried to absorb and then to present in a readable way the ideas, experiences, and insights of over a hundred missionary writers, the majority of whom are listed in the bibliography. I am indebted to all of these writers.

I want to expressly acknowledge the following authors as being particularly helpful to me in the writing of certain chapters: Dwight Carlson, Marjorie Collins, Marjory Foyle, David Hesselgrave, J. Herbert Kane, Dennis Kinlaw, David Seamands, John Stott, Christy Wilson, Ralph Winter.

I also want to thank the many wonderful missionary colleagues I have known, who have been for me an inspiration and an example—in particular, my lifelong partner and wife, Cynthia. To her this book is dedicated.

Except where individuals are specifically named, biographical details of people referred to in this book have occasionally been altered to protect their identities. Other than this, the incidents related are true. I write in the belief that there is no higher or more glorious calling than that of being a missionary of Jesus Christ. It is a subject worth writing about.

1

Why Missionaries?

It's easier to write about missionaries than to be one. If it weren't so, I'd stop right here.

Writing a book about being a missionary doesn't mean one has mastered the subject. It doesn't even mean one has been a successful missionary. This book is written by a learner for learners.

Missionaries make a broad subject. They represent almost every profession, prostitution and racketeering excepted. They come short-term, long-term. Some come as students, some are retirees. Some are church-supported, some self-supported. Some come under mission boards and societies; some come independently. They come from the First World, they come from the Third World, and they go to all the world.

In this book we don't talk of "sending nations" and "receiving nations." Almost every nation has become a "sending nation." Indeed, within a few years there will be more missionaries going out from the Third World than from the First World. Already the Third World has more evangelical Christians than the First World, charismatics included. The balance has shifted. The missionary enterprise has become truly international.

Though this book is necessarily written from a First World perspective, much of its content applies equally to missionaries from the Third World. Even those problems which seem peculiarly related to the Western missionary will, with some modification, be faced by most Third World missionaries as well. It is hoped, therefore, that they also will find this book instructive.

Several comprehensive books about missionaries have been written over the past fifty years, but they have been mainly didactic in nature. In this volume I hope to make the missionary experience more real and vivid through the generous use of stories and illustrations. Most of these illustrations are taken from the country of Nepal, where my wife Cynthia and I have worked since 1970; the remainder (with a few exceptions) come from the wider subcontinent of India. However, let it not be supposed that this limits the scope of the book to those working in that region. Far from it; simply change a few background details, and what is written here becomes the common experience of missionaries working anyplace in the world.

This book is not a manual. Marjorie Collins has written an excellent manual filled with detailed advice you won't find here; it's called, appropriately, *A Manual For Today's Missionary.*

This book is not primarily concerned with theology or mission strategy. It is not a handbook on how to plant churches or how to start a mission hospital. Neither is it a treatise on anthropology, comparative religion, or cross-cultural communication. Rather, it is a book about *being* a missionary, what it's like, what the problems are, the challenges, the heartaches, the joys.

This book is written for everyone who has an interest in missions, from the praying and giving supporter back home to the missionary on the field or about to be. It is hoped that through reading this book many will be led to reconsider what role God would have them play in the missionary enterprise. It is hoped that some will be challenged to go, and that others will be challenged to send them. And it is further hoped that those who go will be more fruitful missionaries for their having read about the struggles and failings of their predecessors.

Yes, this book does deal with the problems, struggles, and failures of missionaries. Because it's from these that we learn the most. Missionary life is two parts joy and fulfillment and one part frustration and defeat. We can only hope to reduce the frustration and defeat by facing it, not by denying it. Far from wanting to scare off missionary candidates, we want to insure that when they get to the field they will be able to avoid many of the problems that have plagued others. Being a missionary is one of the most joyous and rewarding careers possible, and this book aims to make it even more so.

Should we still be sending missionaries?

If the answer is "no," then you can skip the rest of this book. But, in fact, the answer is a resounding "yes."

Whenever missionaries go on furlough they are likely to be asked to speak on the biblical basis of missions. It's as if people needed to be re-assured that missions and missionaries were really necessary. After all, a lot of hard-earned money is flittering off into those foreign lands, when what the church at home really needs is a new parking lot. Oddly, when it comes to defending their calling, missionaries themselves are among the most inarticulate. Many simply say, "I was called."

And that is the heart of it. It is not "we" who send missionaries; it is God. Throughout the Bible, God is revealed to be a sending God. He sent Abraham to the land of Canaan; he sent Joseph to Egypt; he sent Moses to rescue his people; and he sent prophet after prophet to the Jews with both warnings and promises. Finally he sent John to announce the coming of the Messiah. And then he sent his Son.

So, what about us? Does he send us too? The answer is "yes." Jesus told us to pray for workers for the harvest fields. The workers are us. Jesus said, "As the Father has sent me, I am sending you" (Jn 20:21). And he means all of us. And at the end of his earthly life, Jesus gave to his followers a final commission: "Therefore go and make disciples of all nations, baptizing them in the name of the Father and of the Son and of the Holy Spirit, and teaching them to obey everything I have commanded you" (Mt 28:19-20). "...teaching them"—that is, new disciples, us—"to obey everything I have commanded you." "Everything" includes the Great Commission itself. Therefore, this Commission is for every Christian. Every Christian is sent, even as Jesus was sent.

What did Jesus mean by saying, "As the Father has sent me, I am sending you"? Certainly we are not sent as saviors. No, we are sent as servants. Jesus "did not come to be served, but to serve" (Mk 10:45). And, in the same way, he is sending us to serve. He is our example. After he had washed the disciples' feet, Jesus said to them, "I have set you an example..." (Jn 13:15).

Jesus went throughout Galilee "teaching...preaching...and healing" (Mt 4:23). He was sent "to preach good news to the poor...to proclaim freedom for the prisoners and recovery of sight for the blind, to release the oppressed, to proclaim the year of the Lord's favor" (Lk 4:18-19). These are all the things that Jesus did, and we are sent to do them likewise. But just doing them is not enough; we must do them in the way Jesus did them. And, in order to do that, we need two things that only Jesus can give us: his love and his mind, or attitude.

First, Jesus' love. Jesus had compassion on the multitudes. Without his love, all our efforts will be in vain. Paul said, "If I give all I possess to the poor and surrender my body to the flames, but have not love, I gain nothing" (1 Co 13:3). Jesus' love is poured into our hearts by the Holy Spirit; all we have to do is ask. "Ask and it will be given to you" (Mt 7:7).

Second, we need Jesus' attitude. Paul wrote to the Philippians, "Your attitude should be the same as that of Christ Jesus: Who...made himself nothing, taking the very nature of a servant" (Php 2:5-7). Jesus' service was sacrificial, costly. He identified with people in their problems, in their sufferings. He didn't merely give a donation; he gave himself.

This is the love and the attitude we need if our service is to be pleasing and useful to God. Equipped with Jesus' love and Jesus' attitude, we will be able to serve as Jesus did. Our calling is nothing less.

So, we have examined the one major and compelling reason why missionaries must continue to be sent: Because it is God's will. It is his method of bringing the gospel of Jesus to the world.

Sometimes two objections are raised at this point. First, some people say: Why not just send money to support missionaries from the Third World? They are a lot cheaper and usually more effective.

True. Supporting a Third World missionary costs a fraction of what it costs to support a Western missionary, and the Third World missionary is often (but by no means always) more effective in evangelism than his Western counterpart. But there are simply not enough Third World missionaries to do the job alone—even given their increasing numbers. And there are many places Third World missionaries can't easily get to. Sending missionaries is the responsibility of the entire worldwide church: "All nations to all nations."

Furthermore, if Western churches were to begin sending only checks, their vital commitment to missions would decrease. Our commitment will only be maintained by sending our own sons and daughters out as missionaries—and ourselves as well. God didn't send a check; he sent his son.

Jesus said, "The harvest is plentiful but the workers are few" (Mt 9:37). It's an absolute shame the way some people say, "Don't send Western workers; just send money. Support only the indigenous church." Should we send money to support Third World missionaries? You bet we should; plenty more than we have been. But it's not a question of "either...or." It's a question of "both...and." The job is enormous. Third World missionaries can't any more do the job alone than First World missionaries. We need to give unstintingly of our resources, both in supporting Third World missionaries and in sending out our own. The day of the Western missionary is not over.

"Ask the Lord of the harvest, therefore, to send out workers" (Mt 9:38). Will you obey Jesus' command to pray for workers? We needn't be concerned about where the workers will come from; we are only told to pray. But sometimes, I think, we're afraid to pray for workers. We're afraid of what God might say to us. For he may say something like this: "Oh, so you're praying for workers, are you? Okay, I'll send *you.* And when I see you out in the fields with sweat on your brow, laboring in the hot sun for all you're worth, then I'll send more workers to help you."

Many is the missionary who will testify that he prayed this prayer for workers—and God sent him!

The second objection raised to sending more missionaries goes like this. People say: "Why not rely more on radio and literature—on technology? God has promised that his word will not return empty. We have Jesus films, four spiritual laws, tracts, and gospel portions galore. Let's flood these countries with literature, videos, radio waves. Then there'd be much less need for missionaries; we can do the job by remote control."

Not true. I do not deny the crucial value of technology. But those working in semi-closed countries (there are no "closed" countries) testify unanimously that without flesh-and-blood messengers the word itself is much less effective in winning people to Christ. The word needs to be embodied in loving and sacrificial service for it to be most effective. God's ultimate method is the messenger. People can hear and hear and hear, but they need to meet the witness. Jesus said, "...you will be my witnesses" (Ac 1:8).

There is hardly a country in the world that is completely closed to Christian witnesses. Yes, they live under heavy restrictions in many cases, whether they be from the Third World or the First. But the fact is that Christians can enter even the most restricted countries as students, English teachers, tentmakers, and tourists. And for years to come, the majority of these unconventional missionaries will be coming from the West. This is hardly the time, therefore, to tell the Western church to stop sending its people overseas!

It is God who opens doors. And he has opened more doors today than there are Christians ready to go through them.

Missions is for everyone

The church is missionary in nature. Missions is the task of every member, not just a few. In the early church, missions gave rise to theology. Missions isn't just one subject in a seminary curriculum; it lies at the heart of all subjects. Missions is what makes theology relevant. It's what makes seminaries relevant. It keeps seminaries and churches from becoming inward-looking and self-absorbed—which is a good definition of putting one's lamp "under a bowl" (Mt 5:15).

There can be no divorce between theology and missions. Theology should inspire missions; after all, God's word is full of missions. As academic disciplines, theology and missions are, of course, distinct, and must be taught distinctly. Seminaries and Bible colleges must offer courses in missions, cross-cultural communication, non-Christian religions, and related subjects. But these should be core courses, not electives. Missions is the province of every Christian, not just of specialists.

Jesus told us to "go." First to Jerusalem, then to Judea and Samaria, and then "to the ends of the earth" (Ac 1:8). This means that *all* Christians are to go and be witnesses—to their families, to their neighborhoods, to their cities. In other words, all Christians are called to be "missionaries" in the broad sense of that word. This is terribly important. The word "missionary" means "one sent on a mission." Every Christian is sent into the world on a mission.

Sometimes you see posters in churches that read: "A few go, some give, all pray." That's absolutely wrong! All go, all give, all pray. That is the biblical teaching.

No one can say: "Since I'm not called to be a missionary, I don't have to evangelize my friends and neighbors." There is no difference, in spiritual terms, between a missionary witnessing in his home town and a missionary witnessing in Kathmandu, Nepal. We are all called to go— even if it is only to the next room, or the next block. We are all called to be Christ's witnesses by word and by deed.

There is no biblical basis for elevating the "foreign missionary" to a superior status. He or she should get no more attention than the Christian who works in the city mission or spends time evangelizing his neighborhood or gives himself in any kind of sacrificial service to the Lord. The value of our work is not based on whether or not we have crossed geographic or cultural boundaries; it is based on our love for Christ and our obedience to him. Very simply, the call is to all, and it is to all places where God has need of us, whether it be "Jerusalem," "Judea and Samaria," or "the ends of the earth."

So let us refrain from glamorizing foreign missionary work. If anything, it's the work in our inner cities that needs "glamorizing." There is no more "real" missionary work than that. It's a hundred times more dangerous living in New York City than living in Kathmandu—unless, of course, you're on a bicycle, in which case it's fifty-fifty. Even for those first disciples Jerusalem was the most dangerous spot on earth. And yet, in another sense, "Jerusalem" is our testing ground. We must always be open to God's voice telling us, "Now is the time to move on."

One goes to church missions conferences where the church is hoping its young people will catch the missionary vision. But what's needed is for everyone to catch the vision. Jesus wants to send every one of his disciples somewhere, whether across the sea or across the street. And as for the young people, when they see their elders going, they'll go too.

"Of course, elders don't need to consider going far away." Don't be too sure about that. Some of the best foreign missionaries are people in their retirement years. There is no age limit on God's call. Furthermore, maturity is something the foreign mission field needs desperately.

In one sense, then, this book has been written for every Christian. Most of the subjects dealt with in this book apply not only to the "foreign field," but also to Christians who stay at home. The book could have almost as aptly been titled, "On Being a Christian."

Having said all this, however, I am going to limit the use of the word "missionary" in this book to its more narrow and conventional sense of "cross-cultural witness." The reason is twofold. First, there are some peculiarities about crossing cultures that set this kind of witnessing apart from witnessing in one's own culture. Second, the vast majority of unreached people are not found in the main Western cultures; they are found in the cultures of Asia, Africa, and Latin America—and, to a lesser extent, the inner-city ghettos of the West. The greatest need today is to reach these people, and to do so requires crossing cultures. If every church were to continue witnessing only within its own culture, these people would never be reached. Thus, in limiting the use of the word "missionary" to "cross-cultural witness," we are highlighting the particularly urgent need for this special kind of witness.

Consider the figures. There are two billion unreached people in the world who have not yet had the chance to hear the gospel presented in a way they can understand. Then when we look at what we Christians are doing about this, we find that of every hundred dollars raised in Western churches, ninety-nine are spent on Christians; only one dollar is spent directly for non-Christians. And of that dollar, less than ten cents is spent to reach these two billion unreached people. As someone has said, "We Christians tithe to ourselves."

On the personnel side, taking into account evangelical Christians alone, only one in a thousand goes into cross-cultural ministry—that is, becomes a missionary. And of those who do, over ninety percent end up working in areas that have already been evangelized. An almost imperceptible shift (or better, increase) in resources could triple or quadruple the amount of people and funds available for reaching the two billion unreached. And a modest increase could make a hundredfold difference. Is that really too much to ask of the church, which is meant to be the light of the world?

Clearly, if the world is to be reached any time soon, it is going to take, in the words of Lausanne II, "the whole church taking the whole gospel to the whole world." There is no room for bystanders.

Clarifying some issues

We have said that every Christian is a witness, but that not every Christian is a missionary (by our definition). A missionary is any Christian who crosses cultural boundaries to further the building of Christ's church and the expansion of God's kingdom. The title "missionary" presupposes that one has crossed cultures for the express purpose of advancing God's kingdom and has received God's call to do so. True, one may get such a call some time after arriving in a cross-cultural situation, but one cannot properly be termed a missionary without having been called, and without having made a purposeful decision to obey that call. Missionaries don't happen by accident. You're not a missionary simply because you wake up one day in a foreign country. You're not a missionary if you're simply out for a joy ride, or for adventure, or to get away from your in-laws or the Internal Revenue Service. You are a missionary only insofar as you are obedient to a call.

Though the missionary's work differs in many respects from the work of those who stay at home, the missionary will still be rewarded on the same basis as every other Christian. To what extent was his or her purpose the glory of God? To what extent was his or her motive the love of Christ? To what extent were his or her means the power of the Holy Spirit? Let the missionary not build with "wood, hay or straw" (1 Co 3:12).

In this book there is no differentiation made between short-term and long-term missionaries. I want to avoid any implication that short-term missionaries are somehow "second-class," while only the long-termers are "first-class." All of us are called to be first-class witnesses all of our lives wherever we are.

It used to be, before the days of air travel, that a missionary went out "for life." Today, that concept no longer holds. We need waves of missionaries coming and going as the Lord directs. One thing, however, must be clearly said in favor of a long-term commitment: as a general rule, the longer one remains in a given culture, the more fruitful he or she becomes. Thus we would urge that those who are now witnesses in a second culture remain within that culture until God clearly leads them out.

However, aside from that one important advantage of longevity, there is much room for flexibility and mobility in today's missionary endeavor. This removes the opprobrium formerly directed to missionaries who "left the field early." Today there is no opprobrium, as long as one is in God's will. I will even go so far as to say that there are no "failed missionaries," only relocated Christians.

A final word about the use of the term "mission field" in this book. This term conjures up an image of the white missionary going out to primitive lands to preach the gospel. Because of this connotation, the term has fallen into disfavor in certain quarters. However, it is very hard to write a book on missions without using it. In this book the term "mission field" will be used to refer to the entire world wherever nonbelievers are found, especially those areas where there are few or no Christians. Thus the mission field is any place where missionaries are working—or need to work—whether overseas or at home.

Myths to puncture

In any field, especially one as broad, varied and misunderstood as missions, there is bound to develop a body of myths. Every missionary on furlough must contend with the mythical notions of his home constituency. Let us examine the common ones.

Myth number one: "Missionaries are becoming extinct." I think we've exploded this one already. While the number of Western missionaries (excluding the very short-termers) has not risen much in the last thirty years, the number of Third World missionaries has jumped from nearly none to over thirty thousand. It hardly seems as if missionaries are a dying breed—especially considering that today there are more people that need to be reached than ever before in history.

Myth number two: "The church has been planted almost everywhere; the local believers can finish the job." Both statements are, of course, false. There are dozens of countries where there is no indigenous church. More important, there are approximately eleven thousand distinct cultural groups (the number varies according to how the groups are subdivided) that have no permanent indigenous witness within them. In other words, there are as yet no "local believers" in these groups.

Furthermore, many already established Third World churches have not yet caught the missionary vision themselves. They have become self-governing and self-supporting, but they have yet to attain the third "self"—self-propagating. Maybe they *could* finish the job, but they are not doing so. They are simply not reaching out.

Myth number three: "The Third World churches don't want Western missionaries to help them." This sentiment was voiced some years back, but except in a few isolated areas where Western missionaries are still stifling the development of the indigenous church, it is no longer heard. To the contrary, the vast majority of Third World Christians are asking for the help and partnership of Western missionaries.

Myth number four: "The responsibility for evangelism in each country belongs to the national church." The term "national church" is subject to misunderstanding. Properly, there is no such thing as a "national church." It is Christ's church. It's all well and good to speak loosely of the "Nepali church," for example, as long as the Nepalis don't begin to act as if it were exclusively theirs. The church in every land belongs to Christ, and in Christ there is "neither Jew nor Greek" (Gal 3:28), national nor foreigner, Nepali nor American. The responsibility to evangelize Nepal does not rest solely with the Nepali believers, though they must naturally bear the greatest part of it. No longer is the worldwide missionary movement hobbled by narrow nationalistic concerns. This is not to say that the leadership of the church should not be local; locals are more permanent, and they understand their people better. Foreign helpers should come as servants. But the harmful and unscriptural notion that foreign missionaries are merely guests in the national church is on the way out. Christ's church has moved beyond such nationalism.

Myth number five: "The 'heathen' are eager to hear the gospel and be released from bondage." Try this line in a Muslim country! Or a Hindu or Buddhist country. Or most anywhere else, for that matter. Except for a few animistic tribes, the "heathen" don't think they're in bondage and, what's more, they think their religion is superior to ours. And as for those who might otherwise have been open to listen, they are often so busy just keeping their bodies alive that they have little time left over to think of their souls.

Myth number six: "Missionaries are misfits." There's at least an ounce of truth to this one; people that bounce back and forth between cultures might be expected to have a little difficulty "fitting in." But to suggest that missionaries as a group are second-rate or "couldn't make it" back home is pure fiction.

Myth number seven: "Missionaries are super-spiritual." To dispose of this one, just keep reading.

Pressing on

Yes, it's easier to write about being a missionary than it is to be one. I know.

I make no pretense of having successfully followed all the precepts laid out in this book. But I have tried to. Daily, and sometimes many times a day, I have prayed that I might be a missionary pleasing to God. I have striven to be that missionary. I have striven in the sense that all of us must strive to be Christlike. Some people say we shouldn't strive, but that's wrong. With the Apostle Paul, we must "press on...straining toward what is ahead" (Php 3:12-13). It's salvation we mustn't strive for, but for holiness and maturity we must strive. And to the extent I have "attained"—whether little or much—I attribute totally to God's grace. And it is also by his grace that I have ventured to write this book.

The reader will observe that throughout the book much of what is written is really about Christian living, applicable to any Christian, not just to missionaries. For missionaries are preeminently engaged in the business of Christian living, only in a cross-cultural setting. They have the same physical and spiritual equipment that any other Christian has. When missionaries get together, they talk about the same things other Christians talk about: discipleship, obedience, consecration, prayer, holiness, temptation. And I'm not sure the temptations on the mission field are any worse than those at home—only more varied.

So let this book not merely be a text on the missionary life. May it also help the reader enter into the struggles of missionaries, and to more effectively support them and pray for them. And beyond that, may all of us—whether at home or overseas—be encouraged to become more like Christ and to follow him more closely. For that is the primary goal of each one of us; all else is secondary.

A tribute to our forebears

We get so wrapped up in the problems and exploits of our own generation that you'd think no generation preceded us. Missionaries, of all people, should acknowledge their debt to their forebears. Jesus reminded his disciples of this very thing. He said to them, "I sent you to reap what you have not worked for. Others have done the hard work, and you have reaped the benefits of their labor" (Jn 4:38). And so, before going on, let us pause and acknowledge our debt to those who have gone before.

David Garrison in *The Nonresidential Missionary* tells a recent story of targeting one of the many unreached people groups of Asia. The young "nonresidential missionary" assigned to mobilize mission outreach to this group had never heard of any prior efforts to make contact with the group. So he sent out over two hundred letters to various mission agencies working in Asia, asking for information about these people. As the replies came back, one after another wrote that they had never had any work among the people in question. But they offered to contact still other agencies and individuals to ask if they might have any information. Within a month, a second series of letters began coming to the nonresidential missionary. These were now from agencies and individuals the missionary was not familiar with; they were the result of his "networking." Most of the letters contained only encouragement and the promise to pray for his efforts to reach that people.

One letter, however, was different. It came from an eighty-two-year-old retired missionary named William Scott, who was living in England. More than forty years earlier he had worked among those people, until being driven out by revolutionary forces. The young missionary's heart quickened as he read the old man's shaky handwriting.

Mr. Scott wrote: "I have been praying for these people all these years—that God would raise up new laborers for the harvest. You see, when I was younger, I led some to Christ and planted churches among them. I never knew if anyone would ever be able to follow up on my work."

The letter went on: "Before I was expelled from the country, I translated the gospel of Mark into their language. I know that God had a purpose in my preserving this little translation all these years. When I left the country I was searched nine times, but miraculously the manuscript was never discovered! I'm sad to say that for the past forty years no one would take my translation and publish it.... And so, for forty years it has sat in my desk drawer. But now I am sending it to you. God bless you, my brother."

The young missionary went on to successfully place several Christian tentmakers among those same people. Then one day two years later, one of these tentmakers happened to tell the missionary about a young man who was struggling over whether to place his faith in Jesus. The young man's parents had told him to forget about the Christian faith, but he kept asking the Christian tentmaker more and more questions. Yet he couldn't make a commitment to believe. The tentmaker urged him to pray and ask God to reveal himself to him.

"Then," said the tentmaker, "the young man accompanied his parents to their ancestral cemetery. It was a special holiday, commemorated throughout much of Asia, during which time families sweep the graves of their ancestors. It was there that God chose to reveal himself. As the young man pulled the weeds away from the tombstone of his grandfather, he was stunned to see the image of a cross and a Christian benediction engraved on the stone marker. His grandfather had been a believer."

Tears came to the eyes of the young missionary as he listened to the story. In his mind he envisioned the face of old William Scott. Almost certainly it had been he who had brought the now-deceased grandfather to faith in Christ.

The tentmaker ended his story by saying, "When the young man saw his grandfather's grave, he gave his heart to Christ."

We shift now to the country of Nepal, and to another story. The year is 1952. Nepal had just opened to the outside world after being closed for almost a century. Of its ten million inhabitants, not one was a Christian.

Then one day two Western missionary women working in northern India, Hilda Steele and Lily O'Hanlon, crossed over the border into that hitherto unknown land. The two women walked across the border—there were no roads into Nepal at the time—and they continued walking northward toward the majestic Himalayan peaks. After trekking six days up and down row after row of lesser mountain ranges, the women came to the top of the last range. Beneath them lay a beautiful valley, and across the valley rose the towering Annapurna mountains, 26,000 feet high. As they descended into the valley, they met people who had never before seen a white face. They had no schools, no medical care, and they had never once heard of Jesus Christ.

Lily was a medical doctor, and so she and Hilda started a small dispensary in the main town of the valley, Pokhara. Their work grew. Other missionaries, both Western and Indian, came to help them. They formed a small mission called the Nepal Evangelistic Band. And eventually they established a hospital. They built the hospital out of cast-off World War Two Quonset huts made of shiny aluminum, and so it came to be known as the "Shining Hospital." And over the years thousands upon thousands of Nepali patients have come to that hospital for treatment, many of them walking for days over the mountains from their homes.

One of the patients who went to the hospital in its early years lived nearby on the outskirts of Pokhara. He had been very ill, and the missionaries had treated him and prayed for him, and he had recovered. The missionaries had also given him a Bible and a hymnbook in his own language.

Some time after that this man's nephew came to visit from his tribal village four days' walk away. His uncle told him of his experience at the hospital, and how the missionaries had prayed for him and taught him something about the Christian God who answers prayer and can heal the sick. The nephew became sufficiently interested in this new God of the missionaries that when it came time for him to return to his village he took the Bible and hymnbook back home with him.

When the nephew reached his village four days later, he found that his daughter had taken ill during his absence. The witch doctor had been called in to treat her, but she was getting worse. Finally, when the family had given up hope, the nephew remembered the God of the missionaries he had heard about from his uncle in Pokhara, and so he decided to pray to this God asking that his daughter might be spared. He prayed for her healing in Jesus' name, and by the next day his daughter had completely recovered.

Following this event, the nephew began to be called to various village homes to pray for the sick. And time and again as he prayed in Jesus' name, people got well who otherwise would have been expected to die.

News of these healings spread rapidly to the surrounding villages of the tribe, and soon many more were learning about the living God who answers prayer and heals the sick. The nephew taught the people from the Bible he had received from his uncle, and before long clusters of be-lievers began meeting together. They met in secret, because it was against the law in Nepal to change one's religion; the punishment was a year in jail. The believers faced intense persecution from their neighbors; some were driven out of their homes. But in spite of all this, the number of believers continued to grow.

Today, twenty years later, that community of believers has grown to more than thirty different congregations totaling over five thousand Christians. And this has all happened without outside aid or influence, and it has happened in spite of opposition from both the Nepali govern-ment and the surrounding community. It has all happened as a result of the prayers of that nephew, who heard the gospel from his uncle, who'd been healed at a mission hospital started by two woman missionaries who had trekked over the mountains into Nepal in 1952. Look what God can do with such small beginnings!

This isn't the only story we could tell about Nepal, or even about this one hospital; there are dozens of others. In fact, in countries around the world you can hear hundreds of stories like this. But more than that, there are yet hundreds of stories left to tell, stories that are simply wait-ing to happen—and all it takes to get the ball rolling are two missionary women, or two missionary men, or a missionary couple. It could be you.

Today, as we view the rapidly growing Nepali church, over one hundred thousand believers located in almost every district of the land, we pause to pay tribute to the pioneers on whose shoulders we now stand. May each of us be found as faithful in the tasks that God has given us. The work is God's; but, wonder of wonders, he has chosen to accomplish it through us.

2

The Call

Being a missionary begins with being called. You don't choose to be a missionary; you're called to be one. The only choice is whether to obey.

Right off the bat people will begin to question the use of this word "call." They say that "call" should be limited to Christ's "general call" to all Christians to follow him and to offer their bodies as living sacrifices to God. They fear that if we talk too much of this "missionary call," those who don't receive it will sit back and feel they are relieved of any further obligation to missions. Their fear is well-founded. So I need to emphasize at the outset that all Christians without exception have been called to give their lives totally to Christ with no reservations. All Christians are called equally to be disciples, to follow and obey Christ. And that is going to include obeying the Great Commission. Because, as we have said in Chapter One, the Great Commission has been given to every Christian. Thus our "general call" as Christians includes not only following and obeying, but also "going"—to someone, somewhere, even if only across the hall.

Therefore, let no Christian ever say, "I have received no call." The call has been given; you don't need to wait around for it.

So far, we've been talking about God's general call to all believers to follow and obey Christ. Now the question immediately comes: Where

16

are we to follow? What specifically does Christ have for each of us to do? In other words, does he have a "specific calling" for us?

This distinction between God's "general call" and his "specific call" is very similar to the distinction between God's "general will" as revealed in Scripture and his "specific will" for the individual. God's general will (call) is that I be a witness. His specific will (call) is that I be a witness in Nepal, or Chicago, or wherever.

Our general call comes primarily from Scripture; our specific call comes primarily from the Holy Spirit. Of course, the Holy Spirit often uses Scripture to confirm and refine our specific call. Before we went to Nepal, my wife Cynthia needed her own individual confirmation that she too was called to that particular country, and one day she found it in her daily Bible reading, Psalm 67 in the Living Bible. The Holy Spirit spoke to her through that Psalm and gave her the assurance that it was his will for her to go to Nepal.

Before we talk anymore about the "specific call," we need to distinguish it from "guidance." Some say that the so-called "specific call" is simply a form of "guidance," which all Christians need daily anyway. These people prefer not to talk about a "call to the mission field," or a "call to the ministry." They say that all Christians should be "called" to do whatever they're doing, so why insist that pastors and missionaries need a special call to their vocations? "It's all a matter of guidance," they say; "the only time the word 'call' should be used is in its general sense."

I disagree. First, the "specific call" is a much more profound and life-changing event than ordinary guidance is. Second, certain types of Christian workers, such as missionaries and pastors, do need a special anointing, a special empowerment, in order to carry out their duties. These workers carry the tremendous burden of spiritual leadership; they are on the forefront of the spiritual battle. Their vocations demand more than the ordinary perseverance and spiritual maturity. Missionaries, in particular, are led out of their own cultures into often uncharted waters. Simple guidance into these vocations is not enough; these people need to be set apart. They need a clear and certain call that this is the course God has laid out for them. It is my experience that those who arrive on the mission field without this sense of call are much more vulnerable to doubt and discouragement when the going gets tough. Therefore, in this book we will continue to use the term "specific call" or "missionary call." And then, once called, "guidance" will determine the details of how we should fulfill our calling.

What, then, is the nature of the "specific call"—in particular, the missionary call?

In a minority of cases, the call to missions will be striking and unmistakable. It may involve a dream or a vision, or a prophetic word, as in Paul's case when he received his call to be an apostle to the Gentiles from Ananias. (Some refer to Paul's vision of the man of Macedonia as a "call"; but that, by our definition, would be "guidance," not a call.) In other cases it might be a chance circumstance or "coincidence" that constitutes the call. My own missionary call came two days after I had become a Christian. I picked up a pamphlet describing the opening of Christian medical work in the closed land of Nepal, and concluded that God wanted me to go there as a medical missionary. So I said, "Yes." As simple as that. It was about as dumb, naive, and immature a decision as a sixteen-year-old could make, but I am as sure today as I was then that it was God's call.

In still other cases, a call may be a gradually increasing conviction and assurance that God has laid his hand on you for a special purpose. This will be accompanied by a deepening desire to serve a particular people, or to meet some particular need. It may be hard to tell at what point all this becomes a "call," but the person who has experienced it does not doubt that he or she has indeed been called.

A favorite pasttime whenever a bunch of missionaries get together is finding out how everyone got called to the field. Each one has a different tale to tell. Most, it's true, are not dramatic, but invariably they will speak of God's wonderful faithfulness in calling them out and then guiding them step by step to their place of service. The initial call may simply be to full-time Christian service, or to work among the poor, or to serve a certain people. And then God has steadily narrowed the vision and added in the place and the profession.

Abraham was called in this way. God said, "Leave your country...and go to the land I will show you" (Ge 12:1). And the writer to the Hebrews adds: "Abraham...obeyed and went, even though he did not know where he was going" (Heb 11:8). Abraham's experience underscores the truth that we are not called to a place so much as to a person, Christ. As long as we stick with him, the place will pretty much take care of itself. In other words, our "general call" to follow Christ is fundamental; our "specific call" is derived from that.

God's call doesn't register in a vacuum; only a person who is committed to doing God's will can receive a call. If you aren't sensing a specific call, maybe it's because you don't want to. Maybe you're afraid God will upset your plans. You're right there! It's amazing how otherwise intelligent people think that they can make better plans for their lives than God can!

Once a missionary call is sensed, one must do everything possible to nurture it and stimulate it. Read, go to meetings, attend mission conferences. Keep the fire alive; the devil will try to snuff it out.

A word of caution: Any call must be confirmed by others, including one's local church. There are lots of Lone Rangers out loose in the world who have "gotten called" to do this or that, but they don't fit in with anyone. They are often disruptive to the work of others. We missionaries quickly learn to beware the colleague who terminates every discussion with "I've been called to do this; therefore...." If your call has not been confirmed by at least one other mature Christian, you should put it on hold until it has been. There is no place for totally independent missionaries.

Furthermore, all missionaries are accountable to some sending church, even the "independent" tentmakers. A missionary cannot simply say, "God called me to do this," and expect the sending church to automatically agree. The sending church must share in this call; they have the duty to examine the call and modify it as necessary. And together with the missionary, they will need to evaluate the results of the call. An isolated call in itself never justifies a missionary's activities.

There will be times, of course, when you are in the minority—even a minority of two. Don't abandon a call just because you've run into opposition, or what you're doing seems out of fashion. Many missionary pioneers have endured periods when they seemed to be all alone, with little or no support; but they have remained faithful to their vision, to their call. The Apostle Paul himself wrote to Timothy that "everyone in the province of Asia has deserted me" (2 Ti 1:15). "At my first defense, no one came to my support" (2 Ti 4:16). But as we hold onto our vision, it is easy to become defensive and strident. Remember that "the wisdom that comes from heaven is first of all pure; then peace-loving, considerate, submissive..." (Jas 3:17). Let the Holy Spirit do your arguing for you.

The question of "need" on the mission field should be mentioned here. You hear some people say that the need constitutes the call. This is not strictly accurate. God's word, together with the urging of the Holy Spirit, constitutes the call. But the need certainly gives people an extra mental and emotional impetus for heeding the call. The various needs will direct us to the place where our gifts can be put to the greatest use. First of all, God isn't going to send us where we aren't needed. This is why we say: If you're not called to stay where you are, you'd better think missions, because that's where ninety-nine percent of the need is. As one wit has said, rephrasing Jesus' parable: "We need to leave the one and search for the ninety-nine." Why should ninety-nine percent of the shepherds stay with one percent of the sheep? Secondly, God isn't going to send us where our particular gifts can't be used; and determining where our gifts can best be used is a matter of knowing the need, knowing our gifts, and then using common sense.

The needs are overwhelming. If we were to look only at the needs, we'd be paralyzed, or go nuts. God knows all about the need; he only gives us responsibility for a very tiny part of it. We must be assured by the Holy Spirit that the need we are setting out to meet is the need that God has actually assigned to us.

A final question about the call to missions: If you are not certain of your call, should you go anyway? Yes. Go short-term. You don't need to commit yourself to the mission field for life. It is only to Jesus that we have a lifetime commitment.

Guidance

Having indicated the importance of a specific missionary call, we must avoid the opposite danger of over-emphasizing it. People can become immobilized waiting for some "experience" or "special confirmation" that they are heading in the right direction. Don't panic. Just keep moving as far ahead as you can see. God will reveal the route to you as you have need. He knows the end; we don't have to.

For most missionaries, the daily, weekly step-by-step guidance is at least as important as the call, if not more so. Sometimes the call just seems to crystallize out of many individual pieces of guidance. God may begin by burdening our hearts with some group of people, or some need, or some locality. As we respond in prayer, asking, "Lord, what would you have me do?" his answer becomes clearer and clearer. He sends us confirming signs that we're on the right track. We read articles, hear speakers, meet a missionary or a national from the country we are becoming interested in. All of this presumes, of course, that we are actively seeking God's will and not just sitting back waiting for God to write his instructions on the ceiling. As the old saying goes: God can't steer a parked car.

Many young Christians have trouble with this matter of guidance. They say they're not getting clear signals from God; they're confused. In a few cases, the problem is one of patience: they are hurrying God. But in the majority of cases the problem is that they don't really want to do God's will above all. They haven't yielded themselves to God; they're holding back. They are putting conditions on their service. "I'll do anything, God, but.... I'll go anywhere, God, but...."

Sure, maybe they don't want to do "that" or go "there." Maybe God doesn't want them to either. But God isn't going to show them what he wants until they have removed all conditions and reservations from their offer of service.

So, how to receive guidance?

First, present to God your body, your total self.

Second, choose to know God's will.

Third, promise God you'll do it. Knowing it is not enough.

Fourth, be obedient to what you know is God's will right now.

Fifth, listen to the Holy Spirit. If we don't listen, he won't lead.

As long as we do these things, God will unfailingly lead us step by step. If we obey God where his will is obvious, we will discern his will in areas that are not so obvious. Jesus said, "Whoever follows me will never walk in darkness" (Jn 8:12).

If you are not "getting through" to God, it is most likely because you haven't fully yielded your life to him. As long as that situation persists, you will not get clear guidance, much less a clear call. You will never have the confidence you are in God's will.

Praying for guidance isn't a matter of asking God to bless plans you have already made. It's a matter of saying to God, "I want your plan." And remember, God may reveal no more of his plan than you need for today. We keep worrying about the future—what we'll do after our training, for example. God says, "I want you to do my will today." It makes no sense to pray about God's will for our future if we are ignoring his will for our present.

Funny, but for those who are totally yielded to God, discerning his will isn't such a big thing. It's only when our will gets in the way that we have to "struggle' to know God's will.

Are some worried that they might get out ahead of God, misread his call, and dash off to Nepal or wherever by mistake? Yes, it may be possible, but not common. For every person who jumps the gun on God, there are ten people who don't get off the starting line. Don't worry so much about making a mistake. God can easily stop you. His problem is starting you. You can't wait until you're "absolutely sure" of God's leading, or you'll never move. Christians "live by faith, not by sight" (2 Co 5:7).

For how long is the call?

The "general call" is for life. We give our lives to Jesus; there's no taking them back. "God's gifts and his call are irrevocable" (Ro 11:29).

The "specific call," however, can change; it doesn't need to be for a fixed time. As a practical matter, we divide up our lives into segments—two-to-four-year terms of service—but that is only for administrative convenience. It's ordinarily best to keep a light grip on one's plans, and to always be open to change them as the Holy Spirit leads. The one certainty about the mission field is its uncertainty.

Some people are led by the Holy Spirit to commit themselves to lifetime service on the field, and they should be encouraged in this. Only a generation ago it was the rule. The advantages of long-term service are obvious. One has the time to learn the language and culture well, and to truly identify with the people. They can readily see your love for them; you live with them year after year. As the years go by, contacts and friendships increase, and opportunities for ministry multiply. In the experience of most missionaries, spiritual fruitfulness accelerates from the second term on. Indeed, we often refer to the whole first term as orientation, because most of one's energies during that term are spent learning the language and making a string of fantastic mistakes from which one has to recover—like the missionary who almost killed a cow in the world's only Hindu kingdom, where the sentence for such an exploit is life imprisonment. I know about that case; I was the the missionary.

Most missionaries today say to God, "I'll go out for as long as you want me there. And if you want me to move on, I'll trust you to show me when and where." And when that time comes, the call to leave the field should be as definite as the original call to go.

Short-term missionaries

Short-term missions—three months to three years—is a new phenomenon, and it is a welcome one. Though year for year the long-term missionary's contribution is more valuable and his or her fruitfulness greater, nonetheless the contribution of the short-term missionary must not be undervalued.

For starters, there aren't enough long-term missionaries; we urgently need short-termers, especially to staff ongoing projects such as schools and hospitals. Short-termers bring special skills to the field. They bring enthusiasm, and then take it back to their home churches. If they are retirees, they bring maturity and spiritual insight. Short-termers bring new visions, and sharpen old ones. Short-termers free up the career missionaries to expand their ministry opportunities. Short-termers build wells, bridges, schools, hospitals. They witness to English-speaking nationals. They enliven the missionary community—which at times, I can tell you, needs enlivening. And in addition to all this, short-termers often come back as career missionaries.

Such was the case of Gerry Hankins, an eminent surgeon from Calgary, Alberta, who in 1970 came out to Nepal for three months to serve in a rural mission hospital while the regular doctor was away. It was during the rainy season, and I don't think he saw the Himalayas once. He couldn't sleep at night because of the nuts falling from the great *baar* tree onto the tin roof of the hospital prayer room, which was the only place they could give him to sleep in. His clothes became mildewed, he slipped in the mud, he was eaten by leeches. He took one day off—his last day in Nepal—and went on an excursion to a nearby temple, where some monkeys stole his lunch and ate it in front of him, just out of reach. I thought he'd never want to see Nepal again. But within two years, he had left his surgical practice in Calgary and was back in Nepal as the chief surgeon in the large mission hospital in Kathmandu, a post he filled for the next twelve years until his retirement. In the process, he became one of the most respected surgeons in Nepal.

Some years ago I might have been skeptical of the spiritual impact of short-term missionaries. But then our younger son Chris joined Youth With A Mission and went with a small music and drama team to India. Within four months, in conjunction with local Indian churches, they had won three hundred people to the Lord. That's more than most missionaries win in a lifetime.

Am I in favor of short-term missions? You bet! But before everyone decides that this is the way to go, let's look at the downside. Short-termers don't master the language. Their spiritual ministry is often limited. Their motivation is sometimes self-centered: a desire for adventure, experience, fulfillment. Short-termers can be disruptive to the work. They are in a hurry to accomplish their personal agenda, and when they fail, they end up frustrated and disillusioned. They frequently criticize older missionaries, and in so doing sow the seeds of conflict.

When a mission has too great a proportion of short-termers, its character changes. Continuity in the work is lost. Tremendous energy is expended just in turning over personnel and in orienting new workers. Such a mission can become inward looking. I remember once when Michael Griffiths of Overseas Missionary Fellowship came to speak at our annual Worker's Conference in Nepal. He at once noticed among us an underlying attitude of "we" (missionaries) and "they" (Nepalis). He told us that among OMF missionaries, the average duration on the field was nineteen years. Our average was under five years—and it showed.

One sad thing that can occur in a "high turnover" mission is that older and experienced missionaries get left out. Let them go home on furlough for a couple of years and there may well be no place for them when they are ready to return; new missionaries have filled their posts. We were in language school with a wonderful missionary family who went on to serve seventeen faithful years in Nepal. Then they went home to get the kids through the last years of college. When they reapplied a few years later, they were told there was no post for them. Good grief, you *make* a post for people like that! They are now working in Africa.

Long-termers, we still need you most of all, even if we don't always act like it!

There is a special group of short-termers which we could call "very short-termers"—those who come out, say, for less than three months. These would include students taking electives, working people on holiday, and church groups on special projects. Very short-termers are also to be encouraged, but here the reasons are different. The greatest benefit of these programs is not to the field but to the short-termer and his or her home church. Yes, they often accomplish useful projects and provide timely assistance; but that cannot be the primary justification for sending them, because the benefits to the field simply do not make up for the trouble and expense of transporting and orienting so many people for such a short time. No, the benefit is more long-range. Many of these people will come back as longer-term missionaries; and even if they don't, they will usually be better Christians for their experience. Many churches have been rejuvenated and their missionary zeal rekindled after their members have gone on short-term mission projects. So, keep them coming. Only remember to keep the reasons in focus.

Some people dabble in missions. They like to "test the water" before making a real commitment. That's all right as long as they are truly seeking God's will. For while they are testing the water, they will likely receive further direction from God about what he wants them to do with their lives.

But all too often this dabbling indicates a lack of seriousness about God's will. Too many Christians are mainly interested in what's good for them, not what's good for God. They "check out" missions as if they were trying on a pair of pants for size. Like the rest of the world, they move from place to place, job to job, without any sense of lifelong commitment to Jesus. Missionaries are used to moves, to changes, but their commitment to a lifetime of service to Jesus must remain unchanged. The person who is not serious about serving Christ needn't try out the mission field—even for a very short term.

Some short-term missionaries think to themselves: "I'll serve as a missionary for a few years and then I'll have paid back my debt to the poor, to the Third World, to society." Such thinking is faulty. Our debt is to God, and we can never pay that back. One missionary to Nepal spoke of his five years there as a "tithe," as if to say that now he was free to do as he pleased with the rest of his life—an idea that is no more true of our time than it is of our money. All of our money, all of our time, all of our lives belong to God—whether we're short-term or long-term, whether we're paying for groceries or giving to missions.

False calls

No missionary's call is pure; the deeper we look at our motive the more of self we see. I had lots of reasons for going to Nepal: mountains, adventure, the chance to be the only surgeon for half a million people, a healthy life. I wanted to go to Nepal so badly that for months before we went my daily prayer to God was that he'd stop us from going if it wasn't his will. When he didn't stop us, we correctly concluded that he was a loving Father, whose yoke was indeed light. We can echo the experience of countless other missionaries who have been sent by God to places they would have been quite happy going to anyway. God takes our natural inclinations and interests and sanctifies them for his purposes. Don't wait for your motives to be one-hundred percent pure before heading for the mission field, or you'll never get there. But once you get there, expect God to begin purifying your motives in earnest! The Himalayas may draw people to Nepal, but they surely won't keep them there; only the grace of God will do that.

However, I'm not suggesting that we don't have to check our motives before we go; we certainly do. Those who go to the mission field for predominantly wrong reasons cause a lot of grief to themselves and to others. What, then, are some of the wrong reasons?

First, the desire to meet other people's expectations. Missionary kids may feel obliged to follow in their parents' footsteps. Others may fear disappointing seminary or Bible school teachers, or the home-town church people. Others may feel they need to outshine their peers in holiness and dedication. Although these feelings are not in themselves unworthy, they do not constitute proper reasons for being a missionary. Don't do what you think you "ought" to do; do God's will.

Second, the desire to meet your own expectations—to prove yourself, to prove your worth, to accomplish something worthwhile. There is a little of this in all of us, but when it gets out of hand it becomes destructive. The mission field is not the place to go on an ego trip.

Third, the desire for a change of scene. Something is wrong at home: in-law trouble, job dissatisfaction, boredom, you name it, and you see the mission field as a solution to your problems. Well, you'll be in for a surprise.

Fourth, a desire to earn favor with God. This is an incorrect motive for any Christian, not only missionaries, but few of us are completely free from it. A "works" mentality subtly affects much of what we do as missionaries.

Fifth, a feeling of guilt. This is the reverse side of number four, the feeling that we "have to make it up somehow," either to God or to the downtrodden masses whom we Westerners have "exploited and oppressed." Guilt should never be a motive for missions. In the first place, 1 John 1:9 gives us the solution to our guilt before God. In the second place, you and I are not personally guilty of exploiting the Third World—unless, of course, we're living too luxuriously. But you solve that by determining to live simply, not by going to the mission field.

Sixth, aroused emotions. This is a tricky one, because emotions are God-given and essential to our well-being. They are often unselfish, and when they are, they are valid motivators for mission. The "needs" of the field play upon our emotions, and we feel sympathy, distress, compassion. Our hearts go out to the starving children and impoverished masses, and this is good and right. But human emotion is not enough; we need God's love which is poured into our hearts by the Holy Spirit. Without that love as our prime motivator, our good works cannot be sustained.

What's holding you back?

Are you in debt? You have to pay it off. No missionary board I know of will take on your debts. This is a major problem for many—especially in the medical profession—and there is no easy solution in sight. Training is crucial for today's missionary, but that often means going into debt to pay for it. Just don't get too comfortable while you're paying it off, or your missionary vision will soon fade away.

Are you getting too much education? First your Bachelor's, then your Master's, and then surely that Ph.D. is necessary, or else God wouldn't have given you the chance for it—and then, boom, you land that once-in-a-lifetime research job, and there's another potential missionary lost to the field. Yes, of course, it can be God's will, but just remember: the devil is a master of rationalization. Ph.D.'s are needed as tentmakers, you say. You're right; so let those who are already Ph.D.'s fill those slots. The point being: don't use education as an excuse not to obey God's call to go now.

Are you falling in love? And your boyfriend or girlfriend has other ideas than the mission field? If you are truly called, you know who you'd better put first. It's no sacrifice for the man: he'll find dozens of single missionary women on the field just waiting for him. The ratio of single women to single men on the mission field approaches ten to one. But for the women it will most likely mean remaining single. For those struggling with such a choice, to say, "God will provide all your needs" sounds like a platitude. But over and over again, when you talk to single women missionaries who have made that choice in God's favor, they will say that God has indeed provided, and more wonderfully than they ever imagined.

Are you worried about your children? You say, "They weren't called. Is it fair to inflict that life on them?" Gracious, you're not going to the Gulag. And besides, what's so great about raising kids in the USA? The fact is that from almost every point of view, kids raised on the mission field are better off than kids raised at home. We'll have more to say about that later. In the meantime, don't believe that bit about the kids "not being called." If God has called the parents, you can be sure he has called their children also.

Are your parents opposed to your going? No parents, Christian or non-Christian, are entitled to block God's will for their children. Furthermore, the command that children obey their parents is given to young children, not adult children. The problem of feeble or ailing parents is much greater, of course. Paul says, "If anyone does not provide for his relatives, and especially for his immediate family, he has denied the faith and is worse than an unbeliever" (1 Ti 5:8). If there is no other family member to care for one's parents, then the missionary candidate must meet that need. But Paul's admonition cannot be applied in the case of parents who simply want their children nearby for convenience.

Are you worried about your safety? Don't ask if a particular field is safe. Did the early church do that? Don't say: "We must wait until the soil is prepared, until the doors are open." Did the apostles wait? No, they went out and were beaten, jailed, stoned, killed. People aren't going to invite us. And what are these "closed doors" that people talk about today? They are merely barriers put up by Satan, "gates of Hades" (Mt 16:18), which are powerless against Christ's church.

Many other things hold up the missionary candidate. Fear of failing, of not being able to stick it out. Fear of losing one's independence. Fear of poor living conditions. Fear of deprivation. Even fear of deputation! And the list goes on.

Don't suppose it's God who is creating these obstacles in your path; it is far more likely the devil. He'll do anything to keep you from the mission field. Yet God allows you to be tested in this way. He wants to test both your faith and your obedience. Get used to testing before you go; you'll get plenty of it on the field.

Someone will say: "But we shouldn't just rush into a missionary commitment. Didn't Jesus say to count the cost?" Yes, he did. There is a clear sense in which we must follow Jesus with our eyes open; he doesn't want blind followers.

But on the other side, we don't read of Peter, Andrew, James and John sitting down and calculating the cost of following Jesus. They simply got up and followed. Nor did David appear to worry about the cost when he went out to meet Goliath. If these men did, in fact, count the cost, they also decided to pay it. Today the expression "counting the cost" is too often used as an excuse not to obey Jesus, not to heed his call. A calculating spirit will always kill our zeal for missions.

There is indeed a cost when we follow Jesus, and it's not small. The world needs men and women who will count the cost—and then obey.

All the fears and obstacles listed above which hold us back from missionary service are centered around self. Jesus said, "If anyone would come after me, he must deny himself and take up his cross" (Mk 8:34). The missionary call involves *self*-sacrifice. Whenever we hold anything back from God, our own spiritual development is arrested until we give it over. And when we give it over, God either gives it back for our good— as he gave Isaac back to Abraham—or he gives us something better.

My wife Cynthia was once a concert pianist. She abandoned a promising career to become a medical missionary. When she learned we were to be assigned to a rural hospital at the end of a fifteen-mile trail, she gave up all hope of continuing her music. But unbeknownst to her, the Lord had a piano waiting for her in Nepal. A German doctor was just leaving Nepal as we arrived, and sold Cynthia her piano for a song. We crated it up and brought it out to our village. It took thirteen men two days to carry it up our mountain, but Cynthia got her piano. And over the years it has provided not only Cynthia but also numerous listeners much joy and refreshment.

Why, then, should we fear to make the sacrifice involved in becoming missionaries? Do we believe the Bible or not? Is God faithful or not? If he calls, will he not provide? Ask any long-term missionary on the field, and they will without hesitation answer, "Yes."

Jesus made a remarkable promise: "...no one who has left home or brothers or sisters or mothers or fathers or children or fields for me and the gospel will fail to receive a hundred times as much in the present age...and in the age to come, eternal life" (Mk 10:29-30). Countless missionaries have proven this true.

Mary Cundy was an English social worker who went to Nepal in 1957 and stayed thirty-three years. Almost her entire time in Nepal was spent in remote and difficult areas. For much of that time she lived without any Western companion. Her living conditions were utterly primitive. The nearest road was a full day's walk away. She labored from dawn to dusk running a dispensary, though she had no proper medical qualifications. And yet no patient ever died under her care.

When Mary went to Nepal she gave up everything. But today in Nepal there are a hundred homes where she is welcomed as family. She has gained a hundred brothers and sisters, mothers and fathers, and probably a thousand children. Today a Christian Nepali couple carries on her work. A growing church has been established. Mary is rich beyond reckoning.

And if that weren't enough, when she retired back in England someone gave her a lovely cottage, and someone else gave her a new car. And what may have been the greatest miracle of all, she passed her driver's test and got her license! I was her first passenger.

Mary's story is typical of many. What we give to the Lord, he gives back with interest.

The only way to bear fruit is to die. "...unless a kernel of wheat falls to the ground and dies, it remains only a single seed. But if it dies, it produces many seeds" (Jn 12:24). Yes, the power of the Holy Spirit is needed, but that power can only be fully displayed when we have died to self.

The biggest hindrance to the missionary task is self. Self that refuses to die. Self that refuses to sacrifice. Self that refuses to give. Self that refuses to go.

3

Preparation

Anyone who ventures into cross-cultural missions without some kind of preparation is nuts. One can be self-taught to some extent through selected reading, but almost always one will need to go through a training and orientation program, and in some cases attend a Bible college. And all this is in addition to one's own professional qualifications or expertise.

What is written in this chapter applies equally to the traditional missionary and to the "independent" tentmaker who does not go out under a mission board or society. In many ways, training and preparation is more crucial for the tentmakers, because they will lack the ongoing field support the traditional missionary enjoys.

The nature and duration of training and preparation will depend on where the missionary is going, what he or she is going for, and for how long. The different training regimens are so numerous and varied that it is not possible to discuss them here. Candidates will be guided by their local church and by the mission organization they join. The point is that no one should begrudge the time spent in such preparation. It will cut out half the stress of arrival on the field, keep one from making needless mistakes, and make one a much better missionary. The day is long gone when one could just put on his pith helmet and sail off to preach to the natives. Missionaries have learned a thing or two since then—and so have the natives.

Training and preparation fall into three categories: professional or vocational training, field-specific orientation, and general missionary training. Let's look at these briefly.

Professional training

Every missionary needs to have some kind of skill or profession. It could be as basic as knowing how to witness cross-culturally or running a guesthouse.

Three points need to be made. First, whatever you do, do well. Shoddiness, carelessness, and incompetence are not honoring to Jesus. Furthermore, host countries are no longer willing to put up with people who are clearly unqualified for the jobs they have been assigned to do. Gone are the days when missionaries could go out and "just make do."

Second, try to get some practical experience during the training process, either on the field or in a similar situation at home. One month of good practical training can be worth a year of book work.

Third, your skills and training should be appropriate to the field where you are going. Sounds obvious, but in practice it is a complex question. What's "appropriate" to the field may change rapidly. New opportunities open, and old ones close. Job descriptions are often vague. It is best, therefore, to take to the field enough breadth of training to equip one for a variety of openings. Surgeons need to be able to run a general clinic; nurses need to be able to deliver babies; teachers need to be able to teach above or below their ordinary grade level; and seminary professors need to be able to plant a village church.

How much training should one get in his or her chosen field? The answer depends both on one's own aptitude and interest and also on the needs of the field. If you are pretty sure you are going to need a particular level of training, then it's best to get it before you go. However, if you are uncertain, then such training is better postponed until your first furlough, or even later. You will usually benefit more from the training once you have been on the field and seen the needs firsthand.

While it's true that one can be under-trained, the more common tendency is to get over-trained. Often the higher up the educational ladder we go, the less useful we become on the mission field. We get highly trained and then decline to do anything "beneath" our training. There are few openings for super-specialists in missions—the main exception being semi-closed countries which welcome only highly trained personnel.

So while it's tempting to go for that one last degree, don't think it will open more doors of ministry; it's more likely to do the opposite. A Master's is fine, but the Ph.D. should be reserved for just a few, and then only with God's very clear guidance.

If you're headed to a semi-closed country, why not consider going as a student, and staying on as a student as long as you can? You'll likely be more effective for the kingdom of God than if you waited another six years and went out as a professor. There are many factors involved in these decisions; one can't set rules. But we mustn't fall prey to making education an end in itself. Keep checking your motives. Are you getting further training just in order to keep one professional foot back in the home country? Are you using education as a means to delay going to the field? The danger is very great that you will lose the vision. Procrastination equals disobedience.

Professional qualifications give rise to a subtle temptation: We rely on them too much. Missionaries wage a lifelong battle to keep from doing things "in the flesh," and having a bunch of degrees makes the battle that much harder. We all "resolve" this conflict after a fashion, much as we do when we're ill—we both pray and go to the doctor. But the missionary must maintain constant vigilance lest he begin to rely on his own skill and not on the power of the Holy Spirit. Did the skilled surgeon work "in the flesh" or "in the Spirit" when he saved the patient's life? Both, of course: flesh consecrated by the Spirit (using flesh in its morally neutral sense). But for the surgeon and for all other "qualified" workers, every activity every day must be done with the conscious sense of God's enabling. Our qualifications are not what produce the fruit that lasts; only the Holy Spirit working through us can do that.

Field-specific orientation

Some field-specific orientation one gets at home; the rest is given on the field. This orientation would include the "do's and don't's" of living in a particular society, along with any necessary warnings that might relate to that society. Here, too, is where one's own reading is crucial. There's hardly a place in the world that you can't find something to read about. Know the history, the culture, the religion of the place where you are going. Learn about its politics and economy. Use your library.

However, knowing all about the country and people you're going to doesn't guarantee that you're going to like them or they you. It doesn't guarantee that you're going to fit in, or identify with the people, or be an effective witness. And it certainly doesn't guarantee that you'll get along with your fellow missionaries! Facts are important, but they're not most important. Most important is learning to be a missionary, and we turn to that next.

General missionary training

All missionaries, short-termers included, need: 1) a sound knowledge of the Bible and their Christian faith; 2) a knowledge of themselves; 3) cross-cultural communication skills; and 4) basic interpersonal skills. Any general training program should provide these things. For anyone going long-term, a thorough knowledge of missions, church growth principles, and non-Christian religions should be added as well.

The purpose of training is to strengthen weak areas, to improve attitudes, to provide problem-solving skills, and to hasten spiritual and emotional maturation. Training should improve our learning ability, make us more adaptable and flexible, enable us to trust and appreciate others, and above all, deepen our spiritual life.

Now all this sounds fine, and it is. But it's not stuff you get merely by reading. The practical aspects of such training are crucial. You can read a thousand books on interpersonal relations and still be convinced you're the easiest person in the world to get along with—until, that is, you get into a training program with a bunch of people who think the same of themselves.

My sons once got a stone-polishing set for Christmas. You know how it works? You put a bunch of rough stones of different shapes and colors into a tin can, attach the can lengthwise to a spinning device, and let those stones roll around inside that can for one week. That's where the term "taking off rough edges" comes from. It's a service we render one another—though not always appreciated. A week later when we looked at those stones, they hadn't come along like the book said they should. We'd forgotten to add the sand! The sand is the mission field.

The best training programs are like that tin can. How about one or two years in a Bible school or a missionary training college—that will work changes in you! You'll come out self-disciplined, compliant, submissive, humble, patient, adaptable.

Did I hear you say you're all those things already? Okay, let's assign a little project. You are an orderly, meticulous, and deliberate worker. You are assigned to work on a joint writing project with a flamboyant, disorganized genius with indecipherable handwriting. Let's say, just for fun, that the project is to write a 1500-page commentary on the New Testament. See my point? You think I'm exaggerating? It happened to me—

except the commentary was in Nepali! That's the sand.

Of all the serious debilitating problems one faces on the mission field, the great majority are related to interpersonal conflicts among missionaries. Anything that can be done in advance to minimize these inevitable tensions is going to pay high dividends in peace and fruitfulness on the field. Hence, the great value of training programs which to some extent replicate the situation one will encounter on the field. Even the very short-termers should have a program like this. One of the best is the Discipleship Training School run by Youth With A Mission in some fifty cities around the world. But there are many others designed to meet just about any need a candidate might have.

Learning to understand each other's strengths and weaknesses is fundamental to developing interpersonal skills. Every strength of character and temperament has its corresponding weakness. We need to learn to overlook and cover for our neighbor's weakness, even when it adversely affects us. It is our own weaknesses we are responsible for correcting, not our neighbor's. The more all these things can be learned and practiced at home, the greater the chance we will survive on the mission field.

There are additional advantages of missionary training of this sort. One is the exposure a person gets to people of quite different background and outlook. You may have a highly-trained, scientifically-oriented physician rooming with an individual who has less education but much deeper faith. They both need to get to know each other before they hit the field and start calling each other names.

Another advantage of training programs is the opportunity they provide candidates to witness and to lead people to Christ. If you think it's hard in the home country, you can be sure it's harder overseas. Every bit of experience is valuable. Ministering to international students is another ideal way to get such experience. Mission agencies will want to know if you have ever led anyone to Christ.

Many other things need to be learned: how to use the word of God as a sword; how to wrestle and persist in prayer; how to practice the presence of God; how to be filled with the Spirit. No one dare go to the field without having learned these things.

For most of us, learning these things will take a lifetime. No matter how much preparation we get, we're going to arrive on the mission field very imperfect specimens. So when will you be ready to go? That will be decided between you, your church, and the mission organization that sends you out. If you wait till you're fully ready, you'll never go. But if you go too unprepared, you will create difficulties on the field—not to mention offending the nationals, who will rightly wonder why we send such ill-trained people to work with them!

It's one thing to be imperfect; it's another to have a grave flaw, a major relationship problem, serious compulsions, fears, and phobias. Even quirky personality traits can be a severe liability. These problems must not go to the mission field with you. There they will be exaggerated, and the consequences much worse. Take as long as necessary, but get the problem straightened out at home. One of the many purposes of the training period is to detect and correct such flaws.

We talk about the urgency of the missionary task, and rightly so; but somehow God doesn't seem to be in such a hurry as we. He took eighty years to prepare Moses, and fourteen to prepare Paul after his conversion. And he knows how long it will take to prepare each one of us.

In the meantime, what are you doing now to help prepare yourself? You don't need to wait for a special training program three years down the road to begin getting ready for the mission field. There is plenty for you to do right now in terms of reading, witnessing, deepening your spiritual life, studying the Bible, and taking part in church fellowship. Your commitment isn't to some far-off event; it's to the Lord day by day. And finally, don't put off contacting a mission organization in consultation with your local church. The mission organization needs to get to know you, just as you need to get to know it. Mission societies aren't so keen to have people drop by and say they're ready to go out next week!

Choosing a mission organization

The mission organization you choose should have a perfect balance of order and spontaneity, discipline and freedom, tradition and innovation, evangelism and social action. If you come across such an organization, let me know.

People take four routes to choosing a mission, all of which are valid; the Holy Spirit leads in different ways. The first group is led initially to a particular mission organization. Perhaps a family member suggested it, or one's home-town pastor. So you'll want to find out what and where their openings are.

The second group is called initially to a country, and so they will want to find out what missions are working there.

The third group is called to a particular people group or a religious group—Tibetan Buddhist, for example. Again, they will need to find out

what missions are working among those people and what the opportunities are.

Finally, people in the fourth group choose a mission on the basis of
their own vocation. Someone with a Ph.D. in math may want to inquire if
Wycliffe Bible Translators can use him in linguistics. Or an experienced
executive may look for a mission that needs an administrator. All this
matching up of call, need, location, and mission is ninety percent a matter of common sense. Today even computers aid in the process; Inter-
Christo offers a computerized service that helps match individuals with
opportunity.

One of the best places to find out about mission societies is at the tri-
ennial Urbana Missions Convention. Other places will be your church
missions conference, or, if you go to a Christian college, your college
missions conference. You can also find a description of all evangelical
overseas mission societies in the *Mission Handbook*, put out by MARC.

Choosing a mission organization is like choosing a spouse. First of all,
the choosing is going on in both directions. Next, you obviously want to
find out all about the organization you can. What is its doctrine? Is it denominational or interdenominational? What are its support and financial
policies? Where does it serve and in what ministries? What is its policy
on children's education? Are its books audited?

Going deeper, you want to find out what the organization majors in:
unreached peoples, church planting, discipling, works of compassion.
How do the members relate to each other? Are differences of opinion regarded as disloyalty? Do new people have a voice? Are members encouraged to reach their potential? How much responsibility is given to wom-
en? Are there too many rules? If the "Manual of Administration" is over
four inches thick, watch out! Is the organization rigid, or is it chaotic—or
is it in between, that is, flexible, the "in" word today. Well, these questions and more you will want to find answers to. This is going to be your
new family; it's important you choose wisely.

But once you have chosen and been accepted, then enter into the life
of the mission wholeheartedly. You're not an employee, you're a family
member. You be loyal to them; they'll be loyal to you.

One additional matter will need looking into before you sign up: How
will the mission utilize you? Are they more interested in assigning you
according to their needs on the field or according to your own gifts and
sense of calling? If you feel called as a doctor to go to Nepal, will they
instead insist you go to their understaffed hospital in Mozambique?

This is an important question for you; the day is past when missionary
candidates accepted docilely whatever assignment was handed to them,

even if it went against their own judgment. You have the right, even the obligation, to speak up. You want to make sure you join a mission that will listen to you, and not just fit you into their empty slots. After personality conflict, job incompatibility is the next greatest source of unhappiness on the mission field.

When the candidate and mission do not agree on the assignment, both sides need to spend much time in prayer and seeking God's will. It is a test for both the mission and the candidate. The mission is not always right, but it is more likely to be right than the candidate is. This is a good place for the candidate to put into practice the submission and compliance he learned during his preparation. Thousands of missionaries will testify to the times they have submitted to their mission's decision and trusted God, and the decision has either proved correct or God himself has caused the decision to be changed—usually to something better than either party had envisioned. Let missionary candidates walk humbly and trustingly, and not feel they have to take everything into their own hands.

Mission organizations have personalities just like people do. Some are laid back, others are austere, still others are gung-ho. Some are quiet and serious; others are daring and aggressive. Just look at the differences in style between Navigators, InterVarsity, and Campus Crusade, or between Operation Mobilization and Youth With A Mission.

It is not necessary to choose a mission that exactly fits your personality anymore than it is to choose a spouse that exactly fits your personality. A slight (I emphasize slight) "mismatch" would broaden you and also add a little balance to the mission. Short-termers, in particular, needn't fear to join a mission with a different style than their own; in fact, in the case of young people, I'd recommend it. But obviously, when longer-term commitments are involved, overall compatibility is essential. Some people do remain "oddballs" in an organization and run against the grain, and if the organization truly appreciates their gifts they thrive and make a great contribution. But if, as more commonly occurs, their gifts and calling are continually stifled, then such people should find an organization that will fully use and appreciate their gifts.

Sometimes candidates who offer themselves for service to a mission organization are taken aback by the caution and reserve of the mission people. Perhaps they will not at once recognize that you are God's answer to Asia, or wherever. This is only natural. They are not only taking on responsibility for you, they are also responsible to the folks on the field and to the national church for the caliber of missionaries they send out. They will want to get to know you. And to that we turn next.

What does a mission organization look for in a candidate?

An individual's own subjective call must be objectively confirmed by others. The candidate makes himself available; it is for the mission to determine his suitability.

Below are listed the key qualities necessary for any missionary. Mission organizations do not expect perfection, but they do want to see these qualities in any candidate they accept. And, for that matter, wouldn't we want to see these qualities in our spouse, and in the members of our church? These are qualities any Christian needs, not only missionaries. It's just that their absence seems much more noticeable on the mission field. You might want to grade yourself on each of these qualities and see how you do, which might show if you have the first quality on the list, which is—

1. Insight. Insight is the ability to assess your own and others' strengths and weaknesses. It prevents you from both overvaluing and undervaluing yourself. It keeps you from false guilt when you cannot live up to expectations.

Insight is the ability to recognize the source of a problem and then work out its solution. Insight is a good part of wisdom, and as such, it is an essential part of the missionary's equipment.

2. Adaptability. Adaptability and its two cousins, flexibility and versatility, remain crucial throughout a missionary's career, but at no time more than in the first months after arrival on the field. The field doesn't adapt to you; you adapt to the field. Brittle, rigid people usually experience great frustration and unhappiness on the field; if they can't change they end up going home.

The need to adapt hits you from every side. You have to learn new ways of shopping, cooking, sitting, talking. You may suddenly be given a job assignment you didn't expect and don't feel qualified for. You have to adjust to a new pace of life, almost always slower (unless you're assigned to Tokyo). Everything slows down: mail, visa applications, decision making. Back home you thought you were a patient person—another illusion popped. Where is your patience when you need it?

And then there are the unexpected schedule changes. I once had to fly Royal Nepal Airlines from Kathmandu to a city in western Nepal. The flight was scheduled to leave at 7 A.M., so I duly arrived at the airport at six. There was no one at the ticket counter, so I just stood around and waited a bit. Seven o'clock passed, and then eight, and still no activity at the counter. I wasn't surprised; I had brought a book. An Indian gentleman was getting progressively more agitated at the delay, as were several

Nepali civil-service types. Finally at nine a clerk arrived at the counter and announced that the flight would be delayed.

"How long?" several voices asked.

"Until tomorrow," said the clerk.

"Why didn't you tell us before this?" asked the Indian gentleman.

"It was announced on Radio Nepal this morning," said the clerk. This didn't help those who hadn't brought their radios to the airport (Radio Nepal only goes on the air at seven) or who didn't own one, as in my case.

Thinking to console the irate Indian, I said lightly, "All we've lost is time."

He looked at me as if I had just come from Baffin Island, and said with scarcely concealed rage, "Time is money." He then steamed off to the central bus station. I wondered how much the twelve-hour bus ride would cool him down.

You can lose your time. Just don't lose your patience.

3. Perseverance. Whatever one does on the mission field will almost always take more time and effort than a similar activity at home. Obstacles abound; discouragement is an occupational hazard. And the first test of perseverance begins the day one arrives—with language learning. For a few, that's the hardest test of all.

Perseverance includes more than just "sticking with it" until the job is done. It also implies endurance, the willingness and capacity to suffer hardship, physical discomfort, opposition, and worse. When you endure these things it is evident that being a missionary is costing you something, and this is very important for nationals to be able to see. It's worth many sermons. It is only as we have sacrificed and given of ourselves in this way that our witness becomes authentic. Then we can say to our national friends, as Paul did to the Thessalonians: "...we were delighted to share with you not only the gospel of God but our lives as well" (1 Th 2:8).

Ever since the beginning of the church in Nepal in the early 1950s, Nepali Christians have been suffering for their faith. They have been driven from their homes, deprived of their land, denied employment, and thrown into prison. We missionaries have shown them the verses from Scripture that teach that suffering is an essential part of following Christ, and that Christians can rejoice in it. But given our own comparatively minuscule sufferings, our words encouraging them to bear up joyfully have had a hollow ring. "It's fine for you to talk about 'bearing up,'" they'd tell us. "All that happens to you foreigners if you get in trouble for your faith is to be sent back to your home countries. We get thrown in jail."

Then one day several years ago, two missionaries from North America got thrown in jail. Western Christians wrung their hands and prayed for their release. True, conditions in Nepali jails are not pleasant; their health was at risk; no one could say how long they'd be in. But God didn't want them released at once. Their going to jail did more to authenticate the witness of missionaries and bind us to our Nepali brethren than any other single event I can think of. The Nepali believers suddenly realized that we also were at risk, that we, too, were willing to suffer for our faith.

The two missionaries stayed in jail four months and then were released. Their example has shown us that we missionaries, too, need to have our faith tested; we, too, need to learn to rely on God's faithfulness, to learn obedience through what we suffer, to learn not to back out when the going gets tough.

4. Zeal for sharing the gospel. It is not enough to witness solely by good works. Though many missionaries spend over ninety percent of their time and energy doing these good works, they still need to have the burning inner desire that people meet Jesus and have the chance to hear or read his Word. Every missionary must be ready and eager to share the gospel at every opportunity. An older generation of missionaries called this zeal a "passion for souls."

Two obvious corollaries accompany this zeal for communicating the gospel: one is a knowledge of the gospel, and the second is the ability to communicate. Without knowledge or communication skills, one's zeal will spell disaster. Knowledge and communication skills are learned; zeal, on the other hand, is from the heart.

5. Ability to get along with others. Three quarters of all significant problems a missionary confronts are caused by relationship difficulties with other missionaries. Mission organizations, therefore, will be very concerned to know how well you relate to others.

Most of us are quite sure we relate very well. "I certainly don't bother anyone," is a universal assumption. It's also universally wrong. We all have relationship problems.

On the mission field these problems are intensified by the high level of stress and frustration missionaries face and by the closeness of their living and working conditions. Add to that the fact that missionaries, as a class, tend to be strong-willed people. This is not to make excuses, just to lay out the facts. It must be high on the agenda of missionaries and mission organizations to prevent such interpersonal conflicts; they are a major cause of unfruitfulness in mission work.

It is essential that missionaries not only be able to get along with each other but also be able to work with each other. One must be able to work in teams, and that implies interdependence. Both the dependent person and the independent person hamper smooth teamwork. Dependent people need constant support and direction, and rather than contribute to the team they will sap its energy. Independent people divert the team's energy as they yank this way and that to pursue their own agendas. It will be important to the mission organization to find out where you fall on the line between "dependent" and "independent."

The interdependent person is able to relinquish his own agenda and interests for the good of the team. At the same time he is able to reach out and be a support to others. He is a self-starter. He is self-reliant in the healthy sense of being outgoing, of loving instead of always needing to be loved.

6. Emotional stability. Are you prone to mood swings, to periods of discouragement or depression? Are you easily upset by irritations, by loss of sleep, by being cheated—or can you see things as having come from God's hands? Do you have self-discipline, or do you need to be prodded by a regiment of rules in order to function? All questions the mission people will be asking.

7. Humility. It's hard for a missionary to be humble when he or she comes from a "superior culture." And I'm not thinking only of Western culture. Asian missionaries have just as much of a cultural superiority complex as we Westerners do. In Nepal we have had missionaries from India, the Philippines, Singapore, and Korea who, the Nepalis felt, were culturally insensitive. Unconscious cultural superiority is something every missionary must strive to overcome, and the only way to do it is by maintaining a deep sense of one's own unworthiness and weakness and sinfulness before God. This is where humility begins.

But it is not only cultural superiority that undermines our witness. We come out as professionals, we start projects and then lead them, we have the skills, the competence, the money...and we're supposed to be servants?

The most useful and welcome missionaries are going to be those who come out and say to the national church leaders, "How can I help you? How can I fit in with your plans?"

It takes humility to recognize the deep spirituality of our national brethren, the depth of their prayer life, their faith, their endurance of suffering for Christ's sake. We missionaries are spiritual children compared to some of them. We need to learn at their feet.

Lack of humility shows up in many ways. It shows up in our disdain for products made in the host country. It shows up when we disparage the nationals' customs, standards, ethics. It shows up when we criticize national church leaders—and fellow missionaries. It shows up in our unwillingness to submit to authority.

Some mission organizations today may be catering too much to new missionary recruits. After the sales pitch, the candidate begins to enjoy the attention. Things like "submission to leadership" are played down, while things like self-expression and self-fulfillment are played up. And the new missionary comes out to the field expecting full say from day one, and when his ideas are overridden he cries, "Authoritarianism," which is a very bad name indeed. And the new missionary launches out on a journey of discontent and dissension, which may well lead to the destruction of his missionary team. What is lacking? Above all, humility.

Two additional qualities can be included under the general heading of humility: teachability and open-mindedness. Teachability is an absolute necessity if you don't want to end up looking like an idiot. I landed at a tiny hospital out in the boondocks, a highly trained surgeon, but knowing little of general medicine. I learned most of what I know about running a general medical clinic from an English nurse named Valerie Collett. The idea of a doctor being taught by a nurse to be a doctor wasn't one I'd have jumped at ordinarily, but it proved to be a valuable lesson, and not just in medicine. Val was a gracious teacher, and over the ensuing years thousands of my patients became the beneficiaries of her teaching.

Open-mindedness is another essential quality, sometimes too little noted among Christians of more conservative persuasion. I use the word open-mindedness here not only in its intellectual sense but also in the sense of an accepting attitude, an open-heartedness, a lack of prejudice. Do we really accept the nationals in our hearts? Do we respect them? Do we enjoy them? Do we socialize with them? Are they our friends?

8. Spiritual maturity. In this and the following item we are entering an area that is more important than all of the above qualities put together—the spiritual. Because it is the spiritual side of the missionary that is going to give rise to the seven qualities listed above. And it is the spiritual side of the missionary that is going to determine how much fruit he or she will bear for Christ. As the saying goes: Missionary work is spiritual work and must be done by spiritual means.

Spiritual maturity is much too large a subject to even summarize here. But there are two special things that mission organizations will be looking for in their candidates: first, the assurance of their call; and second, a strong devotional life.

Every missionary encounters periods of testing on the field. If the missionary has no assurance of his call, the first thing he'll do when testing comes is to doubt his call. He'll think he's made a big mistake. And he may well come home. Any mission organization is going to want to guard against this possibility. If one does not at present have such an assurance of call, then one should pray for it.

A strong devotional life is another necessity—even more for missionaries than for other Christians. On the field most of the "props" of the devotional life are missing: the home church, the pastoral staff, the conferences and speakers, the support groups, the multitude of books, periodicals, and cassettes. This lack is most heavily felt in rural areas, but one can feel equally isolated in the cities too. For strength and for growth, then, every missionary must be able to draw directly upon God, without the help of these other means. It is very common for missionaries to get depleted spiritually; they are constantly ministering, but seldom being ministered to.

Of particular concern to any mission organization will be the candidate's prayer life, and in the case of a couple, their joint prayer life. For it is prayer that releases God's resources to enable the missionary to do God's work. Prayer is no more necessary for the missionary than for any other Christian, but its lack will be felt more acutely on the field than at home, where it is easier to "get by."

9. A Spirit-filled life. I have separated the "Spirit-filled life" from the eighth quality, spiritual maturity, only for purposes of emphasis. It is, above all, the filling of the Holy Spirit that is going to make the difference in our spiritual effectiveness. Missionary candidates who have not experienced the reality and power of the Holy Spirit in their lives should not go out to the mission field until they do.

The most important qualities of the missionary are the nine fruits of the Holy Spirit. These are not natural qualities. We may have many other good natural qualities, some of which have been enumerated above: a humble disposition, a sensitive and caring temperament, courage, fortitude, and a host of others. But all of these good qualities are inadequate. We need the Spirit's qualities, and among them we need love the most. Love will make up for many lacks.

What does all this add up to? A Christ-like life. The missionary's entire life is like a message, a light. The life of Christ needs to shine out from each one of us. That is the only final test of our missionary careers: Did people see Jesus in us? That is the ultimate measure of success or failure for any missionary.

One of the greatest missionaries to India, John Hyde, was on his first voyage out to India when he received a letter in his cabin from a friend saying that he intended to pray for Hyde until he was filled with the Holy Spirit. Hyde was chagrined that someone should think he lacked the filling of the Spirit. But on that voyage Hyde came to realize that his motivation for being a missionary was "self"—to be a great missionary. And so he, too, began to pray in earnest for the filling of the Spirit in a way he never had before. And when the filling came, what a difference it made. The rest is history.

Screening for problems

A mission board or society is not going to be able to determine the presence or absence of all these qualities in an hour interview. Or a hundred-hour interview. They will do better if they see you function in a three-month training program, or better yet, a year-long program. But what is going to guide them most is the quality of your Christian life up to the present. What do the people who know you best say about you? Because the single most important factor in predicting one's future missionary performance is one's past performance as a Christian.

The mission organization not only evaluates strengths; it must also screen for problems, both potential and actual.

Physical health is one area. You don't send an overweight, aged diabetic with high blood pressure and failing eyesight to a rural outpost at the end of a ten-mile trail. Would that all calls were so easy! My own feeling is that if there is doubt over the issue of physical health, it should be resolved in favor of sending the candidate to the field. But if the doubt concerns emotional or spiritual health, then the candidate should not be sent—at least not until the matter has been resolved.

It's well to remind ourselves again that we all have emotional and spiritual "problems" to some degree. There is no perfect candidate, and even if the home people think there might be, the field people know better!

One of the ways missions in recent times have been screening their candidates is by means of psychological testing and interviews. Though too great reliance has been placed on these means in the past, they are still useful tools in assessing missionary candidates. Psychological test and interview results, however, should never be the determining factor in selecting or rejecting a candidate; they are simply too liable to misinterpretation. They can "fail" a good candidate and "pass" a bad one. They should be used only in conjunction with other more traditional and reliable means of evaluation. And a test alone, unaccompanied by a psychological interview, should never be resorted to by the mission, nor agreed to by the candidate. The result of such a test is called a "blind diagnosis," and indeed it is that.

Psychological testing and interviewing are particularly helpful in highlighting potential strengths and weaknesses of a candidate's personality. It first of all helps the candidate better evaluate himself and directs his attention to areas that need working on. Next, it draws the mission's attention to those same problem areas, which can then be probed further. It also guides the mission in the eventual assignment of the candidate; ideally the assignment will be one where the individual's strengths will be enhanced and his weaknesses minimized.

One example will show that this business of psychological evaluation is not a simple matter of punching items into a computer and coming up with a scientifically objective score. For instance, it is quite easy to mistake determination and single-mindedness for rigidity and inflexibility—and vice versa. Is the candidate resolute, or is he stubborn? More likely both together. Here is a case of similar personality traits producing both a strong quality and a weak quality. It is obviously important to distinguish which quality predominates in a given individual. The person who is predominantly determined and single-minded will be an asset on the field, as long as he is also willing to listen to others' ideas and to adapt and compromise when appropriate. The predominantly rigid and inflexible person, on the other hand, is threatened by new ideas and unable to adapt, and thus would be a liability on the field. Complicating the matter further, people aren't consistent; they don't stay in our neat categories. They oscillate back and forth, one day one quality predominating and the next day another. When you come down to it, psychological evaluation is one-third science, one-third art, and one-third guesswork.

Strict guidelines are necessary when missions employ psychological testing and interviews. Somehow the notion has crept in that psychological evaluation is just like any other kind of medical evaluation. That is not so. Psychological evaluation is not a blood test. A blood test is objective and value neutral. Psychological evaluation, on the contrary, is an imperfect probing of a person's deepest thoughts and feelings, an intrusion into one's inner life. It should be carried out only with the full agreement of the candidate, in total confidentiality, and with the guarantee that the candidate will be informed of the results and be given a copy of any report produced. Anything less than this is unethical—unless, of course, the candidate is psychotic or threatening criminal activity.

Finally, any psychological testing based on non-Christian presuppositions is inappropriate for Christians, and should not be used. Christians are new creations; their orientation is totally the reverse of the world's orientation. There is no way a humanistic psychological test is going to accurately portray the psychological make-up of a Christian.

The only tests a Christian mission should employ are those that have been developed by Christians for Christians.

With these provisos, there should be no problem with using psychological evaluation as a screening tool for all first-time candidates. Candidates should not object; they should welcome it. However, such evaluation should be waived in cases of personnel transferring from one organization to another. In those cases, conventional interviews and references are sufficient.

People ask: "Am I 'psychologically suited' to be a missionary?"

The answer is: "Certainly not! No one is." Unless, of course, you're a complete screwball to begin with. In which case you'd fit right in with our motto in Nepal: "You don't have to be crazy to work here, but it helps."

Why is no one psychologically suited to be a missionary? Because being a missionary means denying self, and that is contrary to the teaching of modern secular psychology, which says, "Affirm self." Secular psychologists preach self-fulfillment; Jesus preached self-denial. But Jesus was a better psychologist than them all. He knew that the only path to true fulfillment lay in denying self. The only way to find truly abundant life is to throw your life away for Jesus' sake.

This is why I am concerned that Christians and Christian organizations should never, except in the rarest circumstances, utilize the services of non-Christian psychologists. Though the non-Christian psychologist may be sympathetic, he can never fully understand the psychology of one who has been born again of the Spirit. As Paul wrote to the Corinthians: "The man without the Spirit does not accept the things that come from the Spirit of God, for they are foolishness to him, and he cannot understand them, because they are spiritually discerned" (1 Co 2:14).

A final question: Is there such a thing as the "gift of being a missionary"? Some say there is, but I cannot agree. Our definition of a missionary is "one who is sent to witness across cultures." It is dangerous to speak of cross-cultural witnessing as a "gift." That means anyone who finds it the slightest bit awkward to relate to a person of another culture could conclude that he doesn't have the "missionary gift" and thus doesn't need to think further about being a missionary. There wouldn't be many missionaries at that rate. The point is that cross-cultural skills are learned, not given. And there is such a variety of needs and positions on the mission field that it is hard to imagine anyone not having some natural gift that could be utilized in a cross-cultural setting.

Think of the high proportion of missionary kids who return to the field as adults. They didn't inherit a "missionary gift"; they learned to be missionaries from their parents.

Take language learning: That's not a gift, it's something we work for. Sure, some receive gifts that make language learning easier, but it's still primarily a matter of learning. No one can say: "I don't have the gift of language; therefore, I'm not meant to be a missionary." We all have the "gift" of language.

Some say further that a major cause of missionaries dropping out is because they went to the field without having the "gift." I don't believe it is so. We'll be looking at the subject of "dropping out" in another chapter.

The calling is primary; the gifts are secondary. God calls us to a work according to the gifts he has given us. He knows our gifts better than we do. I was called to be a missionary when I was sixteen; if you had asked me about my "gifts" back then, I would have shown you my watch and my record player. The primary issue is not an analysis of our gifts or our psyche, but simple obedience to the voice of God. The gifts will fall into place.

Getting to the field

All missionaries, including tentmakers and those who go out with a denominational board, need to speak in churches. If the thought is terrifying, the reality may be even more so. All missionary candidates should read E. Stanley Jones' account of his own first deputation speech in his home church. He thought he should do without notes, in the manner of good speakers, and so he memorized what he was going to say. On the fateful day, he started out in fine form until about the third sentence when, he says, he used a word he'd never used before nor ever used since. As soon as he spoke it, he noticed a college girl smiling in the front row—and at that moment his entire speech departed from his mind without a trace. After a minute or two of anguished silence, he said to the congregation, "I am very sorry, but I have forgotten my sermon." And so began the career of one of the greatest missionary spokesmen of this century.

So, why deputation? The main reason, even while you're a candidate, is to bring a blessing to God's people. Nothing impresses church people more than the sight of a young person dedicating his or her life to God's service on the mission field. And who knows what other young person is listening to you, and through your words is hearing God's call for the first time. Don't underestimate the blessing you can bring to a church.

You don't have to give a dissertation on missiology; the main thing to give is your personal testimony. The Holy Spirit said to the mortified young Stanley Jones, "Even if you've forgotten your sermon, you can still tell the people what I have been doing in your life." And that is what you have to share as a missionary candidate. You're not an expert; you're not proven, tested, tried. Everyone knows that. But you still have a message, and it's as powerful as that of any gray-bearded missionary. You still have one foot in the congregation; you're one of them. You are their link to the mission field. So don't be afraid to share yourself. Don't be afraid to tell them what God is doing in your life and that he's ready to do the same in anyone else's life too.

A few tips. If you can borrow slides, do so. If you have some maps, show them. If you have heard some stories, tell them, and tell them well. If you just don't feel you can speak, ask to be interviewed. Above all, prepare. Especially be prepared if you're only given a couple of minutes to speak; those times are often the hardest. And should you decide to dispense with notes and deliver your twenty-minute speech from memory— I'm glad I won't be there!

One caution. Don't even remotely entertain the thought that just because you are going to the mission field you are therefore holier than those people sitting in the pews. That's a dangerous thought, and besides, it's not true. After having been on the mission field, I sometimes wonder if the holiest people aren't those who stay at home!

There are yet two subsidiary reasons for going on deputation: one is to gain prayer backing; and the second, for those who belong to inter-denominational mission societies, is to gain financial backing. I say subsidiary, because our main focus in Christian ministry must always be on what we can give, not on what we can get. But there is a reciprocity in Christian ministry: As much as you give to others of what you have, they will give to you of what they have. Paul wrote the Corinthians: "If we have sown spiritual seed among you, is it too much if we reap a material harvest from you?" (1 Co 9:11). This is not a gimmick; it is a spiritual principle. It takes from us the false onus of feeling we are going around with a tin cup begging for alms, always on the receiving end. Some of my family used to say to me, before they became Christians, "Why can't you work for a living? Why do you have to ask for other people's hard-earned money?" Well, missionaries are in good company. Luke tells us that Jesus and the apostles were supported: "These women were helping to support them out of their own means" (Lk 8:3). Jesus said, "...the worker deserves his wages" (Lk 10:7).

By presenting yourself as a missionary of Christ, whether or not you explicitly state your needs, you are offering people an opportunity to share in building God's kingdom. That is not a small privilege. As much as people give, they will be blessed. You need not feel personally in their debt; they are giving to Christ more than they are giving to you—or that is how it should be.

The principal object of deputation from the missionary's standpoint, then, is not the "raising of support" but rather the laying down of stones on which the missionary will walk for the rest of his or her life. Through deputation you gain increased faith, valuable training, lasting friends, and a home in cities all over the country and even the world. You cement a relationship between yourself and a few key churches—especially your home church—so that you have the sense of being sent out not just by a mission organization but by your main supporting churches, which is the New Testament pattern. And, above all, you gain a team of prayer partners, whose main task, aside from praying for specific needs, will be to pray that you be continually filled and empowered by the Holy Spirit throughout your missionary career. You will not succeed as a missionary without their prayers.

So do not fear that initial period of deputation before your departure for the field. The money will come in—it virtually always does—though God may occasionally make you wait one or two years for it. And through the "ordeal" of speaking and traveling, God will make you a stronger Christian and a better missionary. And remember: the first round is the hardest. Each furlough down the road gets easier and easier.

A final word about who sends the missionary. There are a few missionaries who say they are sent only by the Holy Spirit and are therefore not under the authority of any other Christian body. There is no scriptural warrant for such an attitude. Yes, the Holy Spirit is the ultimate Sender, but he sends us out as members of Christ's body, the church. The local church, as in the case of Paul and Barnabas, is the primary sender of missionaries. Since most local churches cannot easily maintain and supervise their missionaries on the field, they either rely on the mission board of their denomination or they turn to specialized mission agencies to do the job for them. But in doing so, the local church in no way relinquishes its responsibility as the primary sender of its missionaries.

Thus all missionaries, tentmakers included, must be answerable to a church or churches. And on the field they need to be linked with other Christians and, if possible, to be accountable to some form of field structure. To remain "independent" is to cut oneself off from the body of Christ, and that will guarantee that the missionary will not bear fruit and ultimately will not survive.

4

Into the New World

Imagine flying over the Ganges plain of northern India, the parched, sun-baked land beneath you hardly visible from the airplane window. You have completed somewhere between eight and twenty hours of air travel, made even more memorable if you have three young kids in tow. You have just left the suffocating heat of Delhi—or perhaps the suffocating traffic of Bangkok—and you are heading toward Kathmandu, capital of the fabled kingdom of Nepal, and the site of your new mission assignment.

Ahead, those "clouds" you noticed along the horizon begin to assume a sharper aspect, and soon you realize they are not clouds but mountains—the Himalayas. Eight of the world's ten tallest peaks lie within Nepal. As you get closer, you can make out Everest and Kanchenjunga to the East, and Annapurna and Dhaulagiri to the West. The plane descends. The foothills rise higher and higher. It seems as though the plane will brush their tops—and suddenly, you are through a gap, and below you see an opaque sea of brown haze. What is that, you wonder. It is Kathmandu.

Down through the haze you go, and when you finally land and alight from the plane, you might as well be in the middle of Kansas for all the mountains you can see. You look around. Things looked so different from the plane. What will this new world be like, you wonder. How will you react?

Usually, at this point, one launches into a graphic description of the host country and the horrors of culture shock. Indeed, so much is made of culture shock during orientation and training that the new missionary becomes preoccupied with it. In fact, it's not how the missionary reacts that is so important, but rather how the host people react to the missionary. And so that is where we shall begin our discussion of the missionary's new world. The graphic descriptions will come later.

What will the people think of you?

Once out of the airport and onto the street, you are immediately surrounded by runny-nosed urchins. You recoil. Clamorous porters reach for your luggage. Are they honest? You feel under siege. Your face shows it. And within a few seconds of leaving the airport you have made your first impression on the local people—and it is not favorable.

The problem with first impressions is that they last. It can take months for people to overcome that first impression and see you as you really are. They feel you don't like them. They see you as arrogant, unteachable, irritable, rigid, impatient. Everything they later observe about you is colored by these first impressions.

Adding to your problem is the fact that you will be stereotyped—regardless of the impression you yourself make. The local people already know what all Americans are like from watching "Dallas." If they've seen one Western businessman, or tourist, they've seen them all. And if your mission field is a former colony of a Western power, you will be stereotyped as a colonialist or imperialist. Even missionaries from Third World countries can't escape this. Indian missionaries to Nepal, for example, are seen as overbearing, mainly because their huge country seems "overbearing" in relation to tiny Nepal.

A further problem you face is that the people are bound to misinterpret your motives for coming to their country. I remember a party of Japanese mountain climbers who came to scale the small 21,000-foot mountain overlooking our mission hospital. The local people were sure they had come to "steal rocks," as it was patently obvious that no one in his right mind would ever climb a mountain just to get to the top of it. Not that the locals lacked for rocks, of course; it was the idea that these climbers were "getting away" with something. As I recall, they had to leave by a different route to escape being waylaid by irate villagers.

Down at our mission hospital, we were not without "motive" problems of our own. The people were sure we were getting rich off the backs of poor patients. After all, we charged fifteen dollars for removing a gall bladder, and ten dollars for a Caesarian section. Where was all that money going if not into our pockets?

It takes a long time for people to understand your motives, to overcome their preconceptions, and to see through the first stumbling bad impressions you have created. It's like coming into the batter's box with three strikes against you.

Your attitude is the key to overcoming such a disadvantage. It's the key to building any kind of relationship with the local people. And attitudes are revealed in little things that we may think no one is noticing: how we treat our spouse, how we discipline our children, how we deal with our household help, how we handle frustrations. It's revealed in the little things we do for people, the little gestures that cost us almost nothing. It's revealed in our interest in the people, our entering into their joys and sorrows. It is revealed, above all, in our love for them. It's not our skill in the language or our competence in our work that is going to win their hearts: it's our attitude, especially our attitude of love, that is going to influence them. And by the opposite token, it's our bad attitudes that are going to repel them: our inconsiderateness, our condescension, our criticalness, our indifference. Such attitudes will neutralize months of ministry.

I once knew an American missionary in Nepal who was in some ways a classic "ugly American." He was brusque, crude, loud, boisterous, and aggressive. The British missionaries (and even the American ones) sniffed and said, "Tut-tut." But the Nepalis loved him—because he loved them. He did things for them. They could see through his rough exterior. You'll be forgiven much if you have love.

One helpful attitude to cultivate is that of a guest. Missionaries are, in fact, guests. Guests are reserved, gracious, grateful, and discreet. Guests are dependent on their hosts for many things. Guests honor, not denigrate, their hosts. Too often missionaries have acted as if they were schoolmasters and the nationals were children. Sometimes the reality is the exact reverse.

So, as guests, we learn to treat the nationals with respect. Love is not enough; love can be condescending and belittling. We must add to love an attitude of respect.

This should not be difficult if we look for the many good points of the host people. They usually have high standards of morality and social behavior—often higher than ours. They are courteous; they respect their elders, value family, and are loyal to their tribe and community. Their endurance, hospitality, and friendliness put Westerners to shame. And they have high aspirations for their future, just as we do.

The second thing that should help us develop a respect for the people is putting ourselves in their place. Why do they do the things they do? Could we do things better? Often not. Many a brilliant suggestion by a foreign expert has turned out to have ludicrous results. Why do the nationals react the way they do? Can you imagine what the loss of a buffalo or even a goat can mean to a subsistence farmer? Empathy is a crucial attitude which will allow the missionary to truly enter into the lives and feelings of the people as an equal, as a friend.

Do the people seem backward? Your great-grandfather was backward too. Only a hundred years ago, housewives were emptying chamber pots onto the streets of Edinburgh from upstairs windows. The only difference between that and present-day Kathmandu is that in Edinburgh they used to shout a warning to the passers-by below, "gardyloo," a word still in our English dictionaries. In Kathmandu, there is no warning.

It's all well and good to talk about empathy, respect, and love, but what happens if you don't feel it? You can't fake these things; the nationals would see through it in a minute. The only solution is to pray urgently, persistently, for the love that comes from the Holy Spirit. Yes, we may not like some particular aspect of the host people, but we must like *them*. If not, the game is up as far as relating to them is concerned. Oh, we could do office work or Bible translation and make a contribution; but we'll have little personal impact without a naturally flowing love and respect for the people.

There is nothing sadder to see than the missionary who plainly does not feel comfortable with the people, who doesn't like them. Such was the case with a missionary schoolteacher assigned to a rural area of Nepal. She was a committed Christian, she had read the books, she knew the right things to do, but she felt acutely uncomfortable when Nepalis were around. By her standards they were unschooled, unclean, unmannered. She developed a distaste for them, which gradually became evident even to onlookers. She was dreadfully unhappy, and left Nepal after one term.

What went wrong? I can't say in her particular case, but some general observations can be made. Some missionaries have relied too much on their own motivation, their own human love, and it has deserted them when they've come in contact with the people. Perhaps they failed to realize that the love they needed was a gift of God, the fruit of the Spirit. That gift is something missionaries need not only at the outset of their careers but every day thereafter.

Another reason missionaries fail to develop or maintain their love for the people is that they have come to give a witness or to give aid, but they have not been prepared to give themselves. Those who have only words and works to give will feel discouraged and repelled when their aid is rejected. But those who give themselves will continue to love the people no matter how they respond.

Gifts and help are frequently rejected when there is no giving of self. Gifts are condescending; they are handed down with little chance of reciprocity. The receiver loses self-respect.

But if the giver is giving himself along with the gift, if he is reaching out, making himself vulnerable, sacrificing comfort and convenience, the people will see that and will be more likely to respond favorably. And the giver, in turn, will be encouraged to give more.

Superiority and paternalism

The giver. We missionaries are the givers. That makes us superior. And right here we have fallen into an attitude which plagues virtually every missionary, those from the Third World not excepted: the attitude of superiority, of paternalism.

There is hardly a missionary who is not infected with this malady. Usually we don't even recognize it. And we've been warned of its evils so much that we would fiercely deny we possessed even a trace of it. Well, forget the denials. Any missionary coming from a larger, richer nation to a smaller, poorer one is going to have at least unconscious traces of paternalism, and sooner or later an incident will occur when it will raise its head. And even if we can't recognize it, the nationals surely will, and they will be repelled.

What's wrong with paternalism? First, it is a manifestation of pride; second, it lowers the person toward whom it is directed; third, it prevents that person from developing. It's all right to be paternalistic toward your children (while they are children), but not toward other adults.

Paternalism is rooted in a feeling of superiority. I have something you don't. I can do something better than you can. How can we rid ourselves of this feeling? The same way we must rid ourselves of all prideful feelings: by acknowledging our own sinfulness, our own impotence, our own need for forgiveness, holiness. If we truly feel deep in our hearts that we are unworthy servants, that all we have is of God, that we are merely beggars showing other beggars where to find bread, then the paternalism issue will largely disappear. Yes, we have riches, true treasure; but it is not ours, we didn't earn it, and we can't give it. We can simply introduce people to the One who can.

We have become so sensitized to the problem of paternalism and feelings of superiority that many missionaries have gone too far in the other direction. They refuse to see anything wrong with the host culture. They bend so far over backwards trying not to be condescending that their refusal to see people's defects becomes, in itself, an act of condescension.

For defects they will have, just like you and I. In fact, some of the nationals are outright scoundrels—about the same percent you find in every other country. Some are lazy, incompetent, unreliable, dishonest—just like people elsewhere. Some missionaries think that to point out such problems is to show disrespect to the nationals. But quite the contrary, to overlook people's defects is to show disrespect. It is to treat nationals like spoiled children. It is paternalism at its worst.

Paul said to speak the truth in love. Truth without love is hard and hurtful. Love without truth is mushy sentimentalism; it neither builds up nor edifies. Instead, we need to treat the nationals as equals. We should be as easy or hard on them as we are on ourselves. We need to show them a natural respect based on mutual understanding.

One of the best examples I know of how to relate to nationals on the basis of mutual respect was given by the Scottish nursing superintendent at our mission hospital. Sister Mabel ran a training program for assistant nurses, and she demanded high standards. She called the students "her gar-r-rals and boys," and she didn't let them get away with anything. "Her girls and boys?" How maternalistic can you get! But no, at closer look, Sister Mabel treated those young Nepalis just as if they were young Scots, and there was no greater respect she could have shown to anyone than that!

No pampering; no patronizing; the nationals are our equals. Just treat them naturally.

Yes, but I never found it quite so simple; I could never pull it off like Sister Mabel did. I'd be diffident one day, assertive the next—and usually on the wrong days.

I remember two trees that needed cutting down, and I ended up on the wrong side of both of them. We were extending a corridor into our hospital's central patio, in which was growing a tall papaya tree laden with nearly ripe fruit. The tree needed to be removed. It stood at one end of the patio, which was a narrow rectangle running east and west. The fruit was clustered on the south or sunny side of the tree, probably forty pounds' worth. Some villagers had been hired to cut the tree down. I was in the midst of my medical work when I noticed they had tied a rope part way up the trunk and were attempting to pull the tree down into the patio. It was a good plan as long as the tree fell due east down the length of the patio. But the dozen or more large papayas clustered on the south side of the trunk dictated that the tree would fall to the southeast, with the papayas hitting the tin roof of the hospital, directly over five of my post-operative patients.

I edged quietly up to the man with the rope and asked if they were going to pick the papayas off the tree before pulling it down.

"Not necessary," he said.

After a pause, I said, "What would you think of pulling a little bit to the right to keep the tree from falling on the hospital roof?"

"Not necessary."

I looked at the five other men on the tree-felling squad, and five sets of eyes answered, "Not necessary."

Meanwhile, patients and staff had gathered around the patio. None of these people had studied vectors of force in high-school physics—or if they had, they betrayed no thought that they might apply to papaya trees. As hospital director, I was completely within my rights to prevent certain disruption to the hospital roof and to the equilibrium of patients reclining beneath it. But intimidated by the anti-paternalism lobby, I said nothing.

Down crashed the tree onto the hospital roof, badly denting and dislodging two large tin sheets and splitting the supporting two-by-fours. A collective gasp went up from around the patio.

The man with the rope seemed a bit miffed. "Now, look at that would you," he said—as if the tree were at fault, or at least fate.

A few asked, "How did it happen?"

Most simply said, "Wow." They had thoroughly enjoyed the diversion.

I was the only one who felt badly. Dumbo! Anyone with a grain of sense, much less high-school physics, would have just clumped out and said, "Whoa, buster, you pull thataway," and been done with it. We didn't even get the papayas out of it; they were smashed to pulp.

Some time after that, a huge bunch of bananas on the tallest of the banana trees in our yard became ripe. The bunch contained over 280 bananas, and must have weighed eighty pounds. Since a banana tree bears only once, you simply cut the tree down to get the fruit. This tree stood on a steep terraced hillside off the side of our house. I told the gardener to cut half way through the trunk, and I'd stand down below to catch the bananas. I told him where to cut and how far through; I wanted him to cut just deep enough to let the tree slowly bend over and deliver the bananas into my arms. I'd been told how to do it.

The gardener mumbled a few words, but I said, "Just get on with it. Do as I say." The next thing I knew, the bunch of bananas was crashing down on my head, followed immediately by the tree itself.

As I crawled out from beneath the banana leaves, our cook, who never missed anything, said, "Doctor, you cut the wrong side of the tree. If you'd cut the side toward the bananas the tree wouldn't have snapped like that."

"That's what I was trying to tell you," said the gardener, more cheerfully than necessary. I was sure I detected a trace of paternalism in his smile.

The nationals are our equals. That means we are free to dislike some things about them without feeling guilty, or superior.

For example, I don't like the way Nepalis eat with their fingers. I especially don't like it when I'm invited out and have to eat with my fingers, and they serve me first and then sit around and watch me make a mess of it. I usually end up with a quarter of the rice down my shirt front. And then every time you lick your fingers you taste soap, because there wasn't enough water to rinse the soap off your hands. My wife Cynthia, however, loves eating with her fingers. She says the food tastes better. So much for objectivity.

A trivial example, to be sure. But it illustrates the point that many cultural differences are not a matter of "better" or "worse," but rather a matter of taste. Furthermore, it is irrelevant whether a certain custom is good for you, the foreigner. What's important is whether the custom is good for the people of that culture. For poor people it's an advantage not to have to buy silverware—or shoes, for that matter. Never assume that your ways are better for them than their own ways.

Take the matter of blowing one's nose. You know the "free-style blow," where the thumb blocks one nostril and if the wind is contrary or the mucous especially tenacious half the stuff ends up on one's hand— and then along comes that person and opens your door. Don't immediately consign to the shrink the missionary housewife who wipes her doorknob after the visitors leave. Yes, she has a problem, but she also has good grounds for what she is doing. And she is waiting until after the people have gone so as not to give offense. There are plenty of missionaries with far worse problems than that.

And how does our civilized custom of the handkerchief measure up? Why, to any self-respecting national a used handkerchief is utterly repulsive. And come to think of it, they're right.

Remember, we can like the people without liking all their customs. And we'd better hope they do the same for us!

There are far more important aspects to culture than eating and nose-blowing. Take the matter of the caste system in Hindu society. For the lowest castes, this amounts to institutionalized slavery. It is an appalling violation of basic human rights and decency. There is no way one can tolerate it or overlook it. Even the Indian and Nepali governments have outlawed it; but it is still entrenched, especially in the villages.

Take the matter of marriage. We in the West have no room to talk; divorce is very rare in Nepal, in contrast to our divorce rates. Yet the lot of the Nepali wife is often sad indeed. She is a possession, obtained on contract. For the early years of her marriage she is the servant of her mother-in-law. Husbands show tenderness to their wives so rarely that whenever we noticed it at our hospital it became a matter of comment. And even if divorce is rare, many husbands think nothing of taking a second or even a third wife.

And we have said nothing of tribalism and extreme nationalism, of bribery and corruption. Let us not bend so far over backwards to avoid cultural superiority and bias that we throw out all objectivity and discernment as well.

Some missionaries are so determined to eliminate any sense of superiority over nationals that they deny the virtues of their own cultures. That is clearly going too far. Speaking as a Westerner, I can clearly state that in some areas Western culture is indeed superior to other cultures. Western culture respects the individual and his rights; it emphasizes an individual's responsibility to society and to God; it fosters a work ethic, individual initiative, honesty; it promotes health, hygiene, and scientific knowledge. Much of this comes from our Christian heritage in the West, and far from denying it, we should want to pass it on.

Western culture has been the most successful in meeting man's physical needs, in producing material prosperity. Western culture has been the most self-critical, the most objective, the least ethnocentric of all major cultures. To respect other cultures doesn't mean you have to say they are better than your own; in the above areas they are clearly not.

Missionaries, however, are not in the business of promoting their own culture, no matter how superior they think it is. We are not out to promote Western capitalism, Western democracy, a Western way of life; we are out to promote the kingdom of God and to invite men and women to enter it. The kingdom of God is not related to any political, social, or economic system.

All cultures are under God

Missionaries are often accused of changing people's culture. The charge is often made by anthropologists who have little care for the people except to study them as objects. The charge is false; we can't "change" people's culture anyway. Change comes from within; it's not forced from without. Look at what has happened to three generations of enforced cultural change in the former Soviet Union: it has largely evaporated.

And yet our very presence as missionaries does affect the host culture. The missionary is, in a sense, a catalyst for change. People see what we have—both material and spiritual—and they want it. Why not? Cultures are continually changing and being enriched (and occasionally impoverished) by exposure to one another. What's the alternative? To preserve cultures by fixing them with pins like we do butterflies?

All cultures are marred by the sinful nature of man. Thus they all have weak points along with their strong points. No culture is intrinsically superior to any other. All cultures must be measured by God's standard. There are biblical absolutes, and all cultures and all people must conform to them. The means and methods of conforming will vary from culture to culture, but the basic laws of God are transcultural. One of the major tasks of the missionary is to expose the host culture and host people to the light of God's word. It is that word which will then work to transform those areas of the host culture that are out of line with God's standards. It won't happen overnight; William Carey devoted many years of his life trying to eliminate widow burning in India, one of the most horrid examples of sexual oppression ever devised. The missionary is merely an instrument of change; the power and timing are of God.

Thirty years ago, Jonathan Lindell came to the Nepali village of Amp Pipal, seventy miles northwest of Kathmandu. He asked the people what they needed, and they said health, education, and better agriculture. So Jonathan started a community development project to help meet those three felt needs. But he added a fourth element: God's word.

The people had invited him; they wanted what he and his colleagues had to offer. As a result of the mission's work, the culture of that area has changed—by all accounts, for the better. It is still being changed. But the lasting and most important change will come as a result of that society's exposure to God's word. That change has barely begun in Amp Pipal, but it will soon accelerate, as it has been accelerating in other parts of Nepal.

The thing the missionary must remember is that he is a representative of Christ, not an advocate of his home culture. We need to be sure that no particles of our own culture are mixed up with our gospel. Furthermore, we must not reject elements of the host culture that do not oppose biblical teaching. Indeed, we must do all we can to insure that the Christian faith springs up in as culturally congenial a form as possible.

The less people have to break with their own culture, the more ready they'll be to come to Christ. Let Christianity never be considered a "foreign religion" in any country.

We must keep cultural issues in perspective. In the last analysis, cultural differences are secondary. But Christ's presence in a life is not. When the people we serve accept Christ, when the love of Christ is manifest in their lives, when their spirituality exceeds our own, as it so often does, then cultural differences become insignificant. Standing before Christ, who of us can claim our culture is best? Standing before Christ, who of us can feel superior to anyone?

5

Making the Transcultural Connection

In Chapter Four we dealt with the one overriding requirement for being a successful missionary: that we subdue our pride, superiority, and paternalism, and receive the mind and love of Christ. This is a life-long process, but the more it takes place, the greater will be our fruitfulness.

However, loving the people is not enough; we must also know and understand them. They are very similar to ourselves. They have similar hopes and aspirations, similar sins and temptations, similar fears, similar motivations. Their psychology is the same as ours. Understanding the biblical picture of man and understanding ourselves will carry us a long way toward understanding the people we have come to serve.

Yet we must go further than that: we must also understand their culture. Each culture is unique. It has its own worldview, its own thought framework. If we do not understand the distinctive attributes of the culture in which we are working, we will not be able to fully understand the people, nor will we be able to effectively communicate the gospel to them—which is our supreme concern.

Appreciating cultural differences

There are a number of basic differences between the West and most

Third World cultures that must be recognized. First, the West is time-oriented, while the Third World is event-oriented. This means that church in Nepal begins half an hour late and runs for two to three hours. Church is an "event." People who have to walk two hours to church don't want a one-hour service! If someone comes to your door just as you're leaving for work (as frequently happens), you get to work late; it's as simple as that—though a terrible frustration for the busy Western missionary. Time-oriented people like to come to decisions quickly; event-oriented people talk and deliberate forever in order to reach a consensus. Both orientations are valid; adopt the orientation of the country you're working in.

A second basic difference is that the West is "crisis-oriented" and the Third World is not. Westerners place high value on avoiding crises, on planning and preparing, on preventing problems. They have routines and procedures. Third World people are decidedly non-crisis oriented. Patients don't come back for medical check-ups because they don't feel sick; they need an illness to move them. Our hospital staff have great difficulty understanding why there are so many procedures to follow. They prefer to deal with problems as they arise. After all, why prepare for problems that might never arise? A non-crisis orientation is perfectly valid—unless you happen to be running a hospital.

A third difference between the West and the Third World is that the former is task-oriented and the latter is person-oriented. In the Third World, relationships are more important than performance. It's very hard to fire someone on the mission field—think of the loss of face! Relatives and friends of powerful people get jobs whether they are qualified or not. Speed, efficiency, high standards are all of secondary importance. Discipline in the work place is not appreciated. Confrontation is to be avoided; communication is often indirect. Again, both orientations are valid—unless you are running a hospital or a business. Obviously as modernization comes to the Third World, they will have to become more task-oriented—yet, one hopes, without losing all the virtues and strengths of their own culture. It's a trade-off.

Certainly missionaries should bend over backwards to be people-oriented. Our goal is to win people. If in the course of running a project we trample on our staff to get the work done, we are defeating our larger purpose. It's true, the project itself is for the benefit of people, so whether it be a school or hospital or a literature project, the work must be done well. But usually this can be accomplished without sacrificing our staff along the way.

There are other examples that particularly involve the East and West.

For instance, in the West we promote individualism and distrust authority. But in the East, community is most important, and elders are respected. In the West romantic love is supreme; in the East courtships are most likely controlled by parents. In the West we minimize class division, we accept mixed marriages, we make room for upward (and downward) mobility; but in the East one is expected to keep his place. The West is eager for progress; the East is more resigned, more fatalistic. And we could go on. All of these different orientations affect people's basic assumptions and values, and color the way they think and react, usually without their knowing it.

The greater the difference between our culture and theirs, the greater will be the opportunities for miscommunication. We say one thing; they understand another. We misunderstand their reaction, and they misunderstand ours. Communication breaks down and mistrust and hostility build up. If it can happen in single-culture marriages, it can certainly happen on the mission field!

How can we get to know the people? First, by reading about them, their culture, their history, their religion. Much of this reading should be done while one is still at home, but it will obviously continue on the field—especially during the field-based language and orientation programs organized by most missions.

Books in the national language selected for study in language school should major in the culture and history of the people. One of my favorites was a little book of lurid "cultural tales," through which I got a vivid glimpse of what was in store for me ahead. One story told of a man driven to distraction by a seven-day, non-stop religious service, complete with loudspeakers and chanting priests, being conducted in his next-door neighbor's back yard. "His eyes looked like over-ripe tomatoes," the story said, and I can well believe it, having since had a similar experience myself.

And then another story introduced me to bus rides in Nepal. A boy and a girl returning to Nepal from school in India met at the bus station while waiting for the bus to take them the final leg of the journey over the mountains to Kathmandu. They got a seat together, and as the bus ascended into the mountains they fell in love. Near the top of the mountain pass the boy took out a precious chocolate candy bar, and putting one end in his mouth, he invited the girl to put the other end in hers. Then they slowly bit toward the center of the bar until their lips met. The bus reached the top of the pass and began its descent. As the driver went to slow down for the first curve, he found he had no brakes. Faster and faster went the bus around the hairpin curves, and finally, two pages of oohs and ahs later, off it catapulted into the valley thousands of feet below. The story ends with a graphic description of the deceased, including the two young lovers whose heads were found crushed together with their mouths still full of chocolate.

With stories like these to read, who wouldn't want to study a foreign language?

Orientation on the field is essential to supplement what one has read at home. You may have read all about Hinduism, but you need to learn how it is practiced in Nepal. You need to know what this religion you call Hinduism actually means to the average Nepali. For example, it means, among other things, circumventing little stone gods when you build roads; it means having two sons, so that at least one is available to perform your funeral rites; it means that government functions must be held on religiously propitious days; it means a fatalistic acceptance of one's condition of life. This and much more you may not find in texts on comparative religion.

It is important to distinguish between the idealized religion of the textbook and the "folk religion" actually practiced by most of the people. Hinduism does acknowledge a supreme God, but most of the people worship stones. Religious practice will vary from country to country, and even from village to village. We need to learn as much as possible about what the local people believe and why they do the things they do. And don't forget, every religion has its nominal followers, just as ours does.

More important than reading, of course, is talking with the people and observing them firsthand. We'll get some things wrong at first, but the more we are with them, the more we will come to understand them.

Below are some practical warnings to heed when questioning people.

First, be casual with your questions, not nosey.

Second, try not to read your own preconceived notions into their answers.

Third, don't ask leading questions; you may get misleading answers. Medical doctors know this; they are taught to avoid asking questions that have "yes" or "no" answers. One missionary doctor who hadn't yet gotten the language down asked a patient if he had pain in his umbrella, to which the patient replied in the affirmative. "Yes" answers will often lead you astray, and particularly so in spiritual matters. "Do you believe in Jesus?" "Yes," comes the answer. What do they mean? They believe in Krishna and Shiva too.

Fourth, don't exclude facts because they don't fit with your theory; your theory may be wrong.

Fifth, don't make generalizations based on what may well be exceptions. It is best not to make generalizations at all until you've been in a place for some time.

Finally, in gathering information, talk to someone as close to you as possible in education and status if you want reliable answers. This is particularly true if you are seeking advice on your own behavior. People are so polite they will rarely criticize you; your only hope for feedback is from an equal.

As we seek to understand the people, we are hindered by our own unconscious cultural perspectives. We, as they do, tend to think our own culture is the norm by which to judge behavior. For example, we Westerners like to tease and kid each other a lot; it's a sign of trust and friendship. But to the Asian, such teasing would be an insult and result in "loss of face." With the help of colleagues, both missionary and national, and with the insight of the Holy Spirit, we must work on removing our cultural blinders. Otherwise, we will not be able to enter into the people's way of thinking. We will never be able to put ourselves in their shoes.

Crossing into another culture means learning all over again the kinds of things we have learned from childhood up: the manners, the courtesies, the sensitivities, the ordinary "do's" and "don't's" of interpersonal relationships. This takes time, and some of us are slow learners. Every missionary has his or her own list of embarrassing faux pas. But we must learn as quickly as possible. Much will be forgiven us in the beginning—but just don't make the same mistake twice with the same people.

Mistakes there will be, and Christ will cover them, just as he put back the ear that Peter cut off. But he may not cover mistakes made because of our laziness or carelessness, or because of our lack of concern for the feelings of the people. Too many nationals have been turned away from Christ because of the needless mistakes of missionaries.

What kind of mistakes are we talking about? First, causing people to "lose face." Now we all know that saving face is a matter of bald pride, but in Asia it is given so much importance that the equation of interpersonal relations is shifted in favor of saving face at almost any price. This is one reason why, in meetings and discussions, confrontation is avoided and consensus is sought; with confrontation someone must lose face. Better no decision at all than that! We foreigners need to be gentle and indirect in our approach to issues. This fear of losing face will be found among the national Christians as well; it is, in fact, cultural.

Then there is the matter of common customs. In Asia, the externals of behavior assume great importance, and it is highly disrespectful not to heed them. If the people take off their shoes before entering a house, be sure you do too. If they eat with their fingers, be sure you do too. Don't ask for a spoon; if they don't have one, how embarrassed they will be! And if you are invited to eat, try not to refuse. In many cultures you are not a man's friend until you have eaten with him.

Then there is common courtesy. Don't speak in your own language when nationals are present; that's rude. They may think you're talking about them. If you do have to speak in your language—to your child, for instance—be sure to tell the national what you said, or he will likely imagine the worst.

Don't neglect to practice hospitality. Third World people make it a high art, and missionaries should too. Take time for it. Invite the nationals in; make them feel at home—by their notion, not yours. Feed them the food they like, and let them eat it the way they want. Treat them like valued friends.

Understand the tone of the society you work in. In Asia, dignity and reserve will never be misunderstood; it is the norm. (In Latin America, of course, it will be seen as unfriendliness.) A show of anger or impatience, a forcefully articulated thought, an overly spontaneous gesture will all strike a wrong chord. Strict discipline and uncompromising justice will also be seen as faults. Asians would rather overlook a little dishonesty or immorality than confront it.

Then there are common-sense matters that apply to any culture. Think the best of others. Give people a second chance. Err on the side of trusting a person, even knowing you may get stung. That's not gullibility; better to get stung ten times than mistrust an honest person once.

In short, be a decent, positive person. Remember the prayer of the little girl, who said: "Dear God, please make bad people Christians, and Christian people nice."

A final example concerns respect for elders, something deeply ingrained in Asian society. You'd think this would never cause missionaries trouble, but it has. One missionary couple in Nepal, with twenty years of language translation under their belts, once attended a conference of a hundred church leaders and Bible translators at which an ancient and highly venerated patriarch had been invited to speak. The couple, not known for levity yet possessing a good American sense of humor (which we are taught is indispensable for missionaries) were sitting near the front of the conference hall. When the old man's turn came to speak, a young man in the front row helped him to the podium. The gentleman was very frail and unsteady, and he was some time getting to the speaker's platform. He evidently was failing in sight, as well, for the young man felt obliged to place each of the old man's hands on the edge of the podium. Then the young man returned to his seat.

For a while the old man said nothing. He seemed to be having a problem in his throat that prevented him from speaking. The missionary couple watched him work his jaw and neck back and forth a bit, and then they realized that he had collected a large bolus of phlegm in his mouth, and was uncertain what to do with it. Spying a window to the left of the podium, the old man turned and unsteadily made his way to it. Everyone held their breath as he stepped down off the speaker's platform. The young man assigned to help him froze in his seat. The old gentleman finally made it to the window, and giving his throat a loud and prolonged clearing, he let loose the bolus of phlegm. There was only one problem: the window was shut. The bolus of spit hit the glass six inches from his nose.

As he turned back to the podium, the missionary couple glanced at each other—a fatal mistake—and began to quiver and shake. They looked around; the entire audience sat expressionless, eyes straight ahead. The couple bit their lips, got out their handkerchiefs, tried all the tricks to keep from laughing. Their ordeal did not last long, mercifully, for the old gentleman's speech was brief. It was one of the rare times a missionary sense of humor could have been dispensed with.

Crossing into another culture and getting inside the minds of the people of that culture involves so many details of thought and language that it is impossible in any general book to do justice to the subject. It is a career-long learning process for the missionary. You start from scratch. A wonderful Swedish nurse who has worked in Nepal for more than thirty years and has identified with the people more than most of us, hired a new cook not long ago. The cook worked out well, but one thing perplexed the nurse: the cook repeatedly put the table cloth on the table wrong side up. The cloth had a colorful Scandinavian design, and the back had neither design nor color to speak of; there was no mistaking which side should be up.

After a few months passed and the cook still hadn't caught on, the nurse explained to her which side went up. The cook merely shrugged and said, "Who made that rule?"

Precisely. When you cross cultures the rules change: rules of behavior, rules of aesthetics, and above all, rules of speech. And obviously we play by the rules of the culture we are working in; we deal with people on their terms, not ours.

Let's say you ask a question. The Asian, much more than the Westerner, will wonder why you asked it. What answer are you looking for? And he will instinctively give you the answer he thinks you want to hear.

Is that dishonest? Yes, to you; but not to him. Oh yes, truth is truth. But to the Asian, manners are more important than truth.

So you call a man to fix your pump. "Can you fix my pump?"

"Yes."

"Can you do it today?"

"Yes."

He knows you want this answer; he doesn't want to offend. And, of course, he ends up coming next week. These are your new rules; learn to enjoy them.

Sometimes we don't even ask the right question. During our first five years in Nepal I started work each day by making rounds with one of our Nepali assistant nurses. I'd arrive on the ward and ask, "Who will go with me today?" And the nurses would smile and giggle in a charming way, and then one of them would accompany me on rounds. At our pre-furlough farewell party, one of the staff, dressed in my coat, walked in and asked, "Who will go with me today?"—at which point the place erupted in laughter. Come to find out, I'd actually been asking the girls each day, "Who will marry me?" No wonder they always seemed so cheerful! Beware of lurking idioms. They trip up every missionary sooner or later, but most people don't take five years to figure it out.

Bloopers aside, what is most important is our ability to communicate spiritual truth to people of another culture. And though our lives speak louder than our words, words are still necessary to communicate the gospel.

How do people understand our words? To find out we need to listen to the people. We need to understand their view of spiritual matters. We need to take their interpretation of events seriously. A patient who tells you his jaundice is caused by an evil spirit should not be brushed off. I've heard patients say about Western medical staff: "They don't understand our diseases." So the first three rules of communicating are: listen, listen, and listen.

If you listen to a Hindu in Nepal, you will discover that sin is the violation of a ritual law. In the moral sphere, it means getting caught. Repentance means feeling sorry for getting caught. God is an unknowable, ultimate power. Eternal life is an endless cycle of births from which one longs to escape. Good works are done to gain merit. Reality is illusion.

It is immediately apparent that the words in question will mean radically different things to you and to the Nepali. Your basic thought processes are the same; you simply have different starting points, different definitions.

In order to explain our definition of these words to people of other cultures, we need to start with their definition, their presuppositions, just as Paul did in Athens. But even as we do this, we must continue making sure that our interlocutor is talking about the same thing we are talking about; we can never assume that he is.

How does one best present the work of Christ to a Nepali? One could present it as victory over Satan and death, or as substitutionary atonement, or as reconciliation for the alienated. But the best way, the one which speaks most readily to the Hindu, is to present Christ as the one true and pure incarnation of God, who came to help, heal, and save. This means most to a Nepali, and will get the greatest response. The other presentations can be added later.

Thus, in communicating spiritual truth, one wants to look for points of contact, or cultural parallels (sometimes called "redemptive analogies"). There are such parallels in virtually every culture. God has left his witness among all peoples. Hindus already believe in millions of incarnations. Through the use of cultural parallels, the gospel becomes immediately relevant to the person of another culture. The entire process of making the gospel relevant to those of other cultures is called "contextualization." The gospel becomes part of the cultural context of the receiving people.

Don't be afraid to use the host people's own religious words. As Paul did, to the Jews become like a Jew, and to the Gentiles like a Gentile. But when using their word, qualify it. "Incarnation" becomes the "one true incarnation." If you use unintelligible words, your message will be unintelligible.

All missionaries need some initial training in communicating Christ cross-culturally, and then they need to keep on learning. Too often, missionaries have communicated a Western gospel, and have had few takers. Even their converts have been taught to pass on an essentially Western gospel. No wonder the gospel doesn't take root.

We will always color our message to some extent; we can't help it. But we certainly can avoid presenting Christ as a foreigner, irrelevant to the people's needs. Instead we must present him as a person of great relevance, who fits easily within any culture. Let no one refuse Christ on the grounds that "he is fine for Westerners, but not for us."

Entering into dialogue with those of other faiths

Now that we have gotten rid of hidden pride and prejudice and have entered into the mental world of the national, we are ready to talk with him. With him, not to him. Dialogue is at least fifty percent listening.

And we will get no hearing unless we are respectful, tactful, and gentle. There is never a place for forcing our beliefs on people. We live our beliefs, not force them. Neither is there any place for disparaging or scoffing at another's beliefs. Our interlocutor's beliefs may be as sincerely held as ours are; he may be as earnestly trying to please God as we are. We need to honor that.

To respect the person doesn't mean we have to accept his beliefs. To try to understand the other person's faith does not diminish our own faith. Some Christians are afraid even to talk about other religions, as if such exposure would contaminate them or allow the other religion to get some power over them. Such fears are unjustified; the Holy Spirit is greater than any other spirit. Some Christians find the practices of other religions so repugnant they can't help showing their distaste. But the moment they do so, dialogue will end, and with it, all hope of winning the other person to Christ. Remember that those of other religions are sincere; they feel that if they don't worship the way they do something terrible will happen. Instead of distaste, show sympathy and understanding; show love. How would you feel if someone ridiculed your religion?

All religions contain some truth. God has revealed himself in many ways. People of other faiths do receive divine light, and seek to follow it. As Christians we must say that that light is insufficient and often clouded by superstition and fear and corrupt practices. However, it is never fair to compare the best of Christianity with the worst forms of other religions. This is taking a cheap shot. Approach other religions with reverence. Take off your shoes when you enter another's holy place. This attitude will open for you many doors of opportunity for dialogue and friendship.

E. Stanley Jones, the great missionary to India, taught us much about the importance of building on the good that is found in other religions. The higher forms of Hinduism, for example, contain ethical teachings that are very close to those found in Christianity. Indeed, Hinduism points to an ideal—an ideal which has been fulfilled by Christ. Pointing this out can be an effective way of opening the Hindu's mind to the claims of Christ. This is an example of "concept fulfillment"; Christ is the fulfillment of many of the yearnings of other faiths.

Because all religions contain some truth, it is incorrect to condemn them wholesale. In dialogue, one can speak about the false beliefs and evil practices that have arisen from other religions—including, don't forget, Christianity—but at the same time one should acknowledge the true aspects of other faiths. Even in talking with new converts about their former faith, be gentle; they have just come out of their old religion, and they will be sensitive and hurt if you belittle their former beliefs. Let *them* belittle them, but not you.

Remember, in dialogue you'll never get anywhere with a frontal attack. There are occasions when confrontation will be indicated—but then, that's not dialogue.

In dialogue, you look for openings. After listening, you could ask, "Have you found peace?" or "Have you found cleansing from sin?" If the answer is "No," you have your opening.

Be sensitive to any area of spiritual need in the one you are speaking with. Share what Christ has done to meet your own need. He can meet the other person's need too.

One spiritual need frequently encountered in the Third World is the need for release from fear and bondage. This is especially so among those with animistic elements mixed with their beliefs. In the "folk" forms of the major religions and in all animistic societies, the people are held in fear by spirits and by the shamans or witch doctors, who are in league with the spirit world. This fear of the spirit world is all-pervading. In rural Nepal, families won't bring critically ill patients to the hospital at night, because nighttime is when the spirits are out. In the rare cases when they do bring a patient at night, fifteen or twenty men accompany the party carrying pressure lanterns and talking and laughing boisterously—all this to keep the spirits at bay.

Many customs in such societies arise from this desire to ward off spirits. Farmers will plow their fields in curved lines, because spirits are believed to move in straight lines. High-caste families will give their children low-caste names so that the spirits won't bother with them. Some Western missionaries have pooh-poohed belief in these spirits, but that is a mistake; the spirits are real.

Obviously our words are going to have much greater effect if we can demonstrate that Christ has power over all spirits and can release people from bondage, fear, and sickness. We shall have more to say about this later on. For now, however, we can say that Christ is indeed all-powerful and can meet every need.

As we communicate with people of other religions, there comes a point when dialogue no longer is sufficient. Proclamation becomes necessary. The purpose of dialogue is not simply to bat ideas back and forth; its purpose is to present Christ, and to invite people to consider his claims. Our ultimate aim in dialogue is to persuade (Ac 18:4).

We have been appointed to call people out of darkness. As missionaries, we enter territory that is spiritually hostile, not neutral. Not only will the spirits oppose us, but the shamans and priests will oppose us too, since we threaten their position. We cannot have fruitful dialogue with those who are confirmed enemies of Christ, and who draw their power from spirits hostile to him. We may not always have occasion to oppose such forces publicly (though sometimes we will be called to do so), but certainly in our daily speech and actions we cannot remain neutral when it comes to those aspects of other religions that are directly contrary to Christian beliefs and values.

I recall a time when my wife Cynthia and I were conducting a health survey in the three districts served by the mission hospital in which we had worked for twelve years. We had been on the trail three weeks and were on our way back to the hospital. Two schoolteachers from a neighboring village heard we were in the area and chased us down in order to invite us to their village to discuss health needs. The village was a six-hour walk out of our way and required adding an extra night to our trip. But because the young men had literally run after us for over an hour, and because one of them had been a former patient of ours, we agreed to come to their village that evening.

When we arrived, the family of our former patient put on a fine feast on their front porch. Afterward about twenty Brahmin elders of the village assembled to talk about how the mission might be able to help their community. The discussion went on for two hours, during which time they repeatedly brought up the backwardness of their village, and their need for health teaching, clean water, better nutrition, and of course, a clinic.

They did most of the talking. Then, around midnight, they asked what I thought the mission could do for them. I started off very slowly, carefully choosing my words. I told them that outside help alone would not be enough to overcome the village's problems; rather, a change of attitude within the village was the most important thing. They needed to take responsibility themselves—they were not a poor village. They didn't have to remain "backwards" (their word). They didn't have to remain held back by the fatalistic idea that they were ordained to continue as they were. Cynthia told them that most of their children's illnesses could be adequately diagnosed and treated by their mothers—provided that the mothers were given responsibility for their care instead of all decisions being made solely by the men. We mentioned that the poor nutrition of the children was largely due to religious food restrictions. We spoke about the low-caste part of the village having no incentive or even chance to improve their lot. We spoke about the lack of community spirit, the lack of hard work—except among the women. I obliquely suggested that the whole social structure of the village was perpetuated mainly for the benefit of high-caste males. I concluded by saying that until some of these things began to change, introducing outside help was going to produce little lasting difference in the village.

The meeting ended after my speech. It was well past midnight. The Brahmins filed off. Our hosts politely put us to bed. Cynthia said to me, "Maybe you shouldn't have spoken so strongly at the end."

Did we lose them? Did they walk off because they were offended—or because it was merely time to go to bed? Did those things need to be said? Then? To them all? They had agreed they were backward, but no one likes someone else to say it—certainly not a foreigner. My speech had been polite, earnest, true, friendly; but they had perceived me in the end as an alien with a philosophy hostile to theirs. I had trodden on sacrosanct ground. They, the Brahmin elite, were the ones responsible for their village's backwardness. They were the beneficiaries of the system. They were, in fact, the oppressors. They held the poor in bondage. Fearful villagers gave them money and animals to ward off evil spirits. Low-caste people kissed their feet.

The Brahmins had felt challenged. They were not ready to be told these things, even by someone who had been serving their area for twelve years. We had spoken sincerely and in love. But perhaps we said too much too soon. We find dialogue to be a constant balancing act; we are continually cast upon the wisdom and guidance of the Holy Spirit. And we indeed do say things we later regret. Yet we believe God is faithful to use even our ill-advised remarks for his purposes, or to counteract any harm they might produce.

Some mission groups have been accused of "inviting" confrontation. Yes, sometimes missionaries in their zeal have created a needless backlash, but more often than not they are just getting what Jesus said they would get—opposition, and even persecution. Older missionaries look askance at their "recklessness," and remind them to be as wise as serpents. But we mustn't be so "wise" that we never dare to confront Satan, never dare to draw opposition. If you are not being opposed, then you should begin to worry. It means Satan can afford to ignore you.

While there is some truth in other religions, we cannot ignore the error. Other religions cannot lead men to a full knowledge of God. Other religions point to heaven; Christ takes us there.

Although Christianity has been corrupted from time to time throughout history and has given rise to various evils, even uncorrupted forms of present-day religions around the world contain evil elements. Hinduism, for example, has given rise to the caste system. It teaches the doctrine of karma with its fatalism, which impedes development and keeps the poor mired in their poverty. And many of its gods, according to Hindu teaching, have committed immoral acts and are intent on bringing harm to people rather than salvation. In our desire to show respect and to avoid confrontation, we must not at the same time veil the truth or in any way hinder our national friends from finding it themselves.

We do not need to be apologetic in stating our beliefs—provided we give the national equal time to state his. Neither do we need to apologize for the exclusiveness of the Christian gospel. The gospel is exclusive; it states there is only one way. The gospel is a stumbling block to Jews; it is foolishness to Gentiles (1 Co 1:23). And it is an offense to Hindus, Buddhists, and Muslims. The person of another religion says that such exclusivity blocks dialogue; but it is not so. Dialogue is between two individuals with distinct beliefs. Indeed, the Hindu or Buddhist is equally "exclusive" when he demands that we adopt his relativistic position that all religions are basically one. If we were to accede to his position, then the dialogue would end; there'd be nothing left to dialogue about. Because the crucial issue of the dialogue is the very thing the Hindu or Buddhist desires to avoid: namely, are the claims of Christ valid for all men, or are they not?

We believe they are. And to hold to this belief is not intolerance; it is being true to our faith. And this faith is the only eternally useful thing we have to offer as missionaries.

We must not forget that those who do not know Jesus cannot know God in the fullest sense. Their sins have not been forgiven. They are not in God's family. Insofar as other belief systems point men away from Christ, they are tools of Satan. It is Satan who leads men to worship idols, to create caste systems, to oppress women, to perpetuate tribalism. Our struggle is against him, not against the people and their customs. Behind the idol, the stone, the shaman, is Satan.

Men are not lost in the first instance because they never heard about Christ and thus can't believe in him. They are lost because they do not live according to the light they have received. Thus all are condemned, and justly so. The Bible clearly gives only one means by which men can escape condemnation: faith in Christ. Thus, rather than argue about whether there is possibly some alternate way of salvation that God has chosen not to reveal to us, it would be better to just get out and show people the one sure way we do know about.

Given that we believe that Christ is the only way, how can we avoid being dogmatic and narrow in the eyes of others? How can we hold to the truth and yet at the same time be humble and sympathetic? The answer is love. The motive for all we say and do is love, God's love, which is given to us by the Holy Spirit. As we talk with people, that love needs to radiate out from us. That love will draw people to get in touch with its source, God. How will they do that? Simply by taking hold of Jesus, who is the evidence, the proof, the embodiment of God's love.

And if people reject this love, reject our message? We shall love them regardless.

Indigenization: How far should it go?

For what reasons do people reject our message? Several reasons are possible. Perhaps they didn't understand the message. Or perhaps it wasn't relevant to them. Or perhaps the manner of the messenger put them off. Perhaps they didn't think the messenger was reliable, or believable. Perhaps they believed that the messenger had an ulterior motive. Missionaries can encounter all of these reasons for rejection.

All of these reasons we as messengers can do something about. Yet none of these reasons are true rejections of the message itself. It's tragic, indeed, if people reject the gospel because of us—because of our air of superiority, our rich life style, or our foreign way of thinking. Our model is Paul, who came "in weakness and fear, and with much trembling...not with wise and persuasive words, but with a demonstration of the Spirit's power" (1 Co 2:3-5). Might every missionary commit these words to memory.

As we minister the gospel, then, the only obstacle to acceptance should come from the gospel itself. The gospel will raise objections. It demands that people shift their allegiance from self to Christ. This is naturally perceived as a threat to people within a given culture. Their social stability is threatened. For example, for a Hindu son to become a Christian brings dire consequences to his family; it invites intense opposition from the local community. For the father there is the added fear that there'll be no one to perform his funeral rites, which he believes are necessary to assure his passage into the next life.

Among most non-Christian groups, conversion to Christianity is a momentous step. The dislocation experienced by the new Christian can be enormous. There are ways to minimize the trauma, but it cannot be eliminated completely—nor should it be. After all, the new convert is leaving one kingdom, one set of values, and entering another kingdom with a new set of values. He's being born again, and anyone who has observed a delivery knows that being born is traumatic. However, it is the missionary's task to smooth away all unnecessary difficulties. If resistance to the gospel arises because of some unavoidable demand of Jesus, fine. But if it arises because of a perceived threat to one's culture over an unnecessary issue, then that threat should be removed.

A major question for all new churches is how far to adapt the gospel to the existing culture. We have said earlier that the gospel should not appear "foreign." That means that the church planted in that culture should retain all aspects of the original culture that are not in conflict with the Bible. This is called "indigenization"—preserving the true gospel content, but in an indigenous form. The whole purpose of indigenization is to remove all unnecessary cultural barriers that might keep people from turning to Christ.

One danger of indigenization, however, is that the new truths and concepts of the gospel lose some of their meaning and sharpness when they are put in old cultural forms. In fact, if great care is not taken, the essential truths of the gospel can be altered and even lost as they blend back into the traditional culture. This is syncretism, the mixing of gospel and culture together in such a way that the gospel itself is changed. This obviously must be avoided.

When a new church is planted in a society where there is already a strong, established religion such as Islam or Hinduism, it is tempting to seek a "common ground" with the other religion, hoping thereby to make it easier for the adherent of the old religion to become an adherent of Christ. The problem is that there is not much common ground between Christianity and any other religion except Judaism. The two central elements of the gospel, Jesus Christ and salvation by faith and grace, are lacking in other religions. By trying to build on "common ground," we risk losing the central features of our faith—and all the while our national friends will be complimenting us on how similar our religion is to theirs! We must never compromise on fundamentals in order to win converts.

It is much better to err on the side of too little indigenization than too much. The gospel is radically different from all other human philosophies and religions. We must preserve its uniqueness at all costs.

Thus indigenization is not an end in itself; it can never be total, nor should it be. Christians must remain distinct from those around them. Their attitudes and ethical behavior should stand out. Christians are salt and light. They are in the world, but not of it.

It is true that churches generally attract more people and grow faster the more indigenous they are. But there are exceptions to this generalization, one of the most striking being the Korean church. Few national churches have grown faster and more dramatically than the Korean church, but many of their church services are almost carbon copies of Western services. "Lack of indigenization" hasn't held the Korean believers back at all. They have happily adopted many Western forms and have thrived on them. Just because an Eastern culture adopts Western forms doesn't keep it from being truly indigenous where it counts—indigenous in leadership, in vision, in fervor, in prayer. We in the West need to copy the Korean church in these regards!

One time Cynthia and I helped arrange the marriage of a Christian Nepali couple. Because of their particular family circumstances, we were "adopted" as parents of both the bride and groom, and thus ended up "giving away our daughter to our son." Naturally, Cynthia was involved in the planning for the wedding. At the time, there was little precedent for Christian weddings in Nepal (Christianity was illegal). What should the bride wear? Red is the Nepali custom, but the couple wanted white, after the Western manner, to signify purity. But in Nepali culture, white is a symbol of death—which is why you seldom see nurses in Nepal wearing white. Every detail of the wedding was scrutinized; should it be Western or Nepali or something new? In the end, though the marriage wasn't mixed, the wedding sure was: a Nepali groom and a "Western" bride in a Nepali church with a Western service in the Nepali language. It was a beautiful wedding.

As the years go by, these words "Western" and "Eastern" and "American" lose much of their edge, as we more and more come to enjoy and marvel at the multicolored family into which God has called us. Cultural differences cease being barriers and become, rather, sources of interest, of joy, of mutual enrichment. We can freely give and take of each other's heritage to the benefit of all. Let us see to it that the church in every locality is free of cultural domination or division. We say to all Christians everywhere, in both East and West: There is no place for tribalism or nationalism in the family of God.

As people from non-Christian cultures turn to Christ, we can expect the Holy Spirit to lead them in a wide variety of paths. Even members of a single family will have widely different experiences. We must beware of setting rules for them. We must not straitjacket the Holy Spirit. Grace gives freedom. Some new converts will want to utterly break away from their past. Others, by contrast, will make a less pronounced shift to Christianity. These latter may be part of a people-group movement, where a whole clan accepts Christ en masse but retains most of its old culture. In such cases the change in each individual life will be less dramatic, but the total impact of the large number of conversions will be far greater. Let the Spirit have his way. Let us not quench him by a rigid, critical, and legalistic attitude.

A newly established church in a non-Christian culture will often take a generation or two to sort out what aspects of the old culture to reject and what aspects to retain. It is a more complex matter than simply deciding which parts of a culture are neutral (and can be kept) and which parts are contrary to biblical teaching. Hinduism in Nepal, for example, is inextricably mixed with the national culture. Almost everything in the daily lives of the people has religious significance, from bathing to eating—even going to the toilet, concerning which it's believed that the spirits will get you if you go in the same place twice. (This belief has scuttled many a latrine-building campaign in Nepal.) Must all of their culture, then, be thrown out? Many of the customs are quite harmless in themselves; it is the meaning and significance that people attach to them that is contrary to the Bible. Can some of these customs not be invested with Christian meaning? For example, one of the favorite holidays in Nepal is the festival of Tihar, during which the people light up their houses with strings of colored lights. Now Tihar is a Hindu festival involving idol worship, and therefore many Nepali church leaders feel that Christians should have nothing to do with any of its observances. But others say, "What's wrong with just having lights? To us, it signifies that the light of Christ is shining out from our homes." And there you have the debate; a hundred similar examples could be cited.

First generation national Christians often reject more of their old culture than the missionary might feel necessary. But, remember, the national knows the heathen roots of his culture, and desires to be totally free of all that once held him in bondage. We need to respect that. Take, for instance, the common Nepali greeting, *"Namaste,"* which means both "Hello" and "Goodbye." Its Sanskrit origin means, "I greet the god in you," a typically pantheistic Hindu expression. Therefore, many Nepali Christians prefer not to use the term, substituting instead a more biblical expression, such as "Peace."

The missionary needs to stand back as this debate goes forward; he must never try to impose his way. It is the national Christians who know their culture best and who will in the end be best able to find a balanced path between the different points of view. The debate is as old as Romans 14 and 1 Corinthians 8, and needs to be resolved with the same grace and tolerance. Let all alike—both missionary and national—remember the freedom we have in Christ to choose according to our conscience. Let us heed the well-known saying: In essentials, unity; in nonessentials, freedom; and in all things, charity.

6

Nepal 1, Visitors 0

Culture shock is like a game in which you are always one point behind. The only way to win is to join the other side.

Culture shock: you can read all about it in advance, and you should. Reading will help prepare you mentally, though it won't, of course, prepare you fully. Then after you have read, listened, and looked at slides, let your imagination run loose. Imagine the worst; you'll not be disappointed.

The trauma of culture shock has been overrated. Any reasonably balanced person and many unbalanced ones can adjust to a new culture; the human organism was built to adjust. So missionary candidates or new missionaries need not dread this rite of passage. If their call is sure and their faith strong, they will sail through with little problem. Indeed, they might even enjoy it.

Remember that transitions are God's natural pattern for man, both on a physical plane and on a spiritual one. We are pilgrims here. God wants us to be ready to move. Let us not fear the new and unfamiliar; let us only fear to be out of God's will.

The stress of culture shock for most missionaries is a positive experience, if not always pleasant. It is character building and faith deepening. It increases one's motivation to learn. It increases one's knowledge of oneself. It increases one's ability to adapt. It is a stretching and maturing experience.

In fact, one of the worst things about culture shock is its name. Few people like it; some prefer "culture stress." But this book's purpose is to describe things, not rename them; so we shall continue to use the term "culture shock."

Culture shock works in any direction. Foreign students coming to America have culture shock. Some of the worst forms of culture shock are experienced by Third World missionaries who are sent to another part of the Third World, usually a part that is less affluent. Going from a poor country to a rich one is not so hard; it's going from rich to poor that creates the greatest difficulties.

Where does one begin his description of culture shock? With the customs agents at the Kathmandu airport who are searching for gold smuggled in from Bangkok or Hong Kong? Or with the ride to mission headquarters through billows of smoke, exhaust, and cement powder; past road sweepers raising clouds of dirt into the air, past coverless manholes, rubbish heaps, rickshaws, children, cows, cyclists, dead dogs, people—and more people? Or should one begin with the mission guest house, that special form of culture shock specially designed for the new missionary?

Yes, the guest house is where we'll begin. Because here for the first time you will be meeting face to face with real, live missionaries in situ, modern-day Peters and Pauls, flesh-and-blood saints of the kingdom, untouched by the temptations afflicting ordinary Christians. Talk about shock!

Our guest-house hostess was a semi-retired psychiatric nurse from Switzerland named Lilly. She was a warm, friendly, loving soul with a strong German accent, and she kept a clean and tidy house. In addition to a few unmarried missionaries, there were three families in our "group." One family had three angelic daughters; Cynthia and I provided two rowdy boys; and a Norwegian couple contributed a four-year-old named Odmund, who, not knowing either Nepali or English, got along in the guest house by means of his fists and a bottle of ketchup with which he flavored every meal.

From the third day on, the family with the three angelic daughters was placed at Lilly's table for meals, while we and the Norwegian family were consigned to the table at the far end of the dining room, where we remained for the next five months.

One time Lilly received from Switzerland an allotment of sausage meat of distinct and abiding flavor, which she promptly served up at the next meal. Most of it was left on the platter, so the following day it appeared again disguised as stew. The stew also went uneaten, so the third day the sausage returned hidden in a casserole. Three more reincarnations followed before the stuff was either consumed or, more likely, thrown out by the cook. Though not by intent, Lilly had given us one of our first lessons in missionary life: Never throw anything out.

A year after we all had graduated from Lilly's guest house and been assigned to our various projects in different parts of Nepal, the Norwegian family had occasion to visit the guest house again on a trip into Kathmandu. Lilly greeted them in her usual jovial manner, and singling out Odmund she said, "And here's my friend Odmund."

Odmund, now six and possessing a working knowledge of English, replied solemnly: "You are not my friend, you never were my friend, and you never will be my friend." Poor Odmund; even Druk's Quality Ketchup hadn't been able to sweeten his memories of the guest house.

Odmund aside, the guest-house memories of most of our group are sweet indeed. All of us went on to serve many years in Nepal—and some are still here over twenty years later. Some of our best life-long friends have come from that group. A mission guest house produces a special kind of bonding among each new batch of missionaries. Overall, the guest house is a positive experience, and for most of us it eases the passage through culture shock.

During the first week the new missionary will make his or her first forays out of the mission compound and into the city. For some, the lack of sanitation will be "shocking." In some parts of Kathmandu valley, sewerage still flows in open trenches. Chickens and dogs compete for human excrement; one can see dogs licking off children's bottoms after consuming the main business. My brother-in-law paid us a three-month visit once, and on his second day in Kathmandu he witnessed a chicken gobbling up a loose stool. He was unable to eat chicken for the rest of his stay in Nepal. But, on the other hand, think what the streets would be like without these feathered and furry assistants to the Sanitation Department!

For others, the smells will take getting used to; even your apartment in the less congested part of the city will not be immune to smells: the spicy food being cooked next door; the garbage piled at your corner of the street; the trash burning in four adjacent back yards; the dead rats. All of these can be partially neutralized if you are lucky enough to live downwind from the nation's main shoe factory with its belching smokestacks.

The new missionary will also be struck by the pervading atmosphere of the local religion: the multitude of temples, the strangely garbed holy men, the fearsome six-armed gods at whose feet people leave offerings or burn incense. Suddenly the missionary realizes he belongs to a tiny minority religion in the midst of a sea of Hinduism; he feels isolated, alone. This feeling will be especially acute if Hinduism is the state religion, as in Nepal, and if the nationals must break the law to become Christians. You sense for the first time that you are in hostile territory. You feel a little like the king who went to war but forgot to count the enemy's troops.

The feeling of isolation is further magnified if one is assigned to a rural area, especially if one has to walk the final fifteen miles to his station. I vividly remember looking out from our living-room window across tier after tier of foothills, an area of two thousand square miles comprising hundreds of villages—and not one Christian. Our mission project with its dozen missionaries and handful of Nepali Christians was a minuscule speck in that vast expanse. Imagine what it would be like if you were the first couple, or the first pair of schoolteachers, to come into such an area. For most, the experience is exhilarating—the sense that God has put you in one of the darker regions of the earth where there is no other light but you and your tiny team. But for others, the isolation is unsettling, oppressive. It is very much an ingredient of culture shock.

You say the kinds of things I've been describing won't bother you? Maybe not. But—be sure of it—something will! Everyone is vulnerable in some area. There is no place for finger pointing. One man doesn't like crowds; another doesn't like solitude. One likes it cooler; one likes it hotter. My wife doesn't like smells; I don't like dust. I generally keep the windows closed to shut out the noise of radios and barking dogs. She likes to keep the windows open to fill the house with fresh air. Fresh air? In Kathmandu? Or Mexico City? That's like asking for dry rain.

And the thing that finally gets to you won't necessarily be a big thing. It will more likely be an accumulation of little things: trying to extract a parcel from the Foreign Post Office; trying to talk on the telephone; just trying to talk—you can't even speak the language!

The telephone is a special delight. I once lived next door to a garment factory, and the Indian manager would yell into the phone with such vehemence that I thought he might communicate with his party better by just putting his head out the window and shouting across town. Muffled, indistinct sounds crackling with static and interrupted by poor connections is the usual course served up by the telephone systems of the developing world. Indeed, the clearest thing to come over our phone is the recorded message: "Sorry, all lines are engaged." It's no wonder that after a while missionaries begin talking *to* their phones, as well as on them.

Culture shock usually hits the wives hardest—especially those with small children. How to shop, where to shop, what to shop for? You can't even communicate with people. What do you do when your kids get sick? How do you break in a cook who can't read, count, remember, or smell? How do you dry clothes in the rains, or in the winter? They dry fine in May and October if you can save up all your wash for then. How do you light a wood stove in the monsoon—or even the matches? Or how do you cook on an electric stove in the city when the power goes off? And so it goes. And all the while your husband is off "in the work."

Well, wives, cheer up! Your husbands are getting some shocks themselves. There is not only domestic culture shock; there is also professional culture shock.

Imagine His Majesty's Government inviting you to enter the previously closed land of Nepal to start a mission hospital. You are given an old palace to work in, with murals of tiger hunts on the walls and chandeliers in the waiting room. You are being scrutinized closely by the government; you are foreigners, and what's worse, you are Christians. The day of your very first operation comes; it's an umbilical hernia repair, one of the simplest operations in the book, to be done under local anesthesia. You inject the anesthetic—and the patient dies.

Thus began the story of modern missions in Nepal.

Missionaries learn that whenever something goes wrong, they look for God to work. Well, he's been working in Nepal ever since. Never be afraid of failure; God will use it.

"Getting into the work" means unlearning half of what you learned in the West that is useless or inappropriate, and relearning the other half all over again—in a new language. For highly trained doctors and nurses this is an enormous adjustment. From playing with sophisticated electronic gadgets in Western hospitals, you suddenly find yourself in a mud-and-stone facility in the middle of nowhere having to spend a third of your energy just keeping the dust, dogs, spit, and bugs out of your patients' wounds. And then along comes the sweeper raising clouds of assorted dried filth into the air to settle gently on your patients lying downwind.

Schoolteachers face their own kind of traumas. One of the first things the mission did out in our village in Nepal was to start a primary school. One of the first teachers was a fiery Englishman who was assigned to teach a class of seven-year-old Nepali boys who had never so much as heard of school before. The school building was an open-windowed, one-room, mud-walled affair located in the middle of a corn field. The slowness of the students' academic progress was taxing the patience of the Englishman, and one day, after a student failed to respond correctly to a question they had been over a dozen times in the past week, the teacher threw his arms back in exasperation. Unfortunately, he struck his watch against the portable blackboard standing behind him, and his watch fell in pieces onto the floor. The students took fright, jumped up, and leapt out the windows, half of them wetting their pants on the way out. The teacher ran outside, but there was not a student in sight. They were hiding in the cornfield. So he went up and down the rows calling, "Come back, come back, I'm not really angry; don't be afraid." And finding them one by one, he finally managed to coax them all back into the classroom. This was one eventuality, surely, that had not been covered in his teacher's training course.

The rural church planter will fare no better. He may use that same school building for his church. The few Christians who come are mainly women and children, and the few men are only there hoping to get a job. You doubt if any of your teaching is getting through. You are a drop in a big, wide pond—a pond not favorably inclined to your new religion.

Culture shock isn't something one gets over and never has to think about again; it can affect old-timers too. I recall a veteran missionary who was responsible for finishing the construction of our mission hospital. I was new, and he had been all his life serving in India. One day I heard him sternly rebuking the carpenters for shoddy workmanship on the window frames. They looked pretty good to me, given the fact they were hacked out with hammer and chisel. He said to me, "This is intolerable. You can't let them get away with work like this."

I couldn't understand how this experienced missionary could be upset by such a relatively small matter, but I've since come to understand why. He had become sensitized to poor carpentry. He had been fighting malfitting windows for all of his thirty years in India, and it was bothering him just as much now as it had in the beginning.

Well, you say, he shouldn't have been fighting those windows all that time; he should have been accepting them. It's a spiritual problem, not a carpentry problem. Well, yes, everything is at root a spiritual problem. We shouldn't get upset with anything God isn't upset with. But the fact remains, we do. And we need to understand and be patient with each other. Because while bad carpentry may get to one person, something else will get to you—something that wouldn't in the slightest bother anyone else. We must resist the temptation to label another person "unspiritual" simply because he is vulnerable to a particular irritation. Now if it's five or ten irritations that are tripping him up, that's a more serious matter; but most missionaries have one or two intractable hang-ups, and that doesn't seem to hamper their overall ministry. Not that we should treat hang-ups complacently, of course; we must pray for each other.

Let's say you're a Bible translator working in a new language ten to twelve hours a day. You spend a fair part of your time in Kathmandu. Working in another language requires concentration. Your landlady owns a big dog named Tiger, whose chief purpose in life is to stand on the roof over your office and bark at passers-by, other dogs, squirrels, birds, and moving leaves. There are few moments in the day or night when this dog is not at its post doing its duty; you wonder when it sleeps or eats. You get along all right for the first month, but by the second month you are having trouble concentrating, partly because of the barking, but also because you can't sleep. You mention the matter to the landlady, but she sees no problem. When Tiger barks, she knows her house is safe. Nepalis aren't troubled by barking dogs; in fact, at night if their dog stops barking they wake up and wonder what's going on.

By the end of the second month, you have become sensitized to Tiger's bark. Even Mack's Finest Pillow-Soft Earplugs will not keep it out. The only solution is a Sony Walkman and a tape recording of a waterfall or Mahler's Eighth Symphony played at full volume.

But Tiger is only part of the problem. There are the neighbors' dogs, perhaps twenty of which live within barking distance of your office. Then there is the carpentry shop that operates in the empty lot next door. Aside from the laughing and talking and hammers and saws of the eight carpenters, there is their radio, played at sufficient volume so that all can hear it above the din of their work. The fare is mainly Indian popular music, and the female vocalists reverberate through your windowpanes as if they were right in the room with you. And there are the children at school down the block, and the singing mendicants that stand under your window and sing until you toss money down on them, or bricks. And best, there are the Hindu worship ceremonies in which people place loudspeakers on the tops of their houses and edify the community with chanting and religious instruction. The bigger the loudspeaker and the more people edified, the greater the merit accruing to the family who has paid the priests to perform the ceremony. But that is not all. These ceremonies last either one day, three days, five days, or seven days: hence they are called "one-ers," "three-ers," "fivers," and "seveners." They say there is also a niner, but I have not met anyone who has survived it. At the end of the first twenty-four hours, there is a moment of tension; if the ceremony continues a minute beyond, you know you will be in for another forty-eight hours of it. The tension is greatly heightened at the seventy-two-hour mark, and it is almost unbearable at the end of five days, as you wait to see if your ordeal will continue yet another forty-eight hours. And after you've experienced five or six of these ceremonies, your heart sinks every time you hear a new one start up. Will you be able to stand that loudspeaker one more day, one more hour, one more minute?

And so if, by chance, you should see an otherwise mild-mannered, scholarly missionary standing on his roof hurling stones at loudspeakers or passing dogs, don't rush to judgment. He may indeed be losing it, but it is not without reason.

Of course, people at home have irritations too. The only difference is, really, that irritations on the mission field are ten times greater, both in variety and in intensity. It's all part of this thing we call culture shock.

A final example of professional culture shock awaits those missionaries who are assigned to work in government institutions. Most developing nations are blessed with bright, well-trained leaders and an abundance of low-paid manpower. The problem lies in the middle level, with that collection of civil servants, clerks, and secretaries who actually run the machinery of government. The most powerful ministers cannot budge this entrenched mass of bureaucrats. If you think it's bad in the USA, come to Nepal.

Not long ago my wife Cynthia, who teaches in Nepal's only medical school, was scheduled to conduct examinations for several of the classes. But early that morning a former prime minister died; a national holiday was hastily announced over Radio Nepal. The medical school dean, together with the heads of the various departments, decided that the examinations should go on as scheduled, and they notified all key people by phone. All duly arrived, only to discover that the gatekeeper was observing the holiday. To a man they were all locked out, and the examinations had to be rescheduled. If the man with the key is not there, you can be a Ph.D. from Harvard or the Health Minister himself, and it will do you not one whit of good.

And indeed, Cynthia has found life in the Institute of Medicine a daily adventure in trying to make the system work. A week after beginning work, her boss was in jail as a revolutionary; two months later he was the new Health Minister. After six months Cynthia finally got her own desk. Three months later it was given to someone else, together with her books and papers. After a year, she was asked to be the coordinator of the Bachelor in Public Health program, a job none of the Nepalis wanted—they knew what a headache it would be. Professors would agree to teach a certain class, and then at the last minute announce they couldn't make it—or just not show up. The coordinator gets blamed, of course. Scheduling field trips was a particular challenge: professors would begin falling like flies when their turn to go to the field came up. They'd have attacks of migraine, depression, gastritis; or their wives and children would become ill and require their presence at home. And, in case you're feeling sorry for the students, don't bother. They were as much at fault themselves. Professors would come to teach, but there would be no students; they'd be off at a class picnic or a political rally. Or they'd be holding a "pen-down"—that is, refusing to take notes in class. Or they would decide to skip class in order to study for an upcoming exam in another subject. In spite of all this, Cynthia assures me that quite a few classes continue to be attended and taught, and medical education does continue to take place. The larger issue, of course, is what spiritual fruit will result from Cynthia's efforts, for without that she will have accomplished little of lasting worth.

What is culture shock?

Culture shock is primarily a sense of disorientation, together with the uneasiness and anxiety that such disorientation produces. You discover that you must learn to do many things differently: working, eating, talking—just daily living. There are so many new customs and procedures to master that you can't seem to do anything right. This can place a high degree of stress on a new missionary, especially one who has always put a premium on doing things right.

People experiencing culture shock are anxious about how well they'll be able to cope with their new environment. Will they make fools of themselves? How will they set up house? How will they provide good meals for their family? How much should they pay for pineapples, kerosene, firewood? When the questions come by the dozens each day, one can feel overwhelmed.

Lucky is the new missionary who has a sympathetic and helpful older friend who can answer questions and smooth the way. Unfortunately, many senior missionaries seem to have forgotten their own battle with culture shock, or if they haven't, they feel the new people should experience it for themselves.

Culture shock often begins to take hold in earnest six to eight months after one's arrival on the field, at which time the initial romance and excitement of the new country has mostly worn off and the new missionary is trying to set up house and get into the work. The language is coming slowly; he has already had seven bouts with dysentery. He doesn't like the food. There are inconveniences and problems at every turn. He thinks: "Three (or thirty) more years of this!"

Culture shock is magnified when we enter a culture that is very different from our own; the necessary adaptation we must make is that much greater. The values of the people, their temperament, their life style may be markedly different from our own. The climate of the country, the crowding, the clamor, the lack of amenities, the poor hygiene, the poverty, the sickness—all these may be utterly foreign to our experience. The greater the difference, the greater the culture shock.

Obviously if we suffer from emotional instability or insecurity, the stress of culture shock will be increased. A heavy work load, illness, fatigue, worry about children, interpersonal conflict, and job dissatisfaction will all aggravate culture shock.

Culture shock and its attendant anxiety produce a number of symptoms, which missionaries old and new need to be aware of.

The first is fatigue. The struggle to adapt to a new culture is wearing. The associated anxiety itself is wearing. The missionary is tired out before he's even begun. Wrinkled, white-haired missionaries have more energy than he does. And this further increases his anxiety, which further increases his fatigue. He begins to think he made a giant mistake in coming to this country!

The second symptom is discouragement, depression. The more we sense we're failing and the more we compare ourselves to others, the more we shall become discouraged. The problem with discouragement is that it leads to paralysis. But paralysis is exactly what we must break out of if we are going to make friends with people and overcome culture shock.

The third symptom is a critical spirit. When we feel anxious and under pressure, one of the commonest defense mechanisms is to blame the other guy, in this case the nationals. We may begin to dislike them, resent them. It's their country, after all, that is causing our distress. If only they'd introduce some efficiencies, if only they'd run things on time, if only they'd keep their word, if only...if only....

Our critical spirit may spill over onto our mission leaders or other colleagues. If one looks, one can always find fault. "If they had arranged for a better orientation, or a more suitable assignment, I wouldn't be having these problems," goes the refrain. But blaming others isn't going to help solve the problems.

The fourth symptom, oddly, is a feeling of guilt. This occurs mainly in missionaries from richer countries, especially those countries that have been accused (with partial accuracy) of exploiting the Third World. They have bought into the line that the over-consumption in their own countries is somehow responsible for the poverty of the country they have come to. There is very little truth in this idea. The causes of poverty are many, but the missionary and his countrymen are not among them. Don't fall prey to that sentimental feeling that wealthy tourists sometimes get: "I'm so rich; they're so poor." Guard against the urge to give money here and there to salve your conscience. This is a false guilt you are experiencing. Money given under such circumstances will usually do more harm than good, and it won't eradicate the economic difference between you and the nationals anyway.

The fifth symptom of culture shock is pessimism. You look at the need around you and think, "My contribution is a drop in the bucket; it's worthless." It's always more than a drop, of course. Missions, for instance, have provided twenty to fifty percent of the medical services in many countries, and that's more than a drop. And even if it were only a drop, that drop would be precious in God's sight. Those five loaves and two fish were only "drops," but Jesus used them to feed five thousand men and their families.

The sixth symptom of culture shock is self-pity. Things are stacked against you. Everyone overcharges you. You have trouble getting your visa. You are charged double duty by customs officials on equipment you've brought into the country to serve their own people. Many times the people you're serving couldn't care a hoot whether you came or not. And so you begin to feel unappreciated. The best cure for that is to remember that Jesus was unappreciated too. He didn't come to get appreciation, and neither did we. Our job is to follow where Jesus leads, to love, and to expect nothing in return.

Overcoming culture shock

Many new arrivals to the field have the misconception that they can protect themselves from culture shock in the early days by minimizing their involvement with the host people. For most, however, this is unwise; because in the long run the best way to overcome culture shock is to expose oneself to the culture and the people. Sooner or later, if one is to feel comfortable in—and ideally to enjoy—the host culture, one must more and more reach out, make friends, and adapt, adapt, adapt.

The need to reach out, to expose oneself, cannot be emphasized too strongly. New missionaries do this at different rates of speed, but all must do it if they want to avoid remaining forever in a missionary subculture or forever throwing stones at dogs or yelling at carpenters because the window frames are crooked. We must at all costs prevent a "we-and-they" mentality from taking root. If it does, we shall always be only foreigners, visitors, guests. We are all of those things anyway, but we want to be more: we want to be friends, colleagues, partners, and equals with the national people.

I have earlier mentioned Michael Griffiths' visit to Nepal as a guest speaker at one of our mission conferences, and how within a day he had detected a "we-and-they" attitude among us. There were few Nepalis present at the conference, so what tipped him off? It was the way we talked about the Nepalis—as if they were a different species from us. We criticized them, dissected them. Maybe we justified this by saying we could thereby pray for them in a more informed way. But we are not entitled to pass on criticisms about anyone—even if they are disguised as "prayer concerns."

There's another reason not to criticize nationals, or anyone else for that matter: for every defect you find in them, they are finding one in you—or, more likely, two or three. Criticism breeds criticism. It is all too easy to become preoccupied with the faults of others, and when that happens you can forget about relationship building.

The natural tendency with all of us is to stay within the security of our own culture and support group, and merely make forays into the unfamiliar culture around us. It takes an active effort of the will to overcome this ethnocentrism. Ethnocentrism is as harmful to intercultural relations as egocentrism is to interpersonal relations. If we are to achieve the most fruitful possible relationship with nationals—a relationship of partnership, friendship, and equality—we need to consciously break out of our culture and enter theirs.

Now this entering into the host culture does not mean that we deny our own culture, or try to hide it. We are who we are, and there's nothing wrong with that. Instead, entering into another culture means enjoying and respecting that culture, and participating in it. To go back to the analogy in the very beginning of this chapter, it means "joining the other team." I may be white and have a funny accent and funny mannerisms, and I may have had utterly different experiences in the past, but I am invited to play as a member of their team. And that is a very great joy and privilege. And just as a member, don't forget, not as the captain.

To a practical extent, I want to minimize the differences between me and my teammates. I'll wear their uniform, and play according to their rules. I'll practice when they practice. But there are some differences I may want to preserve. I don't want to forget all the tricks of the game I learned in my own country. I may have something unique to offer the team, which, if offered in the right way, will be gladly accepted. This is one reason I was invited to be on the team in the first place.

The team concept is an ideal which in some situations is hard to realize. In Nepal, for example, missionaries were invited in by the government to set up hospitals and schools and various development programs. We are the experts. We are managers and captains of the team, and in many cases the first-string players as well. We set the rules. Why? Because very few Nepalis in the beginning knew how to play our games of building hospitals and schools. So from the beginning, we have set out to teach the Nepalis to play, we have invited more and more of them to join our team—and our goal is that, in the end, our team will become their team. And we trust that they'll invite us to keep playing.

This whole matter of how far to integrate with the host people is largely a matter of common sense. We're not called to adopt the host culture, only to adapt to it. Some missionaries, depending on their temperaments and work situations, will integrate to a greater extent than others. It is futile to try to integrate totally, to "go native." Except in rare cases, we can never really become insiders. We will always be slightly different. But if we reach out in humility, in respect, in friendliness, in love, those differences will become irrelevant. We'll be accepted. The "we and they" will disappear; it will all be "we."

Remember, too, that we have vastly more things in common with our national friends than we have differences. We share all the basic human characteristics: the same body, the same emotions, the same joys, sorrows, fears, and hopes. And above all, we have the same spiritual needs for forgiveness and salvation. We will all one day stand before the same God. Let us focus on our similarities, and the differences will fade into the background.

So now we can see that some of the principles of overcoming culture shock are falling into place. Remember, we don't want to just cope; we want to overcome. Let's look at some of the practical ways to stay on top of this bugaboo called culture shock.

First, recognize it. It's normal. You will survive it. You will simply get used to the things that shocked you at first. Some things take more getting used to than others, but in the end you'll say: "It was no big deal."

Experiencing culture shock doesn't mean you weren't cut out to be a missionary; it happens to anyone who crosses cultural boundaries. The only people who can escape culture shock are missionary children and very short-termers. It's hard to have real culture shock when you've got an air ticket out of the country in six weeks.

Second, pray earnestly for God's grace and enabling. The struggles you are facing are not only cultural; they are also spiritual.

Third, determine that in all but ethical and religious matters you are going to adapt to the nationals; you adapt to them, not they to you. Cultivate a positive attitude; don't adapt grudgingly. Look for the good things in their culture; there will be many.

Fourth, go out of your way to make a circle of friends. Start from day one with the cooks in the guest house, or with your landlord. (These friendships may yield you some important dividends to boot.) Extend the circle to shopkeepers, neighbors, and other people you engage in conversation. The more national friends you make, the more at home you're going to feel in their culture, and the more opportunities for witness you are going to find.

Fifth, put yourself in the nationals' shoes. We have mentioned this before, but it bears repeating. Try to see things through their eyes. Think about their needs, their limitations, their aspirations. They are not happy with many things in their own culture. Poverty limits their choices. Poverty makes good sewerage systems impossible. Don't complain; understand.

As you grow to understand the nationals better, you will begin to respond to them with sympathy, with caring. You will be less judgmental. You will begin to identify with the people and their problems. Instead of focusing on how much their strangeness is threatening you, you will begin focusing on them as people in need, as people you can befriend and help—and, in addition, as people who can befriend and help you.

As the bonds between you and the people increase, you will no longer feel you are alone in an alien world. You will feel part of your new environment instead of threatened by it. You will become a member of the team.

Sixth, cultivate an attitude of exploration, of adventure. Be willing to try new things, new foods. As you do this, culture shock will give way to culture stimulation. Adaptation isn't only a passive process; it's an active engaging of a new situation and reaching an accommodation with it. You are no longer just a pawn or a victim. And even when you have failed your first language exam, and your baby is sick, and you can't locate that crucial parcel in the Foreign Post Office, you won't feel that "the world is against me." That's when you'll know you are on the way to overcoming culture shock.

Seventh—and this I include with caution—maintain close links with your fellow missionaries. It is not a cure for culture shock, but periodically we need the refreshment, encouragement, and counsel that can best come from those of our own culture. In addition, it is perfectly normal to enjoy other reminders of our home culture: favorite household objects, old family traditions, familiar toys for the kids. A few have even brought a dog with them, though I confess to feeling this is rarely necessary. We have plenty of dogs in Nepal, after all!

Retreating back into our own cultural milieu, however, can become habitual; this is its danger. We come to rely more and more on the people and things of our own culture, and thus become more and more isolated from the people we've come to serve. Retreating in this way may shield us from culture shock for a time, but in the end it will prolong our adaptation, and may, in fact, prevent us from ever making deep contact with the people.

Eighth and last, don't take yourself too seriously. Learn to laugh at yourself. That's hard to do for those who lack self-confidence, but it's worth the effort. It's also hard to do when you're red-faced with embarrassment or feeling totally incompetent. Still it is possible—maybe after a few moments, or after a few months. But there will always be those few things which one can't laugh about even years later.

Though we've spent a whole chapter on it, let's not make an overly big thing of culture shock. Yes, it's real, and for some it causes real problems. But for the great majority of missionaries it is but a temporary phenomenon. We said earlier that culture shock was basically disorientation. The solution to it, then, is to get oriented. That means getting oriented to a lot of little things, which can be dealt with one by one. Learn from your mistakes. Learn to buy Great Wall pencils instead of Squirrel pencils. They're both made in China, but the lead in Squirrel pencils is off-center, so when you sharpen them you end up with pointed sticks more suitable for spearing cockroaches than for writing. Getting over culture shock is learning to buy the right kind of pencils.

Learning the language

I have deliberately left to the end two extremely important subjects related to culture shock and adaptation, the first of which is language acquisition, and the second, bonding.

Everything that has been discussed in these past three chapters is dependent on our gaining some measure of fluency in the host language. Lack of language is a major component of culture shock. "Help! I can't talk! I can't understand! They're laughing at me!" Hence, learning the language is clearly essential if we are going to move beyond culture shock and adapt to the host culture.

Those coming to the mission field for under six months or those who have been called to perform some special task do not need to study the language—though they'd do well to pick up a few common phrases. Those who plan to stay on the field one to two years should definitely try to learn something of the language, if only to show that they care enough about the local people to spend that effort. Learning the language is a sign of friendship and respect. It will reveal the missionary's attitude, which the nationals will pay even more heed to than the words he learns and the work he does.

For all missionaries staying more than two years, language acquisition should be required except in the rarest cases. Anyone joining the United Mission to Nepal is expected to spend five months in language school and then study the language quarter time for the next year. This is the minimum requirement, and for most of us it is only the beginning. Much more time and study and practice is needed before one can become fluent to any degree. Lucky is the missionary who is assigned to a rural area where no one speaks his language; he is forced to use the local language just to survive. If I, for example, had been assigned initially to Kathmandu, where thousands of Nepalis are trying to practice their English, I doubt I would ever have learned Nepali well.

Anyone with half his marbles can learn a foreign language. As we said earlier, difficulty in mastering languages is never a valid reason to shun the mission field. For some, learning language is more difficult than for others, but everyone will learn in time. Learning a language is one-third natural ability, one-third exposure, and one-third motivation. If we have two out of the three, we'll succeed. We all ought to have the motivation, and we can all get the exposure. The natural ability is nice, but not necessary.

Often people inquiring into missions say to me: "I'm terrible at language; I don't think I could be a missionary." Well, they are talking to the wrong person. I usually say to them: "Nonsense. If I could learn the language, any idiot can." Well, I may not use those exact words, but the sentiment is the same.

I spent five thousand hours studying Nepali, and my wife Cynthia was speaking it better than I in one-tenth the time. I derive some consolation from knowing that women generally do better at language than men— though not that much better. Even our children made me look like a dunce. For a whole year the gardener had to communicate with me through our five-year-old son.

There are no shortcuts to learning a language. It takes discipline and persistence. Don't be discouraged. You may apply yourself for six months and see no progress. Then, all of a sudden, you will notice you are speaking and understanding more easily. Progress becomes a series of upward jumps rather than a steadily ascending line.

A major hindrance is our self-consciousness—or, more accurately, our pride. We, the great missionary teacher, health professional, economic expert, don't like being laughed at. We don't enjoy talking like a four-year-old.

And it doesn't help that the nationals won't correct you—even if you ask them to. They are so polite; they assure you that you are doing fine. Or maybe they just don't want to lose the entertainment value of your bloopers.

Just mix up two little endings, and you'll soon be saying things like: "The ball picked up the boy and threw him through the window." Or, if you are into more complex sentences, you might say: "After eating the cow, the cabbage hit the stick on the head with the shopkeeper."

Sometimes it's years before you discover you've been saying something wrong. A veteran medical colleague of mine used to give her patients careful instructions to start taking their medicine "yesterday," leaving not a few of them even more bewildered by the mission hospital than they had been to start with.

At least Nepali isn't as bad as Chinese. Marjorie Collins tells of the missionary pastor in China who thought he was saying, "Our Father, who art in heaven," but was actually saying, "My pants are in the field." If I had been a local, I think I'd have tried to enjoy that one as long as I could!

Don't think to yourself: "Almost all the nationals I deal with speak English, so I don't really need to learn this language." Yes, they may speak English, but they will rarely speak it well enough to understand spiritual matters. If you want to communicate with them on a spiritual level, you will need to do that in their language, not yours.

It is in one's mother tongue or "heart language" that one most readily receives and comprehends spiritual truth. This is why workers are translating the New Testament into many of Nepal's tribal languages, even when the people know Nepali. It is when people are spoken to in their mother tongue that they become truly stirred.

How fluent do you have to be? You can "get along" with only a little bit of the language, but you will never become an effective teacher or evangelist unless you become fluent.

If you're "lucky," you may end up in a situation which requires that you learn two languages. Like Nepal, many countries are made up of tribes, each with its own language. But the people of the different tribes all speak a "trade language," in order to communicate and do business with each other. The missionary may have to learn that trade language, as well as the tribal language of the people he works with. In other cases, as in the former Soviet Union, the official language is Russian, but the many nationalities within the former Soviet empire each speak their own national languages. A missionary, then, may need to learn both Russian and a national language. So, don't complain if you have only one language to learn!

A final word of encouragement: language learning needn't become drudgery; it can be enjoyable. Yes, drills and memorizing vocabulary words aren't one's usual idea of fun, but reading and writing can be. Treat them as puzzles and tests of skill. And if you get the right book, reading can be downright hilarious.

The final and most important part of language learning is conversation with nationals, and that also should be an enjoyable and stimulating time. I recall conversing with a young Nepali schoolteacher one afternoon, after we had been in Nepal about five years. His mother supplied us with milk. We talked two hours on a wide range of subjects, and I was privately congratulating myself on my mastery of the Nepali language. When it was time for him to go, he stopped on the way out to greet Cynthia.

Cynthia said to him, "We appreciate the good milk your mother sends us."

He replied, "Oh, it's nice to hear you talk. It's a pleasure to listen to someone who can speak Nepali well."

Cynthia had spoken only one sentence. So much for the pleasures of conversation. I could have kicked him down the steps.

Pleasures or no, the best way to really learn a language is to immerse yourself in it. Observe; listen; and speak, speak, speak. It won't come naturally to introverts and perfectionists, but there is no other way to become fluent. Many missions are today using a method popularized by Thomas and Elizabeth Brewster, "Language Acquisition Made Practical" (LAMP), in which the new missionary from almost day one is sent out to live in a national home. Not only has this method proved to be the most rapid and effective way to learn a language, but it facilitates the bonding of the new missionary to the host people, a subject to which we now turn.

Bonding

In discussing how to overcome culture shock, we have already mentioned the need for the missionary to reach out, to enter the new culture, to join the host team. Bonding is not something different from this; it is simply carrying the principles we have talked about to their deepest level of application. For joining the team is one step; developing deep bonds of love and mutuality between teammates is the next step.

Missionaries form a continuous spectrum in the degree to which they bond with the host people. On the one extreme are those few who remain isolated in a missionary subculture. In the broad center are those who participate in varying degrees with the host people. Their degree of participation will often be determined by the host people themselves, but they are on the team; they have been accepted. Finally, on the other end of the spectrum are those who fully bond with the people. At the outset, we can say as a generalization that the greater the degree of bonding, the more effective will be the missionary as a Christian witness. Thus bonding is to be encouraged. It is not only the final solution to culture shock; it is also a tremendous asset to one's ministry.

Remaining isolated in a missionary subculture is obviously undesirable. A subculture tends to become more and more ingrown, and less and less interested in things outside the group. There is a big difference between a subculture and a support group. A support group supports you as you reach out; a subculture encloses and isolates you. Missionaries must preserve the proper balance between retreating for support and reaching out for ministry.

Finding one's spot on the bonding spectrum is not a once-for-all matter. During their careers many missionaries will move back and forth along this spectrum depending on their family situation and the nature of their assignment. Missionaries with children usually find that a lesser degree of bonding is better for their family; unmarried missionaries can generally bond with the people to a greater degree.

The best time for bonding to begin is within the first few weeks of arrival on the field It can happen later, but in those early days new missionaries are uniquely prepared and motivated for bonding. They are filled with anticipation and excitement; they desire acceptance; they have as yet had no bad experiences.

What is bonding? Bonding is a deep level of identification, wherein one feels himself at one with the host people. He feels comfortable among them. He spends much of his leisure time with them. He draws emotional support from their friendship. And these positive feelings are almost always reciprocated.

Even though bonding is desirable, it should not be made a rule for all. Some are temperamentally and emotionally unable to handle bonding. They should not be made to feel guilty by those who do bond fully.

By the same token, those who don't bond must never criticize those who do. Sadly, this often happens. Some criticize out of jealousy, when they see how easily the bonded missionary relates to the people. Others are suspicious, defensive; they feel threatened by the bonded missionary's success. Indeed, alienation from one's fellow missionaries is a price some have to pay for bonding.

The best way to facilitate bonding is to place the new missionary with a national family during the language learning period. New missionaries should never be pressured into this, especially if they are shy and diffident, or have families. It must remain a matter of choice. If a new missionary is uncertain whether he is the "bonding type," let him try it—let him take the risk. There is no shame if it doesn't work out. He can always come back into the mission guest house.

The rate of bonding also varies from person to person. Many do well with the "dive in" approach; others prefer to "get wet gradually." If in doubt, dive. There is no intrinsic advantage to prolonging the period of adaptation, and there is always the chance that one never will adapt as fully as he might have if he had just dived in to start with.

One of the main advantages of "diving in," to moving into a Nepali home, is that you, as a foreign missionary, become vulnerable; you have needs. You become dependent on your hosts for many things. This is very important in building a truly reciprocal relationship—the key to successful bonding. No longer are you simply the foreign expert with something to give. One of our mission nurses who had run a medical clinic for many years once broke her arm. When she went next day to the clinic with a cast on, people volunteered to help her do her work; they befriended her in a new way. She said, "Breaking my arm changed my relationship with the Nepalis for the better. I wish I had broken it years ago."

Bonding is an identification with the people on a psychological level, as well as on a physical or external level. The external level is important as a sign of our desire to bond. We wear the national hat, we eat with our fingers, we learn the language and customs of the nationals, and in so doing we show them our respect. They naturally respond to this. They say of us: "That missionary understands us; he wants to be our friend."

Some new missionaries start out getting all the externals right, but they can't seem to go deeper than that. They often look askance at older missionaries who don't live exactly like the people do. But they themselves, after a few years of "doing things right," end up going home. True bonding never took place.

In other words, it is not enough to live like the people; we must also think like them. It is possible to live exactly like them, but be miles apart from them in mutual understanding, appreciation, and caring. After all, bonding isn't simply identification with some idealized cultural group; it is identification with individuals, real people. Bonding is personal.

Successful bonding does not require total identification or "going native." As we said earlier, this is impossible anyway. We will always be different.

One missionary schoolteacher living in a Nepali village made an almost total adaptation to the local people. She lived exactly as they did—except for one thing: she owned a plastic bucket. That plastic bucket was the talk of the village women. The missionary was indeed different from them!

But that missionary teacher did know what was required to bond with those village women. That is, she had genuine love for them, a desire to be with them, a willingness to serve them, to sacrifice for them. If we manifest these things, then it will matter little whether we wear the national cap, whether we eat Western food once a day, whether we have two or twenty shirts in our cupboard, or whether we own a plastic bucket.

Since bonding is an identification with the host people on a psychological level, we need to know what are the components of such identification. First is a willingness to see things from the people's point of view, to get inside their minds. This means that we start where they are at. For example, if they have "felt needs," we start there, even though those may not be their real needs. Second is respect and appreciation for the people and their cultural heritage. Third is a desire to receive from them, to learn from them, along with the acknowledgment that they have much of value to give us. Fourth is reciprocity, mutuality. Even as we seek to enter their lives, we invite them into ours. This means that we are open and welcoming. Fifth, and most important of all by far, is love—specifically love from the Holy Spirit. When these five components are present, real identification, real bonding has taken place.

In the process we do not lose or give up our own identity. We remain unique bearers of the good news of the gospel. Neither must we identify in every way with our hosts. We cannot identify with them, for instance, in those aspects of their culture which are contrary to Scripture: caste observance, debasement of women, bribery, and of course, the worship of false gods and idols. We must retain our objectivity, our ability to discriminate. But if we have identified with them in most other ways, bonding will occur. And when it does, we will have reached the hearts of the people. The barriers of foreignness, of misunderstanding, of different lifestyles will have been removed. The people will be ready to listen to us. We, in turn, will be able to communicate the gospel to them in the most effective way possible. This, above all, is why bonding is so important.

It is often difficult for nationals to enter into our lives the way we seek to enter theirs. We shouldn't expect them to. They have had no exposure to our culture apart from us and from movies and magazines. They can't imagine what life is really like in the more developed nations. I recall when one of our closest Nepali friends went to a conference for itinerant evangelists in Amsterdam some years back. It was his first time in the West. He said to us, "My goodness, now I know what you gave up to come to Nepal!" It would help moderate our "rich missionary" image if more of our national colleagues could visit the West.

It is often assumed that missionaries from the Third World will have a much easier time bonding with the host people than missionaries from the First World. But, in fact, this is not the case. Many times Third World missionaries have a much greater problem establishing close relationships with the people. In Hindu culture, for example, it is extremely difficult for Indian missionaries to bond with those of other castes, even within their own country. Korean and Japanese missionaries are not automatically welcomed in Nepal simply because they are from Asia. They have just as much difficulty bonding with Nepalis as Westerners do—perhaps more, because they come from mono-ethnic societies and aren't used to mixing with those of other cultures. So don't buy the false line that only Third World missionaries can relate to the people of Third World countries, and that therefore First World missionaries should stay at home!

When we bond or identify with the host people, we are simply following the example of Paul and Jesus. Paul wrote to the Corinthians, "To the Jews I became like a Jew.... To those under the law I became like one under the law.... To the weak I became weak.... I have become all things to all men so that by all possible means I might save some" (1 Co 9:20,22). Paul identified with the people of whichever group he was trying to reach. In doing this, he never compromised on fundamentals. But in all else he was prepared to. He had Timothy circumcised, not for salvation, but so that he would be more acceptable to the Jews (Ac 16:3).

Jesus is our primary example of identification. He forsook the prerogatives of heaven and made himself like us—even the lowest among us, a servant. He shared our predicament in everything except our sinfulness. He paid a high price; he gave his life as a sacrifice. In all of this, he is a model for us. "As the Father has sent me, I am sending you" (Jn 20:21).

This is what is meant when missionaries speak of the "incarnational model." It is the fullest manifestation of all we have been talking about. When we come to the people in sacrificial love we are modeling the incarnation. The people may or may not see our sacrifice, but they will sense it. It may involve family separation, broken health, physical deprivation, the loss of advantage, reputation, security, even life. But it is this kind of sacrifice and the love which motivates it that wins people to Christ.

As we seek the Holy Spirit's help to model these aspects of Christ's incarnation, let us also seek to model Christ's character. This is our first and primary calling—"to be conformed to the likeness of his Son" (Ro 8:29). Without this conformity, all else is empty words. As one old man said to a missionary: "We have heard much preaching. Can you show us the life of your Lord Jesus?"

7

Kings, Cooks, Beggars, Saints

Together with getting over culture shock and learning to relate cross-culturally, the missionary must get to know the various classes of people he or she is going to be dealing with. Situations will arise that will demand much tact and wisdom. And there will be dilemmas to which there is no one right answer. It's all part of the ongoing learning experience called "being a missionary."

Dealing with national authorities

If it is necessary to leave our ethnocentrism at home, it certainly is necessary to leave our national pride and politics at home as well. Never should a missionary be seen as an advocate of his own country. And he certainly must have nothing to do with his country's intelligence service! Yes, we can continue to love our own country and be grateful we were born there; it is the pride we must leave behind. After all, being a citizen of America or Norway or Korea is a very small thing compared to being a citizen of the kingdom of God.

A missionary must scrupulously obey the laws of the host country—unless, of course, a law violates a clear scriptural principle, in which case we must follow the example of Peter and John when they refused to obey

102

the Sanhedrin's orders to keep silent. God's law always supercedes man's law.

Missionaries are guests, and as such they must not entangle themselves in matters that do not directly concern them. They should limit themselves to activities for which the government has given them permission. They should, in particular, refrain from siding with any political faction in the country—even if it seems to embody righteousness and justice. All political movements clothe themselves in righteousness and justice, but once their leaders gain power, most of them are just as bad as the "villains" they threw out. There is no advantage in antagonizing one party in favor of another. The minute the antagonized party takes power, the missionary will be out on his ear. And what makes us think we'll be able to understand the politics of the host country? It's difficult enough understanding the politics of our own country.

Therefore, be respectful toward all who are in authority; respect their position, even if you can't respect the individual. But do not identify too closely with those in power. They will lose their power one day, and you may lose your place as well. The rule is: don't do anything that will jeopardize the advance of the kingdom of God. Even be careful what you write in letters; mail is often censored.

These, then, are the principles. Putting them into practice is another matter. What do you do, for example, if the government in power is clearly abusing human rights?

First, keep your priorities straight. Paul had to deal with one of the wickedest governments in history, and yet he avoided confronting it head-on, except where his own rights as a Roman citizen were concerned. He surely opposed slavery in his heart, but he didn't publicly fight against it. His sole objective was to build God's church, and he refrained from doing anything that might jeopardize the fulfillment of that objective.

We, too, need to take that same stance in dealing with governments that abuse human rights. We need to choose carefully what we are going to oppose publicly, and we need to be sure that such a stand is essential to our Christian witness. In all cases, we must act in concert with and under the leadership of the national church—being careful that we are not following just one faction of the church leadership. We as foreigners must never take the lead in criticizing the host government. Even national Christians who agree with us in principle will not appreciate hearing a foreigner criticize their country.

We Westerners are very self-righteous when it comes to human rights, and too quickly get fired up when we hear of their abuse. Remember, we often work in countries which do not have a tradition of Western-style democracy. They may have signed the United Nations Declaration on Human Rights, but they may not have adopted it in practice within their own borders. The national people may not see things as we do. They may view our human-rights activism as an attempt to import a Western political agenda. If we get this reputation, our larger spiritual purpose for coming to their country will be frustrated. The first objective is to change men's hearts; their respect for human rights will quickly follow.

Missionaries' ill-advised involvement in human-rights activities and other worthy political causes can lead to three grave consequences. First, they may implicate the local church in their activities, and expose national Christians to persecution. The Western missionary takes little or no risk; he merely gets expelled, while the national believer may be harassed, jailed, or worse. The national Christians must take the lead, and if they are reluctant to do so, the missionary should be even more reluctant.

The second consequence of ill-advised human-rights activism on the part of missionaries is that they may end up supporting a cause they hadn't bargained for. Before the revolution of 1990, most human-rights organizations in Nepal were dominated by Communists, whose track record in the field leaves something to be desired. To align ourselves with such groups would have been harmful to our ministry in the country.

The third consequence of missionaries becoming involved in political causes is that such involvement can lead to splits in both the missionary community and the national church. In one Asian country in the late seventies, a number of missionaries felt they should oppose the autocratic government in power at the time—in spite of the fact that it was one of the more progressive governments in Asia. These missionaries were, in effect, joining the political opposition; their actions were fueled, in part, by their own Western political biases. They split first the missionary community, and then contributed to splitting the church along the same lines. Their activity ended up doing considerable harm to the advancement of the gospel in that country. If their consciences did not allow them to cooperate in any way with the government in power, they should have left the country quietly, instead of making it more difficult for those missionaries who felt called to carry on.

The United Mission to Nepal prior to 1990 represents a case study in working with a restrictive regime. Previous governments denied their citizens certain basic freedoms, most prominently the freedom of conscience and religion. It was against the law for any Hindu Nepali to convert to another religion; the punishment was a one-year jail sentence. Yet successive governments repeatedly renewed their agreement to allow Christian missionaries to work in Nepal, as long as they did not "proselytize." (Proselytizing was defined as "converting another by means of coercion or material inducements"—something no missionary would ever do anyway.) We were allowed to witness to Christ by word and deed. Local churches grew up in connection with our schools and hospitals. The national church developed alongside the mission, but independent of it, the mission playing mainly a supporting role. The mission did nothing to actively oppose government policies; to do so would have resulted in our being asked to leave the country. Church leaders themselves refrained from opposing the government. The church was more or less being allowed to exist; it was growing. Why rock the boat?

But as the church grew, hostility to Christians on the part of both the government and the local populace increased. Christians were thrown in jail in greater numbers. Many others had cases brought against them. Others lost their land, their inheritance; others were driven from their villages. How could we, as missionaries, stand by quietly and watch our brothers suffer?

The national Christians were themselves divided as to what we should do. Some of the more aggressive among them advised us to stop being neutral and to use our influence with the government to ease the persecution. But others opposed such action because they feared it would provoke a backlash and thus bring even more persecution down upon their heads. Still a third group said that Christians were called to persecution, that we should not resist evil, but rather turn the other cheek. In doing so, they said, the witness of the churches would be enhanced; Christ's power would be released through suffering.

The mission ended up taking no official public position. A small number from both mission and church registered individual protests, but by and large no action was taken. Then in 1990 a revolution occurred, which led to increased political and religious freedom. Looking back, I don't think anyone regrets our having taken a cautious, non-confrontational approach.

Did the mission support the revolutionary forces in Nepal? Absolutely not. We remained neutral, praying that whichever side prevailed, the church of Christ would continue to grow in numbers and in influence. And that it has.

Missionaries must hold in check their desire to protect their national brethren from suffering. The story is told of an Indian Christian who was being persecuted by his fellow villagers. One night they burned down his house. As the man was trying to put out the flames, the villagers seized him and cut off his hands for trying to thwart their will. Some time later the missionaries of the area took up a collection so that the victim might take legal action against his persecutors. But the man refused the money, saying to the missionaries, "This is not what you yourselves taught me when I came to Christ. You taught me to love my enemies, not prosecute them." If our national brethren are led of the Holy Spirit to suffer for Jesus' sake, who are we to try to deny them that privilege?

There have been, and will continue to be, situations in which missionaries must stand up and oppose blatantly evil actions on the part of host governments—and take the consequences. But it should only be done after much consultation and prayer, and only after there is oneness of mind in both the missionary community and in the national church. If there is not unity of mind, then no strong action should be taken.

Some missionaries feel they cannot accept any limitation on their freedom to preach the gospel and plant churches. That's fine; only let them not join mission organizations that believe it is better to have a limited witness than no witness at all. In fact, it's been the experience of most missionaries working in Nepal that there has been no real limitation on our personal freedom to witness. And since none of us is primarily a preacher or a church planter, we have not felt limited in a professional capacity either.

The missionary may face still other dilemmas in dealing with government authorities. What about bribery? In many if not most Third World countries very little gets done without some financial incentive being offered. If the incentive must be offered before the service is provided, then it is indistinguishable from a bribe. But if, as is often the case, the incentive is to be given after the service is rendered, it becomes indistinguishable from a tip. In either case, the person receiving the service is equally obliged to provide a financial reward—in the first case, if he wants the service provided; and in the second case, if he ever wants the service provided again!

It's not so different at home. Whenever you take a flight and check your suitcase at the curb-side check-in counter, you give the man a tip. Why? In order to encourage the man not to ticket your bag to Sydney, Australia—unless, of course, you happen to be going there. Don't you have the feeling that you need to provide the tip in order to get the proper service? Or have I been living in Asia too long?

It is well for the missionary to be somewhat relaxed about this matter, or he will cause himself needless grief. A new business manager once came to one of our projects near the Indian border. It had been the custom for years to provide a little "token of appreciation" to the man at customs for expediting the passage of mission goods across the border. But the new business manager—a wonderful fellow, but prone to see things in black and white—regarded this as bribery, pure and simple. He put an end to the practice. And that put an end to the passage of mission goods across the border. There was a face-off, naturally; the mission re-instituted the practice and the business manager went home. The issue may have been black and white in his country, but it certainly was not so in Nepal.

Bribery does exist, but the person who says, "I know bribery when I see it," doesn't know Asia. Give "tips" and "tokens of appreciation" a wide definition. In Asia, you give "tips" before the service, as well as af-ter. Reserve the term bribery for those cases where extortion is clearly taking place, or where you are being asked to give beyond what's cus-tomary or beyond what is stated in a published price schedule. If in doubt, consult with mature national Christians.

Another dilemma that Western missionaries face is whether or not to treat officials with "extra respect." This is certainly the expectation in most Third World countries, but it is distasteful to our Christian sensibil-ities. We call it favoritism, and regard it as a form of injustice.

Not long ago one of Pakistan's chief ministers showed up at the clinic of a famous missionary eye surgeon, who had been working in Pakistan for many years. The minister demanded to be seen at once, but the mis-sionary politely and gently told him he must wait his turn, that in his clin-ic all people, high and low, rich and poor, received exactly the same treatment. The minister apologized, and agreed to wait. Not many years later that eye surgeon, recently retired, was flown back to Pakistan at the government's expense to receive from the president himself the nation's highest award.

Does this story make you feel good? Over in a nearby country at about the same time, another missionary doctor was holding a clinic when in walked a member of the royal family. The personage, a princess of junior rank, demanded to be seen at once, but the doctor courteously said she would have to wait her turn. The princess walked out in a huff, and a week later the doctor was expelled from the country.

Now the first doctor had acted wisely, we'd all agree. But supposing he had ended up getting kicked out of Pakistan instead of receiving her highest award? Would we then have thought him so wise? The fortunes of these two doctors could easily have been reversed. Is there a lesson to be learned here? The lesson I learn is not to draw conclusions from just one story. There are times when it is indeed wise to show "extra respect" to people in authority. Don't set absolute rules in this matter. When the time comes, trust in the wisdom and guidance of the Holy Spirit.

Back in the 1950s, one of the first missionary doctors to come to Nepal experienced the most exquisite dilemma in relating to government authorities that I have heard about. In this case, the government authority was the king of Nepal. The doctor in question was Edgar Miller, who for nine years served during the formative stages of the United Mission. On several occasions during his time in Nepal, Dr. Miller had the opportunity to treat members of the royal family. And for his service he was selected to receive Nepal's highest award.

The award is presented to several recipients each year, and it is bestowed by the king himself. On the auspicious day, Dr. Miller was waiting his turn at the royal palace. He noticed that the king, after presenting the medal, placed a "tika" on the forehead of each recipient. In Hinduism, to place a tika on someone is to bestow god's blessing on that person—the blessing of a Hindu god. For this reason, Nepali Christians refuse to receive the tika; it is one those critical customs a Nepali gives up when he becomes a Christian. Dr. Miller vaguely knew this—though at that time there were hardly a hundred Nepali Christians in the country. He didn't know what he should do. To refuse the tika would be a horrible offense to the king. Would accepting it be as horrible an offense to God? Dr. Miller's last thought was reassuring: "The king will not give me a tika, because I am a foreigner."

The king presented Dr. Miller his award. Then, without a pause, he reached out and placed the red mark on Dr. Miller's forehead.

The awards ceremony concluded, and everyone took his leave. Dr. Miller had received a high honor; not only that, but the mission also had received recognition for its services. It was a great day all around.

But the next day was not so great. Dr. Miller's missionary colleagues had found out about the tika. They were scandalized, and made no effort to hide their feelings. He had betrayed Christ, betrayed the church, betrayed them. He had bowed to Baal.

I don't think it's quite so simple. Was there some special power in that little red mark? Did the king himself believe he was bestowing a god's blessing, or was he merely carrying on a tradition? Even if he did believe it, did that god have any reality as far as Dr. Miller was concerned? Was Dr. Miller acknowledging a false god when he received the tika? Was he giving a demon entry to his life? Would he really have brought honor to Christ by refusing to accept the tika? Was he looking for glory for himself?

I believe the answer to all these questions is "no." On the other hand, I can imagine that for another person under slightly different circum-

stances the answer could be "yes." In the present case, however, if anyone is absolutely sure he knows what Dr. Miller should have done, he
has more knowledge than this writer.

Dealing with other nationals

In the world's two Hindu countries, India and Nepal, and in many other Third World societies as well, people are stratified into castes or other
forms of class divisions. While developed countries have their own type
of class divisions, they are generally less pronounced than in the Third
World. In Nepal, even the language provides four levels or forms of address: the lowest form is used for addressing animals, low-caste people,
children, and wives; the middle form is used for friends and servants; the
upper form is used for teachers, bosses, older men, and anyone of rank;
and, finally, the highest form is reserved for the king. This last is a long
and complicated form, and unless you are into seeing the king regularly,
you are sure to botch it when the critical moment comes. However, aside
from poor Dr. Miller, I'm not aware that any Nepal missionary has ever
had to use this form except in a language exam.

In Hindu society the different castes and sub-castes are well de-
lineated, and there is very little mixing of their respective roles. If you
are on a trek in Nepal, don't ask the cook of the party to carry a load;
he's the cook, not a carrier.

The sweepers at our mission hospital, as part of their job description,
were expected to bury the bodies of dead patients whose families failed
to take them away. But when the time came, they always refused; it was
beneath them. It took a small "financial incentive" to overcome their
scruples: ten rupees for a big body, and five for a small one.

Some of the mission's low-caste workers have escaped from their
bondage to caste and gone on to great things. One low-caste lad hired as
a houseboy in a missionary's home has now become an important leader
in the Nepali church. Some have gone on to high positions in government; others have become skilled professionals. This fact underlines the
missionaries' major contribution toward breaking down caste barriers
and creating new opportunities for those who work in mission homes and
projects. Those who have so benefited would hardly agree with the anthropologists' charge that missionaries have "spoiled the natives."

Missionaries from the West are uncomfortable with the class divisions
they find in the Third World. The idea of having servants, for example, is
distasteful. It conjures up images of royalty, Hollywood stars, corporate
executives; only such people can afford servants in the West.

Our Western heritage teaches us to treat all men equally. Hiring a servant means getting someone else to do your mean and dirty work that you don't want to do yourself, and because you are rich and the other person is poor you can pull it off. This doesn't sit well, does it?

Why, then, do the majority of missionaries have servants? There are several reasons, the most important of which is that missionaries weren't called to spend six hours a day preparing their meals. For except in big cities, food preparation is tedious and time-consuming. Everything must be prepared from scratch. Nothing is ready-made, all set to be dropped in the pot. If you want rice, you have to husk it, and then pick the stones and worms out of it. If you want spices, you have to grind them; if you want salad dressing, you have to concoct your own. If you want jam, you make it; you want bread, you bake it. Your supporters back home would much rather pay fifty dollars a month to hire you a cook than have you spend half your waking hours in the kitchen.

Furthermore, when you hire a cook, you're giving someone a much needed job. If he or she does well, a long-term relationship is established that will benefit both cook and missionary.

Finally, servants and cooks are commonplace in Asia. Any working professional will have at least one household helper. And if missionaries try to grow their own vegetables, they'll likely need a part-time gardener as well. Having servants does not create the barrier between missionary and nationals that one at first might think. Having servants is completely natural; it is common sense.

Westerners are used to thinking of servants as a luxury, but they think nothing of owning a car. Well, in the Third World, the two are viewed exactly the opposite.

And this same valuation applies to household appliances, the labor-saving devices that help us get by in the West. These are all viewed by the host people as luxuries. It is these things that separate us from the nationals more than having a servant does. Think twice about that washing machine. Washtubs don't break down—though they do leak. Ours had to be patched twice a year, and even then it leaked in between times.

So you have hired your first cook-cum-housekeeper. For the first three months you'll spend half the time wishing you hadn't—especially if she is new to Westerners. On the other hand, hiring a helper who has already been trained by others and then retraining that person to meet your requirements can be equally frustrating. The helper is now an expert, and you are just a green missionary who can't even talk right. Very soon it's you who begins to feel like a servant!

Because of the initial headaches, some wives determine to do their own housework. That's fine for some, but it only works if the wife lives in a city and has no full-time assignment of her own. In most cases, the wife's time and talents would be better utilized in ministry to nationals rather than in doing household work that someone else could be taught to do just as well.

If your helper has never worked with Westerners before, the going will be rough in the beginning. She will have no concept of germs, for example. She won't understand why you boil water, why you rinse the dishes the way you do, why you don't prepare food on the floor. Her understanding of this latter mystery will not be helped by the fact that the same Nepali word is used for both floor and counter. (They've never used counters in Nepal; there is no separate word for counter. Food is prepared and eaten on the floor.)

And about those germs: How will she believe in something she can't see? Even when you explain that the big worm in her stool came from eating an invisible egg, she is likely to remain skeptical.

Then there are lessons on the use of the toilet, the washing of hands, the blowing of one's nose. Next comes the matter of sweeping, a process in which the dirt is lifted high in the air and then allowed to settle in a different location.

And finally, after the basics have been mastered, you start on the menu. Nepali food will come easily, and if you never ask her to cook anything else, your problems are solved. But then you say to your husband, "Wouldn't it be nice if the cook could learn to make your favorite...? Think of the time I'd save." And the incentive to teach the cook is that much greater when you have kids, each with their own five or ten favorite dishes.

If your cook can read, you're way ahead; and if she can read numbers—well, it's hardly a challenge. In no time you'll have her cooking *boeuf bourguignon* and *beurre de crevettes*.

Our cook, however, did not have those gifts. Instead, she had a wonderful way of scrambling Cynthia's instructions into all sorts of interesting combinations—a propensity, one must say, that was due partly to the instructions themselves. Meals were lively in our household, and what was advertised was not always what we ate. My favorites were scrambled eggs with cinnamon sugar, and chocolate-flavored pumpkin pudding, but these had dozens of competitors. Our cook's biggest problem, however, was that she couldn't smell; she couldn't tell the food was burning until the kitchen filled with smoke.

Laughter aside, our cook worked for us faithfully for twelve years. She loved our family, she helped raise our boys. She had the sorrow of being married to an alcoholic husband who abused her. She taught us many things about poverty and hardship that you don't learn in books. And along the way, she became a believer.

What do you do about a missing item? Some servants do steal and cheat—but think of that last. Nine times out of ten you have merely misplaced the item. If you ask the servant if she has seen it, she will instinctively think you are accusing her of taking it. Be most cautious here; say that you yourself have lost it and you are only asking for her help to find it.

But when a real suspicion surfaces, talk about it openly, though gently. Generally, you will have seen a pattern emerging. Rather than accuse, it is better to find a way to make future dishonesty hard to get away with. Remove temptation. Keep accounts. Don't leave money around. Keep a running tally of the sugar consumed, or whatever it is that you suspect her of taking.

Don't worry if your helper cannot understand the reasons behind your rules. Just establish clear, simple procedures which she must follow precisely. Expect compliance. Be consistent.

Avoid familiarity. You and your household servant do not have equal roles. She doesn't have to eat at the table with you; she would feel uncomfortable doing so. Even if she became comfortable, the temptation to abuse her position of privilege would be enormous. Instead, simply show her respect; show concern for her family and her health; listen, sympathize, take an interest in her problems. These attitudes of respect and friendship will count more with your helper than all your specific policies and pronouncements put together. And one more thing: never require your helper to attend Christian meetings or services. If she asks for it, give her time off to go to a meeting, but never force it.

Your household worker is your loudspeaker to the world outside your home. Do you behave one way inside your home and another way outside? Do you lead a double life? Your helper will know it. And so will the whole neighborhood!

Your helper will usually do your shopping for you. She'll get you a better price than you can get. Bargaining is prevalent in Third World countries, and she will be more clever at it than you are. But she's also likely to pocket a fee for her efforts—something you'd call "skimming," but which she calls a "commission." It is another of those Asian ambiguities, like tips and bribes.

We Westerners are allergic to even the thought that we might be getting "ripped off" or cheated. Whenever I begin to have the feeling, I think of Jesus' disciples picking corn from another man's field. According to the Old Testament, anyone could legally pick what was left behind after a field had been harvested. In our Western view, that would be tantamount to stealing. So it's best to leave our cut-and-dried views at home when we come to the Third World; they may lead us to make some wrong decisions.

One of the most tragic decisions I know about involved a young Nepali believer who obtained a job as an accountant with a Western agency in Kathmandu. The young man was severely disabled from an injury sustained years before, which made him unfit for most types of employment. To have landed the job was a remarkable provision of the Lord.

After some years the leadership of the agency changed and a new Western director took charge of this young man's work. After a while, he noted some discrepancies in the books and traced it to this practice of taking a commission on purchases made. The young believer was fired for "dishonesty."

Since I had been the young man's doctor and had known him for many years, I was called upon to help. I was not directly responsible for the young man in any way, nor did I have any connection with the agency that had fired him. But I did my best to ascertain the facts. The new director sent me a long letter detailing the charges; they seemed substantial. I found I could not come to the young believer's defense. I urged him to repent. But he said, "For what? I have done no wrong."

A couple of agonizing years of hardship, isolation, and discouragement followed. Finally he got another good job. The matter seemed laid to rest. But some time later I talked with a person who had been closely acquainted with the original firing episode, and discovered that the director had overstated his case, that the "dishonesty" was not at all clear-cut, and that the problem revolved around the ambiguity of the "commission."

Such ambiguities can be eliminated with strict accounting procedures and controls, and they should be. But, in the meantime, Westerners must tread lightly in these matters, lest they inadvertently ruin the reputation of innocent people with mistaken charges·of dishonesty. Blatant forms of theft and dishonesty, of course, must not be tolerated; but the commission system is harder to define. In Asia, like "tipping," it's a way of life.

For some items missionaries will want to do their own shopping, and it is then that they will encounter the bargaining system firsthand. Bargaining is part ritual, like courting. The shopkeeper starts with double the price he actually hopes to get, though if you look particularly gullible or have white skin, he may triple it. (This is often called a "skin tax.") Then you must offer less than half of what he asks. If you offer too low a price, the shopkeeper will at once resort to histrionics. "I am insulted! I am hurt! You are humiliating me! You despise our country!"

He raises his arms to heaven, or beats his breast. His family appears from the back of the shop. You look nervously up and down the street, expecting to see other shopkeepers pour out of their shops to come to the defense of the national honor. He is hoping, of course, that you will give his initial asking price to avoid further embarrassment, or worse.

Once you have made your final offer and it is not accepted, you may courteously smile and walk away. Bargaining is never an argument; it is a convention whereby two people come to an agreement on a price. No bad feelings are allowed. And once the price has been agreed on, no more dickering; that is unmannerly.

More difficult for most Westerners is the variation of bargaining in which the shopkeeper asks you, the customer, to name your price. The trouble is, you have little idea what the article is worth. So just start with half of what you'd be willing to pay, and take it from there. Or get an experienced "old hand" to go with you.

Not all old hands will be equally helpful. Some people seem congenitally unable to bargain. My wife is one of them. She has been in Nepal twenty-four years and bargains no better today than she did in the beginning. A few months ago she went to the bazaar in Kathmandu to buy a Christmas present for her nephew. She bought a hundred-rupee T-shirt for a hundred and fifty. She was quite pleased with herself. "I got him down from two hundred," she said. Silly shopkeeper! If he had asked for three hundred initially, he'd be a hundred rupees richer today.

A final thing to know about transacting business in the Third World concerns receipts—or getting anything in writing for that matter. People are reluctant to commit themselves in writing, especially if a date and signature are involved. To ask for a receipt or written contract implies a lack of trust. Everyone, from the highest official to the lowest shopkeeper, prefers to conduct business orally. They don't want to be pinned down; ambiguity is desirable. Too many things can go wrong, and then they'll be out on a limb while you're waving your copy of the contract down below them. It is not deviousness that keeps them from committing themselves in writing; it is merely self-protection.

Things are changing, of course; the modern world demands written records. But I remember not too many years ago applying for a license to practice medicine in Nepal. The easiest way to get a license at the time was to join the Nepal Medical Association. A life membership could be obtained for sixty dollars.

It took four trips to the Ministry of Health before I was able to complete my business. The Ministry was then housed in a huge, old, wood-frame palace, reportedly the largest wooden building in Asia. The office of the Nepal Medical Association was hard to locate; the clerk from whom I asked directions sent me wandering up and down the four floors for almost an hour before I found it. The first day the man in charge was not in. His father had died, and he wouldn't be in until next week. The next week I returned; the man in charge was happy to take my money, but as to a receipt, he had none to give me. The accountant would be back from holiday in two days, he said, so if I came back and paid then, I could get a receipt from him.

Two days later I returned to meet the accountant, who informed me it was not their custom to give receipts. I said, "Can't you just give me a piece of paper saying I've paid the money?"

Well, he thought he could do that much. But first I would have to sign an application form and give it to the man in charge, who was out that day but would be in tomorrow.

The next day, my last day in Kathmandu before returning to the hospital, I met the man in charge and gave him my application and the six hundred rupees (equivalent to sixty dollars at the time). I then went to the accountant for the receipt. He looked around the office momentarily, and then drew a crumpled piece of paper out of the wastebasket, tore off a strip along one end, and wrote: "Received 600 rps. from T. Hell."

Several months later the Ministry of Health, along with all the other government ministries housed in that old palace, burned to the ground. It was a terrible blow to the fledgling government of Nepal. As for me, I faithfully carried that little slip of paper around in my wallet for the next ten years. It was my only proof that I was a life member of the Nepal Medical Association and could legally practice medicine in Nepal.

Before we scoff at the absence of legal niceties in countries like Nepal, let us reflect for a moment on the freedom these countries provide—freedom from the piles of paperwork that are suffocating the people of more developed nations. Can you imagine, for example, practicing medicine in a country where there are no licensing requirements, no ambulance-chasing lawyers, no malpractice insurance, no need for voluminous reports and unnecessary lab tests? It's a medical doctor's Garden of Eden. Let us enjoy it while it lasts.

The paying of wages to nationals is something that sooner or later all missionaries will have to face. My wife Cynthia and I encountered it on our first trip out to the hospital where we had been assigned; the porter rate for carrying a load all day 2500 feet up a mountain was a penny a pound—a dollar for a hundred pounds. In the USA, you couldn't hire a man to carry a hundred pounds down the block for a dollar—let alone up a mountain! And yet we were roundly criticized by a "senior missionary" for paying too much, for "spoiling the porter rate" for everyone else.

My first reaction was: "You capitalist scrooge, you're exploiting these poor laborers." But I soon realized that we had entered a self-contained economic system, and that an increase in the porter rate, while benefiting the porters, no doubt, would hurt everyone else. So the first rule in paying wages is: Don't inflate the pay scale, because you'll end up hurting more people than you help. The second rule is: If in doubt, err on the side of generosity.

The missionary will not be long in a country before he is asked for a loan. Remember, you are "Mr. Money-bags" in the eyes of the people. And at once you come up against the words of Jesus: "...do not turn away from the one who wants to borrow from you" (Mt 5:42).

I do not believe that Jesus is giving us a blanket command to loan money to whoever asks. For many years in our community in Nepal, an unscrupulous villager made it his practice to milk each new missionary who came for as big a loan as he could get—without the slightest intention of ever paying it back. It fell to me as project leader to warn each new missionary about this individual, but my warnings were not always warmly accepted. The Nepali seemed so poor, so needy, so honest; and I seemed so calloused, so unloving. One new doctor was offended by my attitude, and quoted to me the above-mentioned words of Jesus. I told him he could do what he wanted, but that his loan would be spent in drinking and gambling. And so it turned out.

It doesn't take many such experiences to sour one on giving loans. I once loaned a Nepali acquaintance five hundred rupees (fifty dollars at the time) to buy a buffalo; his old one had died. But it was all a lie; he skipped town the next day. I gained nothing but the reputation for being a sucker. Surely Jesus did not mean we should loan indiscriminately in this way.

I have come to feel that it is never wise to loan money except to salaried workers, in which case the money can be withheld from their wages over a period of time until the loan is paid back. This pretty much rules out private loans except to your own household help. Such "loans" are really advances on salary, and as such they are not demeaning; the recipient knows that he can pay it back. Such advances may allow an employee to build a house, or buy some land that's up for sale; such opportunities may help him gain life-long financial security. But every other kind of short-term loan is likely to backfire. It holds the borrower hostage; it deprives him of self-respect; it destroys friendship. I don't say there may not be exceptions; just let them remain exceptions.

Then how, you ask, can we meet the needs of the desperately poor people around us? There are a number of ways, the first of which is giving outright gifts. The caution here is not to create dependency, or to take away one's self-esteem. Allow the person to reciprocate in some way. This is not always possible for poor people, but it often is. We used to give much charity medical service to poor people, and when we called them back for follow-up, they would often bring us some fruit or vegetables to express their gratitude. One old man who had recovered from a broken neck and quadriplegia used to bring me two eggs each time he came, not more, not less. Those two eggs meant a lot to both of us.

Much plain charity is given in times of acute need: droughts, floods, fires. In such cases it should be given without calculation. Other types of aid are longer term, and if possible should take the form of "aid-for-work" programs. In such programs the beneficiaries work for what they get and play an active role in the carrying out of the project. The project may be a village water system or community irrigation scheme. The donor supplies equipment and know-how, and the recipients provide the labor. Such projects have long-term value and should be encouraged.

Scholarships are another valuable form of aid, but these are best given anonymously through established channels. Avoid putting people in your debt. It may make you feel good, but it is not good for the other person, and his initial feeling of gratitude may eventually turn to resentment. It has happened many times.

Below are some guidelines in the giving of aid.

First, don't be impetuous; love should be informed by reason. Assess the need; this will take time.

Second, strike a balance between what you feel the other person needs and what he feels he needs; sometimes you will be more right, and at other times he will.

Third, lengthen the golden rule to say: "...do to others what you would have them do to you"—*if you were them* (Mt 7:12). The golden rule by itself is not a foolproof guide; we need to put ourselves in the other person's place. What would I need if I were him?

Fourth, be absolutely sure your help is wanted; otherwise you are just a manipulator. The recipient should have a major part in setting the agenda and in carrying out the program.

Fifth, allow the recipient some way to pay you back. We used to have a deaf-and-dumb neighbor who frequented our doorstep begging for food. In spite of his disability, he was clever and able-bodied. So we began to ask him to collect some firewood in exchange for his supper. As long as he could get a completely free meal somewhere else, he stayed away from our door. But whenever his luck ran out elsewhere, there he'd be, with a bundle of sticks under his arm and a big, wide grin.

Another way people can reciprocate your charity is by offering you hospitality. Most poor people are extraordinarily generous, and one way they show it is by how they treat their guests. Hospitality is a badge of honor throughout the Third World. Try never to reject it; rather accept it warmly and graciously. This may lead you into delicate situations. Accepting such hospitality has led me into eating the most distasteful food under the most unhygienic conditions imaginable. At times I have literally had to close my eyes and pray that I would not throw up. God has answered my prayer each time, and granted me a week of dysentery instead.

It is difficult being a rich missionary in the midst of poverty. We see need all around us. Requests and demands are made of us constantly. And we all have made decisions that in retrospect were wrong. You teeter back and forth between being over-generous and getting caught for a sucker, and then tightening up and turning away someone who truly needed your help. The longer we stay on the field, the fewer and fewer pat answers we have to offer. There are no formulas. A gift to one person will create dependency. The identical gift to another person will enable him to surmount a hurdle and be on his way. Each request, each need must be individually examined, prayed over, and acted upon under the guidance of the Holy Spirit. There is no other way.

There is one pat answer missionaries can give, and that is in regard to professional beggars: do not give. These beggars exist in large numbers on the Indian subcontinent and their trade is little more than a con game. People go so far as to cut out the tongues of young girls so that they might be more pitiable and thus bring their owners greater profit. We have seen these tongueless young women on the streets of Kathmandu; one's heart goes out to them, but the money they receive is not their own.

Other beggars are aggressive and physically block your way until you have given them something. Several times I have been prevented from leaving a shop by a beggar standing in the doorway. Usually the shopkeeper will chase beggars off his premises, but once you're outside you are free game. One old man held me up for ten minutes by squatting down in front of my bicycle and holding onto the wheel. I couldn't run him over. Neither could I talk to him, for he kept up a non-stop lamentation about how poor and hungry he was. I was only released when he spotted another Westerner on the other side of the street who looked like better game than I.

"Let yourself be held up by a beggar?" you think. Yes. You must not express irritation or anger (though I'm afraid I expressed both). Do your best to be gentle and kind. If you have a tract, give it—though few of them can read. People are watching you. Your most telling witness is given at such times.

One thing that grates on many missionaries is the Third World's casual attitude toward work. We have already seen the veteran missionary who was upset by crooked window frames. Such examples could be multiplied almost endlessly. Do not let your sense of humor desert you.

My favorite workers are painters. In Nepal most painters couldn't care less where the paint goes or what shade they use. To them painting means covering something with paint, along with anything else that lies within range. One year we had just moved into a new house in Kathmandu, and I was inside wiping splattered paint off the woodwork. The two painters who had made the mess were finishing up the outside of the house. One of them, looking in through the window, saw what I was doing, and began to laugh. "Oh-ho," he said to his buddy, "look at that. We're outside putting paint on, and he's inside taking it off. Ho-ho-ho." And he began laughing so hard that he nearly fell off his ladder, which would have served him right.

It's not that workmen can't do better; they just don't care. They don't take pride in their work—it's just a job. The most blatant example of this attitude is found among lower-level government employees, the civil service. A government job is widely considered to be the best job of all because there you get a guaranteed salary and don't have to work. Civil servants have no qualms about drawing full pay and then spending most of the day warming a chair; indeed, that is the whole idea. And one look into a typical government office would instantly tell you it was so.

This malady does not affect most Nepalis. Village folk, for example, are not lazy. And the women don't even know what leisure is. Neither is this malady of laziness to be confused with the "slow pace" of Asian life, whereby relationships are more valued than productivity. No, this laziness is limited to a special group of workers—those whose salary and promotion are based not on merit but on seniority and paper certificates. In effect, "job security" means they can't get fired.

This philosophy of employment did not originate in Asia; this is an import from certain thinkers in the West. And many missions have adopted it as well—and with predictable consequences. For as soon as you disengage salary from performance, you will get laziness and lowered standards as surely as night follows day.

It's all the more heartening, then, that even as I was writing this chapter the Prime Minister of Nepal gave a major speech announcing that from henceforth salaries and promotions of all civil servants would be based on merit. What wonderful news! May our mission quickly follow suit! Some years back we made the unfortunate decision to model our employment policies on the government's policies, a move that has gone on to produce much needless contention between the mission and its Nepali employees. Missions should feel under no compulsion to ape unwise government policies, unless, of course, the government itself demands it.

Many missionaries at some point in their career find themselves training or supervising nationals. The principles involved are similar to those in their home countries, though they must be put into practice in culturally appropriate ways.

Training is seldom a problem. Nationals expect missionaries with special skills and academic degrees to act as teachers and trainers. And it is always culturally acceptable to coax, cajole, admonish, and reprimand one's students.

It is the supervising of already trained nationals that causes the problems. It is desirable, as soon as feasible, to train national leaders to take over this supervisory role. I repeat: as soon as feasible. Some missions have been in such a hurry to hand over work to national leadership that they haven't waited until that leadership was ready, and the results have been disastrous. Determining when nationals are "ready" is always a matter of debate, but if you have three views, generally choose the middle one and you won't go far wrong. And remember, people don't become fully "ready" to take responsibility until you've actually given it to them.

However, one faces many situations where there are no nationals to take leadership, and the missionary finds himself required to play a supervisory role. Let's review some of the simple principles that will make his job easier and keep him out of mischief.

First, let the worker know what is expected of him. You don't have to settle for sloppy, careless work—especially in situations that matter, such as medical work. Don't be surprised if your locally trained village staff aren't as concerned as you are about exact measurements, cleanliness, right angles, and straight lines. Why should they be? They've grown up never having bothered with such things. It doesn't enter their mind that these things might matter. The whole concept of "excellence" is foreign to them. Their attitude is cultural. So there is no use blowing up. Patiently, repeatedly, show them where they fall short, explain clearly why it matters (if indeed it does), and demonstrate once more how they can attain the standard you demand. That's point one.

The second point is: only demand attainable standards. It takes considerable experience to know what is practically attainable on the mission field. The more common error here is to aim too low. This implies a lack of respect for the capabilities of the people you are working with. They, after all, are as intelligent as you are. Stretch them; aim high. But be reasonable.

Third, be positive. Encourage, commend good work, give as much responsibility as possible. See yourself as an enabler. Be friendly, though not familiar. Your training is both by precept and example; make your example good. The people you are training will be tomorrow's leaders.

Fourth, discipline firmly, consistently, fairly. Do not tolerate negligence, insubordination, or laziness. Some missionaries feel that we should never rebuke a national. But those who believe that should not work in projects such as hospitals, where discipline and performance are crucial. Indeed, the nationals themselves want us to maintain discipline in the projects we run.

All discipline must be carried out with special sensitivity to this matter of "saving face." Give your discipline in private, and it will be appreciated. Give it in public, and you have made an enemy, often for life. Not only that, the nationals looking on—though they may agree you are right—will instinctively side with their compatriot. In rebuking one, you are, by implication, rebuking all.

Occasionally the situation will arise when you must correct someone in public to avoid a disaster or harm to others. In hospital work, saving a life must take precedence over saving a face. And there will be those times when you must raise your voice, especially when someone is repeatedly negligent or insubordinate—or deaf.

Much is written about leadership style. There is no one style that is appropriate for every situation. In one case, a certain amount of laxness will be appropriate, whereas in another, the same laxness will cause the leader to lose respect. In one case a certain amount of strictness will be tolerated, but in another, that same strictness will antagonize the workers. In the life of any one project, the leadership style should evolve as the project evolves.

Being a firm leader of a mission project is not incompatible with being a servant—though there is admittedly a tension between the two roles. It takes a special anointing of the Holy Spirit to duplicate Jesus' model of servant-leadership. But that is what we are called to do. I think it is one of the hardest roles a missionary is called upon to play. We must rely on God's promise that if he calls us to a task, he will enable us to perform it.

Dealing with national Christians

Missions is the outreach of the church. The church is primary. We, as missionaries, are helping to build the church of Christ, not our own branches of it. There is absolutely no place for denominationalism in missions. By denominationalism I mean such a strong preference for our own denominational stance that we are unwilling to cooperate with and support other denominations in building Christ's church. The church is Christ's. It is not owned by any race, nation, or denomination. As we said earlier, it is technically incorrect to speak of the "Nepali church" or the "American church"; it is Christ's church in America and in Nepal. It is universal. It is spiritual, a spiritual body. Membership is by spiritual re-birth. Ultimately, it is God who decides who is going to be in the church.

So far, this is elementary, and I trust we all agree with it. But when it comes to the local, visible branch of Christ's church, we often act very differently. We establish it according to our preferences, and admit members according to our criteria. We try to make over Christ's church. We become exclusive.

There is only one biblical criterion for church membership, and that is faith in Christ. Judging another person's faith, however, is a risky business; Jesus tells us we are not to make final judgments. But clearly we must have some way to assess the genuineness of a person's faith, and that way is to examine the fruit of his faith, his obedience.

Even here, what standard of obedience do we demand? Where is that line between letting unsuitable people into the church and keeping suitable people out?

The question is made more difficult by the fact that when we are spiritually reborn, we do not instantly change in every respect; some features of our old life remain. How many "old features" does it take to disqualify someone from membership in the church? Obviously, knowing persistence in gross sin without repentance would indicate that faith was not genuine, and would thus disqualify a person. Also, a lack of knowledge concerning the object of faith—who Jesus is and what he came for— would indicate that one's "faith" was in something other than Jesus; that, too, would disqualify the person. But aside from these two basic disqualifications, we are on dangerous ground if we reject someone who says that he has faith in Jesus.

The Bible is full of examples of dreadfully imperfect people who have been welcomed into the household of God. And we need, each one of us, to remember how dreadfully imperfect we were when we first believed— and still are. In ourselves, not one of us is worthy to be a member of Christ's church.

Why this long preamble? Because I believe that both missionaries and national believers guard the gates of the church too closely; in their effort to keep unsuitable people out, they keep many suitable people out as well.

It has been said that the great people movement in northeast India in the early 1900s, in which hundreds of thousands of tribesmen came to Christ, was almost derailed when senior missionaries refused to baptize the new converts because of their lack of teaching. And in Nepal, we find this same hesitancy—not on the part of missionaries, but on the part of the national church leaders.

There are reasons for this hesitancy. Until four years ago, Nepali churches were illegal, and the Christians feared spies. To let a spy into the church could mean the arrest of the entire congregation and a year's jail sentence for all.

Secondly, church leaders were reluctant to admit untested converts for fear that they would fall away in time of persecution and bring the church into disgrace.

Thus the idea has grown up in Nepal that new believers need a period of testing or proving of their faith before baptism is given. But what started as a sound caution is now in danger of being carried too far. In some Nepali congregations, believers must wait years to be baptized. While this is rightly the decision of each congregation, it nonetheless can distress the missionary who may have led such a person to Christ. I know one young Nepali woman who had to wait twelve years to be baptized; we almost lost her. Many others have had to wait a year or more. Such a long wait is discouraging to a new believer; he has broken away from the religion of his family and society, and yet is refused acceptance into the fellowship of Christians.

Sometimes the delay involves a legitimate moral issue, but even here, the Nepali church demands a higher degree of purity for admission than most missionaries are comfortable with. A missionary in our area once led an alcoholic to the Lord. Year after year the local church prayed for him to overcome his addiction, but they wouldn't baptize him until he had had at least two dry years. He would go a year or a year and a half without a drink, and then he'd fall. And all the time he was being kept at arm's length; the other believers didn't want Christ's reputation besmirched by alcohol. A wise Nepali evangelist happened to visit our church after this had been going on for some years and suggested a compromise. He assured the congregation that Christ was quite capable of looking out for his own reputation, and that they needn't be overconcerned on that account. He further said that two years was too long;

just let the man get through one rice harvest without drinking. Why one rice harvest? Because when he sold off his rice, he had money to spend on drink. If he could stay dry during those few months of greatest temptation, then let him be baptized. The church agreed, the man passed the test, and he has now gone on to become the director of Alcoholics Anonymous in Nepal, with a wide and useful ministry.

We all have special sins that bother us more than other sins when we see them in our neighbor. One person can't stand thieves; another can't stand sexual offenders; and so it goes. All sin is equally heinous to God, but not equally so to us. Thus, depending on who is leading a congregation at any given time, the man who has recently taken a second wife might as well forget about joining that church, whereas the town thief or ruffian or drunkard may pass muster more easily.

This all involves the missionary, both as a counselor and as a church member. We must be careful not to let our own biases unduly influence our behavior. Some of our missionaries, for example, have been so upset by various sexual sins that for months they have been unable to even look at the guilty parties—even after they have acknowledged their sin. This was not Jesus' way.

The most difficult church membership controversies we have seen in Nepal involve the believing wives of non-believing husbands. According to Nepali church custom, these wives must first obtain their husband's permission to be baptized. Most husbands, of course, refuse. One of the saddest cases involved a highly competent health educator married at a young age to an irresponsible heavy-drinking Hindu. She is yet to become a baptized member of any church. We need to keep in mind that most of the current Nepali church leadership has come from a background of Hinduism, in which the wife is subjugated to the husband. When we have protested their ruling in such matters, we have been told that "we didn't understand their culture." But here is a case where culture has been placed above the Bible, and the Nepalis have not yet been able to see it. This is one good argument, incidentally, for continued missionary participation in the national church: if we are culturally sensitive, we can add perspective to debates such as these. If our contributions are low-key and offered in humility, they will usually be appreciated—though not always agreed with.

Circumstances vary from region to region and from one period to another. One policy cannot be set for all. But if all of us remember the basic truths about the church mentioned earlier, we will not stray far from God's will when it comes to welcoming new members into Christ's church.

The sign of admission into the local church is baptism. Baptism in Western "Christian" countries is a very significant and joyful event, but it is even more so in non-Christian lands where the contrast between church and surrounding society is much greater. In such countries the baptismal ceremony is significant in the minds of unbelievers also, because when one is baptized his neighbors then know for sure that he has changed religions. It is a powerful public testimony.

Before the revolution, baptisms were some of the most moving events you could witness in Nepal. To start with, you met surreptitiously: the pastor faced six years in prison if he was caught baptizing someone, and the new convert received a one-year sentence. The service began with a series of questions.

"Are you willing to give up your inheritance for Christ?"

"Are you prepared to be driven from your home and village for Christ's sake?"

"Are you willing to be despised by your friends and treated like an outcaste for Christ's sake?"

"Are you willing to go to jail for Christ?"

In each case the new believer had to say "yes," and then the service could proceed. One year during the dry season, they baptized a young man in one of our fifty-five-gallon drums. The church members put too much water in the drum, and when the young man was immersed, gallons of water poured out onto the floor where we were all sitting. The pastor, without so much as pausing for breath, said to his soaked listeners, "Look, the blessings of this baptism are overflowing already, and it's only the beginning." And so it proved. The young man has gone on to become a medical doctor, and on the way he has been an inspiration to many because of his proven willingness to suffer for Christ's sake.

In all such church matters—contextualization, baptism, discipling—the missionary should feel free to function as an ordinary member of the local church. Since the local church is the visible manifestation of the invisible church, it cannot rightly discriminate between races and nationalities, between local residents and foreigners. True, even many missionaries regard themselves as "guests" in the "national church," but in so doing they deprive both themselves and the church of the mutual enrichment that would result from full membership and full involvement. Missionaries should belong to a local church, and feel themselves an integral part of it—the same as they did in their home church before they left for the field.

Today's national church leaders are gradually giving up the notion of "our independent church." They want to be interdependent and integrated with the church around the world. A mature church does not want to "get rid" of missionaries.

However, the missionary's role has changed. Missionaries are servants and supporters of the church rather than leaders and administrators. They are partners with the nationals in the ongoing work of missions. They function both as members of a local church and as members of a mission organization. The two functions exist side by side. There is no reason for a divorce between church and mission; let them carry on their respective tasks, administratively separate but in close harmony and cooperation.

The development of mission work in Nepal is a case in point. The Nepal situation is unique in that almost all Western mission work has been in the "service" areas—health, education, economic development—because that is the only type of work for which the Nepali government grants us visas. But even if there had been evangelists and church planters in the mission, I believe the outcome would have been the same.

From the beginning, the Nepali church has grown up alongside the mission. Indian citizens of Nepali ethnic origin came in with the first Western missionaries and established the church on an independent footing. Today there is a natural division of responsibility: the mission is responsible for capital-intensive technological projects (hospitals, schools, development), and the church is primarily responsible for evangelism and church planting. But there is close and ongoing cooperation between the two. Church leaders sit on the board of the mission; missionaries act as partners in evangelism. Several outside groups carry on evangelism in different parts of Nepal using national Christians recruited and supported by local churches. It is our feeling that in Nepal, mission-church relations approach the ideal.

In Nepal the church is still young and small—though growing rapidly. Some may say that it's fine in Nepal to regard the church and mission as equal partners, but in countries where the national church is strong and well-established, the church should take leadership in all areas, and the mission should limit itself to assisting in specialized fields. Well, if you are talking about Korea, with twenty-five percent of her population Christian, that's one thing. But most mission fields are not like that. Take India as an example. The church there has over thirty million members; in some areas it is strong and growing. But it has only been planted in a minority of India's three thousand culturally distinct people groups. There is an enormous task of evangelization left to do in India, and it is simply raw nationalism to say that "this is only the concern of the Indian church." It is the concern of Christ's church worldwide—just as the deplorable condition of some Western urban ghettos is the concern of Christ's church worldwide.

Furthermore, some well-established national churches are lacking in missionary vision and zeal. To say that missionaries can pull out as soon as a national church is well-established is most short-sighted. Missionaries need to keep on stimulating and inspiring the national church, and volunteering to go into still unreached areas. There is no place for the attitude of "we missionaries" and "we nationals." We are together in the great work of the worldwide church, brothers and sisters, equal partners. We are one in Christ. Yes, we have our superficial differences in customs, temperament, experience, and outlook, but the love of Christ will cover our defects and our differences, and bind us together in the fulfilling of Christ's great commission.

We have called missionaries partners, servants, supporters. They can also be called catalysts, enablers. These are all good and appropriate names; they all describe our proper role in relation to the national church. But having said that, we missionaries often end up "out front." We come on gently with our "humble thought or suggestion," and the nationals feel obliged to follow our suggestion. It's often better not to make suggestions under such circumstances; invite the nationals to make their own— or just keep quiet.

I served on our five-member local church committee for a period— missionaries made up twenty percent of the congregation, so it was appropriate to have one missionary on the committee. But I was very conscious of the weight of my presence. I was older than the others, I knew the Bible better, and I was a leader of the mission project. I resolved to say nothing unless asked. When I was asked my opinion, I limited myself to quoting an applicable verse from the Bible—which either supported or opposed their planned course of action. In so doing, I contributed something of value to the committee's deliberations, but yet managed not to dominate the proceedings. They rewarded me for my diffidence by asking me to conduct all the communion services. I strongly protested, but they told me there was no one else. (One of the committee members was paraplegic, two were women, and the other was often away. Among the missionaries, I was the only man who could speak Nepali fluently.) I reluctantly agreed. Within a few months some of the newer missionaries complained that I was taking too visible a leadership role in the church. You can't win; the main thing is to be a gracious loser.

If we missionaries are to be full-fledged members of the national church, why shouldn't we at times be leaders? The reasons are twofold. First, leadership normally should be held by local people who have some degree of permanence in the area. Missionaries more often than not are transients; they do not have local roots. There are exceptions, of course;

some missionaries spend their entire careers in one area and even become citizens of the country; and then there are missionary kids (MKs) who return to the country of their upbringing. There is nothing wrong with such people taking leadership in the national church.

Second, leadership should go to those most able to communicate the gospel effectively to the surrounding community—those most able to keep the church from appearing "foreign." This will almost always be nationals rather than missionaries. Again there will be exceptions. But these are the reasons we generally encourage national leadership in the church, while we ourselves seek to take a back seat.

The one reason for nationals leading the church which is not valid is the mistaken idea that it is "their" church. This is a harmful notion, not only because it claims for man what belongs only to Jesus, but also because it permits nationalistic pride to take root in the church. This nationalistic feeling will thwart not only the work of Western missionaries but also that of Third World missionaries—often more so. Let no one think that the sending of Third World missionaries solves the problem of nationalism in the church. Nepal is a dramatic case in point. The church in Nepal was established by ethnic Nepalis who happened to be living across the border in India. These Nepalis were basically Third World missionaries coming from India to Nepal. The cultural differences between them and the Nepalis living within Nepal itself were minimal. And yet as soon as the church they planted began to grow and multiply within Nepal, these "Indian Nepalis" were rejected by a large number of the young Nepalis they had brought to Christ. Immature, you'll say. Of course; a nationalistic spirit is always a sign of immaturity. But sooner or later it will rear up against all missionaries, whether they be from the Third World or the First.

As missionaries look at the young national church in various countries, they can find much to criticize. And criticize they do! I've heard missionaries dissect the attitudes and behavior of national church leaders in a most uncharitable and judgmental way. It's slander, pure and simple; it's no different from criticizing one's fellow missionaries—which we do plenty of also. "The nationals are doing things 'in the flesh,'" we say, as if we ourselves had never done anything in the flesh. "They are weak, untaught, carnal, proud"—all of which may well be partly true.

But in the course of criticizing the national leaders, we discourage them, we impede them. We use their failings as an excuse to keep control of the church, and thus further prevent their development. And, worst of all, we set for them an example of tearing apart fellow Christians, an example they are quick to follow in relation to us!

We need, rather, to look at the young church as Paul did. He had to trust the Holy Spirit to guide and equip young leaders. Within weeks he and Barnabas were putting local elders in charge of newly established congregations. And, of course, these new leaders made mistakes, as Paul's letters to the Galatians and Corinthians amply demonstrate.

But Paul treated the new believers as brethren, not as children. He let them make mistakes, knowing that they would learn faster from their mistakes than from his counsel. He wanted the new church to become dependent upon the Holy Spirit rather than remain dependent upon him.

We modern missionaries have often failed to follow Paul's example. We need to place more trust in the Spirit to build and perfect the church; he knows how to do it better than we do anyway. For example, we often shake our heads at the rapidly growing "people movement" churches. "They're hardly Christians," we say. "They sleep with their Bibles under their pillows as if they were magic charms." Well, that doesn't mean the Holy Spirit isn't working among them; we need to rejoice at what the Spirit is doing. And then we need to go out and teach them. Should we tell them to stop winning new converts until those already won are fully taught? Of course not.

In short, we should be treating national leaders as we treat ourselves. We were young Christians once. We, too, had to grow—and are still growing. We continue to be beset by the same failings we so easily see in them. Our motives are often no purer than theirs. Paul's word to the Romans applies to missionaries too: "...you who pass judgment do the same things" (Ro 2:1). Is it any wonder that in some parts of the world nationals want the missionaries to go home?

And then there are those nationals who exceed even the most godly missionaries in faith, endurance, humility, love, and holiness. The best cure for missionary pride I know is to work for a while with one of these saints of God.

Finally, let us not lose sight of the fact that the national church, with all its weaknesses and faults, is God's mighty instrument for calling people out of darkness into light. Just look at the church in Paul's day; a cool assessment of its prospects would not have warmed the hearts of many of today's missionaries. Yet look at what God accomplished through it. Yes, we missionaries have our responsibility to teach, to admonish, to equip the membership, and we must carry it out diligently. But at the same time, we need to stand in awe of what God is doing and intends to do through the lives of these new, stumbling and imperfect believers. As someone has said, we need to mentally hang a little sign on the door of every national church, saying: "Quiet, Holy Spirit at work here."

Missionaries not only harm the national church by criticism; they also harm it by unwise generosity. This leads the church to depend on men instead of on God. It breeds "rice-Christians." It invites the accusation that missionaries are merely "buying" converts, and that converts are merely out for rice, or a job, or a scholarship. Rice-Christians are despised by their non-believing neighbors; they are a black mark on the church. Missionaries are so sensitive about this matter that they often are more willing to help non-Christians financially than they are to help Christians. They bend so far over backwards to avoid producing rice-Christians that they practice a form of reverse discrimination. When a Christian and a non-Christian with equal qualifications applied for the same job at our mission hospital, we generally gave the job to the non-Christian. "Seekers" had a very hard time getting a job, because more often than not they were just seeking the job and not seeking Christ.

I well remember one young man who for months came to our Bible studies and finally was baptized. All the while, we still hadn't given him the job he was hoping for. We were torn between our desire to help this brother get work and our desire to see no spiritual harm come to him or to the church. A year later he finally got his job and has been a faithful hospital employee ever since. But, sad to say, he has not been such a faithful church member. Such dilemmas are the daily fare of missionaries who run projects, who have funds at their disposal and jobs to give away.

Even mature national Christians can be tempted by the patronage offered by rich missionaries. In the Third World "connections" are very important—even for Christians. National Christians instinctively seek to "form a connection" with a missionary or group of missionaries. They don't seek this for base motives; they are not being hypocritical. This is how things work in the Third World.

Furthermore, there is nothing wrong with the missionary establishing a discipling relationship with a national believer; this is totally proper. But while the missionary is looking at it as a "discipling relationship," the national is looking at it as a "connection."

The time inevitably comes when you, the missionary, are in a position to materially help your "disciple." You may help him get a scholarship to attend a Bible college or seminary; you may help him get a job with an international Christian organization that pays a good salary. And in many cases you will be right to do so. Only remember the dangers. In the West, Christian service means sacrifice; but in the Third World it is often the path to an easy life. There have been many worthy young Christians whose spiritual lives have been ruined by the well-intended help of missionaries. They have found themselves with salaries, with security, with prestige far above that of their national brethren, and their heads and hearts have been turned. To have this happen to one's spiritual protege is one of the most painful experiences a missionary can have.

And not only individuals seek "connections," but entire congregations seek connections too, usually with a rich church in the West. And the same spiritual harm that befalls the individual from unwise assistance can also befall a congregation. Indeed, harm is even more likely to befall, because the foreign church can't know as well as the missionary what the situation is on the field. The chance of the assistance being unwise is therefore increased.

One cannot generalize on the giving of assistance. Assistance can do both spiritual good and spiritual harm. When the occasion comes to help national Christians, whether in the form of a gift, a scholarship, or a job, pray earnestly that your assistance will liberate the receiver and not enslave him; that it will draw him closer to you, not drive him from you; and that it will turn his eyes more and more to God as the source of all blessing—not the rich missionary. As we help nationals, both believers and seekers, let us remember that our primary objectives are not church buildings, scholastic degrees, economic advantage, or any other material benefit; our primary objective is to help people find abundant spiritual life in Christ. Our assistance, whatever form it takes, should further that objective.

Sometimes missionaries necessarily play a leadership or oversight role in the church for periods of time. When this is necessary, they should always act in concert with other national believers. They should never make unilateral decisions, especially in disciplinary matters. And they must always seek, as soon as practical, to turn over all oversight and disciplinary functions to qualified nationals.

The missionary must be especially sensitive when financial oversight is involved. Missionaries are often asked to serve as treasurers; they are considered to be above temptation in financial matters. They also channel money to the local church from their home countries. To ask for a receipt or an accounting of such gifts often causes grave offense; it implies a lack of trust.

Third World churches need to become aware of donor concerns for accountability; there must be understanding on both sides. The Third World church cannot demand no-string handouts and then not even give an accounting of how the money has been used. There have been instances of gross misuse of funds by nationals working for the church or other Christian organizations which have come about because of inadequate or absent accounting controls. No donor should give under such circumstances; it is poor stewardship.

On the other hand, donors should not demand strict, Western-style accounting practices to be instituted immediately; some compromise is in order here. Furthermore, it is not prudent for foreign donors to dictate exactly how the money is to be used; how would they know? Let it suffice that the national church agrees to use the money to meet the objectives of the donor; the details can be left in the nationals' hands.

To demand some accountability of the national church is not colonialism or imperialism; we do it among ourselves. We are all accountable, both to God and to each other. Furthermore, accounting controls minimize temptation for national workers; it is utterly irresponsible for us as Western donors to do anything that would draw our national colleagues into temptation. I know of at least one Western-funded "Christian" orphanage where this very thing has happened; and to make matters worse, the foreign executives preferred to believe their own self-serving national staff rather than the missionaries who were trying to expose the evil.

The key to a fruitful financial relationship between rich and poor churches lies in the concept of shared stewardship. When a donor gives his gifts, he is giving up some responsibility for how that gift is used. We cannot treat nationals as if they were unable to take financial responsibility. Let the donor investigate the need, ask some thoughtful questions, ascertain that his objective will likely be met—and then let go. We can no longer say that "he who pays the piper calls the tune." It may work for pipers and for businessmen, but it will not work for the worldwide church of Christ. Yes, make sure those elementary accounting safeguards are in place; that's common sense. But then let us remember that our gift is given to God, and that we must trust God's national servants to use it according to his will.

This is all very straightforward until you try to put it into practice. One of the Sunday-school classes of our home church once raised money to put a roof on a partly constructed church building in Nepal. A newly formed village congregation had rapidly outgrown their crude shelter and needed a bigger place to worship. They had run out of money, and now the rains were coming and without a roof the unfinished walls would be washed away. It was a worthy project, and the Sunday-school class gave generously.

By the time the money reached Nepal months later, the congregation had obtained a gift from somewhere else to complete the roof. So they suggested that the Sunday-school gift be used to procure land for a burial ground. Odd though it sounds, a burial ground is a legitimate need in Nepal: Nepali Christians do not want to be cremated as the Hindus are, and so they need a place to bury their dead. However, a burial ground was not in the mind of the Sunday-school class when they gave their gift, and they were not happy with it being used for this purpose. This was duly communicated to the congregation.

I cannot recall exactly into what account the money had passed on its convoluted journey to Nepal—you don't just write a dollar check and express mail it to an illegal Christian congregation with no postal address or bank account! A nearby missionary served as intermediary in the negotiations. It took over a year before the Nepalis got the gift; they used it in the end to add a Sunday-school classroom to their little church building—a fitting conclusion to the story.

The worst thing that can happen between the foreign donor and the national church is that they get sniffy with each other.

"Well, in that case, we don't want your money!"

"Well, in that case, we won't give our money!"

This is sad, because the rich church should indeed be giving to the poorer church. The biblical pattern is clear. The spiritual welfare of the rich church and the material welfare of the poor church both demand that the gift be offered and accepted. Let us, both rich and poor, not impede the work of God by either our pride or our desire to control others. God is deserving of better from those—both rich and poor—who are totally dependent on him alone for everything.

Finally we must ask: How does the missionary deal with a church under persecution? Our immediate reaction is to pray for relief from the persecution, and we would be quite unloving if we did not. But unless we have clear spiritual direction that such relief is actually God's will in the present circumstance, we should add to our prayer, "Yet not what I will, but what you will" (Mk 14:36).

For we know that persecution is ordained by God for all who would follow Christ. The New Testament writers over and over describe its beneficial effect on our Christian lives. And if it benefits individual Christians it also benefits entire congregations, a truth which has been repeatedly demonstrated down through the history of the church.

The church in Nepal has been a persecuted church—though we must hasten to say, not as badly persecuted as some churches. To my knowledge, no lives have been lost for Christ's sake. The worst is jail for a few believers and social ostracism and financial hardship for the rest. Nonetheless, the church has been continuously and relentlessly persecuted from its inception up until the revolution of 1990.

In 1950, there were no Christians in Nepal. By 1970, there were about one thousand. By 1980, the figure had jumped to ten thousand. And by 1990, the number had gone to one hundred thousand. All this exponential growth has taken place under persecution. In 1990, there were about thirty Christians in jail, over a hundred had cases pending against them, and community persecution was at its peak. Things looked like they would get worse. Yet the church was strong and relatively united compared to other national churches, and most of all, it was continuing to grow rapidly. Under such circumstances, can one pray with any certainty that persecution be lifted? And the national Christians gave us little guidance; they themselves were divided on the matter.

In the book of Acts, persecution seemed to have come in waves, interspersed with periods of peace. During the peaceful periods, the gospel spread rapidly, and many new churches were established; it was a time of rapid advance. Yet when persecution came the church did not stop growing; it merely scattered to new areas; its faith was tested; it grew stronger. God knows what his church needs at any given time. The duty of both missionary and national is to seek his will.

It is difficult to stand by and watch our national brothers and sisters suffer. Our hearts go out to them. We are partly the cause of their suffering, and yet we ourselves are not touched by it. We wish we could suffer in their place and carry their burden.

Twenty years ago a young missionary couple trekked ten days out into one of the remotest areas of the Himalayas to translate the New Testament into a local tribal language. As the translation work progressed over the ensuing years, a small church grew up. Local opposition was intense; the new believers suffered deeply for their faith.

Then with little warning an outbreak of violent persecution struck the church. The believers told the missionary couple to leave at once, which they did. But before they left they learned that seven of the leading Christians had been arrested and thrown into a small, dark, one-room jail.

The missionary couple reached Kathmandu ten days later. They had no peace. They were oppressed by worry and guilt. They were responsible for the suffering of these innocent people. Probably all the believers had been rounded up by now. Possibly the seven leaders had been tortured and killed. Or—had they recanted and been set free?

A week passed. Then one day they heard a knock on their door. They opened it, and there stood a young man from the village where they worked. He said, "I came at the first opportunity. I have been looking for you for several days. I have a letter from the men in jail."

He handed over a small, grimy, crumpled piece of paper. The missionaries opened it up. The note was written in the language of the tribe, the language that the missionary couple had only recently taught the men to read and write. This was the only language they knew; before the couple came they had been illiterate.

Here is what the missionary couple read.

> Dear brother and sister. We know you are worrying about us. So at the first chance we are sending you this letter. Do not worry for our sake. We are well. God's glory is with us. This small cell is God's temple. These chains are God's ornaments. We have been given the greatest privilege on earth—the chance to suffer for our Lord Jesus. Thank you, brother and sister, for coming to our village and telling us about him.

With tears in his eyes, the husband turned to his wife and said softly, "We went out to disciple them, but it is they who have discipled us."

8

A Palace, or a Mud Hut?

Some missionaries in Nepal live in palaces. I mean it literally. There are two hundred palaces in Kathmandu, and in the early days you could rent a room in one of them very cheaply. So a number of missionaries did just that, and they've been doing so ever since. Not to worry—these aren't Buckinghams. Their rooms are dark and musty, the plumbing doesn't work, the roofs leak, and rats, roaches, and termites proliferate. But if you come as a missionary to Kathmandu, you could get to live in a palace. It might be your only chance.

Every year at our Workers' Conference, the missionaries choose various burning issues for discussion. There is one issue that resurfaces year after year and never seems to be resolved: the issue of missionary life style. Since this issue has been exercising modern missionary teams since William Carey's day, we would do well to stir the embers one more time.

Life-style matters are intensely personal. "Who are you to tell me whether I can or can't have...?"

"I'm the chairman of the housing committee, that's who."

"Housing committee? They didn't tell me about that in orientation."

Welcome to the world of 1500-rupees-a-month housing allowances with 300 extra for each child. It won't buy you any luxuries.

What is this? Surely missionaries have a basic right to choose for themselves how they are going to live.

Sorry, I must have missed that verse. The only right I read about in the New Testament is the right to choose Jesus as Lord. After that the New Testament doesn't talk about rights, only responsibilities. If someone is really stuck on this matter of basic rights, then he or she should think twice about being a missionary.

Oh, yes, I have certain legal and moral "rights"—the right to personhood, the right to protect my nose from your fist, and all the other rights that benevolent governments guarantee us. But disciples of Christ are called to forsake those rights for the glory of God. Denying oneself means denying one's rights: the right to self-fulfillment, the right to job satisfaction, the right to health, to a husband or wife, to a good night's sleep, to "having my way"—and to choosing my life style. This is a basic transaction that every disciple makes with Christ. What rights can we seriously expect to hang onto once we have offered our bodies as living sacrifices to God?

So leave your earthly rights back in your home countries, and trust a faithful God to protect your "eternal rights" as his adopted child. Those are the only rights that count, and we never have to look out for them ourselves.

Standard of living

Given the truth that we have forsaken all earthly rights, there are still many practical matters relating to our life style that need to be decided. The major one concerns our basic standard of living: at what level shall we live? This will be determined in part by the mission, in part by the type of people we are ministering to, and in part by the physical and emotional needs of ourselves and our family.

The mission has two interests in your standard of living: first, it wants some parity in lifestyle among its missionaries; second, it wants to enhance your ministry and your sense of well-being. Overall the mission, far from being an interference, is in fact a crucial help to its missionaries—which, of course, is why there are mission housing committees.

The closer you live to the level of the people you minister to, the more effective your ministry will be. Live as much like them as possible without sacrificing your mental or physical health. Granted, we are only talking about externals here, but it is the externals that people see first. If your life style is too different, too elevated, nationals may not even approach you.

It cannot be emphasized too strongly that an excess of material goods and comforts will do lasting damage to one's ministry among the poor. Missionaries who accumulate possessions beyond their needs while their neighbors lack the necessities of life are not living according to the gospel. People will simply not take their message seriously.

If we love the people, we will be happy to make a sacrifice for them and live at a simpler level than we otherwise might have chosen. The question is: How far do we go? Do we give up refrigerators? Electricity? Running hot water? Running cold water? Ovens? Windows? Screens? And the answer is: Each missionary and missionary family has to work out the details depending on their individual situation. There is no place for judgment, one against another. Those who live in mud huts should not criticize those who live in palaces. Indeed, mud-hut and palace dwellers may switch places within a year's time; missionaries are frequently moving from one setting to another. Like Paul, we learn to be content in both huts and palaces (Php 4:12).

It is very difficult to give specific guidelines concerning one's standard of living; witness the repeated discussions of the subject year after year. Let us rather venture a few "reflections."

The first is that nationals, both Christian and non-Christian, view missionaries as being "too rich." This is a perception; how do you define "too rich"? Nonetheless, this perception exists, and it hinders our identification with the people. Therefore, as we work out the details of our lifestyle, let us opt for less "richness" rather than more.

One of the least "rich-living" missionaries I know, a public health nurse, had over many years achieved a great measure of identification with the very poor people among whom she worked. Then one year one of the missionary's more well-to-do supporters came to Nepal for a visit and decided to give the missionary nurse a treat—a night at one of Nepal's posh tourist hotels where they served breakfast in bed. Next morning, as advertised, a young Nepali lad brought in an elegant breakfast. He looked at the missionary nurse and said, "I know you. You work in my village. You taught us health in school." Evidently the young lad had gone out and landed a job at this tourist hotel. But he'd be back to his village before long, and then.... "Guess who I served breakfast-in-bed to at the Royal Himalayan Holiday Hotel!" It does wonders for one's ministry among the poor.

It is not easy for a Westerner to work among the very poor. We want to reach out to them, but we have so little in common. We have books, and pressure lamps by which to read them. They are illiterate; what need have they for books and lamps. We get mail and magazines; we have paper and pens, tables and chairs, shelves and cupboards, and on and on. It takes a special calling and enabling from God for us to really get down to their level. We need to learn about planting rice and corn, about keeping the monkeys away, about telling a cow from a buffalo, and about a whole lot of other things if we are going to feel one with them and they with us. Here is a place where many Third World missionaries have us Westerners at a distinct advantage.

Missionaries tend to make national friends among the middle and upper classes; it's so much easier for both sides. But let us not forget Jesus' injunction: "...when you give a banquet, invite the poor, the crippled, the lame, the blind, and you will be blessed" (Lk 14:13-14). We'd have to say that most missionaries miss this blessing.

The second reflection is related to the first: don't have anything in your house that will inhibit nationals from coming, or make them feel uncomfortable if they come. The easiest solution to this is to have a guest room or sitting room as close to the national style as possible. Make them feel "at home"—their home. Let them relax.

The secret of getting your visitors to relax is to get yourself to relax. That means you'll have to be comfortable with their putting finger marks on the walls, stomping on the cushions, and spilling food and drink around the room. That may be hard to do when you've just moved into a freshly painted (or mud-plastered) house with a new carpet and it all looks neat and tidy.

A new carpet. That's been a snare for more than one missionary. Our first carpet in Nepal was the cheapest you could get: jute. But it was dyed bright red and looked quite magnificent out in our mud-walled mountain home. The day after we had laid it down, four porters came by with some of our goods, and Cynthia invited them in for tea. They were bare-footed villagers, and there before my eyes appeared four sets of perfect golden-yellow footprints on a field of red. Then out came the tea, served in cups and saucers, a first-time experience for these men. Thinking the cups and saucers to be attached, they grasped the edge of the saucer like a handle and drank their cups dry. What kept those cups on their saucers I don't know. I was transfixed by the performance, expecting at any moment to see four cupfuls of tea slip gaily down onto the jute carpet. If one of those fellows had asked a spiritual question just then, I might not have been ready. Anyway, within a week, the carpet had turned a dusty orange-brown, plain plastic cups had been mobilized, and the crisis had become past history.

The third reflection is: your home needs to feel like home to you also. This is doubly necessary if you have kids. Have some favorite things in the back room or bedroom—those special sentimental items you may have brought from home. After all, we aren't called to be ascetics.

Some missionaries have imaginative ways of introducing a "touch of home" to their environment. One missionary schoolteacher living alone in a remote village sponsored a mission-wide, crumble-proof cookie contest; all entries were to be sent to her for judging. The winner would get to spend a week in her village. There were many contestants, but in the end the winner declined the award.

The fourth reflection is this: the choice of lifestyle is not a question of right or wrong but a question of pleasing others. "Each of us should please his neighbor for his good," says Paul (Ro 15:2). Our personal choices are not simply "our own business." Our choices affect others, they affect our witness.

Take, for example, the matter of dress. In Nepal men rarely go without a shirt. And for the women, exposing the back of the knee is as sexually provocative as baring a breast in America. So you do your best to fit in; you avoid giving needless offense. There's no cross-cultural mystery here; this is common courtesy. Courtesy is about pleasing others.

So in the matter of dress, let courtesy prevail—and also common sense. Missionaries don't have to wear loin cloths, even if it is the local custom.

Sometimes our choice of dress can have serious consequences. Amy Carmichael in her early years tells of witnessing to an easily distracted old lady who seemed near to a confession of faith. But then the old lady noticed Amy's gloves. "What are these?" she asked. And Amy was not able to get the old lady back to the gospel. From that time on, Amy never wore gloves. She said, "I never again risked so very much for the sake of so very little."

In the matter of food, generally eat what's available locally. It's much cheaper, and it's just one more thing that helps in your identification with the people. If you come to Nepal, I hope you like rice. But if you don't, there are lots of ways to fix it up to suit your taste. And, of course, you can ask God to change your tastes. He has done it for thousands of missionaries before you.

When mission executives from home come out to visit the field, they usually get the idea that missionaries eat pretty well. Every evening as they visit from home to home they are served meat dishes, special desserts and sweets, and they may get the idea that they'd better go back and review the living allowance of these missionaries. What they need to realize is that those missionaries won't be eating meat and special desserts again until the next visitor shows up—maybe a month or two later. Incidentally, we always enjoyed visitors!

Then there is the matter of possessions—what to bring with you to the field. The best answer is to bring as little as possible; in most countries virtually everything you need will be available locally, either from shops of from other missionaries. Each mission will have its own advice to give on this score.

Once on the field, you will still have more choices to make. Do you get a car, a motorcycle, a bicycle? If there are no roads where you live, your decision will be simplified—but then you need to choose between hiking shoes, sneakers, and flip-flops like the nationals wear. These same kinds of decisions must be made for all household items. If some item is going to save you hours of time, increase your work output, and improve your mental outlook, then by all means get it. But always choose the least expensive and ostentatious model that will get the job done and won't fall apart in two days.

Finally, don't pick at the things your fellow missionary has. "He has *that*, and he's a missionary?" It may be a fine watch, a family heirloom. It may be some favorite jewelry, or an expensive camera. Or it may be a piano. A piano? Sure, quite a number of missionaries have pianos, including my wife. Should Cynthia have turned down the piano that God had so graciously provided? I thought maybe so, but I was overruled by the other missionaries at our rural hospital who were looking forward to some concerts!

Lack of privacy

"Don't fret about lack of privacy," intones the orientation speaker. "Use it to advantage. People will be watching you. It's a great opportunity to witness through your life style. And this is especially true of families."

Right. Now let's see how this works out in practice.

"Let's get away and go on a picnic," the new missionary says to his wife one day. Good idea. You need a break from the crowds. So you pack up a lunch, call the kids, and off you go. You find a quiet, remote place; you look around and enjoy the trees, the birds, the breeze—for about one minute. Two heads pop up from behind a bush, then two more. Before you can spread your lunch out on the blanket you are surrounded by dirty, skinny, runny-nosed, half-naked children and insolent adolescents, drooling and grinning at you and rubbing their stomachs, while a few older folks stand by to see how you'll react. You do pretty well at first, smiling and wondering what you can spare from the lunch basket. Then you try to carry on as if they weren't there. But more gather to see what the excitement is about. They crowd in, laughing, pointing, spitting. Twenty minutes later you decide it might be nice if they would move on. You begin to suggest this by waving your hand and saying goodbye. But they don't understand, or if they do, they don't let on. You're the intruder here. But after a while, you begin to think you have rights too and that they ought to respect them—until you remember you were supposed to have given up those rights.

Finally your kids get fussy and your wife gets cranky. The day has been spoiled. You try to make the crowd understand, but to no avail. Then, with your expression clouded and your voice hard, you begin to speak in earnest. Suddenly their faces change; their mouths fall open; they look surprised and hurt. A sickening feeling comes over you— you've done it again. You remember Christ and his compassion for the multitude and try to smile as if you hadn't meant it. But it's too late; the crowd has backed off, sullen and wondering. It's time for you to go too. With an empty feeling, you pick up the remains of your lunch and go to get your coat that you laid aside. It's gone—stolen. The crowd has gone too. As you stand there with a dozen thoughts tumbling through your mind, you begin to see once again the truth you've always known: the compassion of Christ is a thing of God and not of man.

An isolated incident? Dramatized? Not in the least. It happens daily in a hundred different variations to those who live and work in the Third World. You want privacy? You want "your own space"? Then go back home to Canada, or Australia. You won't find it here.

Privacy is an unheard of luxury in most of the Third World. The people here wouldn't even consider it a luxury—quite the opposite. They do not value privacy. They have no trouble going to sleep with a babble of voices in the background, for then they know, "I am not alone." They certainly can't understand why you, the missionary, would need times of privacy. To them it is a sign of unfriendliness.

This is why missionaries try not to live in compounds any more. If you want to share your life with the people instead of simply preaching at them, you have to go out and live among them. Yes, there will always be the need for a few specialized compounds—around hospitals, for example—and missions should maintain a number of suitably located compounds to which missionaries can repair and find respite from the relentless pressure of people. But overall, everyone agrees today that living in compounds should be avoided as much as possible.

People, people, people. Young people: half the Third World is made up of children getting ready to produce their own children. Curious people—on the streets, on the trails—asking where you've been, where you're going, and why. Needy people, pushing, demanding, begging, knocking on your door, even looking in your windows.

One of our earliest and most persistent visitors was an unpleasant fellow who used to come and put his nose up to the living-room window and stare inside for minutes on end, trampling all over Cynthia's flowers to get a better view. He was invariably dirty and unkempt, and an insolent leer played incessantly across his face. Only after several visits did we come to learn that he was mentally impaired. The villagers called him "Laato." But knowing his condition didn't make his repeated appearances any less troublesome. When he wasn't watching through the window, he'd sit for hours on our doorstep waiting to be fed.

One day, seeing Laato's nose flattened against the windowpane for perhaps the twentieth time, I remembered afresh what Jesus had said about those who feed the hungry and invite the stranger: "...whatever you did for one of the least of these brothers of mine, you did for me" (Mt 25:40). From that day on, I began to see Laato in a new light and no longer resented his intrusions. About that time, his visits began to occur less frequently, as if, having taught me my lesson, he was no longer needed.

God knows we need periods of privacy, of quiet. And he will provide them in the right way and at the right time. But to expect, much less demand, privacy as a right is not for us to do. We must trust God; he knows our needs better than we do.

Closely related to the problem of privacy is the problem of trying to maintain a time schedule. For the average missionary there are fifty interruptions a day. Project-oriented missionaries have more difficulty with this than people-oriented ones; indeed, "people" people often thrive on interruptions. Meanwhile, the project-oriented people quietly go bananas.

Schedules are common-sense things. If you have job responsibilities, you must take practical steps to guard your schedule. But try to treat all unavoidable interruptions and delays as coming from God. Pray against resentment and impatience. Every day say to God: "Lord, this is your day; use me every hour of it as you see fit."

Sometimes God chooses to take up quite a few of our hours in one type of delay or another. Public transportation is one of God's favorite means of letting us cool our heels for varying periods of time. Nepal missionaries have been delayed two weeks sometimes when a plane couldn't fly; a delay of one day isn't worth talking about.

And then there are buses. A bus will not arrive on time for one or more of the following reasons and then some: a general bus strike; the driver is hung over; there are not enough buses; a strike of petrol workers; a war between India and Pakistan (no petrol for Nepal); landslides, washouts, floods; the road has been barricaded by the opposition party; or the bus has broken down for one of as many reasons as there are parts to the bus. If you are in a hurry, you will not enjoy a Nepali bus ride. If you're not in a hurry—well, you may not enjoy it either.

Health matters

This is not the place to write a health manual, but a few general observations are in order. Our health is a focus of attack by Satan. If he can't disable us spiritually, he'll try to disable us physically.

One Canadian family we knew had a non-stop series of health problems. To start with, their arrival in Nepal was delayed a whole year because of a car crash in which the parents were nearly killed. One illness after another—some of them common, some unusual—plagued their years in Nepal, though they accomplished an extraordinary amount of work in spite of their troubles. Finally the husband developed a brain tumor, and the family had to go home. Such stories could be repeated hundreds of times over.

Missionaries from affluent, temperate countries can expect to have health problems on the Third World mission field. Their immune systems have never been exposed to the extraordinary variety of pathogens encountered in warmer countries with lower standards of hygiene. Protection of their missionaries from illness is a major item that churches at home should be praying for.

As we said earlier in relation to other rights, we have no "right" to health, any more than we have a "right" to our bodies; our bodies, our health, our safety—everything has been offered to God. However, that doesn't mean we don't have a responsibility to care for our bodies—for God's sake. He gives us life and strength to spend, not to squander.

Some risks are unavoidable, but most are not. God intends that basic rules of health be followed, except in unusual circumstances. He made the rules when he made our bodies. Trusting God to keep us healthy and ignoring his rules is a mixture of foolishness and spiritual pride. Don't think God will protect you if you break his rules.

A devout missionary couple from India taught school in a village six hours' walk from our mission hospital. The wife's first pregnancy had been complicated, and not long afterward she became pregnant again.

The mission doctor who was caring for her asked her to come and stay near the hospital for the final two months of her pregnancy, but the couple refused, saying it would "interfere with the work," and that the Holy Spirit was leading them to stay where they were.

"Don't worry about us," they wrote. "We are trusting in God instead of in doctors."

One problem is with the little word "instead." Did not God send doctors? Is it not insulting to God to reject the ordinary means he has provided for us? Furthermore, they would have expected us to "worry" plenty if something had gone wrong. Then a whole lot of people's work would have been "interfered with." Finally, the Holy Spirit does not lead one member of a team one way and the rest of the team another. It's a very rare situation when a missionary should disregard medical advice.

The couple in question couldn't understand why we didn't admire them for their faith and spirituality. They remained convinced that to leave the work for the sake of one's body was somehow being unfaithful, carnal. We never convinced them, nor they us. Happily the second pregnancy was uncomplicated, which in their minds merely confirmed the rightness of their decision.

Incidentally, pregnant women are always at greater risk on the mission field. Rural government health services are inadequate to handle complications. The wife of a medical missionary in Bhutan recently died in childbirth—a reminder of why doctors take the risks of pregnancy so seriously. It is one of the costs of missionary service.

Rules of health? They are all written in various mission health manuals. Use screens. Don't eat uncooked or untreated food. Boil your water, or carry iodine drops. If someone offers you untreated water, it's not impolite to refuse, especially if you can eat something else they offer. Everyone knows there are some things that disagree with people. I avoided offending people by claiming a particularly weak stomach, a claim which happened to be true. In fact, I became known as "the doctor with the weak stomach." People, far from being offended, were sympathetic. And there was almost always something they offered that I could eat. That's the main thing: eat something.

Having said all this, there will be times when we face true dilemmas: Do we risk giving offense, or do we risk getting sick? In such cases turn silently to God—and then make sure your choice is made for his sake and not your own.

I have faced many such dilemmas, which even my "weak stomach" couldn't get me out of. The worst occurred in a very poor and remote village where I was offered a plateful of potato balls which had been rolled on the dirt floor amidst ashes, spittle, and chicken droppings. Those were the condiments I saw anyway. The child of the house had a bad case of amebic dysentery—the reason for my visit—and signs of his illness were visible here and there about the floor. I shut my eyes and swallowed the potatos down whole as fast as I could. I must have looked hungry, for the wife promptly brought me another plateful. This I was able to decline, stating that fourteen potato balls was my limit at any one sitting. Just out of sight of the house I took a double dose of amoeba medicine, which I'm sad to report, was not able to ward off what hit me two days later.

In addition to pregnant women, children are particularly vulnerable to health problems. They don't know the rules of health, and the national women looking out for them may not know the rules much better. When the kids get older they go to the homes of their national friends and pick up whatever germs happen to be in residence. But it's not right to restrict and isolate your children; you must take reasonable risks. Furthermore, they need to build up immunity and resistance. Overprotecting them in childhood is merely putting off some illnesses until later, which may then strike in even more serious forms, hepatitis being a prime example. Yes, keep the kids away from known risks—don't send them out to play at Rami's, who has just come down with TB or typhoid. Common sense will carry you a long way. But if you are parents who can't stand the thought of your children being exposed to dirt and germs and all the other various forms of life found in a country like Nepal, then pray that God will send you to Japan or Europe.

A word about teeth. In Nepal, there is one dentist for 500,000 people, so teeth are not given high priority. Standard treatment for an aching tooth is to pull it out, and most anyone can do that. The problem is that missionaries are used to having their teeth fixed, not pulled. Missionaries with half their teeth missing are an embarrassment when they get up to speak in churches at home.

The problem is not a slight one. Missionaries are constantly breaking their teeth and losing their fillings—usually by biting stones lurking in their rice. If that happens, the tooth has got to be either fixed or pulled, and that fairly quickly. One of the missionary nurses at our mission hospital broke her tooth one day, and so I sent her the fifteen-mile walk and eight-hour bus ride into Kathmandu to get it fixed. The dentist there merely pulled it out, which I could have done just as well. But had I pulled it, you can bet the dentist in town would have said he could have fixed it!

So mission organizations say: Get your teeth all fixed up during furlough. And that makes sense. But all these fancily fixed-up teeth are no match for the rocks in your rice. And the problem is compounded when those teeth break, because then they are often very hard to pull out. So if your dentist back home is undecided whether to extract a tooth or try to reconstruct it, I'd vote for extraction—certainly if you're a missionary to Nepal.

Rest and recreation

If people back home in ordinary jobs need holidays, surely missionaries do also. There is an extra stress involved in constant cross-cultural living, and people need periodic relief from that stress. It's a normal and often unconscious stress, but it can build up if we are not careful to pace ourselves, to provide for an outlet, a change, a rest.

Obviously the less integrated we are with the host culture the more stressful living in that culture will be. But even the most integrated missionaries need a break. Timely breaks, far from wasting time, will increase our work output and effectiveness. And if the most mature and integrated missionaries need breaks, you can be sure the rest of us do. It's interesting that one of the most refreshing breaks comes when we can get together and speak our own language for a change.

These breaks take the form of annual vacations and the ordinary daily and weekly "time-outs" we all need. Annual vacations on the mission field need to be wisely planned. It may take you three to four days just to reach your destination, after which you'll need the vacation to recover from the trip. And then the return trip may leave you as exhausted as when you first set out. If your vacation was an ambitious one, you may even have to spend some time recuperating from it! Don't laugh; it has happened many times. And then you can always get sick; illness is no respecter of vacations—certainly not in the Third World. Fortunately in most mission situations, good advice and good holiday spots are both available, and the vacation ends up being as restful, stimulating, and enjoyable as you hoped it would be.

Some missions have a rule requiring their missionaries to "go away" for their vacations. Such rules assume that what's good for ninety percent must necessarily be good for all. This is a false assumption. Some missionaries, especially those with children in boarding school, should not be forced to go away on vacation. The children need to feel that they have a place to come home to, and for their sake the family may do best to spend the vacation at home.

Now how about those weekly and daily breaks we mentioned? They are cumulatively more important than the annual holiday. What do you do on an ongoing basis to keep yourself mentally and emotionally refreshed? Note that I am not including spiritual refreshment here; that will be dealt with later.

One form of refreshment or stimulation will come from your reading. Keep up with your professional literature. Read good books and magazines. Having children is a wonderful excuse to read aloud those classics you may have never read yourself. Cultivate a broad interest in the world, especially in the worldwide church. And keep up with the news. One of our favorite ways of doing that in Nepal is to read *The Rising Nepal*, the daily English-language newspaper. I knew it was going to be a treat from the very first article I read, which told of a recent flood in which "unfortunately only seventeen people drowned." It's been a nonstop treat ever since.

In addition to reading, develop some of those other natural interests we all have: music, photography, crafts. And then there are the hobbies. A senior Nepal missionary has possibly the best collection of Nepali stamps in the world; no great honor, but a lot of fun. Another is a butterfly collector, and Nepal is world-famous for its butterflies. One missionary has raised forty-four varieties of fruit on his quarter acre of hillside. Another collects clippings from *The Rising Nepal*. And so it goes.

Hobbies have an illustrious history in missions. William Carey's hobby was botany; he spent most mornings in his garden, and made significant contributions to the scientific literature of his day. The founder of the United Mission to Nepal was an ornithologist, and his first trip into Nepal, when it was still a closed country, was on a bird-collecting expedition sponsored by the Chicago Natural History Museum. Many other examples could be given in which God has used hobbies not just to refresh his servants, but to further other purposes as well.

Hobbies can assume too much importance, of course, as can any other good gift of God. This is a special danger when one is not really enjoying his work. But abuses are not common. A recent article in a mission journal spoke critically of a south-sea-island missionary who had gotten together the best tropical fish collection on the island. The article referred to him as a "fisher of fish" instead of a fisher of men. Maybe that's what he had indeed become, but I felt the article was altogether too harsh. Maybe he had been going through a rough patch, and those fish had been a real form of therapy. We need to give each other the benefit of the doubt.

Missionaries in isolated settings need social outlets, and these often are simply not available. It's hard to call an evening at your team leader or co-worker's house a "social outlet"—even if they are sociable people.

But a team working together can provide plenty of diversion for its members; cookouts, pantomimes, costume parties, various games, and, if they're partly around the bend already, a five-thousand-piece puzzle will send them the rest of the way. Yes, they have such things. The one we had was forty-nine percent sky and forty-nine percent sea, the rest being a strip of distant coastline on which stood a small red barn that took up one piece. There was not a cloud in the sky and it was a calm day at sea, which is more than can be said for the mental states of those gathered around the puzzle that evening. So much for social outlets.

9

Thoughts for New Missionaries—
And Old Ones

All the adjustments, frustrations, conflicts, and humblings of the early years on the mission field can be included under the heading "discipline." Self-discipline is fine, and necessary. But it is usually insufficient to build our character and prepare us for fruitful service. We need the discipline mediated by circumstances and by others.

Terms like "discipline" and "submission to authority" are about as popular today as fluorocarbons and planned economies. Discipline? What is this? Mission in the nineteenth century? Or worse, a Christian academy? Except for those going out with youth missions, most missionary recruits today have degrees under their belts, they've been around; some are even middle-aged, and have been following Christ for years. What's this talk about discipline?

First, the Christian who doesn't need discipline has already been packed in a box. Old folks need different kinds of discipline than young folks do, but all need discipline.

Second, the mission field provides a new setting, a new set of circumstances that have not yet been encountered. The adjusting to new people, a new culture, a new language, and new living conditions is a very real form of discipline. It should be welcomed, not chafed at. The adjusting to a group of missionaries, especially "senior missionaries," is a form of discipline. The giving up of one's job prospects, the loss of privacy, the need to fit into a mission team are all forms of discipline. Such discipline is always painful, yet it cannot be avoided. It cannot even be short-cutted; sooner or later these issues must be faced.

"Can't a first-rate orientation program eliminate the need for such discipline?" someone may ask. "After all, goes the saying, 'any fool can learn from experience; wise people learn from others.'" This saying is only partly true. If it were completely true, then we'd all be fools, because we all learn the deepest lessons of life through experience, through discipline, and not by reading a book or hearing a lecture.

The making of a missionary "begins in the nursery," said Amy Carmichael. It continues through school and professional training. And it accelerates when one gets to the field. And the essential element throughout is discipline.

As someone has said, a missionary's pilgrimage doesn't end when he gets to the field; it simply gets bumpier. That's when he discovers new weaknesses, new temptations, new sins. These are at the root of most of the emotional struggle and pain we experience as new missionaries. We learn much about ourselves when we arrive on the mission field. Some of our flaws and weaknesses may never have been revealed before in the security of our home country. But now they are. Our defects are exposed. Because of them we sustain wounds. These, in a sense, can be considered battle wounds. As these wounds are healed, the scars remain. They will be signs that we've been fighting on the front lines. They will be scars we can wear without shame.

This is all from the perspective of the new missionary, of course. On the other side stands the older missionary, the mission administrator, the team leader. These people must do all in their power to smooth the way for the new missionary and to prevent unnecessary hardships. In particular, they must do everything possible to meet the expectations of the new missionary, to get him into the situation of his choice or the one best suited to him. They should encourage the new missionary to speak out, and then listen to what he or she says. They must encourage openness. They are to be friends and spiritual guides. Yet even if they perform all these functions to perfection, there will still be plenty of opportunities for discipline left over!

Discipline "produces a harvest of righteousness and peace" (Heb 12:11). The Holy Spirit uses discipline to clear away those things in our life that prevent him from using us fully, those things that keep the fruit of the Spirit from fully ripening.

Four forms of discipline

One of the first means or forms of discipline we encounter on the mission field consists of inconveniences and physical hardships. If we can see God's hand in these unpleasant experiences even as they are taking place, it will be most helpful to us. Then we will be better able to let God use these experiences to refine our character. Our character is revealed most clearly under irritating and difficult circumstances. If we can be gracious during such times, it will be a powerful witness. Love is most manifest when it suffers, especially when it suffers at the hands of the person loved.

Even though God uses difficulties for our good, we don't need to go out of our way looking for them! They'll come on their own. What we need to do is to see them as God's opportunities to work his grace through us as individuals and as missionary teams. This sounds good on paper, but it also has been proven true over and over again in the lives of God's servants. And it will prove true in the most trying circumstances that a missionary will face.

The second form that discipline can take on the field is a sense of disillusionment or disappointment. You recall those fantastic slides of the Himalayas that first got you interested in Nepal—but then when you finally reach your post three to six years later, you find you're in a valley where you must climb eight hours just to get a distant view of the peaks, and then they are usually obscured by clouds. Those quaint, picture-perfect little villages dotting the landscape—they turn out to be crowded, dark, dirty, smelly. And the heat! They told you it would be hot, but you had no idea how oppressive continuous heat can be.

The smiling nationals in the pictures don't seem to smile so much at you. Even the few national Christians treat you warily. And your fellow missionaries—where are those saintly people you read about in missionary biographies? They seemed so easy to get along with!

And then, after a few months, the work becomes routine, glamorless, even tedious. It wasn't the assignment you were expecting. Exciting developments are always taking place somewhere else. And perhaps the biggest disappointment of all is you, yourself. You're not the great missionary material you thought you were. All these disappointments are God's discipline. He is teaching you patience, which is just as much a fruit of the Spirit as joy. He is teaching you to rely on him instead of on externals. He is teaching you to be a missionary.

A third form of discipline is sickness. Air pollution in Third World cities may aggravate your asthma or bronchitis. You may get fungus, boils, three dozen bedbug bites. And you will surely get dysentery. Amebic dysentery is the "best discipline" because it's the hardest to treat and the treatment (Metronidazole) is worse than the illness. And then it can become chronic; it doesn't produce specific symptoms, only a vague fatigue, malaise. And soon you become convinced you've got a spiritual problem, but in the end you find out it was only amebiasis. Of course, you don't need amoebas to make you feel weak and tired; the heat alone can do that. And when you're physically tired, you are emotionally tired too. You think this whole missionary deal isn't turning out right. You become discouraged, depressed. These are disciplines from God.

The fourth and hardest form of discipline comes from our relationships with other people, especially fellow missionaries.

To live above with saints in heaven,
oh, that will be glory;
but to live below with saints on earth,
now that's a different story.

Why does God always seem to mediate his discipline through those we somehow dislike, who are insensitive and unsympathetic, whose authority we resent? We need discipline, yes; but why can't it be given to us by people whom we respect, who are spiritual? I doubt there's a missionary alive who hasn't asked this at least once.

Why do we resist discipline? Because we have not died to self. Amy Carmichael writes: "One day I felt the 'I' in me rising hotly, and the word came, 'See in it a chance to die.'" Discipline gives us a chance to die.

Why is it that so many of us minister self instead of Christ? Because we have not denied self. Paul wrote: "For we do not preach ourselves, but Jesus Christ as Lord" (2 Co 4:5). By means of discipline, God constantly presses us to examine ourselves, that we might put to death the self-life, which so much hinders his work in us. How will we handle God's disciplines—the irritations, the disappointments, the slights and humiliations, the lack of acceptance, the hostility? Will we bridle under these? Or will we be able to see them as God's call to us to die to self?

Again listen to Amy Carmichael, whose words have deepened the spiritual lives of thousands of Christians worldwide: "Think of being the follower of a Savior who was despised and rejected, and yet wanting to escape being misunderstood and misjudged...Oh, that we may die, not in mere hymn and prayer, but in deed and in truth, to ourselves, to our self-life and self-love."

Here we have come to this fundamental scriptural truth: If we would walk with God, if we would serve him effectively, if we would endure the hardships and stresses of missionary life and finish our course, we must take into the very deepest part of our souls these words of Jesus: "If anyone would come after me, he must deny himself and take up his cross daily and follow me" (Lk 9:23). This is a daily crucifixion, a daily dying. The more we focus on our dying, the less we will focus on our selves, on our rights, our injured egos, our self-fulfillment. The more we focus on our dying, the more we will attain true fulfillment, which is to become like Jesus.

Satan's attack or God's discipline?

We have talked about some of the ways in which God disciplines us. But many of those same circumstances we have referred to as God's disciplines can just as easily be called attacks of Satan. The illnesses, the discouragements, the personality clashes—are these disciplines or attacks? Or both?

There is a sense in which we can say that God uses even Satan to discipline us. But I feel that that confuses things. To me it's clearer the following way. God ordains all circumstances. Through these circumstances God disciplines us. Through these same circumstances Satan tries to tempt us to sin. God is constantly desiring to bring good out of all our circumstances. But if we allow ourselves to be led into temptation by Satan, we will end up sinning and miss the good that God intended through that circumstance.

So that terrible headache the missionary is experiencing, is it God or is it Satan who is behind it? My answer is God. God may "allow" Satan to actually deliver the headache, as he did in Job's case, but the ultimate cause is God.

God wants to use the headache to draw us closer to him, to deepen our faith. The headache could even be the result of sin in our life, and God may graciously be using it to send us a warning. Satan, on the other hand, wants to use the headache to discourage us, to shake our faith, and to lead us into further sins of irritability and bitterness.

Circumstances are morally neutral. Circumstances should not be the chief focus of our prayers. The chief focus should be: How are we going to react to the circumstance—by turning toward God or by turning toward Satan, by letting God use the circumstance for our good or by letting Satan use it for our harm?

So when the missionary is buffeted by a difficult circumstance, let him not automatically blame the circumstance for all his problems. Let him not blame the heat, nor the new culture, nor the tiny amoebas in his intestines (they mean no harm, after all); and above all, let him not blame a colleague, that "senior missionary who is the source of all my problems." The difficult circumstance is not the real problem. The real problem is usually in us; it is, at root, spiritual.

Yes, we talk about amebic dysentery and senior missionaries as "problems," but, I repeat, they are not the real problem. And as long as we keep focusing on the circumstances, we will not be able to deal with the real problem; rather, it will end up dealing with us.

Our real problem—that is, the problem that takes away our joy and peace—is always sin of one sort or another. When we are confronting all the difficult and stressful new situations on the mission field, we shall be tempted to sin. We complain about our job assignment; we are irritable with the cook who has burned the bread for the fourth day in a row; we are critical of the nationals, their customs and attitudes; and we resent the authority of our leaders. These attitudes—these complaining, irritable, critical and rebellious spirits—are, after all, sinful attitudes. They are our responsibility.

In calling our "real problem" sin or a sinful attitude, I do not mean to suggest that the circumstances we face aren't real trials; they are. That headache, that psychological depression, that disappointment, that stress—whatever it is—is very real and painful. But it is a circumstance, and God controls circumstances.

Furthermore, I do not mean to suggest that our circumstances are always the result of sin; in fact, they usually are not. One of the worst things you can say to a new missionary (or any other Christian) who is experiencing depression or stress of some kind is this: "It's all because your life isn't right with God; it's because of sin, lack of faith." Yes, maybe it's true; but maybe it's not.

Circumstances may or may not hinder our ministry, but sinful attitudes certainly will. Here follows a number of circumstances commonly faced by new (and old) missionaries that can be used by God to increase their fruitfulness or used by Satan to decrease it. Many more examples could be given than are listed here; but even if we thought we had them all, Satan would choose a new one to attack us with.

First, a personality clash with your roommate. If you are unmarried, you don't usually get to choose your roommate. Mission administrators are expert at matching quiet and sober introverts with relentlessly cheerful extroverts; or tidy, organized, managerial types with spontaneous and disorganized free spirits; or the quick and active with the slow and deliberate; or optimists with pessimists, "morning" people with "night" people—you name it and your mission administrators will hit it on the nose every time. Actually, we encourage our children to marry their opposites; it's more work but it makes for a better marriage. Likewise, God wants you and your roommate to complement each other, to stretch each other. And it sounds absolutely ideal on paper until your extrovert roommate brings home four friends for supper when you just wanted a quiet evening alone.

Second, cultural differences between missionaries. This can be especially troublesome in international missions or teams. We love to stereotype each other—"those tight, stuffy Britishers"; "those loose-lipped, boorish Americans"—but such statements are harmful, not to say inaccurate. The only "tight, stuffy Britishers" I've ever met were in the movies. Humor is always a good way to enjoy each other—provided it's mutually understood. Our hospital team in the early years was half American and half European. One Fourth of July, we Americans got together and celebrated "Leaving Europe Day." We were well into our festivities when we noticed that our European colleagues were having a party of their own across the way: they were celebrating that we'd left!

Third, getting a job you didn't expect. I guess about a quarter of missionaries would raise their hand on this one. Job descriptions are fluid on the mission field, because the situation is usually fluid. One young couple came out to our project expecting to run our guesthouse and do village ministry. The week they arrived we unexpectedly lost our project maintenance supervisor and his assistant, and so guess who took their place. The young husband didn't have much practical experience in maintenance, but he had more general knowledge than any other possible person, so he "volunteered" to help. It was no small contribution to keep the wheels of a busy fifty-bed hospital and community health program turning smoothly—plus keeping all the stoves and toilets of the staff in working order. But it wasn't his calling. It wasn't the "spiritual work" he had wanted to do. He felt caught, trapped. Not knowing the language, he couldn't easily teach a Nepali to step in for him. It was a situation of nobody's choosing. But such situations are part of life on the mission field, and Satan wants to use them to disillusion new missionaries and send them home. God wants to use those same situations too, but for better purposes!

Fourth, conflict with mission leaders. "They seem so old-fashioned; They listen but don't hear." "They make you feel controlled, manipulated." "They are more interested in 'the work' than in you, the worker." These are all common feelings among new missionaries, and there is often some basis for them. These feelings are not wrong in themselves, but the problem is that they lead to lack of trust on the part of the new worker. He begins to doubt the good intentions of his leaders; he questions their motives. And this lack of trust, this suspicion, is fatal. It is almost always fatal to the successful service of the new missionary, and it is often fatal to the continued ability of the leader to lead. It is Satan who takes what are often legitimate feelings and turns them into this lack of trust, this questioning of motives. When we question another's motives we are, in effect, judging that person, and that is sin. God, on the other hand, wants to use these same initial feelings to teach us humility, to encourage us to understand our leaders, to learn from them, and to pray for them.

Fifth, opposition by nationals. I once knew a missionary who had contributed greatly to building up a church in his area and discipling the new believers. He was not a church planter or pastor; he had no desire to lead the church, but only to help train and prepare national leadership. After serving many years in the area, he was one day presented by the nationals with a paper containing nineteen "points"—accusations of wrong doing against them. Every point but one was either totally false or based on a total misunderstanding. The one true point was that three years earlier he had helped raise money to send one of the young Nepali believers to Kathmandu for training in leadership and evangelism. When the individual returned from the training, he refused to serve as one of the church leaders. The missionary had too forcefully tried to persuade the young man to serve, saying, "But we raised money to send you for training; you owe it to the church to do so." It was correctly seen as manipulation—but hardly a reason to have the missionary sent away, as the nationals hoped would happen. When the missionary didn't leave, the main Nepali instigator of the nineteen-point paper left instead, and went to work for a Swiss aid project in another part of Nepal. A couple of months later he stole from that project a huge sum of money and then fled the country. After that, the other believers repented of their action against the missionary and reconciliation took place. God's purposes won out in this case, instead of Satan's. But there have been other cases where a similarly respected missionary has had to leave, or whose ministry has been rendered fruitless. The rejection by nationals is a painful experience indeed; it is like being rejected by your own children.

Sixth, opposition by new missionaries. New missionaries don't stay "new" for long; their turn will quickly come to experience the opposition of yet newer missionaries. I once knew a mission project director who had worked hard to build up a mission institution. Over a ten-year period he and his wife had established good relations with the Nepali community. They had an active and fruitful ministry. But along about their ninth or tenth year, they found themselves the only experienced missionaries in the project; the other dozen or so missionaries on the team were relative newcomers. The Nepalis naturally preferred to deal with the older couple whom they knew, and who could speak their language well. Because of the inexperience of the new team members, more of the management responsibilities for the project were thrust on the couple. The new missionaries quickly received the impression that the project revolved around the couple, and that everything was in their hands. They commenced a murmuring campaign against the couple, reinforcing each other's impressions as they ventilated their feelings one to another. This went on for an entire year, and the couple knew nothing about it. Finally the matter reached the ears of the mission's central administration. But by that time, the slander and false witness against the couple had spread so widely and deeply that they were eventually forced to move from that place. Within two years of their moving, all but one of those missionaries who murmured had left Nepal. The couple, however, continued for many years working in another part of the country. An extreme example, but such trials will come in one form or another to most missionaries who stay on the field more than a few years. Such an experience can be used by Satan to make us bitter, or it can be used by God to make us better.

Seventh, feelings of discouragement, depression. These are very common among missionaries. (I'm not speaking here of the severe forms of depression that require professional help.) They may result from setbacks in one's ministry, failure to accomplish some objective (like passing the first-year language exam), problems in relationships, a sense of spiritual inadequacy—or really any trial such as we have been discussing in this section. But discouragement and depression can take on a life of their own beyond whatever caused them; they can become trials in their own right. Satan wants to turn our psychological depression into a spiritual depression, to decrease our faith and separate us from God. God wants to use discouragement and depression to draw us into greater dependence upon him.

Eighth, a feeling that your work is not appreciated. No one, not even a spiritual person, can go on forever without some acknowledgement that his or her contribution is worthwhile, valued. And yet on the mission field you can go quite a while wondering whether anyone appreciates what you are doing. In Nepal, for example, people rarely say "thank you." They assume that any service you render is only to gain religious merit for yourself—so why should they thank you for that? Rather, they will think you should thank *them*, because they have given you the chance to "earn merit" through your service to them! This takes getting used to. So don't look for gratitude; don't look for rewards. But it sure would be nice to get some encouragement and confirmation from your fellow missionaries once in a while!

Well, we could go on with nine, ten, eleven—physical health problems, loneliness, family stresses, personal loss, tragedy, disaster. William Carey's entire printing warehouse went up in smoke with the loss of many New Testament translations in progress. Years of effort—gone. And things like that have been happening to missionaries ever since— more to missionaries than to those who stay at home. Are we ready for the disciplines of God?

When trials come, we usually resort to what some will call "Christian platitudes" to comfort the sufferer. They may be spoken lightly, as if they were platitudes, but they are not; they are the promises of God. Pain and suffering are God's most effective means for building character, for drawing people close to him, and for cleansing away the self-centeredness that keeps God from fully using us. If we will but respond rightly to these trials, God will replace the pain and suffering with joy and spiritual power. The promises of Scripture are not idle; they have been proven true over and over again.

Let us not, as missionaries, place excessive reliance on plans, methods, and strategies; these are only tools. E. M. Bounds said: "Men are looking for better methods; God is looking for better men." Our sins are greater in God's eyes than in our own; however, our potential is also greater in God's eyes than in our own. God's goal is that we reach our potential. Let us not always expect him to change our circumstances; rather, what God wants is to change us. When through painful circumstances he has helped us change, then we shall be ready to move on to the next level of our potential. We reach our potential only as we yield ourselves to God each step of the way.

One of the great blessings of missionary life is the increased exposure it gives us to this ongoing work of God in our lives. Yes, the mission field aggravates our weaknesses, but it also develops our strengths. It will be different for each person. We need as much as possible to have come to terms with our weaknesses before we hit the field, and to have made a sober assessment of our strengths. This will prevent us from "getting thrown" by the trials that will come. But through each trial, God will be deepening our faith, showing us that he is sufficient, not we. Most of us have no way of learning these lessons but through trial and pain. "Consider it pure joy, my brothers, whenever you face trials of many kinds, because you know that the testing of your faith develops perseverance. Perseverance must finish its work so that you may be mature and complete, not lacking anything" (Jas 1:2-4).

"See in it a chance to die." That we might die to self is God's deepest purpose in sending us trials. There is nothing of lasting, eternal worth that is not born out of trial, travail—out of death itself. That was true in Jesus' life; and so will it be true in the lives of his disciples.

New and old missionaries

One of the most saintly Christian physicians I know was walking one evening along a winding mountain trail toward the mission hospital she had founded several years earlier. She had been, by that time, over twelve years in Nepal, and before that, several years in India. The evening was very still. Before long she heard the voices of two recently arrived short-term missionaries walking behind her on the same trail, but at a faster pace. They were unaware that she was ahead of them. One was saying to the other, "Do you think you'll be able to adjust to these Nepalis?"

The other replied, "It's not the Nepalis I'll have trouble with; it's the doctor."

"Yeah, isn't that the truth," said the first.

Fortunately the trail split just then, and the doctor went one way and the two newcomers went the other. But the doctor was deeply perplexed about how the two short-termers could have gotten such an unfavorable impression of her. They had only arrived the day before.

They couldn't have gotten their impression in one day. Furthermore, they couldn't have gotten it from other missionaries; no one who knew this doctor would have remotely suggested she was hard to get along with. No, these two newcomers had come with a pre-set notion about senior missionaries, and they were already "digging in" in anticipation of a rough time.

Friends, that's not a good way to start a missionary career—even a short-term one.

A generation ago, "junior missionaries" were treated as just that—as juniors. They were put down. They were given no voice until they had passed their second-year language exam, often three or four years after arrival on the field. Some spent their entire first term in virtual silence. Today no one advocates going back to those days.

But the pendulum has now swung too far in the opposite direction, and new people coming out to the field are in danger of forgetting the scriptural injunctions to respect their elders and to submit to authority. We need to regain a sense of proportion in this matter.

Today's missionary recruit is more catered to than formerly. On arrival on the field the new missionary is made much of. The mission administration bends over backwards to protect the new member from upsets and disappointment. From the beginning his input is invited and his opinions listened to. This is all as it should be. But in the midst of this attention, the new missionary may begin to assume that everything is going to bend his way.

The first casualty in the new missionary's rising assertiveness is humility. Part of that humility is the wonder at having been chosen by God to enter this work. It is the wonder that one so unworthy should have been appointed to carry the gospel to other peoples, to be an ambassador for the King of kings. The Apostle Paul expressed this wonder at his own call; if he did it, ought not we to do it all the more?

But new missionaries coming out often do not manifest such wonder. Instead, they have answers; they have just acquired higher education, high-class training, the most up-to-date techniques, the latest knowledge, and they have come to put all this to use. They do not come with the attitude of a learner. They often regard older missionaries as out-of-date. They have too little respect for the accomplishments of the past; rather they are critical of what they see. They regard their untested methods as automatically superior to those that have been used for years.

In some cases they are superior. In other cases, they will work for the new missionary but not for the old one. Older missionaries, often overworked, have found patterns and routines that are helpful to them. These may have been developed over years. But these methods may not work for a new person. The new missionary, instead of just dismissing the old method, should first understand why it is used. Then he should try it out. If it truly is inferior, he can slowly introduce his own method—if possible, testing it side by side with the old. The new person uses his method; the old missionaries continue using theirs. This works fairly well in the professions. New medical doctors—within limits—can practice according to their own style and training. The older ones can carry on as before. There need be no threat to either side.

But what too often happens is that the new missionary can't wait for such a mutual interchange of ideas to take place. He is in a hurry. He may only be planning to stay on the field two to six years. He has a vision, an agenda, and a methodology to accomplish his objectives. He has a short-term perspective. It doesn't matter that his timetable doesn't fit in with those who are long-term, and especially with the nationals, who have no timetable at all.

But even new missionaries planning to stay long-term are not immune to this enthusiasm, this impatience of youth. They have strong feelings. They are at first perplexed that their obviously superior idea has been rejected. Then they may become frustrated, disillusioned. They see that things aren't going to change for them overnight. And instead of settling back and resolving to listen and learn and gain experience, they develop a complaining and critical spirit—often directed not just at methods and practices but also, in a personal way, at older missionaries themselves.

What advice, then, can we give to the new missionary? First, start with a sense of wonder and thanksgiving that you have been called to partake in the work of God. Then, have the attitude of a learner. Observe. Ask questions. Before you introduce your new idea, ask if it hasn't already been tried; it likely has—and didn't work. Older missionaries aren't as "out of it" as you may suppose. Then, set realistic goals for yourself. Idealism is great—it's essential. But it needs to be tempered with realism. Set your goals in conjunction with others; don't be concerned only with "doing your thing." Finally, be patient, be non-judgmental, be humble, be respectful. Above all, do not criticize. Criticism is a poison that destroys teams and will come back and destroy you as well.

And then when you are overruled, and your suggestions and new ideas rejected, how should you react? Accept the situation. To refuse to submit to the wisdom and experience of people who have been around longer than you is a sign of immaturity. Remember, old missionaries were once new; they have a lot to offer you. If you don't let yourself be guided by their experience, you will be the loser.

Finally, adopt a servant attitude. That's not easy to do when you are a highly qualified professional coming out to work among illiterate nationals and a bunch of stick-in-the-mud senior missionaries. But pray for such a servant attitude. Don't think, "I have a great deal to offer these people." Yes, you do; but don't parade it. Others may well think less of what you have to offer than you do. And be willing to "come down a notch" in your professional career—or two or three notches. You'll have to anyway, so you might as well do it willingly! A servant is willing to do this for the sake of those he serves. Be willing to do anything. Be willing to be "used." Be willing to be taken advantage of. It is the servant's way; it is the way of the cross.

I was a new missionary once. When I started working in rural Nepal I was the only surgeon for half a million people. That was pretty important; I was needed. Early on, I visited a large town of five thousand people called Barpak, located in the northern part of our district at the foot of the high peaks. To my knowledge, Barpak had never seen a doctor before. It had no health facilities whatever. Everywhere I looked there was disease, pain, suffering. To visit that town was to step a thousand years back into the Middle Ages. I expected people to greet me with open arms. But half of them regarded me with open hostility and suspicion, and the other half couldn't have cared less that I had come. In their eyes, I was just another practitioner come to take advantage of them, to take their money in exchange for some trifling medicine of untested worth. It was a wonderful place for a self-important new missionary doctor to visit early in his career; every new missionary needs to visit Barpak.

My "senior missionary" was a doctor who had spent all his life in India, a grand old missionary physician of the old school. He had hundreds of tricks up his sleeves I'd never read about. He also had a philosophy different from mine. He told me, "You can't possibly treat everyone, so those you do treat, treat well."

It sounded good, but I strongly believed it was better to give a little treatment to a lot of people than the best treatment to just a few. Many, many more people would be benefited in the end, and at less cost. I was sure I was right. We carried on a respectful but running disagreement the entire year he was there, but of course his view prevailed; I was the "junior missionary." Now, many years later, I still think I am right. But I'm not nearly so "sure."

As a new missionary, don't be "sure" your way is best. I'm reminded of the self-assured Royal Nepal Airlines agent who was assigned to the grass landing strip six miles down the mountain from our hospital. He knew very few English words, but one he had learned was the word "cocksure." He'd be running along well in Nepali, but whenever he wanted to express certainty about any subject, instead of using the Nepali word for "certain," he would use the English word "cocksure." He was always cocksure the plane would come, cocksure it wouldn't rain, cocksure about this, cocksure about that. You can guess what name we gave him! Well, there are quite a few new missionaries coming out these days who, if they're not careful, may wind up with the same name.

In all this discussion so far, the focus has been on new missionaries. But that doesn't let old missionaries off the hook. They have a major role to play in assuring that the relationship between old and new missionaries is harmonious and mutually beneficial.

Older missionaries must guard against getting into a rut; this can happen even to the most spiritual among them. Just because something has worked in the past doesn't mean it will work forever or even that it is the best solution for the present. Humans have a natural tendency toward rigidity, and this quality is a major impediment on the mission field—especially in relation to new missionaries.

Older missionaries, like anyone else, feel threatened by innovation. For some, a new idea is almost an implied criticism: "Why didn't you think of this before?" And it doesn't help when the new idea is presented in a superior and condescending manner. And yet old missionaries must ever be learners. They mustn't retreat into an I-know-best fortress. They must remain open-minded, happy for new insights. They must never squelch the enthusiasm of a new member of the team. They must listen, actually hear, what the new missionary is saying. Their whole attitude should invite the active participation and involvement of the new missionary. They must be encouragers, facilitators. And above all, they must remain gracious and humble. Presumably they are the more spiritually mature; they must then act like it.

But this very issue of maturity can cause division between new and old missionaries. One of the more perplexing problems older missionaries face is how to deal with a new missionary who feels somehow intimidated by their maturity, their spirituality. Clearly such a feeling of intimidation ought not to be. Where is the defect? Is it all immaturity on the part of the new missionary? Or is there a subtle overbearing pride on the part of the senior? Certainly the older missionary must do all in his or her power to be warm, friendly, accepting, positive, humble.

New and old missionaries need each other. The wisdom and experience of the older missionaries combined with the freshness and zeal of the younger ones is a powerful combination. But if the two sides are divided, it is a disaster.

It cannot be emphasized too strongly that the major share of adjustment and change must be made by the new missionary. The new missionary must in the end be willing to submit happily to age and experience, which happen to count for a great deal (as all who are aged and experienced will agree). A new missionary who is not willing to do this will end up causing far more harm than good. And sadly, this has happened many times.

It happened at the very beginning of the modern missionary era. There has never been a more celebrated missionary team than that of Carey, Marshman and Ward of Serampore, India. After laboring many years in proclaiming the gospel, translating Scripture, and establishing educational institutions, they called for new workers to come and help them meet the expanding opportunities opening up before them. In due time the new workers arrived. But before long, they began to find fault with the way things were being done and, in particular, with one member of the senior team, John Marshman. The new workers began to transmit their criticisms back to the Home Society in England. Finally, after several years of correspondence (a letter took six months one way), the Society asked Carey for his opinion of their attacks on Marshman. So critical is this issue to the success of the missionary enterprise, that I include portions of Carey's reply, dated July 15, 1819.

> I disapprove as much of the conduct of our Calcutta brethren [the new workers] as it is possible for me to disapprove of any human actions. The evil they have done is, I fear, irreparable; and certainly the whole might have been prevented by a little frank conversation with either of us; and a hundredth part of that self-denial which I found it necessary to exercise for the first few years of the mission, would have prevented this awful rupture. I trust you will excuse my warmth of feeling upon this subject, when you consider that by this rupture that cause is weakened and disgraced, in the establishment and promotion of which I have spent the best part of my life. A church is attempted to be torn in pieces, for which neither I nor my brethren ever thought we could do enough. We laboured to raise it: we expended much money to accomplish that object; and in a good measure saw the object of our desire accomplished. But now we are traduced, and the church rent by the very men who came to be our helpers....Judge yourself whether it is comely that a man, who has laboriously and disinterestedly served the mission so many years...should be arraigned and condemned without a hearing by a few young men just arrived, one of whom had not been a month in the country before he joined the senseless outcry.

Carey then went on to say that the charges brought against Marshman by these new brethren were false. The controversy lasted thirteen years, and was only "resolved" by the separation of the two groups of missionaries. Carey's own son sided with the new workers, and thereby elicited this letter from his father, dated April 17, 1828.

> From a letter of yours in which you express a very indecent pleasure at the opposition which Brother Marshman has received...I perceive you are informed of the separation which has taken place between them and us. What...you call a 'set-down' [of Marshman] I call a 'falsehood.'

To his credit, Carey's son later apologized to both his father and to Marshman.

So began the modern missionary era. And so it continues to this day. There is hardly an experienced missionary who doesn't have a similar tale to tell. It takes many years to build up a work. It takes but a few days to tear it down.

Hardship and suffering

From New Testament times to the present, obeying the missionary call has meant accepting a greater likelihood of experiencing hardship and suffering. Half of the early missionaries to Africa died within the first two years. William Borden gave first his money and then his life in service to Egypt. He was dead within four months of his arrival on the field. On the flyleaf of his Bible he had written the words: "No reserve, no retreat, no regrets."

Amy Carmichael of India, who suffered great physical burdens over many years, wrote these lines:

But as the Master shall the servant be,
And pierced are the feet that follow me.
Can he have followed far
Who has no wound, no scar?

Suffering is inescapable for the Christian. "In fact, everyone who wants to live a godly life in Christ Jesus will be persecuted" (2 Ti 3:12). Suffering is indispensable to the spiritual fruitfulness of our ministry. As Oswald Chambers taught, you can't drink grapes; they need to first be squeezed. What comes out when we are squeezed? Bitterness, or the sweet juice of the Holy Spirit?

And our response to suffering—what should it be? "Rejoice and be glad" (Mt 5:12). Paul and Silas sang in prison. There is tremendous power in suffering. Jesus looked weak and defeated on the cross, but at that very moment of suffering and death, he overpowered all the principalities and forces of evil in the universe. "...by his wounds we are healed," says Isaiah (Isa 53:5). And by our wounds, our suffering, our humiliation, we too become agents of healing.

Jesus transforms suffering by using it. "The victim becomes the victor; the test becomes a testimony."

All things ultimately originate with God. There are no second causes. So we must say at the outset that all suffering, trial, and hardship has been allowed, even ordained by God for the ultimate benefit of those whom God has called to serve him. We may not see the benefit immediately, nor even in our lifetime. Here we must simply trust in the wisdom and goodness of God.

Such suffering God carefully calibrates to accomplish his purpose. God may want to discipline us in some area of our life; such discipline will always be directed toward our blind spots, and hence will always be unexpected and painful. God may want to redirect us into a new area of ministry; sometimes it takes a jolt to get us out of our ruts. God may want to use our suffering to bring about reconciliation in a team, to revitalize a mission, to draw men and women to faith, to revive nations. The power released through suffering for Christ is incalculable. It is said truly that the greatest power on earth is love. And the greatest manifestation of love is suffering for others. "Greater love has no one that this, that he lay down his life for his friends" (Jn 15:13).

One form of suffering that does not come immediately from God is that which is caused by sin, our sin and the sin of others. We have said that there are no second causes, but there are surely *secondary* causes. God is not the author of sin, nor does he tempt men to sin. But sin has to come from somewhere, and that "somewhere" is our own sinful nature. We cannot blame God for our sin; we cannot even blame the devil. We can only blame ourselves.

The devil tempts, incites, aggravates. He uses our sinfulness to divide, disrupt, and destroy. But he's not the agent of sin; we are.

It is a moot issue philosophically whether a particular trial or suffering has originated with God or has originated in our sinful nature. Ultimately, God uses both kinds of suffering to accomplish his purposes. But as a practical matter, it is important to identify sin in ourselves and in others and also to recognize the activity of Satan. Because we need to oppose sin and Satan, but we dare not oppose God.

The key to differentiating the trial that comes from God and the trial that comes from sin is this: the original circumstance or trial is from God—even though Satan may be used to mediate it. The trial that comes from our sin, on the other hand, is the distress, the consequence, we must endure when we react sinfully to the original circumstance. Thus in every trial, one of our first responses must be to examine ourselves and see to what extent our suffering is caused or aggravated by our own sin or sinful attitude.

It is much easier to bear the trials that come directly from God than it is to bear the trials that result from our own sinful reactions. There may be rejoicing when we suffer for righteousness' sake, but not when we suffer for sin's sake. Surely these two types of trial were in the mind of the one who said: "It's easier to die for Christ than to live for him." Dying for Christ involves a moment of pain followed by an eternity of glory. Living for Christ involves daily dying, daily crucifying our sinful nature, daily warfare against our enemy, Satan.

Thus when we see sin and Satan active on the mission field (or in our church or in society), we must never lightly think that since everything is ultimately in God's hands we needn't be concerned. This thought denies the power of Satan and the destructiveness of sin. Evil is a very strong and active force in the world; Satan does seem to frustrate God's short-term purposes. He does work to render Christians powerless, split up teams, deprive us of fruit. Paul never thought of Satan as a robot. Peter called him a "roaring lion" (1 Pe 5:8). Yes, the lion may be on a leash, but the leash is long enough to permit him to do great harm.

The New Testament teaches that man has two choices, two responses to make to the circumstances that face him. He either responds in a godly way, or he responds in a sinful way. There is no neutral ground between these two ways—though our response may be often a mixture of the two. "Do not offer the parts of your body to sin, as instruments of wickedness, but rather offer yourselves to God...as instruments of righteousness" (Ro 6:13). We either submit to God's discipline and make God our master, or we submit to the impulse of our sinful nature and make Satan our master. The choice is ours. The choice is daily. And the choice faces missionaries on the field just as much as it faces Christians at home.

10

Sin and Interpersonal Conflict

The most difficult forms of suffering on the mission field are those arising from one's own sins and the sins of fellow missionaries. We must deal with this unpleasant but vital issue, because herein lies the greatest cause of fruitlessness and failure in world mission.

Christians as a group, and missionaries in particular, are not known for committing adultery or murder, nor for stealing or lying. These are "big sins," and are recognized as such by Christians and non-Christians alike.

But what all Christians battle almost daily are the sins of the spirit, the sins of attitude, the inner secret sins that are frequently hidden from man, but never from God.

Often we are not even aware of some of these sins, and even if we are, we tend to give them less weight than the "big sins." But we are mistaken when we do that. It is not possible to establish a universal hierarchy of sins from greatest to least. Such a listing is going to vary with each individual. Jesus made it clear that those who are given greater knowledge will suffer greater punishment than those with less knowledge—even for the same sin. And who can say which, in God's eyes, is the greater sin: the murder of a man by a non-Christian, or the murder of a man's reputation by a fellow Christian. Sins of the spirit and sins of the tongue have done far more harm to the cause of Christ than the grosser sins of lust and violence. The missionary who has nothing but contempt for the national caught in adultery is committing just as grievous a sin—the sin of an unloving and unforgiving spirit.

Some sins are obvious; they can't be hidden even from the person committing them. Outbursts of anger, irritability, rudeness, inhospitality—these sins are worn on the sleeve. The missionary who commits such sins almost always feels deeply upset with himself over the matter. However, the inward sins, the sins of the spirit, pass almost unnoticed: the judgmental attitude, resentment, jealousy, pride. These are often hidden from ourselves; we even give them new names: "concern," "righteous indignation," "zeal for the Lord's interests."

Let us not fool ourselves. I once knew a missionary with the all-too-obvious sin of irritableness, who became the focus of criticism by other missionaries who saw nothing whatever wrong in criticizing him behind his back. Did they know how grieved he himself was at his irritableness? Did they know the miles he had come in correcting it from previous years? Did they see him apologize after each episode to the person concerned? No, none of these things were known to them. They remained undeterred. Theirs was a critical spirit, a sin far more destructive because it goes unrecognized.

Even the obvious sins we don't all regard alike. Some sins we readily excuse, some we don't. Those sins we see in ourselves, we tend to excuse in others; those we don't see in ourselves, we tend to judge harshly. We all need to get back to the same starting point, and see our sins as God sees them; in his eyes, all sin is equally inexcusable.

Christians everywhere downplay the sins of attitude. If they have to acknowledge them at all, they prefer to call them "psychological problems": inferiority complex, perfectionism, resentment, depression, a critical spirit, and others. But excepting some deep psychological disturbances, all these are at root spiritual problems. They arise from pride, self-centeredness, or lack of faith. And until the root spiritual problem—the sinful attitude—is dealt with, there can be no final correction of the person's problem.

There is a resistance to labeling all these internal conflicts "spiritual problems" for fear of placing a burden of guilt on a person already weighed down with troubles. But the guilt that is added is not a false guilt. Behind the great majority of psychological problems lies one or more sinful attitudes. The first step in resolving the problem lies in recognizing and confessing the sinful attitude and turning to God for forgiveness and grace.

The New Testament does not focus on psychological diagnoses. It focuses rather on sinful attitudes. Paul wrote to the Colossians, "Put to death, therefore, whatever belongs to your earthly nature" (Col 3:5), and then in the next few verses he gives some examples. In the list of "acts of the sinful nature" in Galatians 5:19-21, over half can be classified as sinful attitudes. And certainly in Matthew 5, Jesus puts sinful attitudes on a par with sinful actions.

It is in changing our sinful attitudes to Christlike attitudes that the greatest battles of the missionary occur. The real problems are not the externals—the heat, the dirt, the difficult co-workers; the real problems are spiritual and need to be dealt with on a spiritual level. Once the deeper problem is dealt with, it's amazing how the external problem seems to lessen and even to disappear.

The success or failure of a missionary's career depends on the extent to which his attitudes are brought under the control of the Holy Spirit. Our attitudes affect every aspect of our missionary lives. Our constant daily priority is to submit our attitudes to the Spirit's control, so that the Spirit's fruits can be manifest in our lives.

Remember, the missionary is no different than any other Christian. He may have a greater variety of temptations, but they all will be "common to man." When he runs into trouble, the first thing he should ask is: How have I let God down? How have I withheld myself from total submission to his will? What other "loves" are there in my life that compete with my love for him and for my neighbor? Who of us can answer these questions with self-confidence? Yet it is on these questions that our missionary careers hang. When trouble and conflict come, don't first look elsewhere for the source of the problem; first look within. It is there that the source of the problem will most likely be.

This chapter deals primarily with those sins which lead directly to interpersonal conflict and a breakdown in relationships among missionaries. For it is interpersonal conflict that is the number-one cause of missionaries leaving the field earlier than planned. It is also the number-one cause of unfruitfulness in missionary teams. That is because interpersonal conflict leads to disunity, and disunity is Satan's most effective means of robbing us of our fruit.

All sins affect relationships, however indirectly. For all sins arise in that most fundamental sin of all, self-love; and self-love is the enemy of relationships.

This chapter is going to skip over most of man's sins. Every sin you can find in churches at home you'll find on the mission field. There'll be a new sin lurking around every corner of your missionary career. Satan has cleverly devised temptations for every age group; one you resisted in early years will suddenly reappear and trip you up. Saintly senior missionaries are not immune. Our enemy never sleeps.

Before looking at the most common sins that lead to interpersonal conflict and broken relationships, two observations need to be made. The first is that conflict, in and of itself, is not necessarily sinful or even harmful. In fact, conflict usually precedes any kind of human progress or development.

Conflict stimulates ideas, challenges us to find new solutions, brings out the best (or worst) in us, and generally, if properly controlled, leaves us better people working in better organizations. So far, so good.

Conflict is also inevitable. The trick is to use conflict to our and God's advantage. However, that is not Satan's idea. Satan always tries to turn a "pure conflict" into an interpersonal conflict. In place of a healthy and vigorous debate over ideas, goals, and strategies, Satan wants to create personal differences. He wants to stir up in us negative, sinful emotions directed at each other. This, then, is how we are defining "interpersonal conflict."

The second observation that needs to be made is that everyone has relationship problems, and from time to time they are bound to flare up with one party or another. It is unfair, therefore, to label someone as "having relationship problems," as though it were some kind of medical diagnosis. It's almost like accusing one of having a nose or two arms. It is one of those broad, meaningless accusations we are so prone to level at one another, and against which there is no possibility of defense.

As with conflict, therefore, it's not having a "relationship problem" that counts so much as how you handle it. It's like the old adage among surgeons: It's not the difficulty you get into at surgery that counts; it's how you get out of it! So, how well do you "get out of it" when you are thrust with few amenities into close quarters in a foreign culture with a bunch of strong-minded missionaries with all their foibles, hang-ups, and personality differences? That is the question we want to explore.

Relationship problems with nationals also occur, of course, but they are not nearly so intense as those between missionaries. Missionaries ordinarily don't work as closely with nationals as they do with their own colleagues. Furthermore, we expect to have differences with nationals, we are mentally prepared for it; whereas we did not expect to have such differences with our fellow missionaries. We supposed that they would be as humble and saintly as ourselves.

So why do missionaries, of all people, have so much trouble getting along with each other?

First, they are commonly strong-willed, single-minded achievers—or they wouldn't have gotten to the mission field in the first place. Have you ever tried to work with such people? It ain't easy. Their very strengths can become their weaknesses: insensitivity, impatience, overbearingness. As the saying goes: When strong personalities clash, they clash strongly.

Second, missionary teams are often international these days, and will become more so in the future. You may never realize the differences there are between British and Americans, for example, until you live and work closely together. It's well and good to write in a book that we need to appreciate each other's differences, but in reality those differences can also grate and irritate. Sometimes it seems as though we can love each other but not like each other.

Third, living closely together magnifies what otherwise would be trivial irritations. You can tolerate, even be amused by the idiosyncrasies of others as long as you only have to work with them a limited number of hours each week; but more than that and it begins to get to you. Most mission work is done by small teams working closely together over long periods, and team members do not often have the luxury of "getting away from each other."

Fourth, with the exception of teams that are preformed in the home country, missionaries are not given a choice of teammates. Incompatibilities there will be, and they need to be worked out. One problem is this idea we have that missionaries, being good Christians, should be able to get along with anyone. Yes, they should—and so when they don't, they prefer to deny there's a problem. They muddle along, and all the while things get worse. Denial is never a solution.

So here we have this missionary team, embroiled in conflict, and along come some visitors or short-term people, and they say, "Good grief! These are missionaries?" And they are quickly disillusioned with the spirituality of these choice servants of God, who were supposed to have left all their problems behind them in their home country. Well, if the newcomers had an idealized vision of what a missionary was like, they need to be disillusioned. But they also need to try and imagine what it is actually like living and working in such a place year after year. If they do this, they will be less quick to judge, and they will thenceforth pray for missionaries with more understanding and more fervor.

At the same time, we must never tolerate or gloss over interpersonal conflict; explain it, yes; excuse it, no. It always involves a failure of grace. Those personal incompatibilities we like to blame things on are never absolute; they can always be overcome, some with less difficulty, some with more. Not to overcome them, not to work through the conflict, is to play into the devil's hands.

It's hard to visualize how a team of missionaries can break up until you've actually seen it and experienced it. Before then, you always think it won't ever happen to your team. You look askance at other teams working in different places who are having trouble, and you wonder why they can't seem to work things out. And then, whammo, a year or two later the same thing hits your team, and you suddenly realize it can happen to anyone.

Sins leading to interpersonal conflict

The first two sins are in a special category, because they are more basic than the others, and their presence precludes any chance of resolving whatever conflict is at hand. The first is the refusal to confess wrong, and the second is the refusal to forgive. The first is always rooted in pride. The second is usually associated with other sins, such as slander, judgment, and envy. We shall pass over these two sins for now, because we shall be dealing with the subject of confession and forgiveness in the next chapter.

The third sin is self-assertiveness. In its unvarnished form, this is no more than a move "to get my way." The term self-assertiveness implies that we are putting a higher value on our beliefs and objectives than on those of our colleagues, and that we are prepared to sacrifice our colleagues' interests in order to protect our own. Self-assertiveness is the downside of strong-mindedness; it plays havoc with missionary teams.

Many say that self-assertiveness, together with self-respect and self-love, are part of a healthy Christian life. A person with no self-assertiveness is merely a doormat, and that is hardly the ideal for a Christian. Thus there is a definite sense in which we can rightly respect ourselves because we are children of God; our value and calling are from him. We are Christ's ambassadors. In that capacity we may indeed assert ourselves. But that is different from asserting "self."

Self-assertiveness takes different forms in a team. It may appear as a desire to manipulate or to dominate. Or it may appear as a drive for self-fulfillment. It may be totally unconscious. Strong-minded people must at all times bend over backwards to avoid such tendencies. They must always be willing to back down or compromise for the sake of unity. Aside from morality and basic Christian doctrine, there are very few issues in team ministries that are more important than unity. Furthermore, there will be times when the Holy Spirit calls us to be "doormats"; we need to be ready at such times to humble ourselves and practice self-denial.

Self-assertiveness is more a problem in newer missionaries, freshly trained and filled with new ideas. They hit the field and are eager to put their ideas into practice. And boom—they hit a brick wall called "senior missionary," and when they hit that wall all kinds of demons are released: impatience, criticism, hostility, frustration. Why? Because the young person wanted his own way.

The fourth sin is irritability. We can never blame irritations for our irritability. Irritability is always a sin; if we were completely humble and emptied of self, we would not be irritated by anything. If we are irritated, it means our self-life has been pricked.

Many can go a long time without getting irritated. If we only occasionally meet someone who has an irritating feature, we are unlikely to be irritated. But if we have to live with that person, he or she quickly gets on our nerves. So, little irritations are magnified by repetition.

In other cases, a particular irritation may cause someone to fly off immediately. An observer would call it an overreaction, but what has happened is that the irritated person has previously been sensitized to that irritation. He may have a family member who drove him bonkers, and suddenly he meets a similar person on the field. Indeed, one's own unresolved family conflicts may be carried over onto the field and account for much of the animosity one feels toward certain colleagues—often without knowing why.

The fifth sin is jealousy. Some writers have called it the second greatest sin among missionaries. Seems hard to believe! Missionaries would certainly be quick to deny any jealousy—especially to themselves. But there is no question it exists.

What are the reasons for jealousy? Just about any reason will do. Slow language learners are jealous of fast learners; those passed over for leadership are jealous of those appointed; those with lesser gifts in some area are jealous of those with greater gifts; those who are not respected and sought out by nationals are jealous of those who are. Even wives can become jealous of unmarried missionary women who receive assistance of one kind or another from their husbands. If unmarried women are young and pretty, it only makes matters worse.

If jealousy could be kept bottled up inside a person, it wouldn't be so destructive to the team as a whole—only to the individual involved. But jealousy is rarely kept within. Jealousy always creates a desire to tear the other person down, to take away his advantage. Jealousy leads inevitably to resentment and backbiting. This is what destroys teams.

The jealous person is unable to rejoice in another's success. Yet that "successful" person of whom we are jealous may himself be a very humble person, not seeking any credit for himself, even embarrassed by recognition of any kind. His success may have been due to simple hard work and dedication, not to any desire for recognition.

Among missionaries, the most harmful form of jealousy is that directed toward someone who has been successful in ministry. After some years a missionary may have built up great trust among the nationals. He may have been given leadership responsibilities. The nationals call him the "big teacher" or the "big doctor" or the "in-charge." They know him; they relate to him easily. Then new people come to the project and they aren't treated with the same respect and trust. The nationals repeatedly ask to see the missionary they know. If they are patients, they want to be examined by the doctor they know. What could be more natural?

But to the person afflicted with jealousy, it is not natural. He sees the successful missionary as someone who has sought prominence for himself and who wants to keep it at all costs. The jealous person feels that he himself is being kept back; he feels threatened by the other's success. No matter that the jealous person's perceptions are thoroughly distorted. The seeds of grumbling, dissension, and slander have been planted; jealousy is fertile soil for such seeds.

The sixth sin is really a complex of sins that are closely related: anger, resentment, and bitterness.

Anger itself is not necessarily sinful. The sudden experience of anger is a morally neutral emotion; it is how we handle and express the anger that determines whether we sin or not.

Then there is godly anger, in which we become angered by the things that anger God. But here we can very easily be deceived. In most cases, our so-called "righteous indignation" isn't righteous at all; it is merely our own sinful anger cloaked in righteousness. Whenever our anger becomes personal—that is, whenever it arises on our personal account or is directed against another person—it becomes sinful. The only sinless anger is that which is impersonal and unselfish.

Resentment and bitterness, on the other hand, are always sins. Resentment is prolonged anger, the continued feeling of being wronged even after the wrong has ceased. Bitterness is the savoring of a bitter or painful experience. Resentment and bitterness are often the aftermath of anger. If we handled our anger better, we'd have less trouble with resentment and bitterness.

Let us look further at this emotion of anger. The initial feeling of anger can lead either to constructive consequences or destructive ones—though they will be destructive in the great majority of cases, either to the person angered or to the recipient of the anger.

In the New Testament, there are relatively few instances of anger that we could say were appropriate. And even with appropriate anger, Paul gives a pretty strict time limit for it—sundown!

If one must ventilate his anger, go talk to a tree, or to the cat. Tell God how angry you are. But don't blow up at your fellow worker or national colleague. It may do wonders for you, but it will hurt him or her. The rule is especially important in cultures where the free expression of anger is unacceptable—as in Nepal. The old saying goes: "Beat the cake, not the cook."

Supposing you are responsible for some project or activity and a national worker lets you down, or is negligent, or is insubordinate—say, for the fifth time in a row. You experience anger, which usually arises because you personally feel betrayed or embarrassed or thwarted. This anger is not constructive. Any parent can tell you never to discipline a child when you're angry.

Let the anger subside. Then deal with the bad behavior coolly, yet firmly, and even, if indicated, sternly. Very often, however, your reprimand will be perceived as anger, even by your own missionary colleagues. Some people are sure they can spot anger in another, though they are often wrong. Nationals, for their part, may see anger under an arched eyebrow. Your reprimand may damage a relationship you have taken months to develop. Thus, you need to exercise great caution in administering discipline, especially to nationals. Ask God to set a guard at your lips, that you might not inadvertently offend a brother.

When we feel anger against someone, we become uncomfortable, for we know it is wrong. However, instead of dealing with the anger, we find it easier to rename it. And the name we usually choose is "righteous indignation." Righteous indignation is a convenient cover for personal anger; it may cover for some private vendetta, or for some political or social agenda we are promoting. True righteous indignation, on the other hand, is totally on God's behalf. Very seldom is our indignation free of self, and as long as "self" is present, we should not indulge our anger. We can oppose evil and injustice without getting hot and angry—and usually more effectively.

How do we tell righteous anger from sinful anger? By asking this key question: For whose sake am I getting angry—for God's sake or mine? If we can answer that question truly, then we will know if our anger is pleasing to God or not.

So, what do you do when you feel that surge of anger? Wait. Wait before you act on it. If necessary, temporarily displace your anger onto a non-feeling object. Turn to God with the silent prayer: Lead me not into temptation. Commit your anger to him, and he will show you the way of escape. And if you must kick a tree, be sure your shoes are strong, or you will have fun explaining to your colleagues how you came to break your toe.

Before leaving the matter of righteous indignation, it is essential to comment on a dangerous variant of it: the indignation we feel toward another person on behalf of a third party. We say: I am angry for "X's" sake, because missionary "Y" is treating "X" so badly. This is never righteous anger. This is taking up another's grievance against a third party. Nowhere in Scripture does God authorize us to do this.

Christians often feel quite justified in taking up the grievances of others. "It's not for my sake," they say. "It's unselfish." And so, without a twinge of conscience, they nurture hostile feelings against people. They nurture feelings against the arrogant Brahmins who oppress the lower castes, against the communists who destabilize society for political gain, against the husband who has taken a second wife, against the insensitive mission administrator who refuses to understand so-and-so's problem.... Whoa! Did you say mission administrator? Now we're getting close to home! We're suddenly angry with a brother. We don't feel quite so righteous about that.

The fact is that being angry at someone on someone else's account is no more righteous than being angry at someone on our own account. This indignation, this taking up of a grievance, is usually the outward expression of an underlying personal animosity—though we deny it to ourselves. And the less we know about the actual situation we are taking sides in, the more righteous our indignation seems to us, and the freer we feel to indulge it.

I have often seen visceral anger directed from one missionary to another colleague whom the first missionary perceived to be mistreating someone else. In each case, the one angered did not know the full truth, or even half the truth. The angered person's only source was the "injured party." What's more, the angered person felt obliged to take the side of the injured party against the "wrongdoer," and to talk to others about the problem—all under the cloak of righteous concern. And before you know it, yet another team is split apart.

Whenever you begin to feel angry at someone on behalf of a third party, it's time to search your own heart for the unrighteous source that will almost always be lurking there. Are you reliving a past conflict of your own? Does the person you are angry with remind you of someone who has wronged you in the past? Or you may have a direct grievance against the person involved, but find it more convenient to ventilate it "on behalf of someone else." How cleverly we justify our attacks on a brother or sister! How great is our capacity for self-deception!

Looking further at the matter of resentment and bitterness, all missionaries know that these are poisons for the soul. Most, fortunately, are able to confess these sinful attitudes and receive forgiveness. But in some people, resentment and bitterness go underground, and do great damage to the person's physical, emotional, and spiritual health.

First, resentment or bitterness can be redirected toward God. This, naturally, is not a profitable exercise. We never deliberately do this, but all too often, after having forgiven our human adversary, we end up with leftover, unfocused anger directed basically against God. We blame him for our trouble and disappointment.

Second, we may redirect our resentment to innocent parties or objects. Sometimes nationals do things that "legitimately" make us angry: shopkeepers cheat us, employees refuse to follow clear instructions, children steal fruit from our trees or mutilate flowers in our garden. We find excessive anger suddenly welling up inside us against these people for relatively trivial offenses.

And then there are the dogs that bark outside our window for twenty minutes at a stretch, or the goats that eat our prize hydrangeas. And finally there is the host of inanimate objects that take on almost human characteristics in their determination to irritate us. I once had a kerosene pressure lamp that seemed to say to me each morning: "Just you try to get me lit!"

In addition to these obvious trials and irritations, it is possible to become chronically irritated and angry with a whole group of people, or with nationals in general. Soon the slightest thing they do bothers us, their mannerisms bother us, their very presence bothers us.

In all the above-mentioned situations, our anger is out of proportion to the provocation. When we begin to see this happening, we need to search our souls and see if it isn't really the project director we are angry with, or our roommate. Then, once we are reconciled with that person, we will find ourselves much more cordially disposed to all other humans—not to mention dogs, goats, and pressure lamps.

Criticism, slander, and judgment

Harold Cook, in his book *Missionary Life and Work*, says: "By far the most serious overt threat to missionary relationships, the greatest danger of all, is criticism of one another." That is why I have placed this seventh sin or complex of sins under its own heading—to highlight its importance. If the devil's chief method of rendering missionaries ineffective is to divide them, then his favored means of dividing them is a critical spirit. A critical spirit is the most destructive attitude to be found among missionaries, both because of its commonness, and also because of the great harm even the most casual critical word can do to God's servants and to God's work.

Criticism is basically passing judgment on someone else. Critical people are self-appointed executors of God's judgment. They always see the faults and mistakes. That's good when it comes to evaluating a plan; then we need skeptics, those who can see the problems. But it is not good when it comes to evaluating people.

Some critical people act just like modern-day Pharisees. They are on a self-righteous mission to root up "weeds." Their judgment may in part be correct, but it is delivered without humility, without gentleness, without love. I remember talking with one missionary brother who had been very vocal in criticizing certain national church leaders and mission leaders. His particular concern was that the local Bible Society was not following the Authorized Version in its translation work. So strong were his feelings that he actually believed the responsible leaders were working for Satan. I mentioned the importance Jesus attached to the unity of believers. Looking at me with an expression I can imagine Elijah might have fixed on the priests of Baal, he replied, "Unity without purity is a work of the devil." As I recall, that sort of wrapped up the conversation.

In large part through this missionary's opposition, the Nepali church was deprived of a much needed common-language New Testament for more than a decade. In a land so desperate for the gospel, how grieved must Christ have been! Before we think to charge brothers and sisters with doing Satan's work, we would be well-advised to review a verse from Romans we quoted earlier: "You, therefore, have no excuse, you who pass judgment on someone else, for at whatever point you judge the other, you are condemning yourself, because you who pass judgment do the same things" (Ro 2:1).

Those who criticize reveal much more about themselves than about the one being criticized. It is a common thing that the picking at the faults of others is an unconscious cover for much larger sins in ourselves. Indeed, we often render judgment against others in those very areas in which we ourselves are guilty. We project onto others our own wrong attitudes. "It takes one to know one" isn't just a retort used by schoolchildren; it reflects a deep spiritual truth. And our blindness is the more remarkable because that shared fault we so easily see in our brother we fail to see in ourselves. Beware before you assay to judge another. "For in the same way as you judge others, you will be judged" (Mt 7:2).

This critical, judgmental spirit is by no means confined to new missionaries; it is found in some of the most experienced and saintly missionaries around. It is their blind spot. How many times have we heard a Christian brother referred to with words like: "His motives are carnal," or "He's only doing it for money or fame." How on earth would they know? This is judgment.

Well, you say, "I have discernment." Don't deceive yourself. Discernment does not give you license to judge. Furthermore, most so-called discernment is merely another name for criticism.

This is not to say that such criticism and judgment are always false. There well may be an element of truth in the accusation; it could even be mostly true. But it is the way in which the critical person acts that is wrong. People who criticize act without love. They have not learned how to hate the sin and love the sinner. Even the worst criminals we must love; they, too, are sinners for whom Christ died. And if we must love sinners, must we not love our fellow missionary also?

Those most quick to judge others are also, not surprisingly, the most sure their judgment is correct. "Where there's smoke there's fire," they say; but as to where the fire itself is, they get it wrong more often than not.

Joseph was one of the first victims of mistaken judgment in the Bible. The "proof" of his intention toward Potiphar's wife was the cloak he left in her hands. The household servants all saw it, and I can imagine them saying, "Proof, proof." Fire, fire. But they got the location of the fire wrong, and the innocent Joseph went to jail.

There are not many who are completely innocent of the charges against them; Joseph comes as close as any. But even he once or twice might have entertained a lustful thought toward Potiphar's wife; only God knows. The point is that when it comes to Christians judging Christians, they get it wrong more than they get it right.

A modern parable teaches us further about judgment. An elderly man wrote a letter addressed to God describing his desperate needs and asking God for a certain sum of money. The postal clerks in his town opened the letter and decided to raise the money among themselves. They raised eighty percent of the old man's request, but couldn't raise it all. Rather than wait further, the postal clerks sent the man the money they had. A few days later another letter came addressed to God. The clerks gathered around to see what it said. It read: "Thank you, God, for sending the money. But next time, please send it to me directly, not through the post office. Those thieving postal clerks pocketed twenty percent of it."

Does anyone doubt how true to life this story is? If so, let that person come to the mission field. Many a time we have seen missionaries labor sacrificially for others, and then be totally misjudged concerning both their actions and their motives. In many cases that which they have been desperately trying to correct and compensate for has been the very thing they've been accused of. All of us will experience abuse and slander sooner or later, but the worst kind of all will come from fellow Christians whom we have loved and tried to help.

I first heard the post-office story from the Nepali leader of our village church. Over the preceding months this leader had grown hostile to a few of the missionaries on our team and to me in particular. Then he had gone to a conference in Kathmandu where the speaker had related this story. When our leader got back, he told the story at the next church meeting. When he had finished, tears came into his eyes. He said, "I have been acting just like that old man in the story. I am very, very sorry." A beautiful reconciliation followed. The post-office story may be trite, but for me it is filled with meaning.

"Do not judge" (Mt 7:1). One asks, "Are we never to use our critical faculties?" Of course, we are. We recognize false prophets "by their fruit" (Mt 7:20). John tells us to "test the spirits" (1 Jn 4:1). Thus, we must assess people's words and acts. But these two verses refer primarily to recognizing non-Christians, or false Christians.

When it comes to assessing the fruit of fellow believers, we must proceed even more cautiously. All assessment must be firsthand, never secondhand. Furthermore, we must consider the soil from which the fruit has come. We may be tempted to think people carnal or unspiritual and fail to recognize the marvelous work God has done in their lives. Or we may look at some trait or habit of a person and say, "How can anyone with that habit or characteristic be a real Christian, much less a missionary?" Whenever we quote Matthew 7:20 in regard to Christians, we must never fail to quote Matthew 7:1 in the same breath! Yes, the fruit we can assess; but the person himself, no. External acts, yes; internal attitudes and motives, no. Only God knows these.

Other people ask: "Well, aren't friends supposed to criticize each other? Isn't our sharpest critic also our best friend?" Yes, if he criticizes you alone and to your face and in love. The "wounds inflicted by a friend" are helpful indeed, but when a true friend criticizes he mixes one part criticism with ten parts affirmation. That's a good rule of thumb in dealing with missionaries, as with anyone: ten parts affirmation to one part criticism. Anything less will serve the devil's purposes.

Sometimes people are critical and judgmental because of an inferiority complex. Unconsciously they try to build themselves up by tearing others down. Others may be critical because of resentment or hostility against a person. Still others may criticize out of jealousy.

Criticism is habit forming. It certainly has become habitual in the West; one can even say it is cultural. We have institutionalized criticism. Many Christian leaders have labeled criticism America's number-one sin. It is even rewarded: journalists get awards and "whistle-blowers" get praised for exposing people in public life—no matter that much of what they expose is untrue or is a misrepresentation of the truth.

It's the mentality of tearing others down that is so wrong. Yet in the West we are addicted to it—and Christians along with everyone else. Sadly, missionaries bring that addiction with them to the mission field.

The Nepalis have an expression to describe such criticism. They call it "dogs biting at people's heels." Paul had a similar way of describing it; he called it "biting and devouring each other" (Gal 5:15).

So far in this discussion we have used the words "criticism" and "judgment" in labeling this complex of sins. There is one word left: the "S" word—slander. Somehow criticism and judgment don't sound so bad to our ears, but slander—well, we'd never do that! I once heard a missionary say to a colleague, "Oh, I've criticized you to others, but I haven't slandered you." Well, that missionary was using the word "slander" in a narrow, legal sense. The traditional definition is "defamation." Any criticism, true or false, that is vocalized behind a person's back is slander.

If you have ever harbored a critical thought about a person and then expressed it behind his back to a third party, you have engaged in slander. So consider this advice: if you can't stop thinking critical thoughts, at least stop verbalizing them. It will save you on judgment day from being charged with the sin of slander.

Many people are hardly aware that they are slandering others, but it comes out in every third or fourth sentence. Their favorite topics are the shortcomings of others. And there is never a shortage of material. But the cost of such talk is high. I have never yet met anyone with a consistently critical spirit who was a happy, contented person. Such people only seem to see the imperfect and disappointing. They themselves end up consuming much of the poison they pass around.

Such communal slandering is often called gossip. Gossiping is nothing more than spreading slander. One mission executive in Nepal said that if he ever found a missionary gossiping, he would send that missionary home at once. Such is the destructive force of slander and gossip. It grows like a cancer and finally destroys the entire team.

Slander is a grievous sin, condemned over and over again in both Old and New Testaments. Read 1 Corinthians 5:11 to see what company it keeps. And given the fact that slander is almost always partly false, the slanderer is guilty of a double sin: he is giving false witness as well as slandering. When people do this they are serving Satan. Satan is the chief slanderer and accuser. What a tragedy that God's children should be working for the devil!

And the greatest tragedy is that they hardly realize what they're doing. The devil blinds them. They sit in prayer meetings and slander their fellows—under the guise of "Christian concern." They meet in small groups to discuss and pray for other members of the team not present. They confirm one another in their negative feelings for certain individuals. They fancy that they are the more spiritual members of the team, and that the team depends on their prayers. But, in fact, the team may well be suffering from their prayers. Mini-groups are usually detrimental to a team or church, unless all are invited and there is no slander permitted in any guise.

Slander can begin its work before we even get to the field. The story is told of a retired missionary couple who visited a younger couple several days before their scheduled departure for the mission field for the first time. Afterward the older couple wrote to the field about their "leisurely visit" with the young couple. They reported that the young couple seemed "uptight and unfriendly"—not surprising in view of their imminent departure.

This word spread rapidly through the mission community, and resulted in the young couple being shunned when they got to the field. They figured this was the "normal behavior" of missionaries, so they too stuck to themselves—thus "confirming" the slander.

Let this story encourage us to go out of our way to befriend anyone about whom we hear a bad report. The bad report will never be completely true, and may well be mostly false. In any case, we will have been an agent of healing, and helped a soul in need.

Slander leaves a deep wound in its victim. For some who have been slandered, it is years before they are able to trust others again. For years they remain fearful, unable to step out. Slander is akin to murder.

Of all the forms of slander, the most subtle takes place during our private prayers. We slander people before God. How is that possible? John (Praying) Hyde of India learned how it was possible one day. A man given to long hours of private prayer, Hyde was in his room praying fervently for an Indian pastor who was experiencing some problems in his church. Hyde was praying that God would make this pastor less abrasive, less assertive, more gentle, more understanding. And as Hyde was praying for the Indian pastor, asking God for all the "less's" and "more's" he could think of, the Holy Spirit suddenly broke into his prayers and convicted him of his critical attitude toward his Indian brother. The word from God that came to Hyde was this: "That Indian pastor is the apple of my eye."

Hyde wept in repentance, and began at once to think of everything he knew that was good about that pastor. Then he began to praise and thank God for the pastor and for each of his good qualities. Within a week, revival had broken out in that pastor's church.

Why, oh why are we so quick to think and speak evil of our brother? Maybe the "evil" is partly true; we may even have some "proofs." But our judgment will never be accurate. Remember that Jesus did not say: "Do not judge falsely." He said, "Do not judge." All human judgment, in the nature of the case, is going to be partly false. But we humans, when we slander and judge each other, are usually not that concerned for the truth of what we say. Our regard for the truth varies according to how much we think the truth will serve us. How many times our judgment turns out to be false, but we refuse to change our opinion of the person in question! We have too much invested in our antagonism; we cannot admit our judgment was wrong. Truth, by itself, is not enough to resolve our conflicts.

It is possible with God's help to become a more positive and affirming person. First one needs to acknowledge that he or she has the tendency to be negative and critical. Then one needs to deal with possible causes: feelings of inferiority, jealousy, hostility. And then one must deliberately set about trying to overcome the habit of criticism and replace it with the habit of affirming and encouraging others. Ask the Lord to make you aware not only of each critical word but of each critical thought, and to help you replace those critical words and thoughts with kind and positive ones. Not only will you in this way stop hurting and even destroying others, but also you yourself will become a much more joyful, free, and accepted person. You have nothing to lose, and everything to gain.

"Therefore," says Paul, "let us stop passing judgment on one another" (Ro 14:13). "Do not let any unwholesome talk come out of your mouths, but only what is helpful for building others up according to their needs, that it may benefit those who listen.... Get rid of all bitterness, rage and anger, brawling and slander, along with every form of malice. Be kind and compassionate to one another, forgiving each other, just as in Christ God forgave you (Eph 4:29,31-32).

Things that aggravate interpersonal conflict

All interpersonal conflict arises from some turmoil or stress within one or more of the contending parties. It does not arise from a pure conflict over ideas or policies. Only when someone's turf has been invaded, or his rights impinged on, or his self-esteem threatened do we see the beginning of true interpersonal conflict. Thus, as we have already seen, all interpersonal conflict is rooted in the sin and self-centeredness of one or more of the involved parties.

Now, as if sin and self-centeredness weren't giving us enough trouble already, there are some additional factors that spur the development of conflict and make it all the harder to resolve. And many of these factors can be subsumed under the heading "faulty or distorted perceptions." One of the most basic examples is this: I look at how much I've improved; you look at how much I have left to go. Both perceptions are only half true, and, as is typical in conflict, they focus on the opposite halves of the truth.

A second example shows how one-sided perceptions muddy the waters of conflict. Take a happy, assertive, somewhat insensitive "action" person and team him up with a sensitive, insecure melancholic. In about two minutes the word "manipulation" surfaces.

"You're manipulating me."

"I'm what?"

Now it doesn't matter how hard the "manipulator" tries not to manipulate. People who are not themselves sensitive can't fully put themselves in the shoes of those who are, though they may try. They believe the sensitive person, they take the charge of manipulation seriously, but no matter what they do, the sensitive person continues to feel manipulated—though, hopefully, less so than in the beginning.

But in a conflict situation, the charge of manipulation will be made in earnest. And how, then, can one evaluate that charge? The one says, "I'm not manipulating." The other says, "You are." Do we just split the difference fifty-fifty? Or is the statement, "You are manipulating me," another way of saying, "I'm not getting my way"?

Well, there are hundreds of different perceptions out there. On any issue you choose there will be two or four or more competing perceptions all equally difficult to evaluate. In conflict management, it's not so often the fighters "throwing in the towel" as it is the referee!

However, help is at hand. It comes in the form of innocuous little things called facts. True, all facts are filtered through our perception, but plain uncomplicated facts get through relatively undistorted. And it is in these facts that our hope of sorting out conflict lies. "What specifically did I do that caused you to feel manipulated?" And then—if you're still on speaking terms—you talk about that incident, and you talk about each specific incident until you both come to a resolution of the problem.

However, we have some ground to cover before we reach the resolution of our conflict. These perceptions we have are all, to a greater or lesser degree, distortions of reality—distortions of facts. Perceptions are not reality. Some modern psychologists treat them as if they were, and this muddies the water even more for all concerned. We do people no favor by affirming or reinforcing their distorted perceptions. Yes, they may seem real to the perceiver, and they will have the same effect on the perceiver as if they had been real. But perceptions must be subject to the rules of evidence and the standard of truth. A false perception is a false thought, and if it is verbalized it is a false statement. We are as responsible for our perceptions as we are for our actions. We can't justify ourselves by saying, "That was my perception," because that perception could be true or false. All that statement says is that we're not deliberately lying, should our perception prove to be false.

Our perceptions tell us as much about ourselves as they do about the object perceived. This is especially true when it comes to negative perceptions. Negative perceptions about people are the precursor to criticism and judgment. Hence they are extremely dangerous, both to the perceiver and to the perceived. Negative perceptions are like darts of Satan. A body can survive two or three darts—especially if they're not in a vital area like the head—but more than that and the body will be weakened and die. Perceptions are serious business.

Faulty perceptions come from faulty thinking. Below are seven types of faulty thinking that we all engage in from time to time, and which cause our perceptions to be distorted.

First, we are prone to exaggerate, to magnify circumstances. We are especially adept at magnifying the negative. This leads us to see situations as worse than they really are.

Second, we consciously or unconsciously omit from consideration matters that are unfavorable to our own position. This is also called selective memory.

Third, we commonly think in absolute terms. "He is impossible to work with," or, "Everyone is against me." This type of thinking sees everything in black and white; it polarizes. Nuance, much less compromise, is not allowed.

Fourth, we sometimes simply come to the wrong conclusions; we misinterpret what we see or hear. One example is to take things personally that weren't meant personally, or to interpret a comment as hostile which wasn't meant to be hostile. Or it could be something more clear-cut. I used to do cataract operations under local anesthesia, and often my elderly patients would get confused and move their heads about. After exhausting other means of getting them to stop moving, I would give them a sharp tap on the head with an instrument handle. This usually worked. But one of our hospital attendants who saw me do it went and reported to others that I "hit patients." She had misinterpreted what she had seen.

Fifth, we often react to new people on the basis of past associations or experiences, or on the basis of things we've read or heard. Past experience distorts our perception of the present. A new person reminds us of someone we've had a problem with in the past. Some people with insight can recognize what they're doing, but most cannot; it is subconscious.

Sixth, we project our feelings onto another. I may interpret your sadness as resentment, because I am resentful. I may interpret your opposition as anger, because I am angry. This is usually done unconsciously.

Seventh, we tend to generalize. We come to a broad conclusion without adequate evidence. After one bad experience we say, "I'll never trust him again." Guilt by association is another form of generalization. If you have known one or two rigid administrators, you assume they're all rigid. Everyone you meet you assume will be like your preconceived stereotype, which is usually negative. Everyone has to prove to you that they're not really the awful person you think they are. This is patently unfair.

Armed with the above faulty thinking patterns with their distorted perceptions, we are ready to enter the conflict in earnest. As our stress increases, our perceptions become even more distorted. New missionaries are particularly liable to have distorted perceptions because of their limited knowledge and background, their increased level of stress, and their relative lack of experience in handling conflict. All this makes conflict involving new missionaries more volatile; it needs especially sensitive handling, lest the new missionary becomes unduly discouraged and embittered, and ends up doing harm to the work and ultimately to himself.

The above seven faulty ways of thinking with their associated faulty perceptions lead directly to faulty ways of relating to other people. Once we start relating wrongly to our colleagues, conflict that may previously have been hidden comes quickly into the open. A representative sample of eight wrong methods of relating follows below.

The first wrong method is to attack. Leave on the football field the notion that the best defense is a good offense. I once sat in a small group in which one member attacked another with a long list of complaints, almost all of which were either false or frank misinterpretations of events. When the person got to the last item, the one being attacked denied it outright. So the first person said, "Well, now I know you're a liar too." That is the attack method.

The second wrong method of relating is to attribute blame. Some people start out blaming the devil, but he is not the immediate cause. If we shove the problem off on him, we will never recognize and deal with our part in the problem. Blaming the devil will only insure that the problem will continue.

More commonly we blame the other party; we deny any share of responsibility, even if our share is small. But equally counterproductive is to blame oneself; that usually leads to depression. Blame is not a method advocated in the New Testament; confession, receiving forgiveness, and forgiving are God's methods of dealing with our own and the other party's guilt.

The third wrong method of relating is to try and dominate or manipulate the other person. This is the power-play method. It's a sure formula for winning the battle and losing the war. It is confrontation—but with you standing on higher ground. Confrontation is only healthy when both parties are on equal ground.

The fourth wrong method of relating is to refuse to relate, to refuse to reach out, to refuse to speak face to face. The common justification for this method is the statement, "He wouldn't listen anyway," or, "He's unapproachable." These statements are almost always false. They are a cover-up for our own reluctance to obey Matthew 18:15. Our hesitancy to approach the other party lies within ourselves: Am I being a complainer? A poor Christian? Am I going to reveal my own bitterness or pride or selfishness? Is my complaint legitimate? Do I know what the truth is, or is my knowledge only second-hand? And so with all these doubts we find it much easier to talk behind the person's back. Remember: someone may *seem* unapproachable because he is busy or not a good communicator, but it's a rare Christian who will refuse to listen to another person's complaint.

The fifth wrong method of relating is to attribute bad motives to the other party. This is judgment, pure and simple, and it is always a sin on our part. We say the other party is acting out of pride, out of selfishness, out of anger or vengeance, out of laziness, out of malice—hey, wait a minute on that last one! Missionaries do not act out of malice. It may seem that way at times—when one is hurting and struggling to survive, even a missionary will do some malicious things—but the motive is not malice. Understanding the reason for inappropriate or hurtful behavior does not excuse or condone it, but it does help us to respond in a helpful way rather than to respond in kind.

A common version of the "bad-motive" method is the accusation, "You're using me." The accusation can be made against anyone in a position of responsibility who has people he relies on for the accomplishment of the work. This charge arises especially when the workload is high, or staff are short. It is usually an unfair charge; it implies the leader is running the work for his own pleasure or aggrandizement, and is using the staff as tools. Nurses often feel this way about doctors. The doctor may be deeply concerned for the welfare of the staff working with him, but because his first responsibility is to his patients, the staff may feel used. Worse, they feel the doctor is using them, not for the patients' benefit, but for his own benefit. This kind of distrust can arise even in mission hospitals between missionary doctors and nurses, who, one would think, should be happily working together for the welfare of their patients.

Give people the benefit of the doubt (and there will always be doubt about motives). We need to keep examining our own motives, but never the motives of others. That's God's business.

The sixth wrong method of relating is to mirror the other person's emotions. There is no need for me to be anxious when you are; there is no need for me to be angry when you are. To have empathy does not require that I share your emotions. When I share your emotions, I take your side against third parties; I take up your grievances. And then I lose the chance to be a mediator, which would be much more helpful. To weep with you and rejoice with you does not mean that I must experience your emotions as if they were my own. The best friends remain objective.

The seventh wrong method is to judge the reactions of others by the way we would react. The cool-headed phlegmatic looks at the volatile person's reaction and says, "Gracious, I'd never act that way! How terrible!" But look out: tomorrow the volatile person will call the phlegmatic calloused and unloving—and be equally mistaken. Temperament differences lie behind these wrong judgments. What is obstinacy to one is firmness to another. What is weakness to one is gentleness to another. What is illogic to one is intuition to another. Don't evaluate others on the basis of your own temperament, or you will be evaluating them unfairly. Don't judge others by your own standards. Don't judge period.

The eighth wrong method of relating is to reject the person instead of his viewpoint or his action. In the case of sin, it would be to reject the sinner instead of his sin. Opinions, actions, methods, policies are all fair game for rejection, but people are not. The ad hominem attack isn't even accepted among politicians; it should never be employed by Christians.

Well, lists can be helpful; but even if we memorize backwards and forwards these wrong ways of thinking and relating, when the conflict comes and the stress levels rise, we'll still have trouble avoiding them. Even so, let the lists written here serve as insights, reminders of what not to do when the next conflict comes. If we can minimize the things that aggravate conflict, we'll be that much ahead when it comes to resolving conflict, a subject to which we now turn.

11

Resolving Interpersonal Conflict

The more quickly conflict can be resolved, the better. In the beginning of a conflict people are still talking to each other, trust has not been completely destroyed, the work has not suffered. Hence, the urgency to bring about reconciliation between the participants before emotional hurt or damage to the work occurs. What is involved, then, in resolving the interpersonal conflicts in which we periodically find ourselves?

The first and most important thing to do is to try and see God's purpose behind the conflict, and to submit to that purpose. One obvious purpose, and probably the most common, is that God wants to discipline the participants in the conflict. We need to be sure that we are not opposing God's purpose, that we are not entering into conflict with God. Conflict with our colleagues is bad enough.

It's very easy, as we become more deeply embroiled in conflict, to see more and more of the devil's hand in the matter and less and less of God's. But that is another faulty perception; God is in the midst of even the worst conflicts. He is polishing his gems, an analogy not less true for being well worn. And as the rough stones grate against each other and the edges are scraped away, more "sensitive" surfaces are exposed; the process seems to become more painful as it goes on. It is very hard to

192

joyfully submit to God's hand under such circumstances. For the natural man, it is impossible.

We can give a more gentle analogy of conflict within the body of Christ: we can call it "trouble in the joints." Or maybe a "pain in the neck." Here a different treatment is needed: the oil of the Holy Spirit to lubricate the joints.

Whatever analogy we use, God is at work in conflict, perfecting his servants, creating a stronger and better-functioning Christian team or church. For a while, things seem to go poorly. We are discouraged by our own sins and the sins of others. Some missionaries get so discouraged they just quit. But listen to Paul: "Forgetting what is behind and straining toward what is ahead, I press on toward the goal to win the prize for which God has called me heavenward in Christ Jesus" (Php 3:13-14). If we, too, will press on, and do our utmost to work through and resolve interpersonal conflict, God will reward us with a "harvest of righteousness and peace" (Heb 12:11).

During periods of conflict we need more than ever the ministry of the Holy Spirit in our lives. We also need to be armed with God's word, which will be our weapon to subdue Satan and our guide to resolving the conflict. Let us take these words to heart—in and out of conflict:

"Be devoted to one another in brotherly love. Honor one another above yourselves" (Ro 12:10).

"Love is patient, love is kind. It does not envy, it does not boast, it is not proud. It is not rude, it is not self-seeking, it is not easily angered, it keeps no records of wrongs. Love does not delight in evil but rejoices with the truth. It always protects, always trusts, always hopes, always perseveres" (1 Co 13:4-7).

"Do nothing out of selfish ambition or vain conceit, but in humility consider others better than yourselves. Each of you should look not only to your own interests, but to the interests of others" (Php 2:3-4).

"Carry each other's burdens, and in this way you will fulfill the law of Christ" (Gal 6:2).

"Be completely humble and gentle; be patient, bearing with one another in love. Make every effort to keep the unity of the Spirit through the bond of peace" (Eph 4:2-3).

If we would only follow these verses, we could end this chapter right here.

When the first hint of interpersonal conflict appears, our natural reaction is to hope that it will go away by itself. Confrontation is unpleasant and time-consuming. But one of the surest rules in human relations is that conflicts don't go away by themselves. The people will go away before the conflict will.

At the first sign of uneasiness, friction, strain, or misunderstanding, we must without delay go to that person and try to set things right. It makes absolutely no difference whose fault it is, or is thought to be. The moment I am aware that someone is grieved, offended, or troubled by me, I must go to that person. Jesus made this very clear in Matthew 5:23-24.

If it is I who am troubled, and I have no indication the other person is troubled, I then have a choice. If I can completely forgive the other person, if I can laugh at and sympathize with his foibles or weaknesses, then I am not obliged to do anything further. But if I am bothered by that person, if I feel I cannot be of one mind and heart with him, then I must do something.

And it's not to go to my project director, or the mission counselor, or my roommate, and talk about that person. Nowhere in the Bible does it say to do that. Rather, there is only one person to go to, and that is the person himself with whom I am having the difficulty. To talk to anyone else first is slander. Jesus gives the procedure very clearly in Matthew 18:15. Some people like to jump ahead to verses 16 and 17 and bypass verse 15. But there is never warrant for taking these verses out of order.

In an interpersonal conflict, I am responsible for my behavior, my perceptions, my feelings. I cannot say to the other fellow, "You led me to say that," or, "I would never have done that if you hadn't...," or, "You are making me angry." By the same token, we are not responsible for the other fellow's reactions and perceptions. We are responsible only to make sure that our own attitudes and actions are free of sin.

This gets us away from the impulse to change the other person. In a conflict, we naturally think the other fellow is wrong and needs to be changed. Yes, maybe he does, but not by us. Our only job is to change ourselves, if that is necessary (and it usually is). Once we and our attitudes change for the better, it's amazing how our adversary will appear to change too! Maybe the Holy Spirit will have changed him; but it's also possible that only our perception of him has changed—because of our own change in attitude.

We have seen earlier how our faulty perceptions stir up and fuel conflict. These perceptions can take on a life of their own, as though they were a fixed reality in any conflict. We say, "Those people have to live with their perceptions," implying that their perceptions will necessarily determine the outcome of the conflict. But this is totally wrong. Most perceptions are false to a greater or lesser degree; they need to be changed, not affirmed. And the only way to change faulty perceptions is through face-to-face contact between the parties in conflict. An outside mediator cannot do it by working with only one party at a time.

It is only through face-to-face contact between the opposing parties that interpersonal conflict can be satisfactorily resolved. We may have lots of reasons for not initiating face-to-face contact—fear of rejection, fear of embarrassment, fear of exposure of our own unworthy motives, uncertainty as to the facts, lack of time—but establish contact we must. Below are some guidelines for doing so.

First and most important is to pray for God's grace. Grace is not given in advance. It is available only as we draw on it in time of need. So, move out in faith and in dependence on God.

Pray for the Holy Spirit to search your own heart and show you your own wrong attitudes. This is critical to the success of your meeting with your adversary. You will not be able to camouflage your bad attitudes with sweet words.

Pray for love for your opponent, for understanding of his or her circumstances and feelings. Remember St. Francis' prayer: "Help me seek not so much to be understood as to understand." And along with love, pray for a forgiving spirit. All these things—grace, cleansing, love, a forgiving spirit—are needed to prepare your own heart for the meeting. They are received through faith. You don't have to wait a long time to prepare your heart—a day or two at the most; and you certainly don't have to wait until you're transformed into a model of spiritual perfection. You are going to your meeting as an imperfect person—and that is precisely where you will want to start.

When your meeting takes place—at a quiet, suitable time for both parties—start with yourself. Start with your imperfections. Confess to the other any real sin or shortcoming that you might be guilty of, which has affected your relationship. Apologize sincerely from your heart. When you do this, you make yourself equal with the other person; you show that you do not desire to "lord it over" him, or shame him. He, in turn, will be able to let down his defenses; he will stop feeling threatened. If this state can be achieved early on, the meeting is almost assured of being successful.

Remember the whole point of the confrontation: it is not to win the argument, it is to win your brother. It's not to justify your position, but to restore fellowship. It does not matter if you end up seeing eye to eye on every detail. You may continue to disagree on impersonal matters of policy and method. But all personal animosity and distrust must be eliminated for the conflict to be successfully resolved. That is the goal. If we do not eliminate every vestige of self-interest and sinfulness from our relationship, Satan will continue to destroy our unity and fruitfulness—not just ours, but our entire team's as well.

Once we begin our face-to-face meeting, there are a few "ground rules" to observe. Obviously courtesy is one; it goes a long way to reducing friction. One part of courtesy is to give the other fellow a chance to speak—and then to listen to him!

Second, don't argue; rather explain. Explain not only your position but your feelings. Don't be "above it all." Feelings, after all, are at the root of the conflict.

Third, don't try to defend yourself; be vulnerable. That's a tall order for someone who is already feeling vulnerable, but do your best; pray for grace repeatedly during your meeting.

Fourth, don't put words in the other person's mouth, and don't try to read his mind. That's trespassing.

Fifth, stick to specifics; avoid generalities. If you have no specific complaints to bring up, then the source of the animosity is not in the other person but in yourself.

Sixth, go the extra mile. Don't say, "I'm only ten percent responsible for this problem, and no more." Don't calculate; don't keep score; rather, be generous. And remember, you're always responsible for some sins of omission, as James 4:17 tells us, and those are hard to calculate!

Seventh, always acknowledge that there may be another interpretation of events than your own. Be willing to concede a point. You don't have to prove the other fellow's interpretation is wrong.

Eighth, as much as possible, put yourself in the other person's shoes. What is he fearing? What is important to him? Is that issue more crucial to him or to you? If it's more crucial to him, compromise in order to meet his needs. If it's more crucial to you, ask him to compromise.

Ninth, work on one issue at a time. A relationship problem is not "one big problem." It arises from a multitude of incidents. But don't bring up extraneous matters or old issues that have no bearing on the present problem; they will just distract you, and may cause unnecessary hurt.

Tenth, recognize that part of the conflict may be due to external circumstances over which neither party has much control. Many situations are ready-made to nurture interpersonal conflict. The point is not to blame the situation, but to recognize the role it plays. Then the adversaries will be less likely to think that the "other guy is the cause of all my problems."

Eleventh, allow for the possibility that your adversary will change. Just because he reacted one way today doesn't mean he'll react the same way tomorrow.

Twelfth, remember what you have in common—above all, Jesus Christ. When we get to heaven, our disputes on this earth are going to seem trivial indeed!

In all this, even Christians will do well to remember the three sieves of the Muslim proverb as they choose what they will say: Is it true? Is it kind? Is it necessary? Before we speak, let our words pass through all three sieves.

We started this section by mentioning our need for God's grace, and for the Holy Spirit's help in revealing to us our own sinful attitudes. Now we conclude this section by looking at those attitudes that we will need in resolving interpersonal conflict.

The first is openness, and I mention it only to point out that it is not an attitude which needs specific cultivating. If there is no spirit of criticism and judgment, openness will flower by itself without effort on our part. But if there is a critical spirit abroad, we can talk about openness until the cows come home and it will be in vain. Trust and openness cannot exist in a climate of criticism and judgment.

Sensitivity and empathy are indispensable in human relations, whether cross-cultural or intra-cultural. There is not a single more important thing we can do in a conflict situation than to try to see things from the other fellow's perspective. Even naturally insensitive people can learn to be sensitive to a great extent. If we see a tender spot or weakness in our adversary, we instinctively want to prick him there; but that is a malicious act. Rather, we should seek to protect that sensitive spot. We should seek to "cover for" our adversary's weakness—and hope he'll return the favor. Since we have weaknesses ourselves, we had best tolerate the weaknesses of others.

Being sensitive means sensing what the other person is feeling and applying the golden rule. Don't provoke, don't irritate, don't try to take cheap shots. Rather, be considerate and seek to please. "But this is my adversary," you say. "He has mistreated me. Why should I please him?" Because Jesus said to. He said, "Love your enemies" (Mt 5:44), and he wasn't even talking about Christian enemies! For "Christian enemies" Jesus gave a different command: "As I have loved you, so you must love one another" (Jn 13:34).

Then there are a whole group of attitudes that could come under the heading "humility." Humility isn't simply a passive trait; it is an active force. Humility lowers oneself and elevates the other. Humility thinks the best of the other; it sees the good and appreciates the worth of the other. Humility gives preference to the other in all things.

Humility overlooks irritations; it forbears slights and wrongs. Paul told the Colossians, "Bear with each other" (Col 3:5). It takes humility to graciously accept the barbs of our adversary. Sometimes it's easier to "turn our cheek" to a non-Christian than to our Christian brother.

Amy Carmichael has some good words for us as we go to meet our adversary: "Make up your mind never to doubt the love of another sister or brother in Christ, but always to think the best, to take the best for granted, and never admit an unkind thought in your heart."

Humility also fosters an attitude of acceptance. We don't just forbear; we reach out and accept and embrace—even the person who puts us off terribly because of the associations he evokes in our mind. One year a new missionary arrived at our mission guest house with very long hair, looking quite like one of the hippies who frequented Kathmandu at the time. The guest-house hostess simply could not accept him—not just his hair, but him. There was a generational separation of sides for a few weeks, and then everyone grew up. The anti-hippy contingent realized they should not be treating a brother as if he was a drug addict from Freak Street; and the pro-hippy contingent realized they needed to accept even those who didn't accept them. True tolerance includes tolerance even of the intolerant. In the end, the question of hair length became irrelevant, and the young missionary went on to serve many fruitful years in Nepal.

Then there is the attitude of thankfulness. It's impossible enough doing what the Bible tells us to do in regard to the obnoxious, overbearing, inconsiderate lout sitting across from us without our having to be thankful for him too! Yup. Not only thankful for him, but also for the pain he has given you! "...give thanks in all circumstances" says Paul (1 Th 5:18); "...always giving thanks to God the Father for everything" (Eph 5:20).

Yes, be thankful for your adversary, not only for his many good qualities but also for what he is teaching you about the Christian life. He, too, is the apple of God's eye, and his quirks of temperament and manner merely make the apple more unique. God wants a wonderful diversity of apples in his orchard, but we are always going around rejecting the ones that aren't just like us. And pity those that have some blemish or deformity—we'd chuck them out in a minute if we had our way. But they are God's apples too, and perhaps they have an especially pleasing taste.

When we go to our adversary with thankfulness in our heart not only for him but for the pain he may have caused us, then we can know that our healing is close at hand—and probably the healing of the relationship as well. When I thank God, my attitude is transformed, and my pain and stress diminish and often disappear. No one said it would be easy to thank God for that vile, wretched dog who's been barking outside my window for twenty minutes—much less for my roommate or that project director. But when I finally succeed in doing so, and discover, yet again, that it always works, I can only wonder why it is that I don't thank God more often!

Forgiving and being forgiven

Even if we have followed all the guidelines and have manifested all the attitudes that have been mentioned so far, the keystone of the archway to reconciliation is yet to be set in place. It needs to be set in place by both sides; half a keystone will not do. There must be both forgiving and receiving of forgiveness for complete reconciliation to be accomplished. Yes, I can forgive and then ask for forgiveness, and I will have done all that I can do. My heart and conscience will be clean. But if the other party cannot bring him- or herself to forgive me, then full reconciliation is blocked. From then on I can only commit the matter to God in prayer. Sadly, there are uncompleted archways in every church and every Christian team, and not the least in missionary teams.

Forgiveness will be a necessary element in the resolution of every interpersonal conflict. We have defined interpersonal conflict as any conflict in which sin has played a part, and the only solution for sin is confession and forgiveness. If forgiveness has not taken place, the conflict has not been truly resolved.

For forgiveness to take place we must first have a forgiving attitude or spirit; true forgiveness is from the heart. If we don't have that forgiving spirit, the first step in getting it is to remember how much God has forgiven us. When we have experienced God's forgiveness, the erasing of our debt, then we are free to freely forgive others. It also helps to remember how terribly Jesus was wronged and yet forgave. The wrong we have suffered is much, much less.

True forgiveness is unconditional. Some people quote Luke 17:3-4 to justify setting conditions on their forgiveness. "I'll forgive that so-and-so when he apologizes...or repents...or mends his ways." But in every other New Testament reference to forgiveness, there is no qualifying phrase such as "if he repents." Instead, Jesus said, "...forgive your brother from your heart" (Mt 18:35). Our forgiving does not depend on whether or not the person who has wronged us has repented. True, it may be wise to withhold the verbal expression of our forgiveness from a person who continues to wrong us without repentance, but we must forgive that person in our heart. Jesus and Stephen gave us an example when they forgave their murderers. Even when the person sins against us again and again, we must forgive him again and again—seventy times seven "again's."

To nurse an unforgiving spirit is to commit spiritual suicide. We ourselves cannot receive forgiveness and healing until we have forgiven others, as Jesus makes clear in Matthew 6:14-15. This is one of the basic spiritual principles that govern our relationship to God.

But before we can even forgive the other, we must first have confessed to God our own sins and sinful attitudes. We are not up on a pedestal self-righteously forgiving our brother; that kind of "forgiveness" is nothing more than spiritual pride. Rather, we need that humility and self-abasement that looks first to ourselves for the source of the problem.

So God's basic pattern is this: first, confess; then forgive; and then go to your brother and verbally confess your own wrongs, ask for his forgiveness, and assure him of your forgiveness.

We need to start the process as soon as we *feel* we have been wronged. We may not, in fact, have been wronged. Or, the person who has "wronged" us may not know it or acknowledge it. Still, for ourselves, we must forgive.

Let's say, for example, I am projecting anger on someone. I say, "He's angry with me"—which happens to be untrue. The anger is in me. If I can forgive the other for his non-existent anger, I open the way to receiving forgiveness for my own sinful anger.

You don't have to personally go to a brother to forgive him. This is especially true if he has done nothing tangible to hurt you, or if it has been a one-time offense that you can truly forgive and forget. The only time it is necessary for us to go to our brother in person is when the offense is continuing or when we ourselves need to ask for forgiveness.

We need to take care how we express our forgiveness to a brother. If we bounce right up and say, "I forgive you for your dreadful behavior," we are not going to get far. First, he may not know what we're talking about. Second, he may perceive that we are indirectly accusing him of wrongdoing—which indeed we may be! No, whenever possible, our expression of forgiveness should be accompanied by our own confession of sin (there is surely something we can confess) and a quiet explanation of how we have felt hurt. Only when the other person has been convinced that he needs our forgiveness will he be able to accept it.

Let us beware of extending false forgiveness. There are at least four types of false forgiveness.

One is the "forgiveness" that puts the other person down, or puts him in our debt, or that makes us seem "holy" at his expense.

Second is the "forgiveness" that makes no attempt at reconciliation, but is only given to clear our conscience. Such forgiveness is not from the heart.

Third is the "forgiveness" that is merely a front, allowing us to repress our pain and anger. Remember that repression is a natural and unconscious mechanism, which, though offering temporary relief from a painful emotion, is destructive in the long run. Don't let your forgiveness be a means of repressing feelings that need to be identified, owned, and dealt with.

Fourth is the "forgiveness" that does not forget. True forgiveness forgets the injury. Like love, "it keeps no record of wrongs" (1 Co 13:5). Yes, the injury will be stored in our memory, but it will not gnaw at us. We will not keep bringing it up. The scar remains, which we can see; but the wound is healed. There is no pain. That is what forgetting means. If we have not forgotten, we most likely have not forgiven.

Having completed the first two steps, confessing and forgiving, we are now ready for the third and final step: the going to our brother and asking for forgiveness.

Whether we are the wronged or the wronger, we go first to our brother, according to Matthew 5:23 and 18:15. We don't wait for him. Ideally, if he too is following these verses, we will meet on the road halfway.

And we shall begin with ourselves, with our own confession and repentance for any wrong we might have done. Even if we believe we are only two percent of the problem, we start with that. We may indeed be the victim, the oppressed, the abused, but there is always something for which we are responsible: our own unforgiving spirit, our own sinful reactions of resentment and hurt pride. These we must confess and ask forgiveness for. We are not responsible for what the other party does; we are only responsible for ourselves, for our own actions and reactions.

We must emphasize once again that in dealing with our negative reactions and attitudes—our hostility, our jealousy, our anxiety, our doubt—we must call them by their right name: sin. Then as we confess them, we are promised immediate cleansing and forgiveness. Many psychologists, as we have seen, shy away from using the word "sin" for fear it will increase our guilt and lower our self-esteem. But, in fact, in downplaying sin, they are depriving people of the very means of removing guilt and regaining self-esteem: confession of sin. For in addition to forgiveness, God offers us grace and power to deal with these negative feelings and to overcome them; and in their place God gives us his peace.

To forgive and be forgiven is a major part of loving and being loved. When we withhold forgiveness, we are withholding love. Such is the devil's scheme, that at the very point missionaries need each other's love the most—during periods of stress and conflict—you will often find them caught in a cycle of injury, distrust, hostility, and unforgiveness; instead of helping one another they are hurting one another; instead of loving one another, they are opposing one another. The only way out of this cycle is through confession and forgiveness. Such an elementary lesson in the Christian life! But missionaries need to keep learning it, just like everyone else.

When the attempt at reconciliation fails

In spite of all that has been said above, many interpersonal conflicts between missionaries never see a final resolution, or the resolution is delayed for months or years. This usually comes about because one or both parties refuse to humble themselves and reach out to the other with a forgiving spirit. What do you do when you have done all you can and the other side continues to erect a barrier of hostility against you?

The first thing is to question whether you have "done all you can." But there will come a time when the other's hostility is so deep that no matter what you do it is rejected or misinterpreted. Nothing you can do is "right" in that person's eyes. Then you must withdraw from engagement and wait on the Lord. "Waiting on the Lord" doesn't mean washing your hands of the matter and just sitting back. It means persisting in prayer, persisting in self-examination, persisting in love, and persisting in hope that reconciliation will one day occur.

But we must never withdraw from the conflict out of disgust, anger, fear, or any other unworthy motive. Before we withdraw, our heart must be free of any desire to get even, to punish the other by our silence, or to avoid the inconvenience of continued efforts at reconciliation. When we withdraw, it should be in love, and in sadness that we have not been able to win back our brother or sister.

We need to look at the case where an individual, it may well be a leader, is maligned and rejected by his or her colleagues. All efforts at reconciliations have failed. The individual has withdrawn from combat. Are there words of comfort and encouragement for him or her?

Yes, indeed there are. First, all of us should anticipate that this kind of thing will happen to us at least once during the course of our lives, especially if we spend any time in leadership. A leader acts as a lightning rod for the grievances and frustrations of those under him. Their anger is displaced onto him. All leaders need to expect this. It is commonly said that the proof of good leadership is that your followers follow you; but this is a false saying. It was not so at one point in Jesus' life, nor was it so at many points in Paul's life. Followers can turn against even the best leaders; it is those leaders whom Satan most wants to neutralize.

Second, God is constantly in the business of humbling, breaking, re-molding, and rebuilding his children. His major focus is on our self-life, our self-esteem, our reputation. Richard Foster, in his *Celebration of Discipline*, tells the story of a medieval monk who was being unjustly accused of various offenses. One day the monk looked out the window and saw a dog biting and tearing a rug hanging out to dry. God said to the monk, "That is what is happening to your reputation. But if you can trust me, I will care for you—reputation and all." When our reputation is being bitten and torn, we need to trust God in silence. We need to remember the words of Peter: "But if you suffer for doing good and you endure it, this is commendable before God. To this you were called, because Christ suffered for you, leaving you an example, that you should follow in his steps.... When they hurled their insults at him, he did not retaliate; when he suffered, he made no threat. Instead, he entrusted himself to him who judges justly" (1 Pe 2:20-21,23).

It is often true in life that the victim is blamed for the wrongdoing: it is a double injustice. It is even more painful when the blame comes from one's own brothers and sisters in Christ. They will even say they are "acting as friends"—though true friends never resort to slander and false witness. But if we complain, we are, in effect, complaining against God. To the extent we are innocent of the charges, God will ultimately be our justifier. To the extent we are guilty of the charges—or of others that people may not know about—God will use the experience to discipline us, to prune us, to purify us. In either event, if we complain or seek to justify ourselves, we only compound the problem.

It is well for us to remember that no matter how badly or how unjustly we are criticized, our critics don't know the half of it. Our suffering is always less than our sin deserves. That is something to be thankful for, even in the midst of our distress. Oh, to see God's hand in our trial, even when we are being slandered and lied about. He is humbling us. We know we should be abased; he is merely using our colleagues to do the job.

Some who have been turned against by colleagues may feel pressured to confess non-existent sins, to accept responsibility that is not rightfully theirs. Outsiders may clamor for a resolution to the conflict, and hold the rejected party responsible for the impasse. In this they do the same as Job's "friends" did for Job.

Some who are rejected in this way may enter into a "dark night of the soul." Not only is their pride and sense of worth stripped away, but even spiritual comforts seem to be withdrawn. One never fancied that carrying a cross would be like this!

Thomas á Kempis wrote:

> Jesus hath now many lovers of His heavenly kingdom, but few
> bearers of His cross.
> He hath many desirous of consolation, but few of tribulation....
> But they who love Jesus for His own sake, and not for some
> special comfort which they receive, bless Him in all tribulation
> and anguish of heart, as well as in the state of highest comfort.

Let those who are rejected by their fellows be quietly grateful that Jesus is taking them down into the deepest testing of their love for him. If
they persevere, they will learn the fellowship of his cross. There is no
greater privilege given to man than this.

> But all through life I see a cross
> Where sons of God yield up their breath:
> There is not gain except by loss,
> There is not life except by death,
> And no full vision but by Faith,
> Nor glory but by bearing shame,
> Nor Justice but by taking blame;
> And that Eternal Passion saith,
> "Be emptied of glory, right and name."
> >   Walter Smith

Some principles of managing interpersonal conflict

Debates over policy and programs never in themselves lead to interpersonal conflict. What happens is that one or more of the parties in the
debate begin to feel personally threatened in some way. Instead of looking only at what is good for Jesus and his church, we begin looking—
often unconsciously—at "what is good for me." Now this is not necessarily bad, as long as we bring it out into the open. What is good for
me will often be good for Jesus too. Not one of us can with perfect accuracy discern where our will ends and Jesus' begins. But if we are open
and honest about it, and say that this or that decision is really going to
hurt me or help me, then that need of ours can be put on the table for consideration. This kind of debate or conflict, far from being harmful, stimulates personal growth as well as progress in the organization or ministry.

What goes wrong is that one or more of the parties don't want to express their need; they may not even be fully aware of it. They may be embarrassed to express it; saintly, unselfish missionaries aren't supposed to have needs for job fulfillment, decent housing, a compatible roommate, more authority, more independence, more free time, and so forth. All they sense is that someone is threatening their well-being. They aren't getting what they would like, and so they begin to murmur against the person or persons they perceive to be responsible. Once this takes place, interpersonal conflict has begun.

Sometimes the sequence is reversed. An interpersonal conflict may already have begun over personal issues. Because one of the parties in the conflict is embarrassed to oppose the other party for "personal or selfish" reasons, he proceeds to attack the other's ideas and methods. This gives his side legitimacy. "This isn't just a personal disagreement," he can say; "it's his policies that are all wrong."

Thus, whichever came first, the policy conflict or the personal conflict, by the time one comes to sorting things out, the two types of conflict have become completely entwined. But what came first doesn't matter so much, as long as both aspects of the conflict are recognized. The conflict can then be managed in much the same way regardless of its genesis.

Many missions have elaborate administrative procedures designed to prevent interpersonal conflict or to identify it in its earliest stages. There are annual reports and evaluations, meetings at various times throughout the year, interviews twice a term, and annual workers' conferences. There are various levels of administrators, project leaders, personnel staff, personal counselors, and special speakers. I have no quarrel with any of this. My only warning is: you can't rely on procedures to prevent interpersonal conflict. There is no substitute for genuine open sharing and communication, especially between leaders and their people. Leaders must know their people. But, unfortunately, many leaders are so tied up in meetings that they don't have enough time to attend to this vital area. Almost out of necessity they have had to resort to personal counselors to take care of their people's personal needs. This has resulted in a separation of administrative and pastoral functions, which I believe has been detrimental overall. It is not the New Testament pattern for the church, and I doubt it should be the pattern for mission organizations either. We need personal counselors to help us with our deeper problems; that's fine. And these counselors need to be kept totally separate from the administrative side. But the administrators must not neglect their own pastoral responsibilities. Pastoral concerns must affect their administrative decisions. They must give time to pastoring their people.

"It takes two sides to have a conflict" is a true enough statement. Thus when one sees a conflict in process, one naturally thinks that both sides are partly wrong and that both sides need to give something to work the conflict out. This is still true. But the thinking becomes untrue when it is assumed that both sides in the conflict are equally at fault. This could be called the "both-fault" approach to conflict management, a variation of "no-fault" collision insurance.

There are several reasons why this is a wrong approach. First, in the majority of interpersonal conflict situations, one party is predominantly responsible for the conflict. McSwan and Treadwell, in their book *Conflict Ministry in the Church*, state bluntly: "The person experiencing stress within is the root of conflict with others." Second, the "both-fault" approach is unjust to the person who bears little of the responsibility. Third, this approach does nothing to encourage the one causing the problem to change his or her behavior, and hence does nothing to restore the relationship.

Granted, the "both-fault" approach is an easy way out for busy administrators: everyone's guilty! It saves a lot of time and bother, but it doesn't resolve things. It is like saying, "The truth doesn't matter." Even secular society does better than that.

I once knew a team leader who was having a problem with his assistant. The assistant had come to distrust and even dislike this leader, but had kept things bottled up. When the leader finally discovered that something was wrong, he went to his assistant and tried to talk about it. The assistant said, "You're insincere. You're just trying to manipulate me. I know your type."

Thereafter, the leader tried various ways of restoring the relationship. But each time his gesture was misinterpreted; it merely further confirmed the assistant in his thinking. Half a dozen times the leader asked to talk with the assistant, but each time the charge of insincere motives quickly ended the conversation. On the last attempt, the assistant said, "I do not want to talk to you again."

The assistant, however, had no problem talking to others. And before long, several team members had taken the assistant's side against the leader, and were spreading charges that the leader was unapproachable, insensitive, and autocratic. These charges reached the headquarters of the mission, and someone came out to investigate. This person listened to all the charges and then spoke to the leader, who hadn't heard any of them. The leader refused to talk about his assistant; he did not want to make countercharges. His silence was interpreted as a partial confession of his own fault in the matter. In the end, both the leader and the assistant were reassigned to other projects.

In this case the assistant had a deep emotional problem. He suffered frequent headaches; he was lonely; he was an unhappy person. He stayed on the field another two years and then went home. His own intrapersonal conflict had spilled over and brought an entire team into conflict.

It is essential that those called upon to mediate conflicts keep an even hand. It is so easy to soak up negative talk and then become negatively inclined to the person being talked against, especially if that person does not counterattack. And here we have the very reason that one should absolutely refuse to listen to negative talk without the one talked about being present. To do this is contrary to Scripture. To do this is to be party to slander—even if you are an administrator. (A personal counselor is ordinarily exempt from this rule, but is under a strict professional code not to divulge or use confidential information outside the counseling situation.)

The one seeking to mediate a conflict comes with his own prejudices and preconceived ideas that may prevent him from being totally impartial. This will render him much less effective as a mediator. The mediator must know himself and ever correct for his own bias, in order that he does not unconsciously favor one side over another. The mediator should empathize with both parties in conflict and seek to put himself in each side's shoes, but he must scrupulously avoid identifying with one side at the expense of the other.

At the very heart of conflict resolution lies the truth. Without an honest search for the truth, there can be no final resolution to an interpersonal conflict. Very well, someone says, but who's to say what the truth is? Which is similar to the question Pontius Pilate asked Jesus: "What is truth?" (Jn 18:38).

What, then, is the truth in interpersonal conflict? The truth is a dozen or a hundred details of fact, which can be examined and verified. Facts are far more important than perceptions—though it may take some effort to get at them through the distortion of people's testimony. But get at them we must, because it is only by means of facts that we can learn the truth. Granted, we can never know the full truth (which is why Jesus told us not to judge others), but we can get reasonably close to it in most cases. As we have said earlier, people's perceptions must meet the standard of truth. Conflict mediators who accept people's perceptions as a valid basis for making a judgment are going to be led astray again and again. The only way one can test the truth of conflicting perceptions is to have the two parties meet face to face and bring their perceptions up against each other.

Administrators have to make administrative judgments. These are judgments concerning the conflict in general and the specific behavior of individuals in the conflict. I emphasize specific behavior. No assessment of a person should be based on anything other than his or her specific behavior. Why is this important? Because specific behavior involves facts. Facts can be analyzed, refuted. If a person is charged with wrongdoing in the conflict, he can defend himself. He knows what the charge is.

One common mistake that is made is to label one or more of the parties in a conflict as "having relationship problems." As said earlier, this is a meaningless but nonetheless defamatory label. Who can defend himself against it? To label a person as "having relationship problems" and then to use that as a basis for making a decision inimical to him is the same as a judge passing sentence on a person without due regard for the evidence simply because that person has been dragged into court.

Sometimes we use such vague labels out of fear that specific truths will hurt people who are troubled and under stress. But, in fact, it is the truth gently expressed which is the only way to healing and restoration for that person. It is only when our faults and sins are brought to light and confessed that our lives can be made whole and our relationships transformed. Neither individuals nor communities can survive without truth anymore than they can survive without love. Love and truth are the indispensable pillars of any relationship and of any community.

A leader cannot tolerate hidden conflict. Conflict must be brought out into the open; otherwise it will eat like a cancer. But in dealing with interpersonal conflict as a third-party mediator, certain safeguards must be observed. The first and most important is that one should never entertain criticism or negative comments that have not first been communicated in person to the criticized party. If someone does not have the basic honesty and fairness to directly confront another with a grievance, then that grievance will always be suspect. It would certainly not be accepted in a court of law.

A major problem in mission organizations that have more than one level of leadership is that members with a complaint against their local leader "go over his head" and talk to the next level up. Often this is even encouraged by the upper-level leadership. But it is encouraging one to talk behind another's back. I have heard a top mission administrator publicly urge members of the mission to come to him with complaints if they felt they couldn't talk to their local leader. It may be gratifying to the senior man to play the omnipotent problem solver, but it both undermines the authority of the field leaders and institutionalizes backbiting and slander. Slander is the coward's way. It destroys another from the shadows. Not only should administrators refuse to encourage it, they should also admonish the person who does it and send him right back to his local leader. If both the local leader and the complainant agree to come together to the senior leader, that is fine. If one or both refuse, the senior leader can then ask to see them both together. But letting them air their gripes one at a time without the other being present will lead to nothing but a violation of Scripture.

When a leader, any leader at any level, acts on a complaint passed around the back of another person, he is violating a basic norm of justice which prevails even in secular courts: namely, that the accused has the right to face and cross-examine his accuser and any witnesses. It is impossible to administer any kind of justice without this safeguard. Surely one must expect as much justice within a Christian organization as he can expect in a law court.

Earlier we mentioned briefly some of the reasons why people with a complaint don't speak directly to the person complained against; but when the person complained against is in a leadership position, it is even more imperative that he be approached directly. The welfare of the whole team is immediately at stake when a leader is attacked behind his back. We must put to rest this widespread myth that leaders are unapproachable. They may be busy, they may not give you the response you would like, but it is a rare leader who truly is unapproachable, who doesn't want to know the feelings of those under him. The "unapproachable" charge merely becomes an excuse, then, for bypassing Scripture.

It is understandable why one hesitates to approach a leader with a personal grievance. He may fear the grievance will reflect back upon himself, that he will be labeled a "grumbler" or a "trouble-maker." The leader has power, and if he is displeased he may use it against the one with the grievance. Perhaps the person with the grievance isn't sure that his case will hold up; perhaps he lacks some facts or proof; perhaps he has been relying on hearsay himself—which is especially likely if he is carrying a grievance for someone else. All these things make one hesitant to approach his leader.

Furthermore, one may have gone once to the leader and seemed to have gotten nowhere. The request was denied; the validity of the grievance was rejected; the decision remained unchanged. The leader may have had very good reasons for his position. But what does the person do when his will is thwarted and his demands unmet? He tries to bypass the leader or to talk against him, or both. He begins saying to others, "The leader never listens; it's like talking to a wall." And human nature being what it is, this criticism of the leader is usually believed.

There are two simple responses to give to those who are reluctant to face their leaders. First, if you sincerely believe, as best you know, that what you have to say is true, and that you are motivated by the desire to clear up misunderstanding and restore your relationship, then you have nothing whatever to fear from going to your leader. Second, your leader's authority comes from God; if you oppose your leader unrighteously, you are opposing God. If you go behind your leader's back, you are guilty of slander—whether what you say is true or false.

Is there recourse if you truly feel wronged in any way? Yes. The first recourse is to take the matter to God. You should allow a period of time for prayer, reflection, and searching your own heart. Then, if you still feel the need for further action, Matthew 18:16 is your recourse. If you have first followed Matthew 18:15, then, and only then, are you entitled to follow 18:16. And notice what 18:16 says: "But if he will not listen, take one or two others along, so that every matter may be established by the testimony of two or three witnesses." You take these others "along"—that is, back to the leader or other person who you believe is in the wrong. Scripture does not permit you to speak behind anyone's back. You do not present your case until you and those two or three witnesses are present together with the accused. And if they fail to mediate the conflict, the same rule applies when you take the matter before the "church" in Matthew 18:17.

Why is the Bible so clear on the need for witnesses? "...so that every matter may be established." If every matter "was established" from the beginning of a conflict, if Christian organizations demanded strict adherence to Matthew 18:15-16, then these terrible convoluted conflicts with unsubstantiated charges flying here and there would never need to arise. Senior leaders would never need to throw up their hands in despair and say, "How will I ever get to the bottom of this?" The answer is: witnesses.

What kind of witnesses? The word "witness" implies eyewitness, or firsthand witness. The difference between a first and secondhand witness is often the difference between truth and falsehood. Witnesses are called for, not tale-bearers. And being an "eyewitness" does not mean seeing with your own eyes a person who is upset and then drawing a conclusion as to the supposed cause of the upset. An eyewitness must see the actual cause of the upset, or else his testimony is merely the hearsay of the upset person—which will hardly be objective.

Furthermore, the witnesses must agree. You may have lined up two or three witnesses for your side, but if there are also some witnesses on the other side you have a hung jury and no conclusion may be drawn.

Finally, we must ask about the character of the witnesses. Paul wrote to Timothy: "At my first defense, no one came to my support, but everyone deserted me" (2 Ti 4:16). Paul must have been a terrible fellow that he lost all his witnesses! But the problem was with the witnesses. They were cowards; they were faithless. Deuteronomy speaks of a "malicious witness" (Dt 19:16). We must assess the character of the witness. In a secular court of law the defense is always allowed to cross-examine the witnesses. Such a basic protection must not be denied Christians under attack.

It is often said, "So-and-so worked closely with the accused for a good period of time. Therefore, so-and-so's testimony is sure to be reliable." Well, that is a mistaken conclusion. It is such testimony that is most likely to be biased and colored by personal considerations. So-and-so may have an ax to grind. He may not know things firsthand either, yet he claims to. Witnesses, as well as the defendant and accuser, must be evaluated as to their truthfulness and objectivity.

Why have we gone on so long about this? Because the matter of slander and the improper use of witnesses is the number-one cause of breakup in Christian teams and one of the leading causes of fruitlessness and failure among missionaries. Satan is a slanderer. That is his chief method of destroying Christian work. And we, the workers, are his instruments.

Here are a few practical comments on mediating a conflict. Go slow. Start with the smaller issues that are easier to resolve. Proceed step by step, one issue at a time. Try to avoid a major blowup.

Don't let baseless and false perceptions go unchallenged. You need to quickly ask: "How do you know that? What is your evidence for that statement?" If there is no solid, specific evidence, such perceptions should be rejected.

Allay irrational fears: fear of rejection, fear of failure, fear of going crazy or being possessed by demons. Quiet assurance can calm most such fears—unless, of course, the fear happens to be justified.

Help people see their motives in the conflict. You yourself can't determine what their motives are; that's judgment. But you can help those in conflict to recognize their own motives. Hidden motives just add new layers to the conflict, making it that much harder to resolve.

Focus on the interests and needs of the people in conflict, not just on their positions. Positions get fixed; it is hard emotionally to let them go. But interests and needs are more flexible; they can be traded, adjusted, and temporarily set aside. Furthermore, they are what the fight is all about in the first place.

Finally, a word to senior leaders. Keep working patiently toward a final resolution. It is very easy to get discouraged and impatient, to think things are getting worse, when in fact they may have turned the corner. In such a situation you may well be tempted to just "move people out," thinking that that will solve the problem. But this is the very last thing you should think of doing. First, such action cuts off any further chance for the conflict to be resolved and relationships healed. Second, it merely moves the problems elsewhere. It solves nothing. Nobody grows; nobody learns. Rather, let your people work through their problems. Then they can move on in freedom and victory—instead of in defeat and discouragement.

Yes, there will be rare cases when moving people out or splitting them apart will be the only possible "solution" in the end. Paul and Barnabas split up too. But it is the measure of last resort. If it is resorted to before all other means of resolution are exhausted, it merely becomes an administrative cop-out. The issue of truth and falsehood is neatly bypassed. The innocent are guilty, the guilty are innocent. All are right, all are wrong. A clear river and muddy river come together and all is muddy. No one bothers to trace the mud back to its source.

We must not get cynical about the problems of missionary life. I once met a former medical missionary at a conference, and he told me as we parted, "Keep your eyes on Jesus; all others will disappoint." The tone in which he said this made me wonder if he himself hadn't experienced disappointment with his former missionary colleagues. Maybe it was the reason he had left the field.

But we can avoid cynicism and disillusionment not just by looking at Jesus, but also by seeing what Jesus is doing in our lives through the conflicts, the heartaches, the sins, which are part of our daily existence wherever we are. Through these trials he is conforming us to his likeness. He is making us better witnesses, better ambassadors, better missionaries. The devil cannot stand against a Christlike person. So Jesus needs to make us like himself. And that is not done in a day; and it is not done easily. "You were taught, with regard to your former life, to put off your old self, which is being corrupted by its deceitful desires; to be made new in the attitude of your minds; and to put on the new self, created to be like God in true righteousness and holiness" (Eph 4:22-24).

12

Fitting into the Team

I haven't met many "traditional" missionaries. Most missionaries are buzzing with ideas, eager for new experiences, filled with energy. They come from wide backgrounds; they are capable and intelligent beyond the average. Mix them all together, and you get a stimulating bunch of people. In fact, I can't think of a more interesting group of people to work with.

All these interesting people need to be forged into teams, and as in any good marriage with some spark to it, that takes work. The goal is to lose none of the zest, none of the individuality, none of the creativity, and yet get the whole circus moving in vaguely the same direction. It's almost possible!

Expect rip-roaring (but courteous) policy debates. The hotter the debate, the more trivial the issue as a rule, but no matter; the debates can be good fun and are rarely dull—until you descend into finance matters. Then you learn to be thankful that there are such people as treasurers and business managers who can tell you whether the ten mattresses you have ordered for the hospital should be put on the capital budget or the recurring budget. Don't be afraid of differences. As long as no personal animosity enters the debate, your unity will not be harmed and the devil will gain no foothold.

213

On the other hand, unrestrained individualism is disruptive to the work of others and to the harmony of the team as a whole. Individualism can be channeled without being squelched; this is the ideal. Missionaries should not be "single issue" people: all evangelism, or all revival, or all works of love. They can major in one area, but let them allow others to have their majors too.

A mission does not have to have tight organizational unity in order to be united. The crucial unity we are speaking of here is spiritual unity, not organizational unity. Organizational unity leads rather to uniformity. Missions that veer toward a centralized administrative style run the risk of becoming homogenized, and losing the sparkle of their members. Initiative is stifled, capable people are discouraged, and stimulating ideas dry up. That kind of "unity" no one needs.

Spiritual unity, on the other hand, is energizing. It does not depend on programs and organization; it flows directly from the Holy Spirit to each member. When an organization and its members, under the guidance of the Spirit, subordinate their own interests to the good of Christ's work as a whole, the ministry of both organization and individual is empowered and magnified. Furthermore, spiritual unity will always bubble up in a visible manifestation of warm fellowship and cooperation within the organization.

A beautiful example of the subordinating of one's own organizational interests to the good of Christ's work as a whole can be seen in the formation of the United Mission to Nepal. Back in the early 1950s, eight denominations and independent mission societies joined together to establish a united work in the newly opened country of Nepal. They could have just come in separately and each grabbed up its own little piece of turf (as has happened in most countries). But they sacrificed their own denominational and organizational identity and joined together so that the overall development of mission work in Nepal might be enhanced. It was one of the finest acts of missionary statesmanship ever. And the result has been a large, energetic and diverse yet truly united mission, comprising now almost forty different denominations and agencies from eighteen countries. Even better than that, the church that has sprung up alongside this mission has so far manifested a gratifying degree of both organizational and spiritual unity. It is not splintered into dozens of independent groups, each competing with the other. Like mission, like church. Nepal is one of the success stories of missions in the twentieth century.

For missionaries to be able to work together in such "united missions," they must agree on the fundamental doctrines of the church. It may be impractical to work closely with Christian groups whose basic beliefs diverge at too many points with ours, but we would be on dangerous ground if we tried to judge their standing with Christ. We ought not to compete with such groups, much less bad-mouth them. Rather, we should pray for each other.

The criticism, the competition, the "turf-grabbing" that has gone on between mission groups in the past is a black mark on the history of Christian missions. Whose "turf" is it, anyway? It belongs to Jesus, and we demonstrate a most un-Christlike spirit when we compete for it. Even today in Nepal we are beginning to experience an influx of Western Christians who want to set up "their own work" in Nepal. These may represent individual Western churches who believe that each local home church should do its own mission work. Or they may come from a small "denomination" with some distinctive teaching, such as a recently arrived Boston-based church which is teaching Nepalis that unless they are baptized again in that church they are not true Christians. One problem with some of these groups, aside from their divisiveness, is that they recruit Christians from other established churches to "set up their work." Their reports sound great at home, but often they are doing little more than "sheep-stealing"; there is no net gain in Christians. But there is a net gain in confusion and infighting among national believers. Beware of any group that tells you they are the only ones doing "true missionary work" in such-and-such a place. All they are doing is playing turf-games.

They are like the disciples who said to Jesus: "...we saw a man driving out demons in your name and we tried to stop him, because he was not one of us."

"Do not stop him," Jesus said, "for whoever is not against you is for you" (Lk 9:49-50).

There is still plenty enough work to do on the mission field without our trying to "stop" each other, compete with each other, and talk against each other. Such behavior is not of Christ but of the devil.

Now we all agree that cooperation for the advancement of Christ's work is a good thing. Let's see how it works out in practice. For two years my wife Cynthia and I hosted an evangelistic house fellowship in our home on the north end of Kathmandu. There were no churches in our area, so we and others who were part of the group prayed that a church might be established in our neighborhood. Then a Nepali evangelist with a charismatic group started working in our area, and at about the same time a new missionary from another Asian country settled on our street. The next we knew, our house fellowship had become a "church," with the new Asian missionary footing the bill and the Nepali evangelist installed as pastor. We hadn't even been consulted.

But, of course, we were delighted. God had answered our prayers. This dark end of Kathmandu was now to have a church.

The people in our house fellowship came from a variety of different churches in the city, so they all duly gave the happy news in their respective churches. The day following these announcements several interesting things happened. First, the leader of the evangelist's charismatic group called me, quite upset that "I had taken his evangelist to start an interdenominational church." Then an "elder" showed up representing the church our leading local Christian couple attended, and he let me know that his church would not allow the couple to transfer to "our new charismatic church." Are you confused? So was everyone else—especially the new Asian missionary who understood virtually no Nepali or English, yet ended up being accused of "buying" himself a Nepali church to impress the folks back home! It seemed like a classic case of God marvelously moving to establish his church and then denominational interests coming in and knocking the whole thing down like a house of cards.

I pause here, for thus far this story has been repeated a thousand times on mission fields around the world. The focus is on the word "our": our evangelist, our denomination, our church—our turf. And, of course, it's nothing of the sort. It's Jesus' evangelist, denomination, church, and turf. We know it, but we seldom act like it.

Getting back to our particular story, in case you have sized it up as I have indicated above, I'm happy to tell you that you're wrong. It's a good lesson in not jumping to conclusions on the mission field. Denominationalism was not a factor in this story. It was basically a communication problem. The Nepali evangelist was eager to start a new work, but he hadn't communicated adequately with his leaders. The new Asian missionary had been unable to communicate adequately with anyone. And the "elder" who had come and told me that our leading local couple couldn't transfer to the new church turned out not to be an elder at all but a back-slidden Christian with a personal agenda of his own.

A wonderful reconciliation of all parties took place in our living room. We agreed that the new church should be "dis-established" and that the Nepali evangelist should return to his own church. Finally, everyone went home except for the Asian missionary. He had understood almost nothing of the four-hour meeting except that he had lost his church. It fell to me to try and explain to him what had happened.

He distinctly felt that I was the cause of his disappointment, that I had sided with the others against him. There was considerable tension between us. Then I noticed on a shelf a Christmas card that we had recently received from the president of a seminary in the missionary's country. At the time, that seminary president was the only church leader of that country whom we knew personally. There were probably two hundred seminaries in that Asian country; it was a ridiculously long shot. But, thinking to ease the tension, I got it down and showed it to the missionary.

As he looked at the card, his eyes got big and filled with tears. "My seminary; my teacher," was all he said. The tension evaporated. Thanks to this distant seminary president, we could now trust each other. After that, as I struggled to explain to him what had happened, it was as a friend, not as an enemy. He did finally understand. Further, we agreed to move the house fellowship to his home (which was larger), where it promptly doubled and then tripled in size. We still at this writing don't have a church in our area, but one day we will—or maybe two churches, or ten. Why not? Forty years ago there were no churches in Kathmandu. Today there are forty churches. That's God's work, which goes on in spite of our denominationalism, our misunderstandings, our mistakes. It takes a great God to be able to use people like us.

The mission field provides many missionaries not only with their first experience of denominationalism, but also with their first close encounter with Christians of differing denominational beliefs. Many Western Christians (and Third World Christians too) have never been exposed to anything but their own denomination's teaching. The idea prevails at home that it is best to teach only your own denomination's beliefs, so that the people are not confused. But the implication is ever present that "only our denomination teaches the pure truth." So when people from these denominations get out to the mission field, they look about at other missionaries and think they must be heretics. They simply have not learned that there are a number of verses in Scripture that can be honestly interpreted in more than one way.

Missionaries as a rule are less hung up on fine doctrinal distinctions than their supporting churches back home. When people get out in hostile territory and find themselves a small persecuted minority, secondary doctrinal issues become insignificant compared to the task at hand. Such issues are seen in their proper perspective: fine to discuss in Bible studies, but not to divide over. There is more than a little truth in the saying: Mission unites, theology divides.

Oh, how we need broad-mindedness on the mission field, and tolerance for one another's position. The one who insists that he is right in every detail ends up doing great harm within a community of missionaries. We need people who can discriminate between those principles we must stand for without compromise and those issues concerning which we can welcome different opinions. Missionaries must be able to keep distinct those crucial doctrines that relate to the person and work of Jesus Christ and the way of salvation from the many other doctrines that are of lesser importance. Surely the deity of Jesus is of much greater moment than the precise nature of the bread at the Lord's Supper.

Sadly, there will always be those who place more emphasis on the five or six passages telling us to separate from those we feel are in error than on the five or six *dozen* passages which exhort us to be united and avoid division. These people are usually zealous for the Lord, but their zeal flows down narrow pipes. They may well oppose us, but we must not contend with them. If they speak falsely of us, we should merely state the truth as the occasion warrants. We should not retaliate in kind; nonbelievers will see it simply as Christians fighting among themselves. We do not need to engage in unseemly battles for "Christ's honor"; he is perfectly able to care for his honor himself. We must contend for the faith, not against each other.

The paramount importance of unity on the mission field cannot be emphasized too strongly. We have seen that Satan's chief tactic is to divide us. If he can divide us, he has weakened us, neutralized us. He divides us mainly through interpersonal conflict, as we have seen, but he also divides us through an exaggerated concern for doctrinal exactitude in secondary issues, issues which Christians have been struggling with for two thousand years. Our unity is dependent upon our oneness of doctrine, true; but that means oneness in *essential* doctrines, over which there is little debate among Bible-believing Christians. Nonessential doctrines must not be allowed to divide us.

Our unity is dependent not only on our oneness of doctrine but also on our love for one another. Jesus said, "By this all men will know that you are my disciples, if you love one another" (Jn 13:35). It's pretty important that missionaries be recognized as Jesus' disciples! Disunity gives the lie to everything we say and do. It is ultimately the result of sin. Disunity and love cannot exist together. Remember that we are speaking here of spiritual unity and spiritual disunity. These qualities are internal, not external or organizational. "Make every effort to keep the unity of the Spirit," says Paul (Eph 4:3). And effort it will take.

The effective team

Moving now from theory to practice, most missionaries end up on teams consisting of at least two people, usually more. And it's on the team that this unity business will be put to the test.

Virtually all mission work is done in teams, and so it has been since Jesus sent out his disciples two by two. The reasons are as old as Ecclesiastes 4:9-12. The issue before us, then, is how to make teams effective. The answer is unity—or, to use another word, teamwork.

Below are six practical things that are necessary to make a team effective.

1. A leader. Already I'm in hot water. Why do teams of two and three need a leader? Why does a husband-and-wife team need a leader?—asks the wife. I will concede that many small teams have functioned effectively for long periods without a leader; their members have usually been equivalent in age and experience. But most teams do better with someone assigned as leader, or tacitly acknowledged as leader. The leadership can alternate, but in a crisis or when quick decisions must be made, a leader is very useful.

This is not the place to discuss qualities of leadership. Obviously any leader must possess spiritual qualifications in addition to maturity, experience, and knowledge. But the one quality I do want to highlight here is this: a leader must devote himself to nurturing his team members and enabling them to function at their maximum.

What often happens on the mission field is that the assigned leader of a team is burdened down with his own job responsibilities, and has inadequate time and energy to spend nurturing his teammates. The teammates, meanwhile, begin to sense that their leader has put his own work before that of the team as a whole—which may or not may be true, yet it is so perceived. Thus the team members gradually lose their loyalty to the leader. The problem for the leader is how to demonstrate servanthood and self-effacement even in the midst of busyness and pressure. If the servant spirit is truly there, it ought to come through no matter how busy the leader is. However, where possible, it is better to choose people as leaders who aren't so busy with some specific job that they have no time to lead.

2. Submission. The second thing necessary for the effective functioning of a team is that the team members submit to their leader, regardless of his qualities. The New Testament has as much to say to followers as it does to leaders, and the main thing it tells followers is to submit.

But beyond submission to the leader, team members (including the leader) are to submit to each other. "Submit to one another out of reverence for Christ" (Eph 5:21). It is mutual submission which binds Christ's servants together.

3. Commitment. All members of the team must be personally committed to each other. They must love each other. They must practice body life. There must be truth and openness between them, and this means there can be no criticism or judgment of one another. Independence must be constrained and interdependence fostered. Individualism must be subordinated to the good of the whole. Misunderstandings must be immediately corrected. Clear communication must be maintained. And great care must be taken in handling the inevitable differences of opinion that will arise. Someone has said that Satan doesn't care so much which side you take as long as you take it strongly—so strongly that you become intolerant and judgmental, and split your team. That's what Satan is after.

4. Agreement on basic goals. One can disagree on strategy—as long as everybody gets behind the plan in the end. But the basic goals of the team must be shared by all.

5. Complementarity among team members. The fifth thing necessary for an effective team is that each member recognizes and values each other's strengths. It is generally beneficial if the temperaments of the team members complement each other. You don't want all optimists or all pessimists, or all "project" people or all "people" people. You want some who see the glass half full and others who see it half empty. You want some who expect everything to go right, and some who expect everything to go wrong. (On the mission field you will need more of the latter!) And remember, if you're going to be thankful for your team members' strengths, you also need to be thankful for their weaknesses. This is where your unity will be most sorely tested.

6. Prayer. The final thing necessary for team effectiveness is prayer. Prayer releases God's power to work through your team. Without prayer, all the other five items mentioned above won't be worth anything as far as your team's effectiveness is concerned. Spiritual teams work through spiritual means. If the spiritual means aren't there, the team will do no spiritual work.

"Preformed" teams of missionaries are becoming more common today. These are teams that live and work together for a period of some months before heading out to the field. Team members have the advantage of learning to work harmoniously together before facing the stresses of a new culture. These teams generally go into some of the most difficult pioneer areas in the world, and their record has been impressive. The sending of preformed teams is to be encouraged.

There will always be a few souls who just don't fit easily into team life. If you should happen to be one of these, don't despair. There are plenty of posts available—translation, accounts, teaching, to name a few—where the work is primarily individual in nature. But even so, you'll still be part of a team and will be expected to fit in.

Administration versus the workers

Unity is not only a horizontal matter among workers; it is also a vertical matter between leaders or administrators and those under them. We have said that an individual leader must be devoted to facilitating and enhancing the ministry of his followers. This applies equally to the "administration," a collective body of leaders. The administration is meant to help the workers, not to hinder them. At the same time, workers must be prepared to support and follow their leaders. Unity works both ways.

Administration-worker tensions are as old as the Himalayas, and even mission organizations made up, as they are, of saintly missionaries are not immune to them. Such tensions, and even the occasional conflict that arises from them, are healthy and normal. They are part of the dynamic life of any organization. Keep personalities and sin out, and this tension will lead to constructive and creative solutions. It's okay to say, "I don't like his policies," as long as you add, "but I like him." And make sure you mean it—or else go back to Chapter Ten.

Most people who end up in mission administration never asked for such a post, never sought it, nor did they receive any special training for it. Mission administrators are not politicians. They are asked to run established organizations that already have accumulated a pile of rules and policies that were put in place to help previous administrators cope. The more insecure the new administrator is, the more new rules and policies he will want to institute himself. Rules and policies help administrators help the workers; this is the idea. We all know, of course, that too many rules and policies stifle the workers. The key word, as in all other aspects of Christian living, is "balance."

The recurring practical question, then, is how can we have the necessary rules and policies without being overly bound and restricted by them? We don't want to administrate the Holy Spirit out of our mission. We don't want to straitjacket free spirits—a class into which most missionaries fall. We don't want to be guilty of cramming different-sized feet into the same-sized shoe. Is there an answer?

One answer is to have less rules and more "guidelines." Guidelines give people sliding room; they allow for individualized decision-making depending on circumstances. Tidy administrators generally prefer rules to guidelines, because guidelines require thought and sometimes messy negotiation. Well, let tidy administrators follow the guidelines strictly, if they desire, and let loose administrators follow them loosely. Guidelines give one the freedom to choose one's style. And they also give workers some relief from the regimentation of rules.

Missions need to build into their administrative structures ample room for flexibility. There need to be speedy mechanisms for making urgent decisions, without having to wait months for the multiple levels of committees to grind out a ruling. And there must be a willingness to waive rules when necessary. "Heresy!" I can hear the administrators saying.

I know an experienced, highly qualified and capable missionary who served in Nepal for over ten years and then went home to see his children through high school. Several years later he again offered for service in Nepal. It so happened that there was a great need at the time for an administrator to run a large project the mission had undertaken, and this individual admirably fitted that need. The only hitch was that in the meantime he had had a health problem, which had cleared up but which had the potential for recurring. No one in the current administration knew this missionary; he was just a name and a file. The medical advisor was also new, and couldn't have appreciated how greatly the mission needed this person's services. So the administrative committee responsible decided to stick by the established medical policies and recommended that the missionary not come. It could be said that they had looked at the trees and missed the forest.

However, others in the administration disagreed, and felt that the larger interests of the mission would be best served by accepting the missionary in question. And so, in the end, the missionary was called. This case serves to illustrate the kind of decisions that daily fall upon the heads of mission administrators. For great potential gain they must be willing to bend the policy or waive the rule—to take a risk. Good leadership requires it. Here's a case where we can see the advantage of guidelines over rules. Guidelines are like paths through the forest. Rules are too often trees that stand in our way.

And what about those "free spirits" called missionaries? One particularly free-spirited woman worked for twenty-five years in a remote Nepali village running a dispensary. No other medical help was available within a day's walk. It was a beautiful and fruitful work. Indeed, there was only one problem: It didn't fit into current mission plans.

I remember the director of our health services asking me, "What are we going to do with her?"

I said, "Why not leave her where she is?"

The director looked at me in silence. I couldn't tell whether he hadn't thought of it before, or whether my question was too obtuse to deserve a reply. In any event, the free spirit was left where she was until she retired after several further years of fruitful service.

"What are we going to do with her?" Look out! They may be asking that question about you one day. And then you will know the joy of working in an organization that puts people before policy—or the distress of working in one that does not. People versus policy. When it's a close call and you're down to the wire, you need to choose "people" every time.

I do not want to leave the impression that I am against rules and policies. One of my favorite people in Nepal was a former administrator who used to say: "Rules are for fools." But I decline to go that far! We've all heard about charismatic visionaries who have started works or founded organizations and then been unable to run them. People under them haven't known their responsibilities, or who they were accountable to. They have lost sight of where they were heading. There has been no training of new leadership, no setting of priorities. Chaos has reigned. That's the flip side of regimentation.

Let us aim for the middle ground. We need visionaries and we need managers. We need free spirits and we need plodders. It's rare to find an organization that is perfectly balanced between these extremes—and if you find one, it won't stay that way for long. But not to worry: no one is going to agree on what is "balanced" anyway!

A final word on centralization. Most larger missions have two or more levels of administration: a project level, possibly a regional level, and then a central level above that. In all organizations, as in government, there is a subtle tendency to accumulate decision-making power at the upper levels. This almost always is detrimental to the organization. Middle-level leaders are not developed, initiative is sucked away to the center, the organization becomes top-heavy. If Soviet communists can learn this lesson, certainly mission organizations can too. Let those at the center delegate authority, and build up their people instead of smothering them. And be humble; those at the center do not always know best.

We do well to keep our administrative policies and plans in perspective. Abraham "obeyed and went, even though he did not know where he was going" (Heb 11:8). But he knew who he was going with, and that was more important than where or how. That is true for Christian organizations too. And then we have those two telling passages in which Jesus outlines his program (Lk 4:18-19; 7:21-23). These passages don't bear much resemblance to most of the annual plans and five-year plans our missions churn out. Our plans have a way of taking on a life of their own. Our planning, as well as everything else we do, must continually be submitted to the Holy Spirit for his approval. Let us be able to say with the Jerusalem council: "It seemed good to the Holy Spirit and to us...." (Ac 15:28).

Getting your assignment

The first grand encounter between mission administration and worker is usually over The Assignment. Since up to a third of new workers don't get exactly the assignment they anticipated, the assignment process is the first big test as to how well the worker and the mission are going to get along with each other.

It ought to be apparent that mission leaders can't please everybody. The mission has specific needs, specific openings; and although ideally the new missionary has been recruited with one of these openings in mind, in the two-to-four years it takes him or her to get to the field the situation may have changed: an unexpected person has come to fill the opening, or the government has withdrawn its permission for that new initiative, or someone has gotten sick and it is urgent that his spot be filled—by the new worker, of course, who was expecting to be assigned to something totally different at the opposite end of the country, or continent.

We must start by assuming the general intelligence and good faith of the mission administration, and also the desire on the part of the worker to cooperate and fit in. If these assumptions hold, ninety percent of workers will be well-satisfied with their new assignment, even if it wasn't quite what they expected. After all, mission leaders have an obvious interest in getting workers into positions where they will be happy, challenged, productive, and able to use their training. And by and large, the leaders will know best what position that is—especially in the case of new workers. We can implicitly trust their judgment, certainly for that initial assignment. We can ask the reasons why they chose such and such an assignment for us; they owe us that. But we would be wise not to oppose their decision. Do *we* know for sure what will be best for us? No, we don't. We are more likely to make an error in our assignment than our leaders are.

It is important early in the assignment process that we, the worker, make our thoughts and feelings known to our leaders, and known clearly. Occasionally we ourselves won't have a clear leading as to where we should work, in which case we can simply accept our leaders' decision. But usually we will have a sense of what God wants us to be doing. He may have given us a burden for evangelism, or a burden for discipling, or a burden for the sick or the poor or the fatherless. We need to express these burdens, these callings, to our leaders, and our leaders need to take them strongly into consideration when they assign us.

One special problem occurs with those who feel called to proclaim the gospel in a semi-closed land, such as Nepal, where the only workers allowed in are professional people of one sort or another. We can agree that all Christian work motivated by love is a form of "proclamation" of the gospel, and this satisfies many missionaries who work in these lands. But others feel they must have adequate opportunity to witness by word also, and that they will be betraying their calling if they end up in an assignment where they don't have time or opportunity to do so. Mission leaders need to give great weight to this sense of calling. Major incompatibility between one's call and the situation on the field is obviously best picked up before the worker leaves his home country.

Let us not think that just because we start out as a doctor or a teacher or a church planter that that is what we're going to be doing the rest of our lives. There are numerous delightful opportunities for career changes on the mission field: teachers become administrators, doctors become teachers, church planters become translators. Our leaders will play a major role in these career changes. Furthermore, we will discover that God wastes none of our past experiences as we move into a new career situation—provided we move according to his will.

Our own natural gifts and inclinations will rightly be an important factor in determining our initial assignment, as well as all future moves. God does not ordinarily go against our inclinations, unless he sees that one or more of them need crucifying. But at no point can we assume that our inclinations are the same as God's will! Indeed, we must always mistrust our inclinations, and seek for other confirmation as to what God's will is. For example, missionaries, like everyone else, get comfortable in a certain career or location and are disinclined to move on. But God may use our leaders to move us out into new ground and new endeavors. One of the many wonderful things about a missionary career is the variety of circumstances into which God can move us. We'll find something to stretch us at every turn.

We must always be ready to move on. In 1 Samuel 20, we see David at a critical juncture in his life. Should he stay at the court of King Saul where his life was in danger, or should he move out? Saul's son Jonathan agreed to find out his father's intentions and arranged to give David a signal if he should stay or flee. He would shoot three arrows either to the side of David's hiding place or beyond it. If the arrows fell to the side,

David could stay: he would be safe. But if the arrows went beyond, David would know he had to flee. As with David, God is continually shooting arrows signaling us whether to stay or to move on. We need to be watching for the arrows.

How long we should stay in a post depends mostly on the kind of work we are doing. If we are planting a church, we should build up local leadership and move on, as Paul did. If we are in community development work, we need to get the community to carry the ball and then move on. If we are in teaching, it is not so critical whether we stay or go; a teacher gets a new class every year wherever he or she is. For health professionals, however, and for those who run orphanages, it's unwise to move on without compelling reason. In those cases, longevity and continuity are critical for the success of the work, because so much depends on the building up of confidence and trust over a period of time. Move out doctors or nurses against their judgment who have spent years gaining the faith of the people, and you will likely be moving them out of your mission organization. Don't set rules and timetables in these matters; both leader and worker need to watch for God's arrows.

My wife and I hadn't been in Nepal three months when at our first annual Workers' Conference the cry went out: "Work yourself out of a job." We hadn't even worked ourselves into a job yet. It was one of those slogans we love to use which eliminates the need for thought. What it means, of course, is to train, train, train, and then move on to a new area and repeat the process.

"Moving on" is indeed the general pattern for missionaries, except for health professionals and foster parents, as we have seen. It was Jesus' pattern, and certainly Paul's. But you don't move without leaving something behind, something that will be carried on after your departure. And the most essential thing to leave behind is a church. Simply to go in and do development work, to improve people's physical lot, is not a sufficient justification for starting a mission project. There can be no true development where there is no spiritual development. If a body of believers is not the ultimate goal, then we're better off letting a development agency do the project instead.

Thus the selection of projects and the timing of personnel moves should be based primarily on spiritual considerations. In deploying our resources of money and personnel, our chief question should be: How can we best build up the church of Christ and bring the most people into his kingdom? As for the individual missionary, sometimes it will be best to move, at other times best to stay. Major consideration should be given to the missionary's current spiritual ministry: Is it growing? Is it at a critical stage? What are the needs and wishes of the local people? The local church? Leaders need to be asking these questions; they aren't just running projects.

Handling disagreements

Leaders bear the greater responsibility for communicating with their workers and inviting their input. They have the responsibility to see that the workers feel part of the team, that their needs are being looked out for, that their opinions are valued. The great majority of disagreements over assignment and other policy matters can be quickly settled if worker and administration can come together in mutual respect and talk frankly.

Any mission administration should have in place simple procedures for soliciting the opinions of workers, instead of the worker being made to feel like he has to shout at deaf leaders. There should also be standard mechanisms for resolving disagreements, so that no one in the organization feels that he has no recourse, no appeal, in case of a possible wrong decision. If such a mechanism is already in place, the worker won't feel he is a complainer; it is expected that differences will be aired freely and openly—with the person involved, of course. Administrators should also provide job descriptions with a clear delineation of the worker's responsibilities. The job description should not be confining, but allow each person space to individualize his or her assignment.

This matter of getting incipient differences out into the open and discussing them is crucial in any organization. Don't fear a disagreement; rather, fear suppressing it. For if you suppress it, it will go underground and emerge later as an interpersonal conflict. In all this the administrator needs to take the initiative. But in the event he is not aware that a worker is unsettled or in disagreement, it is then the worker's responsibility to go to the administrator. The goal is to get these practical and impersonal matters settled quickly so they don't lead later to a breakdown in interpersonal relations and the conflicts we talked about in Chapter Ten.

Here are some additional suggestions for leaders when they are discussing personnel and policy matters with their workers.

First, avoid being autocratic. An autocrat misuses his authority. He's unsure he can lead his people, so he tries to drive them. But don't hesitate to use your authority when necessary—even at the risk of being called "authoritarian," a pejorative title that people give to their leaders when they haven't gotten their way.

Second, avoid an "I-am-a-senior-missionary" attitude. This conjures up a lot of unfavorable images in the worker's mind. He may feel you are treating him like a child, keeping him back from reaching his potential. He may feel you don't have a high regard for his contribution, that you are using him to get unpleasant or routine jobs done. He may come to feel undervalued, undertrusted, and overused. And the worst thing you can do is to communicate the attitude: "I had to put up with that when I was a junior missionary; there's no reason why you shouldn't too."

Third, avoid giving the glib advice: "Don't expect your situation to change; expect yourself to change." Now that's true enough, but if you as administrator need to change something in that worker's situation, you'd better do it; otherwise, that statement merely becomes an excuse to neglect your duty.

Fourth, understand where your worker is at. If he's green and dependent, give the needed support; don't push him into jobs where the risk of failure is high. That can come later. The more confident and experienced worker needs to be challenged and given independence. Encourage him to question your own ideas. And then train him for leadership. All this will apply to your dealings with nationals as well. The point is that leadership style isn't a rote formula. It should vary with the individual worker and with the situation you find yourself in.

Leadership is a trust. A leader has no sanction to place burdens on people that Christ himself wouldn't place. A leader must not make such demands of service and loyalty on a worker that the organization begins to supplant Christ as the chief object of devotion in the worker's life. No organization or leader should run a worker's life.

The leader is a servant. That doesn't mean he can never exercise authority; it is all in the way he does so. For whose good is the authority exercised? The answer to that question will determine whether or not the leader is a servant. If the workers can see that the authority is being exercised for the good of others, they will accept it. To use authority for one's own benefit is always an abuse of that authority.

Finally, far from being a burden giver, the leader is a burden bearer. Indeed, the leader is a cross bearer, for he or she is a magnet for the complaints and discontents of others. If the culture, the diet, the work, the nationals are getting you down, you can always hold your leader responsible! Leaders, be ready for it.

One unique problem that occurs in Christian organizations is the so-called "holy war," in which each side is quite sure he or she is doing Christ's will. Short of interpersonal conflict, these are the most difficult disputes to resolve.

I remember when we switched our team's observance of the Sabbath from Sunday to Saturday. The reason was simple. The Nepali government had just taken over the mission schools, and since the weekly day off in Nepal was Saturday, that meant our mission teachers had to work Sundays—and hence couldn't attend church. First the church decided to switch. Then, naturally, the mission hospital followed suit.

A couple of the mission nurses were extremely upset by this. They saw it as a capitulation to the Hindu society around us. They felt we were dishonoring Christ by not following the practice of the early church. They were deeply offended by the thought that they might be asked to work Sundays. And they grumbled against the decision.

Well, we eventually got it resolved. The nurses became convinced that the Bible didn't say *what* day of the week should be set aside for the Sabbath, and the hospital promised to do its best to give them Sundays off. You may think: How silly; I wouldn't have gotten upset over that. Well, you can be sure there'll be something that upsets you, something on which you feel compelled to take a stand. When it happens, whether you be leader or worker, take a good dose of Philippians 2:3.

When disagreements arise, both leaders and workers must commit themselves to settling them quickly and amicably. I use the word "disagreement" here to mark a difference from the personal type of conflict we talked about in earlier chapters.

The first missionary disagreement is recorded in Acts 15:36-41. It follows immediately after the momentous settling of a much greater disagreement by the Jerusalem council. Which reminds us to watch out after those momentous settlings and grand break-throughs: the devil is getting set to lam us.

So along come Paul and Barnabas heading back to Antioch, happy as larks that the Jerusalem council has gone their way, and before they know it they have "such a sharp disagreement" that they part company (Ac 15:39). And they've only taken one missionary journey together! Not an auspicious beginning for the Christian missionary movement.

Well, Paul was a "project" person; he put ministry first, and Mark was a deserter who couldn't be relied on. Barnabas was a "people" person; he put the man first. He had faith in Mark—just like he'd had faith in Paul in the beginning when no one else had.

Barnabas ended up being the more right of the two, and God got two missionary teams instead of one, and we're left with the feeling it wasn't all that big a deal—forgetting how truly painful and unsettling that dispute must have been, and how nearly the devil came to derailing the entire missionary enterprise.

Notice that both Paul and Barnabas had a valid viewpoint. That is the way it is with nearly every dispute on the mission field. So the first step in resolving disputes is to understand the other fellow's viewpoint. And this goes for disputes between leaders and workers as well.

There are certain guidelines a worker should follow in taking a dispute to a leader. He needs to respect the leader's position, no matter what he thinks of the person. It is the position that gives the leader authority over the worker. If the decision or request of the leader is legitimate, it should be honored. If the worker doesn't think it's legitimate and has gotten nowhere with the leader in face-to-face discussion, then he should appeal— but only in the proper way. And he should not write home about the dispute in a critical way, anymore than he should talk behind his leader's back; this is murmuring and grumbling, a practice that got some Israelites in trouble back in the book of Numbers.

It is essential that any dispute be kept impersonal; that is, not aimed at personalities. If the worker feels his leader is "authoritarian," "insensitive," "unqualified," he has to come up with specifics that can be talked about; he must not deal in general impressions, which are nothing more than personal criticisms and which can't be defended against. The worker must examine his motives: Is he trying to cut the leader down to size? Is he debating differences or is he debating the person?

Throughout the dispute, both sides must not only listen to each other but also respect each other's viewpoint. Remember, as with Paul and Barnabas, both viewpoints will probably be valid. Be thinking of possible solutions or compromises as you go along. The point is not to win but to resolve. An especially important point in resolving differences is to determine who has the most vital stake in the outcome. Any compromise should be in that person's favor.

And if no solution is forthcoming, take a break. I worked closely for over a decade with a medical colleague whose opinions differed from mine on numerous occasions. Whenever we couldn't agree, we put off further discussion until the next day. In more cases than not, when next day came I had taken her side and she had taken mine, and we had to go at it again—though it was much quicker the second time around! It got so that after stating our positions we'd say, "Let's talk about it tomorrow." We didn't have a serious difference in all the time we worked together.

A final word for the worker who is having "trouble" with his leader. Your leader is doing his best. Maybe he's not a "natural" leader, but there was no one else and so he was chosen. He's doing his job in good faith. Give him a break. Try praying for him. If you do, you may find your anger toward him drying up. And don't pray that "his many glaring defects" will be rectified! Pray rather that he will be filled with the Spirit and glorify God—and that you yourself will become more loving, less critical, and more submissive.

Submission to authority

This topic won't win a popularity contest with today's missionaries, but the purpose of authority is not to make a leader popular but to mediate God's will in the Christian community. Authority is established by God and is therefore derived from God. It is not a man-made invention. If one has a problem submitting to authority, his problem is basically with God.

That's all easy to agree with until we begin to look at some of the human authorities God puts over us. All are flawed to a greater or lesser degree; all have limitations. The new missionary, in particular, is likely to conclude that the authorities on the home council have a poor understanding of the field; that the authorities on the field are rigid, closed-minded, and living in the past; that the national church authorities have half the spiritual maturity and Bible knowledge that he has; and, worst of all, that his own project leader is domineering and totally unfit for the job.

Hmmm. Let that missionary revisit the New Testament. If Paul and Peter commanded believers to submit to the Neros of their world, can we suppose they would be sympathetic to our rebelling against our project leader?

"But the project leader has no 'spiritual authority,'" the missionary says. It may be true. Spiritual authority is something that God invests on certain individuals whether or not they have actual positions of authority. It is sadly true that many in Christian leadership are lacking in this quality. But the term "spiritual authority" is misleading. The New Testament doesn't tell us to submit to spiritual authority; it simply says to submit to authority. "Spiritual authority" is no more than the deep spirituality manifested by a man or woman who walks closely with God. This spirituality is something every Christian desperately needs and prays for. Sympathize with the one thrust into leadership who does not yet have such spirituality. It is harder for him than for those under him.

Others seek to avoid submitting to authority by appealing to democratic principles. "Place more authority in the hands of the workers" is a widespread sentiment. Some might say, "Place *all* authority in the hands of the workers," but then you have a headless democracy in which no one benefits. Yes, delegate authority to the workers, as the apostles did in

Acts 6:2-3. But final authority must remain in the hands of the leadership.

This still doesn't satisfy our modern thinking, which says that leaders should be accountable to the people, and that final authority should be invested in the people, not in the leaders. This concept may work well in politics, but the Bible gives us no warrant for applying it to either the church or to Christian missions. The weakness of some Christian organizations today may be traced to putting too much authority in the hands of the workers. This gives the opportunity for new and inexperienced people to come in and disrupt the work of the organization. Leaders become discouraged, even paralyzed, and then, of course, are blamed for "poor leadership."

One mission in Nepal sends around an "evaluation paper" to the workers, inviting them to anonymously make comments about their top leaders and soliciting the workers' opinion as to whether a given leader should be reappointed for a new term of office. This procedure is not scriptural, because it invites behind-the-back criticism. You ask, "How, then, can we get rid of a bad leader?" And the answer is that God will take care of bad leaders; it is not for us to take authority into our own hands—even if the mission misguidedly gives it to us. We all must follow Scripture in these matters, in particular Matthew 18:15-17, which is as applicable to problems with leaders as it is to problems with fellow workers.

We come down to this basic fact: all Christians are commanded to submit to the authority over them, up to the point where that authority forces them to violate Scripture. That point is not always easy to determine, but on the mission field, it will virtually never be reached. I have not heard of a mission authority who has knowingly or unknowingly caused a worker to violate Scripture. Mission authorities may themselves unknowingly violate Scripture in the exercise of their duties, but that is a different matter; that does not give a worker license to disobey or rebel against their authority.

Now "submission to authority" is not nearly as onerous as it sounds. It does not mean craven acquiescence to everything your superior says. It doesn't preclude talking things out, or even respectfully disputing decisions. It does not mean you can never resign.

Biblical submission, rather, means to be free of self-will, to be free to let go. Submissiveness is first of all an attitude. It is the attitude of caring for another above self, of being willing to give up one's rights for the benefit of others, of loving unconditionally and expecting nothing in return. Submission is self-denial.

Since true submissiveness is an attitude, it is quite possible to be out-wardly submissive but inwardly rebellious. One cannot live in this state for long. All of us need continually to pray for a submissive spirit.

The willingness to accept a decision or an assignment that is not to our liking is a critical test of our spiritual maturity. Furthermore, submitting to such decisions is the only sure way we have of ultimately knowing what God's will is. In the first place, mission leaders are more likely to be able to discern God's will than, say, a newly arrived worker. They know things we don't; they know of complicating factors we're not even aware of. We need to start out with the attitude of accepting our leaders' decisions as from God. We need, first of all, to tell God that we will sub-mit to *anything* the leadership says, and then trust him with the outcome. Once that is settled with God, then we are freed to enter into frank and open dialogue with leadership concerning those decisions we question. In most cases such dialogue will result in a better understanding of why the decisions were made, or it will lead to a modification or even cancella-tion of the decision.

Remember, your leaders are kindly disposed to those under them. You do not need to question their good intentions, even when their decisions seem to go against you. They may be dead wrong, and often are, but the way to counter them is not head-on, but through patience, humility, di-alogue, and prayer. Leave the issue in the Holy Spirit's hands; he is your leader too.

Leaders do not ordinarily violate a worker's sense of guidance. Indeed, they should do so only in exceptional circumstances. But the guidance of the Holy Spirit can be misinterpreted on both sides. To be certain of the Spirit's direction, both sides need to seek for oneness of mind.

If, after a reasonable period, your own guidance and your leader's guidance continue to differ, fulfill your promise to God: submit to your leader's decision and let God cover the consequences. That is the only scriptural option you have at that point. To resign in protest is merely an act of insubordination. Not to submit is to disobey God's word. "Obey your leaders and submit to their authority" (Heb 13:17). We must state clearly: willingness to submit to authority is indispensable to a successful missionary career. The person who is not prepared to submit willingly to the decisions of his leaders should not come to the mission field.

Many disputes with leaders could be avoided if we were not quite so cocksure about our guidance and calling. Many of us may not understand our own calling as well as we think we do. Many missionaries' calling has changed after a few months or years on the mission field, and they have happily ended up in quite a different line of work than they had ex-pected.

I once knew an experienced missionary who was questioning a leadership decision concerning his next assignment. The missionary was not at peace with the decision. He knew that the leadership had based its decision in part on erroneous information, and he felt that such a decision could not be God's will. Neither did he have any peace about resigning from the mission, which was his other option. In the end he rightly decided to submit to the leadership and accept the assignment—even without being fully "at peace" with the assignment itself. But he was at peace that he was obeying God's will, and that was far more important.

Within three months, before the missionary even had a chance to take up his new assignment, the decision was reversed. New factors had arisen. And with perfect timing a marvelous new opportunity to serve opened up for the missionary, which exactly suited his gifts and temperament.

Variations of this story have been repeated hundreds, probably thousands of times on the mission field. Can we not learn to trust God? If we will only do things his way, we can trust him to give the story the right ending. Let God write your story; he is a better author than you.

When the worker has no peace

Even when both sides, leader and worker, have tried hard to resolve a dispute, there will be times when the worker remains unhappy with the outcome. The worker may already have submitted to a decision which he questioned, and now he feels trapped, bound. What should he do?

His problem is almost always going to be one of attitude. He has submitted outwardly, but not inwardly. Any number of sinful attitudes may have entered his heart: self-centeredness, rebellion, pride, a critical spirit, lack of faith. If these are identified, confessed, and repented of, peace and happiness will come in their stead.

Nowadays workers are more and more concerned with their rights, and less and less concerned with their responsibilities. It is a symptom of our age. Some young people are reluctant to join a mission for fear their freedom will be abridged. They prefer to do their own thing without restriction. But this is nothing more than selfishness. Christians are to focus primarily on their responsibilities, not on their rights. And when we join a mission organization, one of our main responsibilities is to submit to our leaders.

The people who have the hardest time submitting are those who have already been in leadership themselves, or who have worked independently for a considerable time. Some may have been out in isolated areas with little or no supervision, and suddenly they are transferred to the center and the supervision seems suffocating. Or while they are out in the isolated area, they may begin to get instructions from the center; new policies are put into effect that are utterly inappropriate for their setting. And the complaint goes up: "The administration doesn't understand our situation." And the missionaries on the site, who "know better," are tempted to ignore the new emanations from the center. A spirit of insubordination sets in; the missionaries essentially become disloyal, and cease to support their leaders.

This is a very sad state, both for leader and worker. Leaders count on the support, prayers, and loyalty of those under them. There are few things more displeasing to God than the sight of missionaries opposing their leaders. Those who do this rarely go on to a successful missionary career. Most will have left the field within a couple of years.

The worker is not entirely to blame every time there is an unresolved issue. Leaders do not have an exclusive channel to God—though they at times act like it. The leaders may not have been of one mind among themselves. They may have made an arbitrary or hasty decision. They may have acted on the basis of incomplete and erroneous information. They may not have followed scriptural principles. They may have been tactless or insensitive, and have thus given needless offense to the worker. Leaders are busy; leaders are human. This doesn't excuse wrong behavior, but it explains why it occurs. And when it occurs, one loses confidence that they've gotten God's directions right.

There were two fine nurses who directed community health projects in different parts of Nepal. Then, after several years of fruitful service in their respective locations, the central administration switched them. The positions were the same; the work was the same; but the people were now new to both nurses. Relationships just beginning to bear fruit were ended for both of them. It seemed a wasteful decision. It was made mainly because a new incoming project director didn't think she could work easily with the nurse originally assigned there.

Twenty years have passed, and the decision seems no more right to the two nurses today than it did in the beginning. From our human perspective it was a mistake. It probably should have been questioned more vigorously. But God allowed it. Who can say what might have happened had the decision not been made? The outcome could have been much worse. As it is, the two nurses have continued to serve the Lord faithfully ever since that time. That is quite a wonderful outcome in itself.

Your leaders are being bombarded daily with decisions like these. They don't have perfect knowledge; they do their best. They need your help, your support, your advice. But above all, they need your prayers. If Paul needed the prayers of fellow Christians, you can bet your leaders need yours.

Broad policy debates

Most missionaries coming to the field will have read and discussed missionary strategy relating to a whole variety of situations, and these strategy discussions and debates will go on throughout one's missionary career. They are good, useful, and often important. They are never quite as important as they seem at the time, but inasmuch as they determine the general direction, the goals, and specific strategies of the mission, each missionary should expect to be an active participant in these discussions. And any good mission organization will encourage this participation and set up mechanisms whereby the workers' opinions can be fully aired and listened to.

It is much easier in broad policy issues to keep personalities out of the debate. These debates are stimulating, broadening, and they can become quite lively without even a hint of ill feeling or rancor arising. Occasionally, however, some major issue will provoke strong feelings, and some missionaries will inevitably be unsettled by this, even to the point of becoming disillusioned with the mission. And there will always be a few who feel compelled to withdraw from the mission if a policy has been adopted which they cannot accept.

The larger and more complex a mission organization is, the more frequent and vigorous will be the policy debates. The United Mission to Nepal (UMN) is a case in point. With nearly three hundred missionaries working in thirty diverse and widely scattered projects, the UMN is in a constant ferment of debate and redefinition. The workers develop their different views over a period of time and things hum along for few years, and then either from within the mission or from the board members who fly in every year, some new concept or direction is introduced and the ferment is once more stirred up.

The bigger the mission and the more varied the membership, the more difficult it is to reach a consensus on policy matters. Yet a consensus should always be the goal; unity of mind is the surest indication that the Holy Spirit also agrees with the decisions being made. But there will be times when consensus cannot be reached and yet a decision must be made; in that case, a majority vote will carry the day. It is second best, but it's often a practical necessity.

Some of the broad policy debates that have recurred throughout

UMN's forty-year history are similar to debates found in missions elsewhere. Since UMN is involved in development work in a poor country, there is a constant tension between whether we are here primarily as "nation builders" or primarily as "kingdom of God builders." The issue is compounded by the fact that it is still quite illegal to be "building the kingdom of God" inside the kingdom of Nepal. This major debate spawns many subdebates: To what extent can a Christian mission be a partner with government in the developing of the country? To what extent should we be training non-Christian Nepalis to manage our hospitals, schools, and other programs? What is the best way to promote "Christian values" in UMN, when the great majority of our Nepali staff are not Christians? Should a Christian organization give scholarships without regard to the religion of the recipient—which may mean giving ninety-five percent of the money to non-Christians?

And then, in the midst of these debates, the Board flies in with the latest scoop from the World Commission On This Or That and announces that we should no longer be running institutions at all but rather should be putting our resources into "people-oriented projects" (which makes one wonder what a hospital or school is), or that we should be focusing all our energies on the "poorest of the poor" and issues of social and economic justice.

As the years roll by, many of these debates serve as helpful course corrections, and as such should be welcomed and engaged in by all. But the root issue—does a mission exist primarily to build a nation or to build the kingdom of God—must be settled in favor of the latter if any mission is to be a useful instrument in God's hands.

So now we can envision the "perfect" mission. Its leadership is responsive to the members, forward-looking, and open-minded. As to general direction, purpose, and goals, there is oneness of mind. As to strategies and methods for attaining these goals, there is constructive and stimulating diversity. The two missions I know best come wonderfully close to this ideal, though it would be folly to say there was no room for improvement. And since I'm entitled at least once in this book to "put in a plug," I wish the reader the blessing of being associated with a mission as good as my own two missions: InterServe and the UMN.

Resignation

Before you resign from the field or from your mission, you need to be "called" to resign. You need a call to resign just as much as you needed a call to join. Stay put until God calls you out. Remember God's arrows; wait for his signal. If your will is surrendered to his, you will know when and if you are to move on.

A worker need never feel trapped. Resignation is always available to him. There is nothing dishonorable in resigning for the right reason and in the right way. Indeed, in many cases resignation is an act of courage and honesty. But the reasons for resigning and the way in which it's done make all the difference in whether your resignation is pleasing to God or not.

The first caution is this: Do not resign in protest or in reaction to something—a person, a decision, a policy—unless, of course, you are compelled to do so for scriptural reasons. Even here, be humble; some verses can be interpreted in more than one way. If you resign in reaction, it is most likely that you are resigning in rebellion. God did not call us to be rebels. Furthermore, when we resign in reaction, we may set a pattern for the future, and spend years thereafter ricocheting from one organization to the next.

Above all, do not resign in a state of unsubmissiveness. First submit to your leaders for however long it takes to make sure your own attitudes are right before God. All personal conflicts must be resolved. If problems remain unresolved, you will simply take them with you, and they will plague you afresh wherever you end up. You don't escape problems; you resolve them. And when they are resolved, you can move on in confidence and peace.

There are many reasons for resigning, some acceptable, some not. A fuller discussion of the reasons missionaries drop out comes in Chapter Thirteen. For the present we shall limit ourselves to a few observations.

Be suspicious of negative reasons for resigning: discontent, lack of job fulfillment, sense of failure, or dissatisfaction with the mission. These should rarely if ever be your primary reason for resigning. They suggest problems that remain unresolved. Your reason should be positive. You should see yourself as stepping through an open door, stepping out into a new calling, a new venture. And you need the confidence that God is going before you.

Not all negative reasons are bad reasons for resigning. You may have deep differences of opinion over mission philosophy and direction. New leaders may have come and major changes may have taken place that make it desirable that you move on. Then there may be a door that closed, or a work that reached completion, or an illness. These are all natural transition points, and resignation is often suitable at such times.

Beware of "the Lord is leading me" approach. He will not lead you alone. He will not lead you to oppose your mission or your leaders. Especially beware of "holy indignation" at some person, policy, or practice; it is rarely if ever "holy."

Finally, beware of self-deception. We must discern between the promptings of nature and the promptings of grace. Nature is crafty. It will blow up negative reasons. It will make selfish reasons seem like God's leading. Even the maturest Christian needs to be ever wary. We are totally dependent on the Holy Spirit to reveal to us our selfish motives and guide us in God's true path. The battle against the natural man never grows easier. Nature keeps appearing in new guises as we go through life. Let us plead with God that when the time of resignation comes, it will be the spiritual man in us that resigns, and not the natural one.

13

Keeping the Focus

"Mission" has many definitions, both narrow and broad. People speak of "the mission" of the church as one thing, and "missions" (as in "missions program") as another. But "mission" and "missions" aren't two separate things; it is through "missions" that we carry out the "mission" of the church. And "mission," in John Stott's broad definition, is "everything the church is sent into the world to do."

In this book we have defined a missionary as a cross-cultural witness, and we have limited our discussion to cross-cultural missions. But for a moment, I want to rejoin cross-cultural and intracultural work, and think briefly about the overall mission of the church. What is it that we are sent into the world to do? What is the goal or purpose of our mission to the world?

Our goal is to reconcile men and women to God. We are God's instruments in this work. "All this is from God, who reconciled us to himself through Christ and gave us the ministry of reconciliation.... And he has committed to us the message of reconciliation. We are therefore Christ's ambassadors, as though God was making his appeal through us. We implore you on Christ's behalf: Be reconciled to God" (2 Co 5:18-20).

What must be emphasized is that there is but one goal of missions. We

240

could have chosen several other verses and stated the goal in different words, but the meaning would have remained the same: We are sent as a church into the world to reconcile men and women to God. That is the one and only goal of missions. That is, in fact, our primary mission. Everything else we do in the world contributes to and supports that mission.

Why is it important to speak of *one* goal? Because it helps us get our mission into focus. It helps us to set priorities and to make the best use of our resources and talents. And it clarifies the debate over the relative importance of social and evangelistic ministries.

We have a goal; now we need a motive. The motive is love. Love is the engine, the driving force of missions. This is the love that "God has poured out...into our hearts by the Holy Spirit" (Ro 5:5). Without it, missions is just an empty shell. We receive this love only from the indwelling Holy Spirit. Along with love, we need the other eight fruits of the Spirit Paul mentions in Galatians 5:22-23. In order to bear fruit for Jesus, we first need to have the fruits of the Spirit. We can't represent Christ without them. In order to be "ambassadors" for Jesus, we need to manifest his qualities. People need to see Jesus in us, to experience his love through us.

We have a goal; we have a motive. Now we need to look at the means by which we can achieve our goal. They fall into two broad categories: ministry of the word, and ministry of service. Ministries of the word would include evangelism, disciple-making, theological education, and radio and literature work. Ministries of service would include health, general education, and economic development ministries, with special (though not exclusive) concern for the poor and oppressed. Both types of ministry should issue in the formation of new churches.

All ministry, whether "of word" or "of service," is equally acceptable and pleasing to God as long as it is motivated by love. Indeed, it is artificial to draw a sharp distinction between the "ministry of the word" and the "ministry of service." Translating the Bible, after all, is just as much a "service" as treating an illness. And an act of compassion is just as much a "proclamation" of the gospel as preaching a sermon.

The main reason for separating ministries of word and service is that they address two very different kinds of need: spiritual need and physical need. Now some will object to this dividing of man's needs into spiritual and physical; we are taught today to regard man as a whole. We favor a "wholistic" or "integrated" approach to ministry, and this is good. But the truth remains: man's spiritual and physical components are distinct, and nowhere do they become more distinct than at the point of death.

Furthermore, man's spiritual need is infinitely greater than his physical need. Spiritual need involves eternity, while physical need involves only a few years on this earth. An infinite number of years is always going to be infinitely greater than any finite number of years. Ministering to that part of a man that will continue on beyond death is infinitely more important than ministering to his physical body. Eternal life is infinitely more valuable than earthly life.

Ministries of the word are aimed primarily at man's spiritual need. Ministries of service are aimed primarily at man's physical needs. Does that make the former "infinitely" more important than the latter? No, and for two reasons. Much "service ministry" actually ministers the word as well, albeit indirectly. Acts of compassion by people known to be Christians are a powerful testimony; the acts themselves can draw people to Christ. A word hardly needs to be exchanged. Secondly, service ministries tremendously enhance the effectiveness of word ministries. In many parts of the world, there is little opportunity for word ministry apart from an accompanying service ministry. In Nepal, for example, missionaries can't get resident visas to stay in the country unless they are engaged in a service ministry acceptable to the government. And yet those service ministries have made possible a coexistent ministry of the word. In such a situation, who can say that service ministry is "less important"?

One thing must be kept in mind, however: the ministry of the word is always essential at some point if a person is to be reconciled to God. No one can be saved by service alone. Ministry of the word is indispensable to mission; without it, true mission does not exist.

Keeping this in mind protects us from the fuzzy notion that all we have to do is "go out and love people." Michael Griffiths says that a "mission society does not exist merely to bear a general witness to the love of Christ." Yes, love is our motive; it gives validity and power to all we do. But we must love people in such a way that they are drawn to Christ. At some point and in some form, they need the word. Giving "a cup of cold water" will gain us our reward (Mt 10:42), but it will do little for the recipient. What people need is "living water." Jesus said, "Everyone who drinks this water will be thirsty again, but whoever drinks the water I give him will never thirst. Indeed, the water I give him will become in him a spring of water welling up to eternal life" (Jn 4:13-14). From the perspective of eternity, if we do not reconcile a person to God—that is, if we do not lead him into eternal life—we have done virtually nothing for him. So whether we are considering ministry of word or ministry of service, there is only one yardstick by which to measure its usefulness and effectiveness: to what extent is our ministry contributing to our primary goal of reconciling men and women to God? To what extent is our ministry contributing to the winning of men and women to Christ and then making them disciples so that they in turn will go out and reconcile others?

Some people object at this point, saying that we are just using our service as a means to an end, as "bait" to get people to become Christians. They feel this is unethical, and that it will lead to "rice-Christians." Yes, it is possible to use our service ministry in unwise or unethical ways—to "build our own empire," for example. But the fact remains that ministries of both word and service are means to an end; they are "bait," and there is nothing wrong with that. We dislike the term "bait" because we associate it with fishing, where the fish are deceived and end up in the frying pan. But with Christian ministries, the "fish" are not deceived and they end up in heaven. Jesus did say, after all, that he would make us "fishers of men" (Mk 1:17).

In whatever ministry we are engaged, then, it is essential that we keep focused, that we keep our eye on the goal—the goal of reconciling men and women to God. For if we don't, we will quickly find ourselves pouring all of our time and energy and resources into meeting people's physical needs and thereby neglecting their spiritual needs. This is especially true in less developed countries, where we may have set out to address all needs—spiritual and physical—but quickly find that the physical needs are drowning out the spiritual ones. Whenever the meeting of physical need is carried out at the expense of meeting spiritual need, then our ministry has lost its focus; it has lost its balance.

Mission work in less developed countries presents a further dilemma: not only does the meeting of physical needs draw off time and resources available for meeting spiritual needs, but it also in many instances counteracts our overall spiritual ministry.

How can this happen? Take the example of medical work. By its very nature it focuses on physical needs. The patients are thinking about their bodies; the doctor is thinking about their bodies. It's difficult to get patients to think about spiritual needs under such circumstances. Even if we bring up the subject, our words usually fall on deaf ears, and the patients go away from our mission hospitals cured in body but less aware of their spiritual need than when they came.

It's almost as if our medical work was undermining our spiritual goal, and indeed it will if we do not take pains to guard against it. It's pertinent to note that we've often had more success spiritually with those who are not sick, such as the patient's family and relatives.

So there is this danger in all our service ministries of undermining our spiritual goal. By our service we encourage people to seek after better health, better education, better living standards. But Jesus did not emphasize these things. He said, "...seek first his kingdom and his righteousness, and all these things will be given to you as well" (Mt 6:33).

We, on the other hand, have gone out and given people "all these things," with the result that they end up with less incentive to seek God than they had before we began. Jesus warned, "Do not work for food that spoils, but for food that endures to eternal life" (Jn 6:27). But we, through our well-intentioned service ministries, have caused people to seek the "food that spoils" and have by the same measure thwarted their spiritual development. We have taken their eyes off their spiritual need.

Another closely related problem with service ministries is their tendency to produce weak Christians and weak churches. When a person comes to faith as a result of some physical or material benefit received, that faith is usually weak. Take away the benefit, and you take away the faith. In Nepal it is generally true that the weakest and slowest growing churches are those that have grown up in the shadow of a mission project. This is not an argument against mission projects! In many areas there would be no church at all if it hadn't been for a mission project. But it is a warning to us to do everything possible not to divert people from Jesus as a result of our ministries of service.

Numerous instances have been recorded where outside aid from Christian organizations has divided and paralyzed local believers and diverted their attention from spiritual matters. J. P. Masih of Union Biblical Seminary in Pune, India, has given this warning regarding the infusion of such aid: "The primary concern of new churches should be the spiritual growth of their members. Let us not confuse and destroy them with our well-meaning but misplaced emphasis on lesser or unnecessary matters."

There are some practical ways to avoid diverting people from Jesus. We should keep our service projects small and inexpensive. Where possible, we should major in community-based health care rather than hospital-based care, rural development rather than industrial development. People are distracted by our wealth. They are drawn to us by the jobs we offer and the training we provide. In their eyes our projects are big business. The more we can minimize this impression, the less people will be diverted from seeking Jesus.

The second practical way to avoid diverting people is to work in teams. The most effective mission work combines both word ministry and service ministry. Some team members spend most of their time in one or the other, but the total ministry of the team combines both together—even as we find it in the ministry of Jesus. The constitution of the United Mission to Nepal states that we will witness to Christ "by word and by deed." Both together is the best. But always remember: don't lose sight of the primary goal of all ministry—the reconciling of men and women to God. In poor countries especially, it takes constant vigilance to keep that goal in focus.

Meeting spiritual and physical need

All needs—including physical needs—are at root spiritual. The world's need, the world's suffering, is caused ultimately by man's sin, and it has been ever since Eden. Therefore, in the first instance, it is not the alleviation of suffering that is needed but the gospel. The struggle against hunger and poverty and ignorance is first of all a spiritual struggle. Acts of loving service, while necessary and good in themselves, cannot be a substitute for bringing the gospel to every tribe and nation. Indeed it can be said that evangelism is the most effective form of social action, because it deals with the root of the problem and not the symptom. If you want to overcome racism, preach the gospel, multiply churches, until more and more people believe Galatians 3:28 and Colossians 3:11. Then racial prejudice will fade away. If you want political reform, preach the gospel. If you want to eliminate poverty and ignorance, preach the gospel. Bring people into the kingdom of God, and the kingdoms of the world will begin to change. You transform society by transforming people, not the other way around.

This is all well and good until the missionary hits the mission field—a poor country, say—and is immediately swamped by physical needs. The missionary may be a Bible teacher or a surgeon or a secretary, but he or she will at once be surrounded by people who don't have enough food, who don't have enough water to irrigate their fields, whose houses are falling down, whose kids are malnourished, and whose wives have tuberculosis.

And so you pitch in. Love is spontaneous. It doesn't calculate how much time you spend each day in this ministry or that. You minister as you have opportunity, whether by word or by deed or both at once. If I see a need, whether physical or spiritual, and I have the means to meet it, I must do so; love requires it (Jas 3:17-18). What I minister depends on what I have and what I see. As John Stott has written: "The man who fell among robbers needed above all else at that moment oil and bandages for his wounds, not evangelistic tracts in his pockets!"

Yes, we missionaries (and all Christians) go out and minister to the needs we see, using the gifts and skills we have been given. But saying that does not solve our problem. In the first place, as we said earlier, needs are not of equal weight. The man among robbers needed the oil and bandages, but only for a brief moment of time. He needed the gospel for eternity.

And so let's look at our busy doctor, nurse, teacher, or development worker. They have spent all day administering oil and bandages, and evening comes and they are too exhausted to do anything but go to bed. And this goes on day after day after day. And all those people who got their wounds healed, their land watered, their kids fed, are spiritually in the same condition they were in before. The missionary feels utterly frustrated that he cannot go back and follow up those people and give them the words of eternal life. This is a fact of life, a tension experienced by missionaries working in poor countries, especially by those missionaries in the "service professions." And every effort must be made by mission planners, executives, and the missionaries themselves to reduce this tension, this sense of frustration. Either the individual missionary's role must be restructured, or he must have extra help on the team to meet the vast spiritual need that is going unmet.

The tension will never completely disappear; there are not enough hours in the day to meet all the needs that come our way. Some needs we will need to turn away from, not as the priest and Levite did—out of lovelessness—but rather because there are still greater needs pressing upon us. It is as we apportion our time and select what needs we'll meet that we must remember there is one need that is far greater than all the others—and that is man's need for Christ, for reconciliation with God.

Jesus himself experienced this same tension. He had been healing people in Capernaum, and as he was getting ready to leave, the people came to him and asked him to stay and be their resident physician. They had major needs. But Jesus said to them, "I must preach the good news of the kingdom of God to the other towns also, because that is why I was sent" (Lk 4:43).

If Jesus couldn't escape this tension, neither can we expect to. Some of us will be called to stay in Capernaum in our resident medical practices. But let us hope that still more will be called to follow Jesus "to the other towns also" in order to preach the good news of the kingdom of God.

A final word here about "spiritual work" versus "secular work." You'd think any full-time missionary would assume he was doing spiritual work. But for many missionaries, especially those in the service professions—health, education, agriculture, engineering—there is a feeling that they aren't doing "real missionary work." This feeling extends to people in the administrative offices and even to top mission leaders.

This feeling is, of course, false. The work of all these people is every bit as spiritual as the work of the evangelist and church planter. Indeed, everything we do is spiritual if it is done as unto the Lord. Even our holidays are "spiritual work." A. W. Tozer said, "It is not what a man does that determines whether his work is sacred or secular, it is why he does it."

Therefore, let us never think that one Christian work is more spiritual than another. And let missionaries never look down on those Christians at home or abroad who are not "full-time Christian workers." They are serving the Lord through their professions and careers; they are full-time Christian workers just as much as missionaries are. The entire concept of "full-time worker" is off the mark. All Christians are full-time disciples of Jesus, no matter what their profession or where they serve. Our profession and location by themselves have no bearing on our spirituality. The only question we need to ask is: Why do I do what I do—is it for the Lord?" Let us not answer that question lightly.

The sick, the poor, the oppressed

A large number of Christians remain suspicious of "social action," feeling that at best it is an unfortunate necessity, and at worst, an interloper that should not be part of world mission. These Christians, if they could, would leave social action out of their mission planning altogether.

Jesus didn't look at social action that way. He gives us his "three-year plan" for mission in two places in Luke's Gospel. The first is in Luke 4:18-19. "The Spirit of the Lord is on me, because he has anointed me to preach good news to the poor. He has sent me to proclaim freedom for the prisoners and recovery of sight for the blind, to release the oppressed, to proclaim the year of the Lord's favor."

The second is in Luke 7:22. "Go back and report to John what you have seen and heard: The blind receive sight, the lame walk, those who have leprosy are cured, the deaf hear, the dead are raised, and the good news is preached to the poor."

The emphasis on social action or ministry of service in these passages is impossible to miss. It cannot be spiritualized. Jesus was concerned for both the "poor in spirit" (Mt 5:3) and the "poor" (Lk 6:20). He proclaimed freedom not only from sin but also from poverty and ignorance. He gave sight to the physically blind as well as to the spiritually blind. He released both the spiritually oppressed and those oppressed by injustice and exploitation. And in both passages, he says that the good news is specially earmarked for the "poor."

The apostles had only one special request for Paul and Barnabas when the two came up to Jerusalem the first time: that they "should continue to remember the poor" (Gal 2:10). And many other passages highlight Jesus' and the early church's special concern for the poor and oppressed: the widows, the fatherless, the sick, the demon-possessed, and those with leprosy. Theirs was not just a theoretical concern for a class of people; they were concerned for individuals in need.

Likewise, in our various ministries, we must give special attention to the poor. We need not be worried that they make up a disproportionate percentage of new believers. In India, Christianity became known as the "religion of untouchables," because so many of the converts were drawn from that group. I somehow can't think that Jesus would have been displeased. Those are the very type of people he was especially concerned to minister to.

We cannot remain aloof from issues of social and economic injustice, which so much contribute to the poverty we see around us. There will be occasions for us to take a stand. There is a risk involved. In Nepal, up until four years ago, if missionaries had publicly opposed government exploitation, corruption, and curtailment of basic human liberties, all of which existed, they would have been thrown out of the country within the week. But there are discreet ways of stating one's position that in the long run may be more effective. In cases of blatant injustice, of course, one would need to oppose it openly and take the consequences—though always in consultation with the national church.

Without question, our loving concern for the poor and dispossessed is a powerful witness. We will not deserve a hearing for the gospel unless we can demonstrate love for people in their need, whatever that need may be. Nothing speaks so eloquently to our non-Christian neighbors as our love manifested in simple and practical ways.

One year in the area served by our mission hospital a famine occurred, and the mission was able to procure a large quantity of grain and other food, which they then distributed to the people in greatest need. Here was a case where compassionate medical and development work had been going on among the poor for years, yet it was widely said that bringing in this food was the "best thing" the mission ever did. It indeed made a powerful impact.

Most missionaries from the West are middle class. We need to be sensitized to the poor. We are rightly focused on cultural groupings—people groups—but we must not neglect to think in terms of social groupings— the poor and the rich. The poor must have priority in both the hearing of the word and in the partaking of social benefits. They are most in need of the latter, and they will be most responsive to the former.

In giving the poor priority, however, we can make three mistakes.

The first is to neglect the rich. Scripture gives us no warrant for doing this. Their spiritual need is the same as anyone else's. All men stand in equal need of salvation.

The second mistake we can make is to idealize the poor. Poverty alone does not make one more spiritual or more deserving of God's mercy. The poor enter the kingdom like everyone else: through repentance and faith. One can say that they are closer to being poor in spirit than the rich, and that when they cry out for help, God is more ready to listen. But in poverty itself there is no virtue, no glamor. It is degrading, and can as easily make one rebellious and bitter as it can make one humble and contrite.

The third mistake we make is to assign the wrong cause to poverty. Many say that the major cause of poverty is oppression of the poor by the rich, especially the rich West. This is simply not true. Insofar as we Western, middle-class missionaries have ignored our neighbor in need, we are guilty. This is true guilt, a signal given by our conscience that we need to set something right. But, as said earlier, we should not accept collective responsibility for the poverty of the Third World.

There are greater causes of poverty that the West has never been responsible for—even in colonial times. Speaking of the Indian subcontinent, one main cause of poverty is the fatalistic teaching of Hinduism, which militates against any effort to improve one's lot. Second, the socialistic policies adopted by the governments of the subcontinent have played a major role in the perpetuation of poverty. This fact is now finally dawning on everyone. Third, religious and social beliefs on the subcontinent discourage family planning. Overpopulation is, in the opinion of many, the greatest single cause of poverty in the Third World today. Fourth is the exploitation of the poor by the rich and powerful of their own countries. Fifth is widespread corruption.

And there are other causes; we shall be looking at poverty again in the next chapter. But we mention these main causes here so that we are not tempted to blame ourselves for the state of affairs we find in the Third World. Accepting false guilt will only distort our thinking and our strategies. It is not our responsibility to atone for social and economic wrongs perpetrated by others or by past generations. Our responsibility is to model Jesus' ministry, and by loving word and deed invite people into the kingdom of God.

One winter evening, as we were welcoming neighborhood Nepalis in for our weekly house-fellowship meeting, one small boy we hadn't seen before entered along with the rest. We were all muffled up against the cold (no central heating) with our socks and sweaters and shawls. But this young lad had on only the flimsiest torn T-shirt and a thin pair of shorts. There was nothing on his feet.

And it came back to me for the thousandth time that if we have no heart of compassion for such as these, then our whole missionary enterprise is a fake and a fraud. Our eyes must always be open for someone in need whom we can help in a wise and appropriate way (not by throwing money at him, as a rule). One wise and appropriate way of helping this young lad, in addition to giving him a sweater, would be to see if there were ways to improve the living condition of his immediate environment, his community—this being the major rationale for community development programs. In all our thinking and planning, in all our strategies and programs, let us not lose sight of the individual in need. Let us remember the compassion of Christ, and keep it at the heart of everything we do.

14

The Major Mission Ministries

In this chapter we shall look at the common ministries in which missionaries engage. To do justice to each ministry would require a book in itself, so of necessity the treatment here will be sketchy. It is not the purpose of this book to examine the professional aspects of the different types of work being carried out by missionaries. Other books are available on these subjects.

The first three sections below deal with ministries of the word. The last three deal with ministries of service.

Evangelism and church planting

Calling to mind the overall goal of missions—the reconciling of men and women to God—we must state unhesitatingly that the most important, indeed indispensable, means of accomplishing that goal are evangelism and church planting.

No matter what one's profession is, every missionary is a witness, a personal evangelist. It is the same for Christians in their home countries. Our daily prayer must be: Lord, keep me alert for every opportunity to witness. The words we choose and the way we relate to people will vary from culture to culture, but the basic message will be the same, and the spiritual need of the people will be the same.

The essential core ministry in missions is the winning of people to Christ and forming them into congregations—that is, evangelism and church planting. All other ministries depend for their spiritual fruitfulness on this one central element of the missionary enterprise. All those won to Christ through student work, medical and development work, and radio and literature work need ongoing nurture and discipling by a local church body. We must always think of evangelism and church planting together; they cannot exist separately. It is useless to win people to Christ and then leave them on their own as a bunch of individuals; they will quickly fall away. Not only must there be churches for new believers to join, but also it is the church which is going to be responsible for ongoing evangelism. Hence, in the same breath with church planting, we need to include discipling new believers and imparting to them the vision for further evangelism.

The greatest need on the mission field has always been and remains today the need for evangelists and church planters. And the greatest areas of need are obviously among those groups who are most unreached. People speak of doors closing to this type of missionary. Some doors close while others open. And doors closed to Western church planters may open to church planters from the Third World. Don't be troubled by closing doors; God holds the keys. "What he opens no one can shut, and what he shuts no one can open" (Rev 3:7). If a door should be temporarily closed to church planters, then we can send in some other kind of missionary—a doctor, a teacher, a tentmaker—until it opens again. We don't speak so much of closed doors these days, but of revolving doors.

J. Herbert Kane has said that "missionary work that doesn't include evangelism isn't missionary work at all." In many countries the "evangelism" will need to be very low-key, perhaps nothing more than personal witness or Bible studies within one's home to which non-Christians can be discreetly invited. The service ministries of health, education, and development have been aptly described as "pre-evangelism," the introducing of people to the love of Christ lived out in the lives of the missionaries. Whatever form it takes, "evangelism" must be taking place, or we do not have missions.

But even if evangelism is indispensable to missions, it is not complete without the formation of congregations. The ultimate objective of missions, then, is the planting of churches. Missionary work focused only on individuals will by itself accomplish little of lasting importance. It is congregations, not individual believers that bring lasting spiritual change to a people or nation. The church is the primary agent in God's plan to reconcile mankind to himself. The reconciling work that God began in Christ is now being continued by Christ's body, the church. The church is absolutely central to the accomplishment of God's purpose.

Evangelism implies no superiority. We are sinners showing other sinners where to find forgiveness. We preach not ourselves but Christ. It's true, people must be able to see Christ in us. But that doesn't mean we have to be "perfect" in order to evangelize; our job is to point to the "treasure" within our "jars of clay" (2 Co 4:7).

We must not let it pass when people try to put Christianity on a par with other religions. Our treasure is unique; our message is unique. We preach salvation by grace, not by works. We place more importance on motive than on outward action. We tell of a personal and loving God who has come to earth to save us. Our gospel is radically different from all other religions. We can evangelize with the absolute confidence that our gospel "is the power of God for the salvation of everyone who believes" (Ro 1:16).

A final caution about the gospel we bring, whether in its spoken or written or electronic form: it is not living and powerful unless the Holy Spirit carries it to the innermost heart of the receiver. It is possible to make an idol of the written or spoken word, and when we do that it becomes a dead letter. In all our ministries of the word, let us remember that the word itself is but a seed; it is God who gives the increase through the Holy Spirit.

God expects an increase; he expects results from our evangelism. We can't produce the results, but we can sure hinder them. We may mix the seed with alien material. We may stay only on the beaten paths, and so our sowing comes to naught. We may neglect to give water or manure, or to keep the weeds down. These are our responsibilities.

Sometimes God sends us into a field and tells us only to get the rocks out, to prepare the soil (Mk 1:2); but his eye is always on the eventual harvest.

Many missionaries have gone into an area and gotten no response to their message. They come away, reporting that the people are "hardened." But the problem may not be entirely with the people; it may be partly with the messenger. He may not have communicated clearly or relevantly. He may not have followed the customs of the people, and thus needlessly offended them. We can expect opposition, but let it not be because of something we, the messenger, did wrong. Some missionaries have brought rejection and persecution upon themselves—and then claimed they were suffering for Jesus' sake.

Some years back, during a period when propagating the Christian faith in any way was highly illegal, an independent missionary arrived in Nepal who described himself as an "apostle." He had even written the word "apostle" on his visa application, but since the Nepalis didn't know what it meant, they overlooked it. Now, there is a sense in which missionaries, in particular church-planting missionaries, can be called "apostles"; that wasn't the problem. The problem lay in the bluntness of the approach. This brother felt called upon to take the gospel directly to the king. So, within a short time of his arrival he asked for an appointment at the palace. The king was not available, he was told; he would have to see the king's secretary. This was distinctly second best, but the missionary kept the appointment, hoping that it would lead later to a royal audience. He presented the gospel forthrightly to the secretary. The secretary politely informed him of the laws of the land. The missionary expressed his opposition to the laws of the land and to Hinduism in general—including the king himself, who was considered to be an incarnation of the Hindu god Vishnu. It was a tour de force of confrontational evangelism. All this I learned from the brother himself; I believe I was the only missionary he met during his short stay in Nepal. He informed me that he had shaken from his feet the dust of the palace and of the entire country. I wondered where that left the rest of the three or four hundred missionaries working in Nepal at the time. He said it was our business whether or not we stayed on in Nepal, but we'd be wasting our time if we did. This brother got nowhere because of the way in which he delivered his message. Since his visit, the Nepali church has multiplied fiftyfold. I'm glad none of us followed his advice.

If the confrontational style of evangelism is rarely indicated, the arm-twisting style is even less so. Our aim is not to "make converts"; we can't do that anyway. That's the Holy Spirit's prerogative alone. Our aim in evangelism is to offer men and women the opportunity to accept Jesus as their Savior.

Furthermore, we must not induce people to become Christian by offering hope of material gain. We must use no pressure or enticement. But keep in mind that the words "pressure" and "enticement" will be variously defined, depending on who you're talking to. Opponents of the gospel say that the mere mention of sin or hell is a "pressure," and the mention of salvation is an "enticement." By this reasoning, it would also be a "pressure" to inform someone his house was on fire and suggest that he step out the door.

The principles of evangelism don't vary between "closed" countries and open countries. Public evangelism is restricted in the former, of course, but the question of pressuring people to accept Christ gets the same answer wherever we are: we don't apply pressure, for to do so is to violate the other person's integrity. He must remain free to choose Christ or not to choose him. But neither do we present the gospel dispassionately, as if people could take it or leave it, we couldn't care less. "We implore you.... Be reconciled to God" (2 Co 5:20).

All missionaries should have a clear understanding of the conversion process. The last two chapters of David Hesselgrave's excellent book, *Communicating Christ Cross-Culturally*, give a concise and helpful overview of the subject. It is important to note that conversion is a *process*. Yes, at a given *point* a person becomes a child of God and a citizen of the kingdom of heaven; nowhere does Scripture suggest that there is a "no-man's land" between God's kingdom and Satan's. But only God knows that point at which a person begins to truly believe in Jesus.

From our human perspective, we see the process, not the point, of conversion. A person at first turns and listens; then he is drawn toward Christ. He learns more; he ponders; he counts the cost; he wrestles. Then he decides. But it's still not over. There may be a period of doubt after the "decision" has been made. Indeed, if the decision is not sure, the person may fall away. It is in those first days after the decision is made that Satan's attacks are fiercest and the new convert most vulnerable. Oh, how important it is for us to support the new believer in those early days!

Missionaries (and others) often try to speed up the conversion process and to bring people quickly to the "point of decision." Here it is crucial to discern God's timing. The mission field is littered with premature "decisions" that have not held. Many people say they have "tried Christianity and it didn't work." But maybe it was our evangelistic method that didn't work! Those early stages in the conversion process cannot be neglected or short-cutted. People should not be rushed into a decision—so that we can count the hands raised in our meetings and write glorious reports back home.

We would do well to remember how Philip dealt with the Ethiopian eunuch, whom he found reading from the book of Isaiah. Philip could have asked right out, "Will you believe?" But instead he asked, "Do you understand what you are reading?" (Ac 8:30). Yes, we must bring people to a point of decision; but we must also make sure they understand what they are deciding.

As missionaries in foreign cultures, we need to broaden our understanding of the conversion experience. In particular, in many parts of the world people act corporately; they make corporate decisions rather than individual decisions. Heads of families make the decisions for the whole clan. Chiefs make decisions for the tribe. Eventually, each individual comes to share in that decision, but initially it may not seem as if the individual has made a decision at all.

How are we to view "corporate conversions"? With latitude. Nothing, of course, replaces the individual's personal faith in Christ as Lord and Savior. But in corporate conversions that faith takes time to fully develop. Such conversions often take place incrementally. We see this in children, certainly; it is also true for adults. We dare not disparage these group "conversions." These people are taking the first steps of faith, which will eventually lead on to personal commitment. They need encouragement and, above all, teaching. And let us not forget, many individual conversions are also suspect; individuals also come to Christ with a mixture of motives.

In many Third World societies, if you want to get a hearing for your message, you first approach the headman of the village, or the local political leader. Take your time; build up trust. If you do, you may win a village; it you don't, you may get run out of town. Furthermore, if one or two individuals respond to your message, don't rush them right out to make a public confession of faith. It may be wiser to wait until several more have believed, and then to let them make a public confession together. If only one or two "step out" of the culture, they lose their influence, and possibly even their place in the society. We need to leave our Western rules and timetables at home.

Before new converts can have an influence in their own societies, people want to know their motive for becoming a Christian. Were they bought? Enticed? Tricked? Pressured? Are they sincere?

The believers that grew up around our mission hospital were looked down on by the villagers as being "rice Christians." The villagers were sure they all were getting some material advantage out of their association with the missionaries—though many of them were not. Then one day two of the believers were arrested and threatened with a jail sentence and the loss of everything if they did not recant. They stood firm and went to jail; and from that day on the attitude of the villagers toward all the Nepali Christians changed. They weren't any happier that the Christians had "changed their religion" and left the traditional ways, but at least they now respected them for being sincere. As a result, the effectiveness of the believers' witness was greatly increased.

If the sincerity of new converts is closely questioned, you can be sure the missionaries' sincerity will be questioned also. We don't only proclaim the gospel, we demonstrate it. Any discrepancy between our words and our deeds will be noticed immediately, and the credibility of our words will be reduced to that degree.

People will especially be looking for our love. We are not just witnessing to souls but to people. Many an unbeliever has said, "If the missionary had cared as much about me as he cared about my soul, I might have heeded what he said."

On the other side, many a believer has said, "I became a Christian because I saw Christ manifested in the lives of other Christians." The most powerful persuasion comes not from words, but from a Christlike life. We must live the life we preach every waking hour; we're being watched all the time.

Yet people will say of us, "He's just a foreigner. That's his nature." They don't give credit to Christ in us, but rather to our foreignness. That is why nationals are potentially more effective witnesses and evangelists than foreign missionaries. No one can brush off the change in their lives by saying they are foreign. This is why those early converts are so important. Spend more time on them than on your sermons, for they will become "living sermons" to the people around them. It is also one reason, in mixed missionary-national teams, why nationals should do most of the evangelizing: they'll have a greater impact. Plus, they speak the language better!

From the moment people begin coming to Christ, they should be taught to start reaching out to win others. There was a time in Korea when a new convert had to bring two other people to the Lord before he could be baptized. Not biblical, you sniff, but look what has happened to the Korean church! A new convert is a powerful witness; fresh from his old life, he is eager to tell friends and acquaintances about his new life. We should be doing everything we can to encourage new believers to witness.

If each new convert is taught to witness, the new churches are going to be witnessing churches. Too often missionaries have been guilty of creating "country-club" churches, which exist solely to support and entertain their members. We need to be forming mission-minded churches from day one.

There are two restraints: poverty and persecution. The nationals are poor, we say; how can they support evangelists and missionaries? And so we all too often have taught them to receive instead of to give. But even poor churches can send missionaries. Ten members can support a pastor if they tithe, and just ten more can support an evangelist or missionary. Newly planted churches need to see this as their duty. It is a great mistake to underwrite the evangelistic outreach of a new church with outside funds. Timely contributions, yes; but total financing, no. The church must take primary responsibility for its own outreach.

A second restraint is found in "closed" countries where it may be dangerous for nationals to witness openly, much less send out missionaries. We missionaries feel hesitant to exhort them to witness for Christ, because the risks for them are vastly greater than the risks for us. In most cases we'll simply be deported back to our comfortable and affluent countries, whereas the nationals will be disinherited, lose their jobs, be driven from their homes, and even imprisoned. How can we tell them to take risks that we'll never have to take ourselves?

Let Jesus tell them. Point them to the many places in the New Testament where Jesus and the apostles make no bones about the risks and dangers that any follower of Christ must expect to face. And then be ready to stand with them in every way possible if they should be called to suffer.

This is why it was such a great event in Nepal when the first two Westerners (referred to in Chapter Three) were put in prison for evangelistic activities. One of them wrote from jail that he rejoiced at the opportunity to suffer alongside his Nepali brethren. And the Nepali Christians, for their part, finally believed that we missionaries were ready to take the same risks they had been taking all along.

Once a missionary has planted a church, what should his role be thereafter? For many church-planting missionaries the answer will be to move on, as did the apostle Paul. The error is usually made in the direction of staying too long, which creates dependency and stifles the development of national leaders. Even if the missionary doesn't consider himself indispensable, he will feel that the new church needs his continued presence, guidance, and inspiration. In some cases it may be true—provided the missionary takes his hands off the controls.

A good rule is to leave *before* you think the church is completely ready. In fact, it won't be completely ready until you do leave. It is usually the missionary who isn't ready: he's not ready to stand down. Also it's wise to leave before people begin asking you to leave. After all, it's bad enough being dominated by one of your own, but being dominated by an outsider is doubly bad.

Sometimes the newly planted church has asked the missionary to stay on. In such cases the missionary will need God's leading to discern where he is going to be most useful. Many missionaries have served the national church in varying capacities, worked under the national leadership, and made valuable contributions. Other missionaries working under national leadership have felt frustrated and hamstrung. Each case must be individualized. One guideline we can state is that the missionary should not take a post in the church that a national can do just as well.

This is not because the missionary doesn't belong to the church as fully as anyone else. The reason is practical: it is best to let the ongoing work of the church be carried on by the most permanent people in the community, which will ordinarily be the nationals.

A cautionary note is needed here: from the moment the new missionary hits the field he or she will be greeted by the chorus: "Work yourself out of a job." As we said earlier, this is fine as long as it's understood to mean: "Train a national and then move on to another job on the mission field." The idea that foreign missionaries have been so busy working themselves out of jobs all these years that there are now fewer missionary jobs to go around is completely untrue. Wherever we go we are creating new jobs for both nationals and foreigners, because we are constantly opening up new areas. And even so, there are still more people to be reached than at any time in history—thanks to a little factor called fertility. Work myself out of a job? Impossible.

As for the mission agencies and the missionaries who are invited to continue helping the newly established national churches, there are at least four main ways in which they can usefully contribute. The first is the area of technical skills and the giving of specialized training; the second is in financial support for new initiatives; the third is continued evangelism in new areas; and fourth is participation in the ongoing process of indigenization and contextualization. We shall conclude this section by examining these four areas.

First, the technical area is straightforward. Missionaries from developed countries bring skills in computers, literature production, radio and television evangelism, as well as professional skills in the health, engineering, agriculture, and administrative fields. Not only are these technical and professional skills themselves needed, but above all, it is necessary to pass on these skills to the national church insofar as is practical. Missionaries are well-suited to provide this training.

It bears repeating that the greatest and most crucial role that missionaries can play on the mission field—whatever their particular skill or profession—is to train nationals, to pass on their knowledge and skills. Jesus was a great preacher, teacher, and healer, but he spent most of his time and effort training just twelve men. Whatever skill we bring to the mission field, the most important thing we can do with it is to pass it on.

The second area is financial support. Some missionaries go to one extreme and say that the national church should be totally self-supporting. Others go to the opposite side and continue subsidizing the church, hoping gradually to wean it away from outside money. A helpful compromise is to fund new initiatives and other one-time expenses, but let the church be responsible for ongoing expenses and ministries.

It seems hard to be "wise" in this matter of helping national churches financially. There is no question they need and deserve our help, just as the Jerusalem church needed and deserved the help of the Greek churches in Paul's day—though there the money flowed from new churches to old. The obligation of the well-off to channel resources to the poorly off is reaffirmed again and again throughout the Bible.

But experiences differ widely. Some Christian groups have reduced or withdrawn financial support and seen revival break out in the national church. Was it as a result of less outside money? These groups believe so. But on the other side, people like Donald McGavran speak of numerous people movements that have been nipped in the bud for lack of financial support. Missionaries involved have withheld money, and the movement has fizzled. What a horrible tragedy—if indeed a lack of money was the cause.

How do we choose between these two extremes? The best advice is not to. Pray through each case. Pray for wisdom. Don't set fixed policies. But if we could offer one guideline it would be this: Err on the side of not giving when ongoing expenses are involved; and err on the side of giving when unusual need or opportunity is involved. This will give you a basically self-supporting church, which can then count on the timely assistance of the more affluent churches of the West.

The third area in which missionaries can make a contribution to the national church is in evangelistic outreach to new areas. We have already mentioned the possibility of financial support for such initiatives, but here we are talking about the missionary him- or herself. The national church can assign a foreign missionary to head up a new outreach, even a cross-cultural outreach.

In practice this happens too little. If missionaries are conscious of their "turf," you can bet national churches are too; they learned it from us. The ordinary national church, if it does any outreach at all, usually wants to run its own show. If they would just put on a "show," fine; the missionary could go elsewhere. But too often the church doesn't have an evangelistic program, and won't ask for help in starting one. The missionary then has no reasonable choice but to move on.

Because the Third World church has been so far unable and in some cases unwilling to shoulder the burden of reaching out to the unreached people groups around them, it falls to the worldwide church to continue doing so. World missions cannot be dependent on national churches, or else the job will not get done. What is required is a continuing cross-cultural mission advance until every last people group has its own self-multiplying indigenous church. Let all do their share as they are able.

Nepal is a case in point. The church is only forty years old. God has planted his church in about a dozen of Nepal's hundred or more people groups. Vast parts of the country remain unreached. We need to encourage the Nepali church to begin its own cross-cultural mission outreach to these unreached areas. Each area needs its own indigenous church. It's not enough to say the "Nepali church"; a church is needed for every tribe in Nepal.

Meanwhile, foreign missionaries should do their part too. Several groups have been working in Nepal for years, side by side with members of the national church. They have sent out small international teams into every corner of the country. Let such work continue until the job is done.

It's not important who is doing the job; the important thing is that it gets done, whether by the national church, foreign mission societies, small international teams, or a combination. We need to ask: Are we effectively breaking new ground? Are we penetrating unreached cultures and subcultures? If we're not, it's time we started.

A dangerous new teaching is gaining popularity: it says that the responsibility for the evangelization of a country rests solely with the national church of that country. This teaching is not taken from the Bible; it is taken from nationalism. Some Westerners have adopted it out of a misguided desire to "give place" to the emerging national churches. But as we have indicated, in many instances the national churches are not doing the job. The unreached remain unreached. That is everyone's responsibility.

Finally, let us look at the fourth area in which missionaries can have an ongoing contribution to the newly established national church, the area of indigenization and contextualization. The missionaries' chief contribution will be providing historical perspective and biblical scholarship.

All agree that the national church must be "indigenous." By indigenous we mean, at the very minimum, that the national church be "self-supporting, self-governing, and self-propagating." However, these terms can easily become buzz-words, witness the "three-self" church in China, which at times has seemed more a branch of the government than a church. Indeed, it is quite possible to have "three-self" churches that are totally lifeless. So the three-self concept is only the beginning. Beyond that, the church must be alive, growing, reaching out, and sacrificially expending itself. Only then can it be said to be mature. The ultimate sign of maturity is when the church begins sending out its own missionaries.

The word "indigenous" also carries the connotation, "of or pertaining to the local culture." Some national churches carry indigenization so far that they reject everything foreign and isolate themselves from the worldwide church. In doing so, they impoverish themselves. A mature church is free to develop its own indigenous forms and is also free to borrow good things from other cultures.

The new national church must find a middle ground between adapting too much to the local culture and adapting too little. If the church adapts too little, it will remain isolated and irrelevant, a cultural anomaly. Non-believers will be repelled, and even if they are attracted to Jesus, they will not be attracted to his church. This, of course, defeats the main purpose of the church, which is to win people to Christ. The church exists primarily for unbelievers, after all, not believers. Therefore, the church must adapt enough to the local culture that it will be seen as an indigenous and not an alien organization.

Too much adaptation, on the other hand, is just as bad as too little. In this case, the church merges so much with the surrounding culture that it loses its distinctiveness, its savor. This is especially true when the church compromises on issues of doctrine or morality. When this happens, the church ceases to be salt and light. It loses its voice, and along with it, all power to transform society.

It is primarily the leaders of the national church who must decide how far they should go in adapting to the local culture, that is, how far they should go in contextualizing the gospel. They best understand the cultural and religious traditions of their society and can test them in the light of Scripture to see if they can be accepted, or whether they must be modified or rejected altogether. But missionaries can add valuable insight to these debates, and they should not withhold their counsel simply on the grounds that it's a "national-church affair."

The principles are not complicated. All cultures have many aspects that do not conflict at all with biblical principles. Let the church adopt these harmless indigenous forms. Let them have their own style of music: the clapping, the dancing, the popular tunes—though with Christian lyrics. Let them "Christianize" some of the local festivals. Let them have three-hour church services. Let them pray all at once—a cacophony to our ears, but a pleasing sound to God, who can hear each prayer. Let the liturgy, the architecture, the trappings all be colored by the local culture.

But when it comes to morality and doctrine, the bedrock commands of Scripture, there can be no compromise. The ten commandments and the law of love do not change from culture to culture. The worship of idols in any form cannot be tolerated. These and other clear standards of Scripture must be maintained, and any cultural tradition that violates these standards must be discarded.

So far, no problem. The question arises, however: What constitutes a violation of Scripture? For example, is ancestor worship true worship, or is it merely profound respect? What do you say to the believing wife who is forced to carry out the household religious rituals? Could she say, as Paul did, "Idols are nothing; this has no meaning for me"? Or must she refuse and take the terrible consequences? What about the subjugation of Third World women in general? In Nepal, as we saw earlier, a believing woman needs the permission of her husband before the church will baptize her. Can such cultural practices be squared with Scripture?

There are all kinds of ambiguities like these which need to be worked through. But it is no mere theoretical exercise. Some of these issue are life-and-death matters for the individuals concerned. In many cases a missionary's entire work can be jeopardized and the local Christians scattered or imprisoned for refusal to abide by some local custom. In some cases the social pressure on believers can be so great that the only choice they see is to recant, or to die.

Not long after my wife and I arrived in Nepal, a beautiful twenty-year-old girl named Maya was admitted to the mission hospital where we were working. She was one of the few female high-school graduates in Nepal at the time, an especially rare distinction for a village girl. And in addition, she was a Christian. There couldn't have been more than three or four Christian female high-school graduates in the entire country. And the worst of it was: Maya was dying.

Our problem was that we didn't know the cause of her illness. She had a bizarre form of respiratory paralysis, and no matter what we did she kept getting worse. We repeatedly questioned her family concerning her medical history; we pored through the books; we prayed. Finally we inserted an endotracheal tube into her windpipe, and assigned the hospital maintenance man to pump the breathing bag. In this way we were able to keep her alive for two more days. In the end, her family called it quits. If you can't breathe on your own in the hills of Nepal, you've pretty much come to the end of your road. Such was the family's reasoning. So we pulled the tube, and after some agonizing moments of watching Maya struggle to breathe, she passed away.

Maya had been in the hospital a week. All through her ordeal, she had exhibited extraordinary courage and faith. Many people were deeply moved. The testimony of her death seemed to be as powerful as the testimony of her life.

Then the very next day after her death we received two pieces of news, which together had the effect of a bomb going off in the pit of our stomachs. First, a local shopkeeper casually informed us that Maya had bought two cans of bedbug poison from him a week earlier. (She had denied taking poison.) And second, our first issue of the Nepal Medical Association Journal came that day, the lead article of which described all the cases of bedbug poisoning treated over the past year at the big government hospital in Kathmandu. The symptoms described were exactly the same as Maya's. And the treatment? Atropine, of which our hospital pharmacy had a full supply. Her inspiring death had suddenly turned into a depressing suicide. And we had watched her die with the treatment close at hand.

Why had she killed herself? Shortly after she had become a Christian, her family married her off to a Hindu man, who strongly opposed her faith. According to Nepali custom, Maya remained in her own home for a year after her wedding. But the day came when she was required to move in with her husband and his parents. Then she would be forced to follow the Hindu customs. She would be the virtual slave of her new mother-in-law. She would be prevented from seeing her old friends, especially those who had led her to the Lord. She saw no escape, except the one she chose.

In one sense, I have no regrets about Maya, for I believe she is with God; and that, after all, is the ultimate point in becoming a Christian. But often now, when I hear of dramatic conversions and thrilling answers to prayer, I think of Maya and wonder what I've not been told. We talk so easily about the "abundant life," the power, the peace, the joy that is to be found in Christ; and it's all true. But we also need to reckon with the misery, the despair, the isolation that can result from becoming a Christian in a country like Nepal. And we, both missionaries and national church leaders, need to do everything we can to minimize unnecessary hurt, to avoid wrenching people out of their families and setting them adrift from their cultural moorings. And, above all, we need to nurture in new believers a deeper spiritual life, which will enable them to count all suffering but joy for the sake of Christ.

Literature, literacy, radio, and television

I used to feel sorry for those engaged in "literature work"—especially when furlough and deputation time came around. Other missionaries have all kinds of dramatic stories to tell and slides to show, but what on earth is the poor guy in literature work—yawn—going to say to keep his listeners awake? And then in a roundabout way I got into literature work myself. My solution on furlough now is to keep showing my medical slides and talk about literature on the side.

It may be dull to talk about, but no one denies the indispensable role that literature plays in the Christian movement worldwide. Our libraries at home prove it. Our pastors in the West have hundreds of books at their disposal. Bibles are printed in the millions.

But when we get to the mission field, everything is in short supply. Nowhere is the shortage more glaring than on the bookshelves of national pastors. The average Indian pastor owns six books—most of them in English. J. Herbert Kane writes in his book *Life and Work on the Mission Field:* "Why should we not make sure that the national pastors are supplied with the helps they so desperately need.... There is no greater need on the mission field today. Funds invested in this way will pay the highest dividends not only for time but also for eternity."

But we're getting ahead of ourselves. If Bibles and other books are to be utilized, people must learn to read. Thus literacy work must go hand and hand with literature. Literacy campaigns received much of their early impetus from missionaries, most notably Frank Laubach, who developed a simplified method of teaching literacy. In recent years governments have taken over the major share of ensuring that their citizens are literate, but there is much that remains to be done in the poorer nations.

In Nepal, for example, the literacy rate is thirty-three percent. The government is working to improve that figure, but because of meager resources progress is slow. So the churches in Nepal have begun to take matters into their own hands, as churches have done in other lands. It is heartwarming to walk a day or two out to a remote village of a hundred or more Christians and at night, when the field work is done, see them gather around a kerosene lamp to learn to read from a younger church member just back from a literacy teaching seminar in Kathmandu. A strong church is a literate church. If God gave us his written word, he expects us to learn to read it.

But going back one step further, before one can become literate there must a written language to become literate in. And it is in this area that Wycliffe Bible Translators have made their tremendous contribution to missions. Just in tiny Nepal, they have reduced to writing over a dozen of the eighty or so unwritten languages and produced the New Testament in ten of them.

And do these people have stories to tell! No dull deputation talks from this group. One couple we know has worked for fifteen years in one of Nepal's remotest areas; they have to walk seven days just to get to the place. And now those people have a New Testament, and a church—and persecution.

Another couple worked in a village of five thousand people located two days' walk north of our hospital. We used to conduct medical clinics in that village. I remember coming to the village for a clinic not long after this couple had started working there. They were living in one room of the tiny village *panchayat* house, which served as village meeting place. Their presence prompted, in effect, a non-stop "town meeting," as curious villagers stopped by on their way to and from their fields to peer in at these strange white-faced people. Children and old folks stood by for hours monitoring their every movement. One night they invited me to supper. As there was no place to eat inside their room, we ate in the courtyard. By the time we had finished our meal we were surrounded by a large, silent circle of people three deep, the outer rows jostling to get a better view. People speak of missionaries living in fishbowls or bird cages, but I think it's more like a one-ring circus where you are the clowns. Except these people weren't laughing. They had grave misgivings about foreigners coming to their village, and they still do. But not the two or three dozen believers among them, who have sprung up largely because of this couple's work. The believers even publish a newsletter and have just started a youth group. And the church is planted in yet one more village that once was in total darkness.

People often ask: Why spend so many years getting the New Testament into an unwritten language, when the number who will benefit are only a few thousand, many of whom speak the national language anyway? Good question.

The main answer is that more people respond to the gospel when it is presented in their own mother tongue. In Nepal, virtually every male and probably half the females can speak Nepali, the national language. But they may not know it well; they use it mainly for trade. Their vocabulary in Nepali may be limited to matters of business and politics; it would usually be inadequate for understanding spiritual concepts. Thus for the large language groups in Nepal it is definitely worthwhile to give them the scriptures in their own language. And for the women who don't speak Nepali, it may be the only way they will ever understand the gospel.

For those societies that have a well-established written language with its own body of literature, a question arises as to what literary level should our Christian literature be pitched. In many countries there is a "literary" language and a "common" language. In some cases the ordinary folk understand the literary language about as well as we can understand Chaucer. Who should we write for?

The New Testament itself gives us the clue; it was written in everyday Greek. But in less-developed countries even our "everyday" language may be beyond the ready comprehension of many. So the best of all solutions is to produce a " common-language Bible" in addition to the standard translation. After all, when English speakers have over a dozen translations to choose from, two doesn't seem that extravagant.

As a national church is established and begins to grow, it needs an ever increasing supply and variety of literature. Too little attention is given to this aspect of the church's ministry. Financing literature projects is an ideal way in which Western Christians can help the Third World church. And we can get into the business of distribution too. One of the organizations that has done the most to stimulate the production and distribution of literature all over the world is Operation Mobilization. OM'ers establish bookshops, hold book fairs, send out roving teams of evangelists to sell books, and even operate two ships that serve as floating book stores. They rightly say that those who buy books read them. And if anyone is still tempted to think that "literature work" is boring, I suggest he do a stint with OM; he'll be quickly disabused of that notion!

What literature does the church need in addition to Scriptures? First in order of priority is a hymnal. Then come Bible study aids, the most essential of which will be a basic commentary.

At the same time these are being prepared, tracts can be cheaply produced, each targeted to a different group with its own special needs. Don't underestimate the effectiveness of tracts. One of the most respected church leaders in Nepal came to Christ through a tract, and there are many others who tell a similar story. As we have walked the trails of Nepal, we have observed a tremendous hunger for the written word. When you stop at a teashop and give out a tract, it will likely be grabbed up by a young schoolboy who will then begin to read it out loud. Everyone in earshot promptly gathers around—other kids, old grannies, farmers, schoolteachers—and soon you have ten, twenty, or more people listening to the word of life. You hardly need to know the language to pass out tracts.

Once my wife Cynthia and I were walking along a trail a day's walk from the hospital. A man recognized us and called us into his house where he showed us a well-worn gospel of Luke. A year earlier he had been to the hospital for treatment and had taken Luke's gospel home with him. He and his wife couldn't read, but his school-age son had been reading it to them almost daily. He wanted to know if we had another booklet with us like the first; so we gave him the gospel of John. "My word will not return to me empty," says God (Isa 55:11). Let us do our part to make his word available.

Other vehicles for the word each have their important place; gospel recordings on tapes and records are essential for people who cannot read. You can walk through the villages of Nepal and here and there you will see old people, perhaps blind with cataracts, sitting on their verandah, and at their side will be a younger person cranking away at a hand-operated tape player. They will be listening to the gospel.

And then there are the radio and television ministries. Christian missions operate major radio stations around the world, which broadcast in over one hundred languages. There isn't a place on earth that is not reached, including the remotest valleys of Nepal.

Radio and television ministries are so expensive to start up that Western resources will be needed for a long time to come. So capital intensive are these projects that even Western agencies must band together in cooperative ventures to eliminate waste and duplication. Joint organizations have now been set up on every continent to coordinate these large projects.

The advantages of radio ministry in particular are clear. Transistor radios are everywhere; there's hardly a village in the world without one. Literacy is not required to understand the message. Many people can be reached at one time. No country is closed to radio waves, though jamming does occur. In lands where to be Christian invites persecution, the listeners can listen privately to the gospel in their homes. Finally, the radio prepares the ground; it paves the way for the missionary to follow.

Television is now coming of age in Third World cities, and has many of the advantages of radio ministry listed above. Even in Kathmandu, the sign of the upper class has now become a television antenna sticking up from the roof, while the very rich will have a satellite dish as well. The main drawback to television so far is that its audience is much more limited.

We cannot leave this subject without mentioning film—in particular, the Jesus film, which by now has been shown in hundreds of places all over Nepal (not to mention the world). All you need is to strap a portable generator on your back and you can show it anywhere.

All of these evangelistic tools should have one primary aim: to bring people to a point of decision and final acceptance of Christ, and to incorporate them into a nearby church. So whatever the particular message or Bible portion, add at the end an evangelistic exhortation, as well as a suggestion that the reader or listener seek out other believers for fellowship and follow-up. And don't emphasize individual conversion to the exclusion of group conversion; both are biblical.

There is one thing lacking in the media technology we have been describing: the missionary. Sending in only radio messages, tapes, and books is not sufficient: we must send the messenger. Sending in the message without the messenger is like waging a war with artillery and aircraft alone. You need foot soldiers to possess the land. Occasionally the message will do the trick by itself, but not often. You need a person to hand out the tract and then explain it. You need a fellowship group that inquirers can go to for fellowship and discipling. The gospel needs to be personified, embodied. Even God needed to be "embodied." Technology will never do away with missionaries.

Theological education

"Theological education" begins in Sunday school and ends in the seminary. Every bit of it is crucial to the development and growth of the church. Let us not neglect the "less prestigious" forms of training and education, such as Sunday school work. Early in the church's development, the teaching of children should take an important place, and suitable materials prepared for that purpose. In Nepal, though the church is still relatively young and small, an ambitious project is underway to provide Sunday school materials nationwide. The project is being spearheaded by two young missionary teachers, one from the Netherlands and the other from Singapore.

Theological Education by Extension, or TEE, was developed in Latin America to train pastors who could not attend seminary. Thousands of churches in the Third World go without pastors, or have pastors who lack necessary training. Many pastors have other full-time jobs, or have to work their farms to survive. TEE meets their need for further training.

Bible correspondence courses are another teaching tool. Though its purpose is mainly evangelistic, it still provides basic Christian education to new believers, and so I include it here. Correspondence courses are of particular value in countries where Christianity is frowned upon; inquirers can take the course without having to attend public meetings where they might be seen. In Nepal, almost sixty thousand people have taken these courses over the past ten years. And remember, just forty years ago there was not even one Christian in the country!

More formal theological education takes place at different levels. First are the schools of evangelism and discipleship lasting one to three months. These are being conducted all over the world by such groups as Campus Crusade for Christ and Youth With A Mission.

Bible schools and institutes have been established in most of the cities of the Third World, excepting China and some Muslim countries. These schools offer one- to three-year courses. Nepal now has five of these schools.

The final level is the four-year seminary. As with seminaries every-where, there is a natural tendency to emphasize academic disciplines to the detriment of practical skills. On the mission field, this tendency should be vigorously countered. Half of the seminary time should be de-voted to gaining the practical skills needed to lead and multiply churches. The level of education must be geared to the needs of the church in each country. The Western model of seminary education will not be appropri-ate for most of the Third World.

For example, will seminary graduates still be willing to fan out across their respective countries and lead churches, or will they choose rather to stay only in a few large cities in prestigious positions? Will the semi-naries turn out men of God or men of only book learning? A degree is even more coveted in the Third World than it is in the West; it is the passport to a good life. For a church leader, it can be a snare as well as a blessing.

Most Third World seminaries and Bible institutes receive much of their financing from Western churches, and this is proper. The problem comes when each denomination feels it must establish its own de-nominational institution. This is all right when a country is prosperous and has a strong church, as in Korea. Some years back, Korea had one hundred and seventy theological schools averaging ten students each. That can't even be good for Korea, but if it happened elsewhere in the developing world it would be preposterous. In theological education, as in the high-tech communications business, missions and denominations need to cooperate in order to avoid duplication and inefficiency. If the pursuit of our own denomination's agenda leads us to waste God's re-sources, it is a sin against the Lord we profess to serve. And if the semi-nary we have established turns out graduates that refuse to fellowship and cooperate with those of other denominations, we have sinned against Christ's own body. In the former case, we will have only weakened it; in the latter case, we will have cut it to pieces.

One of the finest examples of cooperation in theological education is the Union Biblical Seminary in Pune, India. It was established by a con-sortium of over thirty missions and churches, and has a student body of two hundred. The first six Nepali seminarians were graduates of that in-stitution.

Only rarely should national Christians be sent to the West for higher learning. They should be chosen first of all by their fellow church lead-ers—or else, when they return, they will not find a ready place. Too often a missionary develops a protege, who is then sent off for training in the West by the missionary's home church. Such trainees often do not fit back into the national church, and their potential is wasted. They may even "lose touch" with their own people. It is much better to train people locally or in an adjacent country.

The Third World church does need a few Ph.D.'s, however. They are needed to develop an indigenous theology and to take the lead in contextualizing the gospel for their respective cultures. Nepal just recently acquired her first native Doctor of Theology, a fine Christian man who did his studies at Oxford.

Since Western financing is almost always involved in the sending of nationals abroad for study, we need to look at how that money is used— and misused. In most cases, candidates for higher education are easily agreed upon by both the missionary community and the national church leadership. Funding is then solicited with full consultation between the field and home, and the training takes place with good results. Obviously, candidate selection is the most crucial factor in ensuring a good outcome.

Things can go wrong, however, when the home church or organization takes the initiative and begins "looking for its man," who once found, can be trained and sent back to "head up the work" in Nepal or wherever. The missionary plays an essential role here, because the home people need some advice in choosing "their man." Their man is going to have to be a very mature Christian, who can withstand the temptations of working with a rich Western organization or church. Such a position often gives a national Christian an income higher than that of local doctors and engineers—quite the reverse of the West, where doing Christian work entails a financial sacrifice. Above all, before such a man is selected, let there be wide consultation with the national church leadership. For Western-based groups to make decisions without such consultation with missionaries and church leaders on the field is worse than folly; it is extremely harmful. They may choose a national who is spiritually unqualified. The national will be tied to strings pulled from overseas. The overall work on the field will be fragmented. Other Christian workers supported indigenously at lower salary levels may become jealous of the high-rolling worker with outside funding. Backbiting and division result. And all the while, the people at home remain unaware of the problem they are causing. They say, "Oh, but the national worker's salary is so dreadfully low" (by their standards). They say, "We who give the money should have some say in how it's used." Yes, as long as their "say" does not cause conflict and disruption on the field.

Even in the little country of Nepal we have had our share of national Christians whose heads have been turned by outside money. The most tragic case involved one of the main leaders of the early Nepali church. He started being sponsored by a Western-based agency that specializes in supporting "indigenous workers." This agency, sadly, was not content merely to support this pastor; it persistently misrepresented the situation in Nepal, and in its literature stated that this pastor was doing the only truly indigenous Christian work in Nepal. This was false. Worse, this pastor had fallen out of fellowship with the great majority of Nepali church leaders and had disgraced himself in their eyes. Yet he continued to be invited to the West to "represent the Nepali church." It was a case of the agency needing the pastor as much as the pastor needing the agency.

Missionaries who stay on the field for long will sooner or later find themselves in the middle of such problems. Missionaries know the situation on the field far better than the "experts" from outside. It's a pity that they have to spend so much of their time and energy trying to undo the problems that have been created by well-meaning Christians at home.

Healing

The next three headings deal with the main "ministries of service," as distinguished from the "ministries of the word," which we have discussed above. Service ministries are not poor cousins to word ministries; they are partners. The first of these that we'll look at briefly is the healing ministry.

Medical missions need no justification. Not only was healing one of the ministries of Jesus himself, but also the miracles of healing were one of the major factors attesting to the truth and power of the gospel. John calls them "signs" in his gospel. They were signs of the kingdom, signs of both Jesus' power and his love. As the Father sent Jesus, so Jesus sent out his disciples. The apostles healed many. And the followers of Jesus have been healing people ever since.

Jesus never looked on healing—or any ministry—as an end in itself. "Doctors merely delay death," the saying goes, and when put in those terms, the medical profession doesn't sound quite so romantic. If healing is an end in itself, then the end is death. Surely Christian medical workers want to set their sights on something better than that!

Healing draws crowds, even as in Jesus' day. The crowds can then be taught, not only about physical health but about spiritual health also. The medical team is uniquely able to point people to Christ. It can be done openly through evangelistic services by hospital chaplains and by literature distribution, or in closed countries it can be done more discreetly.

Literature is on racks, doctors and nurses pray for their patients, social workers counsel individually with patients, prayer meetings are open to all.

Healing ministries break down barriers and build trust. People are then more open to what we say, even on non-medical subjects. National evangelists report a greater openness and receptivity among people served by mission hospitals. Many of the people will have been one or more times to the hospital, and experienced firsthand the love of the Christian staff. Then, when an evangelist comes to their village, they are more ready to listen.

The healing ministry touches people at points of crisis, at times of great need. Often at such times the Spirit is able to break through, and the physical healing becomes a spiritual healing as well. Even hardened enemies of the gospel have been won over by the compassionate care of Christian health workers. And then there are the countless other patients who have gotten their first glimpse of Christ in the lives of those who cared for them. One missionary to India recounts an evening when he was giving a talk on the life of Jesus to a group of villagers. After the meeting an old man came up to him and said, "I know that person you were talking about. He operated on me last year."

The number of patients who have come to faith in Christ through the ministry of the world's 2500 mission hospitals cannot be calculated, but it must be in the millions. God has used Christian medical work to call out key people to himself. Some of the early Nepali church leaders were introduced to Christ at a mission hospital on the Indian side of the Nepal-India border before Nepal had even opened its borders to the outside world. Countless other Nepalis have come to Christ at mission hospitals since that time. One young man with a minor sore on his chin journeyed two days to our hospital, stayed a week and found Christ. The examples could be multiplied hundreds of times—and that's just in Nepal, where open hospital evangelism is forbidden. Many times more have been won to Christ in countries where evangelism is not restricted.

Medical missions have always been on the forefront of the missionary movement, and in many countries they have gained for missions broad respect and acceptance. For example, two of the earliest and best-regarded hospitals in India were established by women missionaries, and they continue to be two of the leading medical centers in India today.

In many other countries, especially those that have restricted the entry of Christians, the earliest access into the country has been through medical missions. In Nepal, for example, mission work began with the establishment of three hospitals. That was the only work for which the government gave permission. All subsequent mission activity has rested on the reputation of that early medical work. Indeed, the mission hospital in Kathmandu remained the premier medical institution of the country for more than two decades, until the mission deliberately downgraded it to a lower-level hospital. Government officials went there for care. Its doctors were called to treat members of the royal family. It won respect for Christian missions. It was through reading about the opening of that hospital in 1954 that I received my own call to go to Nepal as a medical missionary.

When new doctors, nurses, or other health professionals arrive at their assignments, they are greeted with an array of vivid impressions. The first impression is of the enormous health needs of the people, especially in the poorer countries. In 1970, when Cynthia and I first reached our place of work in Nepal, we and a third doctor were the only doctors serving a population of half a million people. In the West, you have a thousand doctors for that many people. Our hospital served an area the size of Delaware, but without roads; our average patient walked a whole day to get to the hospital. Half the children died before the age of five. The blind, the crippled and deformed were everywhere; there had been no one before to treat them. People suffered in the advanced stages of every conceivable disease. Simple maladies went untreated. When someone with a toothache finally arrived at the hospital, the tooth would usually be infected, and often their faces would be blown up with abscesses the size of cantaloupes. Why did they wait so long? You'd wait too if you had to walk up and down a mountain a full day just to get to your dentist.

The physical suffering on the mission field is overwhelming. The lines of patients coming each day grow longer and longer, as confidence in modern medicine increases and the people learn to trust the Christian medical team. For many health workers, the weight of this need becomes unbearable; they feel they must carry the whole load. Of course, God doesn't ask that of them. They are not responsible for any more than God gives them strength to do. Yes, health workers need to find practical ways to manage and distribute the workload—mainly by training local paramedical workers; but ultimately they need to rest in God. He controls the load; he gives the resources. The missionary health worker is not alone; he or she simply needs to do what God shows to do each day.

A helpful antidote to feeling overwhelmed is to feel grateful that God has put you in a place where you are really needed. Everyone needs to feel needed. Goodness, some doctors back home are competing for patients there are so few to go around. Be thankful you are not in a rat race like that!

The next impression that will hit the new doctor and nurse, fresh from their spick-and-span, sterile hospitals of the West, will be the conditions under which they are called upon to work. You could have fit our entire fifty-bed mission hospital inside the front lobby of the hospital I trained in at home. Crowds, dirt, dogs, chickens under the bed; non-matching instruments and supplies donated from a dozen different sources; outmoded and non-functioning equipment, cast-off relics of a former generation. Birds fly through the operating room—even during operations; kerosene stoves flare up and deposit soot all over the Central Supply; dust storms and rain storms pass through ill-fitting windows and leaking roofs as through a chicken coop. All this and much more await the intrepid doctor or nurse who ventures to work in a mission hospital in a poor country.

However, let us not over-emphasize the bad. The fact is that the great majority of patients get well in these hospitals—and for one percent of what it costs at home. The infection rate at our mission hospital was a fraction of that found in the average U.S. hospital. We were able to provide as much truly needed service to people in one day as we would have provided in a whole month had we stayed at home in a conventional medical practice. Medical missions, whether domestic or foreign, is the most useful, fulfilling, and challenging career open to any Christian health professional.

But we mustn't forget the heartaches. Doctors not only do patients good; they sometimes do them in. Every doctor has his portfolio of woes. We simply trust God to cover our mistakes; it sounds glib, but it's true. There is no way a mission doctor or nurse can get through a busy day of caring for more than a hundred patients without something going wrong.

As mentioned earlier, Christian medical work in Nepal began with something going wrong: the first operation done in the country resulted in the patient's death. You feel like packing your bags when that happens. The government officials who had just stuck their necks out by inviting these foreign Christians into their country came by to investigate the death. They finally decided that "sometimes those things just happen." It wasn't any knowledge of surgery that led them to that conclusion; this was the first operation ever done in their country! It was their religion that saved the day: Hindus are fatalists.

In spite of the crucial and at times indispensable role medical missions have played in the overall missionary movement, medical work is still subject to the criticism that it is not a cost-effective means of reaching our spiritual goal in mission: to win people to Christ. Certainly, when medicine is the only way to gain a Christian presence in a society, the "cost-effectiveness issue" is not important. But in all other situations, the criticism is basically true. Therefore, it behooves health professionals to do everything they can to cut costs, to make medical missions more cost-effective—both in medical and spiritual terms.

The main way to do this is to focus on prevention rather than cure; it costs one sixteenth as much to prevent a disease as to cure it—not to mention the suffering it saves. Consequently, missions have been cutting back on expensive hospital-based care, which benefits relatively few, and have begun concentrating more and more of their resources on primary, community-based health care. This ideally will reduce the long-range need for expensive hospitals, because most illnesses will either be prevented or be treated right in the community.

Hospitals will not become obsolete, however! They will always be needed; people do get serious illnesses that cannot be prevented. Furthermore, hospitals give credibility to community health work; people get dramatically cured in hospitals, and those cures serve to bolster the teaching of the community health workers. "They brought old granny back to life at that hospital; therefore, they must know what they're talking about."

Nevertheless, the community is where the real health action is. Eighty percent of deaths in children, for example, can be prevented by their mothers—with a little common-sense teaching. Clean drinking water will prevent most intestinal infections. Better use of the land, improved irrigation, more nutritious food will all help to eliminate malnutrition and enable people to ward off illness and become more productive. So suddenly we are thinking in terms of the "individual-in-community," and we need to link up with the community and rural development people to improve the economic base of the community. Everything that goes on in a community is interrelated; you can't tackle one problem effectively unless you tackle all together. Furthermore, it's not enough simply to "deliver health care" or other assistance. Communities need to be enabled to take responsibility for as many aspects of their health and development as they can reasonably be expected to. Outside workers in health and other fields then become enablers, "change agents." This is the only way to effect lasting improvement in a community.

The main focus of health professionals must be on education, motivation, disease prevention, limiting family size, and finally training more health workers. As we have seen elsewhere, any missionary must be a trainer. Not only that, he or she must be a trainer of trainers. Every village needs its own home-grown health worker, and this requires training thousands of such people to cover the villages of the Third World. In Nepal, for example, half the villages in the country have no practical access to modern medical care. We have to train the villagers themselves, so that they can go back and provide basic care and teaching to their own communities.

So this is the theory, and it is all sound. Instead of dealing just with the crisis, get at the cause. But putting it into practice will take time. Meanwhile, there is this guy called a medical missionary out there in the swamp fighting alligators. Don't sit on the edge smugly suggesting he'd be better off draining the swamp. Get out and give him a hand. It takes two to ward off alligators and drain the swamp at the same time.

It is appealing to think of the national church picking up the burden of medical mission work. In parts of Africa, where the church is large and the government is poor, Christians have been taking a major part in providing health service. But in most of the world, it is not practical because of the expense involved; even running a community health program is more expensive than most Third World churches can afford.

This means that if medical work is to continue, it will have to be heavily subsidized from outside. There is no way mission hospitals or community health programs can be self-supporting and simultaneously provide service to the poor. And medical missions can under no circumstances neglect the poor or deprive them of treatment because of inability to pay. Cash-strapped missions all over the world are wondering how, with costs shooting up, they are going to continue running their medical programs. There are only two answers: keep pouring in the money, or stop treating the poor.

In the meantime, let all health care personnel learn how to provide care economically and efficiently. That means, above all, lowering the *level* of care they give (not the standard of care), and providing "minimum essential treatment." Let them leave all their "go-all-out" and "bar-no-expense" slogans back home. Poor patients count the cost of their treatment, and missionary health personnel should do likewise. The greatest controllable cause of mission hospital deficits is the missionary doctor. Let's at least start there.

Any missionary in the health field sooner or later is going to have to grapple with these health policy questions. But beware of isolating health matters from their spiritual context. The United Mission to Nepal once invited a high-powered commission from an international Christian consulting group to come out to advise us on what to do with our hospitals "in the context of Nepal's health needs." But what was needed was advice "in the context of Nepal's *total* need, including, above all else, her spiritual need. And so we got the same advice we might have gotten from

WHO or AID, sound enough in the health context, but missing the mark as far as our Christian mission was concerned.

The hospital where Cynthia and I worked for twelve years was born out of a prophecy given by the Holy Spirit that it was to be a "hospital of the living word." That then was the context in which its role should have been defined; it could not be defined simply in relation to government health schemes and the existing health needs of the people.

Unless mission organizations see their health and other projects in light of the spiritual need of the people they serve, it will be indeed difficult to define their role. Many mission projects have arisen, to all appearances, at random, with little plan and ill-defined purpose. But they arose, in fact, through the vision of men and women sensitive to God's leading. The journeys of Paul appear "random" at first sight; did he cover Asia Minor and Europe in the most effective and efficient way? By our current concept of management, planning, and evaluation, the answer would be "no."

The next question one asks is: Is there such a thing as a "Christian institution"? We too quickly answer that it is people who are Christian, not institutions. True. But our witness is both individual and corporate. We are not only "salt"; we are a "city on a hill" (Mt 5:13-14). Christians, as a rule, have an enhanced personal witness when they work in a "Christian institution." A lone doctor or nurse working in a government hospital will, on average, not make as great a spiritual impact as he or she would working in a mission hospital. Christians reinforce each other's witness. And the same applies to other fields as well.

In saying this, we are not opposing the sending of mission personnel to work in government and other secular institutions; we need Christians in all kinds of situations—especially so in restricted countries. Here we are simply saying that there are unique advantages to maintaining Christian institutions as such.

What, then, is a "Christian institution" or "Christian project"? It is first of all an institution or project which is identifiably "Christian" in the minds of the surrounding population. This would require that the leadership be Christian, and that there be a core of committed Christians on the staff. All staff would have to adhere to basic Christian values, and would not be permitted to oppose the Christian witness of the project. If these criteria cannot be maintained for one reason or another, the mission should divest itself of that work. No Christian mission should be in the business of running projects that are not identifiably Christian at the local project level.

Mission hospitals generally outshine government hospitals. There is nothing wrong with letting them do so! First of all, it glorifies Jesus. Second, it sets a standard that government can aim at. The high-caliber and compassionate service offered at a mission hospital is in itself a powerful testimony to the presence of Jesus in that place.

One approach to the "mission institution" question which has been widely pursued is to turn our hospitals and other institutions over to nationals, either to the government or to private agencies. In line with this, there has been a great push to put nationals in charge of mission institutions regardless of their spiritual qualifications. One argument used to justify this approach is that the "nationals know best." In reaction to the earlier stereotypical "overbearing, paternalistic, and know-it-all missionary," it has become fashionable to defer to the national population as the repository of all wisdom. Of course, the truth lies somewhere in between. In early phases of mission work the missionary will have relatively more "wisdom," not only in things spiritual but also in things technical. As national leaders and professionals arise, their wisdom in technical matters will become more and more predominant. But the general wisdom of believers, both foreign and national, must always be regarded above the wisdom of non-believers—which is the wisdom of the world.

The critical issue is not *if* we should put our institutions into national hands but into *which* national hands. It is not a valid mission goal to set up institutions and programs with a view to their takeover and secularization at the earliest feasible time. We should not be satisfied simply with the fact that our institutions are still functioning after we leave, or that we have contributed so many beds or buildings to the government health services. If these are the results we are willing to settle for, then we become but little different than a government aid agency.

Teaching

Every missionary must be a teacher, no matter what his or her profession. Not to teach is to markedly reduce one's long-term contribution to the field.

As with physical health, education is not an end in itself. Education, above all, should serve to teach men and women to know God and to live according to his word. All else we teach is of little lasting value without that.

There are two broad categories of educational work in missions: first, teaching in Christian or mission schools; and second, teaching in secular or government schools. The latter form of teaching is done primarily in countries where open Christian mission work is restricted.

Together with mission hospitals, the establishment of Christian schools has been a major part of the modern missionary movement. Mission schools have played an important role in the development of the middle class throughout the Third World, and in so doing, they have contributed greatly to the independence movement in many former colonies. They have attracted the elite of society because of the high quality of education they provide. Many of the leaders of developing countries have been educated at mission schools. And finally, mission schools have provided educated leadership for the Third World church. Their influence is incalculable.

Mission schools are run very much on the principle of Christian schools at home. In addition to teaching the Bible as part of the curriculum, the teachers model the Christian life for their students. Character building and discipline are emphasized. Because of the dedication of the teachers, students are motivated and challenged to reach their potential.

On the mission field, missionary teachers have been able to make some unique contributions. On the Indian subcontinent, including Nepal, they have hastened the breakdown of the caste system among the upper and middle classes—that is, among those who have been educated. In many countries they have helped elevate the status of women by giving them equal educational opportunity. Two of the earliest and finest schools in Nepal were girls' schools, both started by Christian missionaries. The girls still have a long way to go in the Third World. Most families don't consider it worthwhile to educate their daughters. They just go and join another family when they marry, or drop out of school altogether; so the family thinks, "What's the use?"

In countries that restrict evangelism, missionary teachers must do their job more discreetly—as was the case with missionary health personnel. But opportunities for personal witness remain. And the teaching of Christian values can go on regardless.

But unless one is careful, a subtle shift can take place in one's educational goals. One can easily begin to teach just plain values, in contradistinction to specifically Christian values. And one begins to think of "making good citizens of Nepal," rather than citizens of the kingdom of God. In either case, once the Christian emphasis is lost, the teacher begins doing more harm than good. Because the students get the idea that now they know what Christianity is all about, so they no longer hunger after the real thing. They've learned "Christian" values, but are missing Christ.

All religions teach "values," after all. For a mission school to teach values without teaching Christ is to give the impression that being a Christian is no different and no better than being anything else—just as long as one holds to these "values." If a mission school is forced to stop teaching Christ-centered values, it should stop altogether, and let another organization take it over.

And what are Christian values? They are described in the New Testament from Matthew through Revelation.

So far, we have been talking about mission-run schools. Let us turn now to the second main category of missionary teaching: that which takes place in secular institutions, usually in restricted countries.

Here the missionaries, either alone or in small groups, are invited to teach in national-run schools. If these teachers are knowledgeable in a special subject that the government particularly wants taught, then the teachers will often be given a salary, and hence become "tentmakers."

The opportunities for such teaching positions are numerous; they exist at all levels, from village primary schools in the poorest countries to Ph.D.-level teaching in major universities. One of the greatest opportunities presently available is in teaching English as a second language. Take a short course, and the certificate you get will serve as your passport into scores of countries, many of them closed to other types of missionary.

A variation of the teaching-English theme is for missionaries to give private English lessons. If this is done, observing a few guidelines will make your teaching more fruitful spiritually. First, team up, if possible, with a national Christian. Second, don't disguise your intentions; state that you are going to use the Bible (in modern translation) not only for its English value but also for its content. Third, charge a fee comparable to what the student would have to pay elsewhere. And fourth, follow-up those who become interested in the gospel.

A final category of missionary teaching is the education of missionary children, either in small tutorial groups in remote projects or in more centrally located schools majoring in MK education. We'll have more to say about this important teaching opportunity when we come to the chapter on missionary children.

Community and economic development

Many Christians do not like the term "development"; they prefer "transformation" instead, and I prefer it too. For convention's sake, however, we will use the word development here, but with the understanding that true development begins with a transformation of the individual from a self-centered, self-serving person to a community-centered or other-centered person. For that to happen the individual needs to meet Christ. If we just go out and "develop" communities, that is, make them economically more prosperous, we are going to leave them more self-centered, more materialistic and covetous than they were before. That cannot be the aim of Christian missions.

Evangelical Christians are often suspicious of development work, but there is a real need for Christians to enter this field. To say that development is needed is to say that poverty exists, and immediately we are back to the Bible's emphasis on serving the poor.

The causes of poverty are the very things that Christian missionaries need to be concerned with. First is religion. We have seen how the fatalism and the caste structure of Hinduism have encouraged poverty. Second is ignorance, illiteracy; Christians can do something about this. Third is overpopulation. I'm sorry, but if you don't include this, forget about community development in the Third World; you'll just be swimming against the flood. Fourth, malnutrition and poor health.

There are some additional causes of poverty which missionaries can do little about: totalitarian and socialist governments, lack of infrastructure, lack of natural resources, unfair trade practices, corruption, war, natural catastrophes. All these above-mentioned causes interlock with each other; some causes may predominate in one country, others in another. It is fruitless to attack just one or two of them. Hence the need for an integrated approach to community development.

In some cases Christian organizations may be called upon to undertake major development work; for example, World Vision has the resources and worldwide respect to carry out large-scale projects. Western governments often channel their aid money through Christian missions, because they know the money will be spent wisely.

But in the average case, missionaries will more likely carry out their development work in more rural areas and on a smaller scale. They will choose (with government agreement) the poorest yet most receptive communities. They will concentrate on things like clean water, agriculture, irrigation, cooperatives, cottage industries, cash crops—and, of course, training villagers in the skills necessary to bring about and maintain these improvements.

Cynthia and I were privileged to be part of one of the earliest integrated rural development programs to be established anywhere. It was started back in the late 1950s. There was medical work; first a dispensary, and later a hospital. The mission ran half a dozen schools. A church was established. And on the development side, the mission built a demonstration farm, which was run by a wheat farmer from Saskatchewan. Since this was a totally agricultural society miles from the nearest road, agricultural development was what the people needed most.

The contribution made by that missionary farmer continues to this day. Half the buffalos in the region were sired by a prize bull he imported from somewhere. Most of the hogs in the area have doubled in size. Better strains of this and that crop are now widely used. Better-yielding fruit trees surround many homes. And there has been the spiritual seed planted by that farmer as well. A beautiful legacy.

Not every innovation succeeded. The fine goats from Israel all died. A special batch of heavy-laying chickens were eaten by leopards. And the farmer's crops were constantly being devoured by neighborhood animals, or demolished by wind, hail, or drought. But thirty years later, the people still remember that farmer with fondness and appreciation.

The chief principle of development is to enable people to help themselves. "Give a man a fish and he will have food for a day; teach him to fish, and he'll have food for a lifetime." One impediment to development is government; governments in the Third World usually do not want to "enable" the people. They prefer to keep the people dependent—grateful for handouts, and happy to vote again for those in power. In spite of lip service, most of these governments do nothing to foster the independence and self-reliance of their people. It threatens their power. "Help people to help themselves" is not the motto of centralized governments, and yet for any lasting progress or change to take place, the people's involvement is essential.

The modern approach to development is the "empty-hand" approach: the worker goes in, not with a handout (which creates dependency), but with empty hands. The worker doesn't burst out with a lot of ideas of his own; he lets the ideas of the villagers bubble up and take expression. Thus the villagers will be able to determine their own needs and take active steps to meet them. The concept is basically sound.

At one of our mission conferences once, the woman heading up the mission's community development work was expounding on the empty-hand philosophy, when her husband asked from the floor, "Do you mean you experts actually go into a village and say nothing at all? It sounds to me like a dialogue of the dumb." We wondered if he'd be coming to the meeting next day in a plaster cast.

Dialogue of the dumb doesn't quite nail it; dialogue of the deaf is more like it. Have you ever tried the empty-hand approach? It goes something like this.

> Development worker: Good morning. We've come to talk to you about the felt needs of your village.
>
> Village leader: Wonderful. Welcome. Our village needs a hospital.
>
> D.W. Ah, er, why do you say that?
>
> V.L. Because our people are getting sick.
>
> D.W. And why are they getting sick?
>
> V.L. Because we have no hospital. We are so grateful that you've come to help us with this need.
>
> D.W. But I'm more interested in why your people are getting sick.
>
> V.L. In fact, we have already set aside land for a hospital. It's right over there on that hillside.
>
> D.W. But what are their illnesses?
>
> V.L. The entire village is behind it. We'll cooperate in every way we can.
>
> D.W. I'll return next week and we'll discuss your need further.
>
> V.L. Thank you very much. We'll have everything ready by then.

Far-fetched? Not at all. This is the kind of fun you can have putting theory into practice on the mission field.

The "big cousin" of rural or community development is economic development, including small-scale industrial development. "What on earth does that have to do with missions?" you ask. And the answer is the same here as it was for rural development: our objective is to raise the baseline economic level enough so that the poorest people can have adequate food, clothing, and shelter.

If you had walked into Nepal in 1950, you would have felt you were walking into the fifteenth century. No roads, no hospitals, no schools, no electricity, primitive agriculture—a nation of impoverished farmers held in serfdom by a family of feudal rulers who used to have grand pianos and Mercedes Benzes carried over the mountains into Kathmandu for their enjoyment. What an opportunity for Christian missions when the country opened a year later! The whole gamut of modern technology was needed to alleviate the suffering of the Nepalis.

So the United Mission to Nepal called out engineers, and in particular, specialists in intermediate technology. And they began to teach the people things like carpentry and auto mechanics. They showed them how to build foot bridges, and mills for husking their rice. They helped Nepalis set up a plywood factory; they helped establish companies specializing in hydroelectric power and dam building. These projects have benefited hundreds of thousands of Nepalis, and Nepalis are now running them. And along the way, there has been spiritual fruit—and that in a country where Christian witness has been severely curtailed.

If you were a Christian engineer, wouldn't it be humanly gratifying to take part in projects that will make a vast difference in people's lives, rather than just a little improvement? I recently visited the dam site of a large hydroelectric plant the mission is currently constructing out in an isolated region of Western Nepal. I almost wished that I was an engineer, the missionaries were having so much fun. Well, it looked like fun to me. They had bought two Indian dump trucks, thinking they'd always be able to keep at least one running with spare parts from the other. But the transmissions of both trucks had gone out within weeks of their purchase, and now the project was three months behind schedule. And this problem had arisen, and that problem.... Add to it the sandstorms, floods, landslides, labor problems, lack of supplies, and all the other interesting things that happen when you assay to build a dam in the hills of Nepal, and you have a whale of a challenge. And all the activity has resulted in yet another congregation being added to the national church.

Let us conclude this chapter on different types of mission work with three final observations. Though we have divided up the work by profession, it is still to be hoped that missionaries will come to the field willing to help out if needed in areas outside their own specialty. Some of the most valuable missionaries in Nepal have been those who were willing to pitch in anywhere. Such a person has the gift of being "able to help others" (1 Co 12:28). It is one of the greatest and most needed missionary gifts.

But just because you don't have this "gift" doesn't mean you aren't going to get called upon to tackle something outside your field. My own field is surgery, but I spent over half my time taking care of a host of administrative matters ranging from tracking down stolen money and equipment to the elimination of stray (and possibly rabid) dogs, not to mention the disposal of deceased patients in the woods beyond the spring along the path leading to the hospital. The jackals used to dig up the dead bodies, and village officials would complain. Cemetery management had not been included in my courses of study. Amputated limbs also caused trouble. One day the officials informed me that there was an arm lying alongside the trail down by the spring, and I'd better look into it. They were right. It was like a signpost: "Welcome to the mission hospital."

The second observation concerns the desire we all have to "get the job done." We feel we have to "accomplish something," perhaps to persuade the supporters back home that they ought to keep supporting us, or, as is more often the case, to satisfy our own need to succeed, to be fulfilled. Neither of these are proper motives. The work is the Lord's, and it needs to be done in his way and in his time. Real fulfillment only comes through doing the Lord's will day by day. Supporters should not demand "results on schedule," as if missionaries were merely business investments. And neither should missionaries hurry to complete projects at the expense, say, of making friends with the nationals they have come to serve. Making friends is part of our "work" too—a very important part.

The third observation is this: missions, with its multiple disciplines, is like an army, men and women with many different skills working together toward a common goal. These days the military metaphor is unpopular among Christians; it's hard to find a church where they are still singing "Onward Christian Soldiers." Yet the fact is, when you consider the enemy we face, the military metaphor is the most apt there is.

It's apt in another way too: in a modern army it takes ten men in the rear to support one man at the front. Ten Christians at home to support one on the field. I wish it were so. But today in the West, there are a thousand Christians at home supporting one on the field. That's too many at home, and too few at the front. The call to mission is as valid today as it ever was: if you haven't been called to stay, you should plan to go.

15

More Recent Developments

Though this chapter is short, that makes it no less important. In the previous chapter we looked at the more traditional or conventional types of mission work. Much of what was said there applies to these newer types of ministry as well, and so will not be repeated here. Also most of these newer ministries are so diverse that it is impossible to describe them in detail. We will merely comment on some of them briefly.

Most of what will be touched on here comes under the general subject of "tentmaking." Paul was the first "tentmaker"; he made his living making tents. But for him, the preaching of the gospel was primary; his tentmaking was secondary, merely a means to an end.

The chief distinguishing feature of tentmaking is that one earns his livelihood by his own labor rather than being supported by a church or mission agency. Both kinds of missionaries are fully scriptural; indeed, Paul was both a tentmaker and a church-supported missionary at different times in his career.

The main rationale for tentmaking in today's missionary movement is to enable Christians to enter countries and seize opportunities which are not open to conventional missionaries. In cases where this rationale is not a factor, tentmaking offers little overall advantage relative to ordinary mission work.

First, the advantages of tentmaking. By far the major advantage is, as we have said, that tentmaking allows missionaries to go through doors that would otherwise be closed. This advantage alone overcomes all disadvantages.

The second advantage is that tentmakers earn their own way. This relieves the church of the need to support them.

The third advantage is that tentmakers avoid the accusation of "making money off religion." The functionaries of other religions do, and so people assume we do too. When they find that we don't, people more readily assume that we are sincere, that we have no ulterior motive; we're not just preaching for money.

The fourth advantage is that tentmakers are free of the stigma of proselytizing; they are simply ordinary working people who happen to share their faith in their spare time. People can see them live their Christian lives as they work.

The disadvantages of tentmaking are considerable. One's employer may place strict limits on evangelistic activity. There is often inadequate time to learn the language. The terms of service are short, and often not renewable. Contacts with nationals may be limited; tentmakers may not really get into the host culture. They may lack fellowship and spiritual support, a lack that can result in failure to bear spiritual fruit. Tentmakers may be self-supporting financially, but they are not self-supporting spiritually. For all of these reasons, it usually is more difficult for a tentmaker to have a fruitful mininstry than for a regular missionary.

Tentmakers must not be "independent" missionaries. Tentmaking is not some kind of private road to the mission field. People who try the independent route are usually unwilling to submit to authority. They desire to do their own thing. They want to be free of accountability to others. People who say they are accountable only to the Holy Spirit are deceiving themselves. Tentmakers need to be trained and sent and kept accountable just like anyone else. And once on the field, they need to establish close links with fellow Christians, both for support and for mutual accountability.

The traditional mission boards and societies are the best, indeed the only, means of providing tentmakers with the spiritual backing and the oversight that they need. The reason for this is that only mission boards and societies are equipped to engage in cross-cultural witness on a large scale. Just being a Christian in a foreign country doesn't make one a cross-cultural witness. Training is necessary, especially in cultural sensitivity, language, spiritual survival, and in witnessing. And once one is trained, ongoing support is imperative: tentmakers do not last without it.

The feeling is abroad today that mission societies and boards aren't really scriptural, that each church should be sending out its own missionaries and tentmakers. This view reads too much into the fact that Paul and Barnabas were sent out by the Antioch church. This does not suggest that Antioch was the sole source of support and authority for the work of Paul and Barnabas. True, they came back after their first missionary journey and reported to the Antioch church, but it nowhere says they did so again. We know that the Philippian church sent gifts to Paul. It is unreasonable to think that each church can effectively maintain and supervise its missionaries on the field—unless the church happens to be enormous, or unless the "field" is limited to a couple of geographic sites. Otherwise, great inefficiency and duplication will result. This is why tentmakers are turning to the established missions for support. Many of these missions themselves are beginning to send out tentmakers. Tentmakers are missionaries in every sense of the word. My own mission, InterServe, has been in the forefront of this development. We are not even referred to as missionaries anymore, but together with our tentmaker colleagues, we are all called "partners." Such missions are "arms" of the local church, specializing in doing what the individual church cannot easily do: that is, getting their members to the field and ensuring that they have a fruitful ministry there.

But having said this is not to lessen the importance of the tentmaker's link with his or her own local church. A tentmaker needs to be commissioned and sent out like any other missionary. The tentmaker needs his church's continued prayer support almost more than the regular missionary does. Just because the local church doesn't have to pay for him does not mean it doesn't have to pray for him.

Since tentmaking is ordinarily a more difficult form of mission work, it is a good idea, where possible, that a missionary start out with a regular mission for a year or two and then switch to a tentmaking assignment.

The openings for tentmakers are nearly unlimited. Almost anything a Christian is at home, he or she can be as a tentmaker on the field. You name the job, and there will probably be a tentmaker somewhere out there doing it. Retirees are also suited for tentmaking. Though they adapt less readily, they bring to the field wisdom, maturity, and perspective—qualities as badly needed in missions as anywhere else.

The concept of the tentmaker has taught the church at large an important truth about being a Christian. We like to divide people into full-time Christian workers and non-full-time Christian workers. But as said earlier, such a division should not exist. Every Christian is a full-time Christian worker, no matter what his or her work. And those who stay at home and earn a living—they are also "tentmakers," only not in a cross-cultural situation. So let not people at home think the tentmaker abroad is any different from themselves; whether at home or abroad, all Christians must witness through their work and through their leisure. Faithfulness in our work and the fruit of the Spirit manifest throughout the day are our major means of witness as tentmakers. But don't forget the ministry of the word. All of us need to be ready and to pray for opportunities "to give the reason for the hope that [we] have" (1 Pe 3:15). The opportunities will come if we pray for them; we never need to lament that there isn't sufficient time.

A recent variation on the tentmaking theme is being put forward by Tony Campolo and others. Here the idea is that instead of working for secular businesses in the Third World, Christians go in and set up their own businesses. In this way they can insure that their business benefits the economy of the host country and also provides jobs for both national and expatriate Christians, all of whom are then encouraged to be witnesses. This concept is now being put into practice in many countries around the world.

Secondment of missionaries to government or other agencies

"Seconded" missionaries are halfway between tentmakers and regular missionaries. They are church-supported and belong to a mission organization, but they are then loaned or "seconded" to another agency, usually secular. This enables the mission to get its people out of purely mission projects and into society where they will have a chance to witness to groups that previously had no exposure to Christians.

As with self-supported tentmakers, this kind of mission work takes a higher degree of initiative, self-discipline, and witnessing skill than that required by missionaries working in mission projects, where the team as a whole enhances the witness of each member. In Nepal we have often sent our more experienced people into this kind of work.

In seconded work the day-to-day support and fellowship of colleagues is missing. You lose the feeling of security the mission organization gives you. With the mission, your life is more predictable; you have a measure of control over what goes on. But once outside the mission, you enter an arena where you have no control, and which is often filled with lions.

The first thing you notice when you go to work in a Third World government institution, for instance, is that the ethos is different. Here the idea is to get paid for doing no work; indeed, that's the beauty of government employment. Work is associated with suffering; popular religion teaches one to avoid suffering, so what better than a government job! This is why the phrase, "busy doing nothing," is never a joke in a Third World government office.

Enter the missionary, usually a work-oriented, no-nonsense, high-idealed person—like my wife. She is an associate professor at the medical school in Kathmandu, a branch of the government university system. It is typical of just about any government-run institution in the developing world.

Today she has spent twenty minutes trying to phone the medical school office to ask that something be made ready for her twelve-o'clock class. Since no one answered, she has cycled down to the school to take care of the matter herself. As she walks in the office, she sees three clerks sitting around. The phone is ringing, but no one answers.

"Why don't you answer the phone?" Cynthia asks.

But Cynthia knows the answer already. The phone is used by more than one department. Thus the clerks feel under no obligation to find out who's calling; supposing it's not for their department. That would be wasted effort.

Yesterday had been the same. Cynthia had tried to call to find out if the medical school would be open at all, because the previous day all the professors in Kathmandu had gone on strike to protest the beating up of one their colleagues by university students.

The medical students have so far not resorted to violence to gain their demands. Their method is the *gherau*, which means, literally, a "surrounding." Last week they surrounded the dean in his office and wouldn't let him out for twenty-four hours. *Gheraus* end when the students get hungry.

In addition to the general lack of coordination, lack of equipment and supplies, and lack of motivation on the part of many students, there is the special frustration of the library. The library is the domain of the librarian, otherwise known as the "lady with the key," whose chief function is to keep the books safely locked up. This is necessary because should a book ever fall into the hands of a reader it would likely disappear, or have a section cut out. Indeed, if you are lucky enough to come across the librarian and actually get the desired book in hand, you may well find that the very chapter you are looking for has been removed.

Enough has been said to convey the idea. If your only reason for working in a government institution is to help improve the way things are done, you will become discouraged and cynical. But if your goal is also to model the life of Christ in the midst of difficulties, God will give you the grace to do so and to bring forth fruit.

And things are never all bad. Cynthia has found some of her students highly motivated. Many of her faculty colleagues are hard working and dedicated, and as frustrated as she is that the system doesn't work better. She has made many friends; she has won respect; she has modeled Jesus. It has all been worth it.

Friendship evangelism

Friendship evangelism is not some specialized entity distinct from other evangelism. Friendship should be at the heart of every personal evangelistic encounter. Establishing a friendship is the best way to gain acceptance, to gain a hearing. Yes, if you are a professional with needed skills, your profession alone may gain you a hearing at one level, but ultimately, to be an effective communicator of the gospel at the personal level, you must become a friend. Otherwise, you will always be an outsider.

Sometimes, it's true, we can lead a person to Christ before a friendship is really started. But still, the seed of friendship was there: the genuine concern for the other person, the respect shown, the personal warmth. But, more usually, friendship comes before the person accepts the gospel. It is the means, the bridge, by which we can lead the other to Christ.

Some people don't make friends as easily as others, but everyone makes them. Friendship isn't a "technique." It's a natural process that follows the same pattern in a cross-cultural setting as it does at home. It doesn't depend on the right words but on a simple desire to reach out, to share, to mutually benefit one another. Its motive, as always, is love. Even the most shy and diffident person can make the effort to win a few friends, and God will bless that effort.

One practical suggestion in a foreign culture is to start out as the learner, as the one who will benefit most from the friendship. Don't start off as the self-sufficient dispenser of new and better ideas. Allow yourself to be vulnerable. You want the other person to reach out to help you also; the best friendships are reciprocal.

Friends help one another. If you are a rich missionary working among very poor people, most of the help will inevitably go from you to them. It will be difficult to establish equal and reciprocal friendships. But don't let that discourage you from giving the necessary help. Even one-way friendships are important in evangelism.

It is said that a hungry man will not listen to the gospel. This is untrue, of course; people in physical need can and do listen to the gospel. But if we have the means to meet his physical need and do not do so, he will conclude not that our gospel is phony but that we are phony. We help our friend not to make him listen to the gospel more attentively, but because we love him and desire to meet his needs.

Making friends, sharing our lives, being with people is part of our missionary "work." For some missionaries it will be the major work they do. That visitor at the door—he's not an interruption, but an opportunity to make a friend. Friends take time. All missionaries, especially those with a gift for making friends, should give time to this crucial ministry. But remember, making friends is not the end, it is a means. It is a means of introducing others to the best friend of all, Jesus.

Student missionaries

Student ministry has always been one of the most strategic and effective ministries in the worldwide Christian movement; it is no less so today. In this section we have in mind particularly Christians who go out as students and enroll in a foreign university. Such "student" missionaries are just as much missionaries as anyone else; their target audience is among the most receptive. Christian missions need tens of thousands of new workers, and many of them should be students.

Advantages of such ministry are many. Tuition and expenses in Third World and former Soviet-bloc countries are minimal. Students are eager to speak English, so the missionary doesn't have to wait until he's learned the language before starting his ministry. Witnessing can begin from day one. Visas are easy to obtain, even for long-term study.

And what courses should the missionary student major in? The language, culture, and history of the people would be most natural—a ready-made orientation course.

Christian students can go out on exchange programs arranged by their colleges and universities. Or if they have finished college, they can join a regular mission and then enroll in a foreign university to do further studies. The combinations are many; the potential impact is enormous.

Nonresidential missionaries

The most important development in missions over the past thirty to forty years has been the increased focus on church growth and on culturally homogeneous "people groups." The church grows fastest within its own cultural group. The more people can maintain their cultural identity, the more rapidly the church grows. Therefore, the most efficient way to reach the world's two billion unreached people is to target and penetrate each unreached cultural group and plant there a self-multiplying church, which in turn can finish the job of evangelizing its own group.

There are an estimated eleven thousand of these unreached people groups (by one commonly accepted definition) which have no indigenous, self-multiplying church of their own. But over ninety percent of all missionaries are working among groups that already have an established church; they are in the so-called "church perfecting" ministries. These ministries are, of course, essential; they consolidate the gains of the church planters. They include the discipling and teaching ministries, which are an integral part of Christ's Great Commission. You can't have church planting without church perfecting; these two are inseparable and equally important. However, at the present time the deployment of the church's manpower between these two ministries has become unbalanced. It's not that we need fewer church perfecting missionaries today; it's rather that we need thousands of additional missionaries who will specifically focus on planting churches among these unreached people groups.

How do you "focus on," much less reach, a group that has no church and which is often closed off from outside Christians? Up until now, the expansion of the worldwide church has seemed "random"; each mission group in each country has moved into new areas and seized new opportunities as the Spirit led. Yet there are still eleven thousand people groups that remain unreached. Missionary strategists are concerned to accelerate the process of reaching these groups. How to do it? Enter the nonresidential missionary.

At first hearing, "nonresidential missionary" sounds like a contradiction in terms. The idea is that certain individuals will be burdened to "take on" one specific unreached people group as their particular "field of ministry." These individuals—nonresidential missionaries—may or may not be able to visit their designated area. But they begin to pray for that group. They read books and write letters in order to learn as much as possible about the group. They search for any member of the group who might be able to translate tracts and parts of the Bible into the language of the group. In a word, they attempt to marshall the resources of the worldwide church on behalf of the group; and above all, they seek for people who will actually go into that geographic area and plant the church.

All this time, the nonresidential missionary is serving as "field coordinator" for this undertaking. He is busy "networking" so that he can obtain all available help and cooperation from other Christian agencies and at the same time avoid duplicated effort. Though all of the remaining eleven thousand people groups may not be suitable for this approach, surely there are enough that are suitable to keep several thousand of these nonresidential missionaries busy.

But let us keep in mind that the nonresidential missionary is a resource person, a coordinator, a facilitator. He does not obviate the need for foot soldiers on the ground. For every nonresidential missionary there needs to be ten, twenty, or more people out there on the spot, witnessing, discipling, church planting. Let us not allow the nonresidential missionary concept to become an excuse for having all chiefs and no Indians.

Third World missionaries

Placing the vast reservoir of Third World missionaries at the tail end of this chapter is not meant to indicate that these missionaries constitute some peripheral, "by-the-way" group in modern missions. They are no more a "special category" of missionaries than are First World missionaries. As we said at the outset, we can no longer speak of First World sending countries and Third World receiving countries; it's now the whole world to the whole world. Already two thirds of the world's evangelical Christians (including charismatics) come from the Third World. And soon the majority of the world's missionaries will too. This is something to praise God for.

Virtually everything written in this book applies, with some allowance for cultural differences, to Third World missionaries. In some areas they have an advantage over First World missionaries; and in other areas they do not. Let's look first at their strengths.

Third World missionaries have the manpower—and it is increasing. Those foot soldiers we talked about in the above section are going to be coming in fair part from the Third World church.

Third World missionaries, on average, have less cross-cultural adjustment problems than Westerners have. There are glaring exceptions, of course, but if the Third World missionaries will concentrate on areas where the culture is not too different from their own, they will do well.

Third World missionaries are less likely to be charged with propagating a Western or "foreign" religion. They will often get a more receptive hearing for their message.

Third World missionaries cost less to send and to maintain than Western missionaries. They come from countries with a lower economic base. They are able to live closer to the level of the host people. Their mission structures are simple and less top-heavy. Third World missionaries are, in a word, more cost-effective than their First World counterparts.

The drawbacks of Third World missionaries are mostly correctable. They have generally not had the intensive training and orientation that Western missionaries go through. Many lack cross-cultural experience; they often develop little appreciation for the host culture. They can be just as guilty of cultural imperialism as we Westerners.

Though they cost less, Third World missionaries suffer from an overall lack of finances. Many Third World churches support their missionaries sacrificially, but it is not enough. And then there are still too many churches in the developing world that do not have a missionary vision, who say, "We are too poor to be sending missionaries. We can hardly survive ourselves."

In some countries of Asia, an Asian missionary may be less accepted than a Western missionary. The people may be less forgiving of the Asian; they will be quicker to pick at his mistakes. They also may experience some nationalistic jealousy: "Who does he think he is, coming over here and trying to teach us? Why, he's only from the Philippines."

Indeed, we did have a Filipino missionary some years back, highly trained in economic development—more highly trained, in fact, than anyone else we had in that field. But the Nepalis didn't appreciate his training; they didn't believe that he was smarter and better trained than the Westerners in the mission. Few people were interested in his advice or his plans. And he left discouraged after a couple of years.

A Third World missionary may also not be accepted in certain parts of his own geographic area. An Indian missionary of one caste may find it impossible to minister effectively to those of a different caste. Or a Christian from one tribe may be unable to witness to people of an adjacent tribe because of longstanding tribal animosities. In such cases, a Western missionary will have a much better chance.

The coming of age of Third World missions is the second most significant development in recent mission history, after the church-growth and people-group emphases. In a few more years it will no doubt become the most significant. The need of the moment is to get the potential Third World missionaries out to the field and keep them there. To do this, the church in the Third World needs its own national mission structures. In addition, already existing international missions need to welcome more and more candidates from the Third World. If a Korean Christian is called to serve in the Middle East, presently the only practical way for him to get there is by joining an international mission that's already working in that area.

The Third World missionary needs every bit as much preparation and training as does his Western counterpart. The idea that the Third World missionary is "ready to go" is fallacious. Those missionaries from developed but monoethnic countries like Korea and Japan may need extra training in cross-cultural adaptation. Third World missionaries are capable of all the mistakes of Western missionaries; most can be avoided with proper preparation.

Third World missionaries who join an international mission must undergo two adaptations: first, to the international mission; and second, to the host country. The first adaptation may be harder than the second. All of the cross-cultural and personal relationship problems we have discussed in earlier chapters will confront Third World missionaries as they try to find their place in an international (but mostly Western) organization.

In larger sending countries a still better solution would be for groups of Third World missionaries to go out as teams. They could be assigned to one project or at least to the same area. The mutual support of fellow countrymen would go far to ease the stress of cultural adaptation.

The relationship between First World and Third World in the missionary enterprise must be one of partnership. It is similar in every respect to the relationship discussed earlier between First and Third World churches. The West's major contribution to Third World missions will be in financial and technical help, as well as in training. It is absolutely imperative that we help, and help generously. Third World churches, for their part, need to set up structures that will allow for supervision of their workers and also financial accountability. If money is to be transferred from the West to the developing world, then it needs to be accounted for. We are asking no more of our Third World brethren than we ask of ourselves.

However, the Third World church needs to do its share of the financing; they shouldn't sit back and expect the West to provide it all. Their people must be taught to tithe. Third World Christians are not poorer than the poor widow who gave "all she had to live on" (Lk 21:4). The Western church could give on an "unequal matching" basis, perhaps contributing double or triple what the Third World church has raised on its own. Partnership implies that both sides do what they can to accomplish the task.

A final word about those who claim the day of the Western missionary is over. Certain Western-based organizations are, in effect, asking people to give less for Western missionaries and instead send the money to them for the support of "native evangelists." To promote one's own work at the expense of another's—especially when the other's work is still urgently needed—is a tactic not worthy of our Lord. Not long ago a young American couple felt called to be missionaries. But then they came across the literature of one of these organizations stating, in effect, that Westerners shouldn't go as missionaries, they should just send money. And so the couple abandoned their call and sent a check instead—to that organization, naturally.

To temper the claims of these organization, four things need to be kept in mind.

First, the overall need for missionaries is greater today than ever. Third World missionaries cannot do the job alone—even if we diverted all Western mission money to support them.

Second, while Third World missionaries are indeed more "cost-effective" than Western ones, this cannot be used as a reason against sending Western missionaries as long as they are needed. Suppose you are fighting an epidemic, and donors are sending you medicine, some cheap, some expensive, to treat the victims—but the supply is not nearly enough. Do you say, "Don't send any more of the expensive medicine; it's not cost-effective"? Of course not; people will die. Not until you have enough medicine can you begin to choose between the expensive and the cheap. And it is the same with choosing missionaries.

Third, there is no evidence to date that Third World missionaries are more cost-effective in reaching unreached people groups—the priority need in missions today. They may be more cost-effective as evangelists and as missionaries reaching out to nearby cultures similar to their own, but they have no proven overall advantage when it comes to penetrating totally new and different cultures.

Fourth, in addition to frontier missions, there are major areas of mission work that First World missionaries are best equipped to handle: literature, high-tech communications, training and education, health and development, to name the main ones. Then, apart from frontier missions, there are still other geographic areas (developed nations, for example) where the First World missionary can go more easily and work more effectively than his Third World colleague.

There is no place for competition between First and Third World missions. Let the one group do what they do best, and let the other group do what they do best. No one is suggesting sending expensive Western missionaries to areas where sufficient Third World missionaries are already working effectively. The point is that the harvest is vastly greater than the present number of workers can manage. "Ask the Lord of the harvest, therefore, to send out workers into his harvest field" (Mt 9:38).

People at home are too quick to pronounce the end of Western missions. "Door closed." "Third World missionaries taking over." Is it because they don't want to be bothered any more? Or that they don't want the responsibility? Or that they're hoping to cut their mission budgets by sending "cheaper" missionaries?

The cause of this "anti-Western-missionary" feeling does not lie entirely with these organizations pushing indigenous missions. It also lies with the Western church. Cries are going up everywhere: "We don't have enough money. Mission costs are skyrocketing. We can't afford Western missionaries anymore."

What kind of talk is this? We pay more for medicine, cars, and televisions and barely grumble; it's just inflation, we say. Well, don't we expect missions to get more expensive too? Don't missionaries eat food and fly airplanes and pay rent just like anyone else? I'm sorry; this lament over the rising cost of missions is simply a sign of misplaced priorities in the church. We're willing to pay for what's important to us. Let's rather think about what's important to God.

After reading about the different types of missionaries and the widely varying work they do, can anyone still think that the doors to Western missionaries are closing? Nothing could be further from the truth. There are lots of swinging doors out there—closing one minute, opening the next—but closed doors? No.

The day of Western missionaries is not over! Changing strategies, yes; but phasing out, absolutely not. The biggest engagements are yet to come. Don't miss the action!

16

Stress

Mission means engagement: engagement with colleagues, with foreign cultures, with the enemy. And engagement produces stress. Stress is an important part of a missionary's existence.

In previous chapters we have discussed God's discipline, Satan's attacks, culture shock, and interpersonal conflict. All of these provoke within an individual the phenomenon of stress, which can also be called "intrapersonal conflict." In ordinary doses, stress is normal, necessary, creative. It is prolonged and excessive stress that is harmful, and it's this which incapacitates many missionaries.

Stress is an internal experience. In this book we do not speak of stress as something outside a person, as in the expression "stresses of the mission field." Stress is our reaction to events and circumstances outside ourselves, and also to our own biologic needs. We can never blame our stress solely on something external, because our own reaction is necessarily a part of the stress and we are responsible for our reactions.

Stress, then, depends on both a provocation and a reaction. The reaction is ours to control; the provocation is usually beyond our control.

Our reaction is determined by our attitude—that is, our thoughts, our emotions, and our will. These it is a Christian's duty to control. Paul said, "...we take captive every thought to make it obedient to Christ"

(2 Co 10:5). The ninth fruit of the Spirit is self-control (Gal 5:23).

Provocations, on the other hand, are not fully under our control—especially on the mission field. Have you ever tried to control the behavior of barking dogs, marching ants, insects, rodents, neighbors with radios—to say nothing of bacteria, amoebas, air pollutants, and disagreeable weather? Some of these provocations can be modified or reduced by ear plugs, screens, fans, and good hygiene; but others we cannot alter. These we must learn to live with, either by accepting them or by adapting to them. In other words, when we can't alter the provocation, we must alter our reaction to it.

Missionaries face a greater number and variety of provocations or "stressors" than people do who stay at home. Here is a partial list of them: loneliness, loss of privacy (the goldfish bowl syndrome), high workload, lack of facilities, financial support worries, unmet expectations, cross-cultural strains, interpersonal conflict, health problems, anxiety about children, and pressure to perform.

An identical provocation will affect two people differently. The same thing that bugs me won't bug you, and vice versa. All provocations are colored by our experiences, our temperament, and our perceptions. We can't do anything about our experiences and our temperament, but at least we can check out our perceptions. If I have a perception that someone is trying to break in through my window but in fact it's only the wind, then I am experiencing a lot of stress for nothing.

The picture is complicated by the fact that when we react to a provocation, our very reaction may aggravate the original provocation or incite a new provocation. If you try to exterminate a column of ants by pouring boiling water on them, they will at once scatter all over the house and you will have damaged the furniture. This interesting cycle of provocation-reaction-greater provocation can be ended either by a short circuit or explosion, or by following the instructions in your Bible.

So, what do we have so far? If you are experiencing stress, the first thing to do is to take practical steps to reduce the provocation. If that is impossible or doesn't reduce the stress level, then see if you're looking at things accurately: check out your perceptions; get the facts straight. Maybe it's not the cook who's been stealing the sugar but the rats. These two practical, common-sense steps will eliminate two thirds of the stress in people's lives.

What happens when they don't? That's when we have to begin to look to ourselves. Don't push it off on Satan. He'll be in the wings stirring things up, all right, but the problem is going to reside in you. Why is it that these provocations are getting to you? The reason is going to be both psychological and spiritual.

The root cause of the stress experienced by people is that their self-life, their self-will, their self-image is being challenged or threatened. And the answer to stress is to replace that little word "self" with Christ.

This is a sweeping statement, but there are few, if any, exceptions to it. If you examine the instances when you have experienced stress, you will invariably find that at the bottom your will was being crossed, or you were afraid you wouldn't get your way, or your estimation of yourself was being reduced; something was pricking pride and self.

This is not to equate the experience of stress with sin. If we meet a bear in the woods we experience stress (manifested as fear); our self-life is threatened. If someone humiliates us, we experience stress (manifested as anger); our self-image is threatened. No sin here. These are the normal stress reactions of "fight or flight" that are part of us all. These are protective reactions, and the emotions associated with them usually subside quickly. This kind of stress isn't what causes problems among missionaries.

It is prolonged stress that does the damage. Stress is prolonged when we fail to deal rightly with the emotion released by the stress. We allow the anger to turn to resentment, the fear to turn to anxiety and unbelief. This is when sin enters.

How can we prevent sin from turning stress reactions into sinful reactions? The answer goes back to the word "self." The Bible doesn't talk about stress, but it talks a lot about self. Deny yourself (Mk 8:34); humble yourself (1 Pe 5:6); do not please yourself (Ro 15:1). Christ even "made himself nothing" (Php 2:7); he emptied himself. The answer to stress is not to build up self or to enhance one's self-image, as modern psychology tells us to do. To "build up self" is the one sure way to perpetuate stress, because self is always going to be threatened in this life. Rather, the way to find release from stress is by denying self, and clothing oneself with Christ instead.

There are people whose normal self-image has been crushed or distorted by childhood trauma, and it seems pointless and even cruel to tell such people to deny themselves. That's already been done. The point is to replace that broken image with the image of a child of God, a disciple of the King of kings. God has especially chosen those with broken self-images to glorify himself. "He chose the lowly things of this world and the despised things—and the things that are not—to nullify the things that are" (1 Co 1:28). We do not need self-confidence; we need God-confidence.

Closely bound up with our self-image is the matter of accepting ourselves. In one way we must accept the body, the life, the circumstances God has placed us in. We not only accept but are thankful that we are his children and have certain gifts. But in another way, we should not accept ourselves the way we are. We should despair of self, because we are beset with a sinful nature. This despair is essential. This is the despair of Matthew 5:3, which leads us to the foot of the cross. It is only there that the Holy Spirit can begin to restore, reclothe, and rebuild us, so that we might become like Jesus.

Two groups of people are particularly vulnerable to stress, in both cases because maintenance of self-image plays an important part in their equilibrium. In the first group are the goal-oriented people, the perfectionists, the achievers. Any setbacks—and there'll be plenty on the mission field—will provoke an extra degree of stress in such people. The second group consists of those who depend on the approval of others for their self-esteem, those who cannot confront others or say "no" to others for fear of losing that approval. The majority of missionaries fall into one of these two groups.

Since concern for self-image plays such a major role in stress, let's look at it more closely. Our self-image is derived from our perception of our self-worth. And right off we can smell a danger: our perception may deceive us. This is why Paul said, "...think of yourself with sober judgment" (Ro 12:3). It is possible, through reading Scripture or listening to trusted family members and friends, to come to a reasonably accurate assessment of our self-worth; it is important to do so.

Our self-image, our sense of self-worth, is based on what we are (a gifted child of God) and on what we do (the fruit we bear). Any dichotomy between being and doing is false: what we are determines what we do; what we do defines what we are. Being is to doing what a lung is to breathing. If we bear no fruit, we cease to be what we were meant to be; the tree is, in effect, dead. It is similar to faith without works; that too is dead (Jas 2:17).

Pride leads us to compare our self-image (what we are and what we do) with the image we have of others, to measure ourselves against others. It is good to do this as long as we compare ourselves to Jesus, or perhaps Paul: to do so will keep us humble. But the problem with comparing ourselves with our contemporaries is that we end up competing with them; we end up either inflating ourselves or deflating them, or both. We begin trying to be somebody we aren't; we set unrealistic goals.

So we cease to be satisfied with a "sober judgment" of ourselves: we must needs improve on our self-image relative to those around us. We decide we must be an Amy Carmichael or Hudson Taylor. We feel we must plant so many churches, treat so many patients, learn the language in record time. And when these goals are frustrated, as they often will be, our self-image is threatened and stress results.

This process goes on daily in many mundane forms. Let's say a medical doctor, whose self-image depends on his successful treatment of patients, comes to feel that the nurses are not cooperating with him (probably a false perception). He experiences stress. And let's say those nurses, whose self-image depends on their ability to give high-standard nursing care, complain that the doctor is admitting more patients than they can handle and has no regard for their feelings (most likely another false perception). Now stress levels are rising on both sides, which further distorts perceptions, and soon we're in a fine tizzy—and why? Where did it start? Back with those self-images, which were so important to protect and to nurture.

Any thing or person or circumstance can threaten our self-image. But the greatest fallout comes when the threat is from another person—in particular, a missionary colleague—because then we enter the arena of interpersonal conflict, which is so devastating on the mission field. Getting into conflict with marching ants and barking dogs isn't a hundredth the problem of getting into conflict with your colleagues!

Why do we attempt to establish better or false images of ourselves? Because of pride. Part of denying ourselves is to deny this self-image that we, not God, have created. All our striving that is rooted in pride and image-creating will lead to stress, frustration, team breakup, and a wonderful opportunity for Satan.

The solution? Confess our pride to God; deny the self-image we are trying to create; and pray for the Holy Spirit to transform us from the bottom up into the image of Christ. We all know we must give up our "Isaacs." Our self-image is the last "Isaac" to go.

Indeed, giving up the "last Isaac" is a life-long process, a process that doesn't end until we die. This is why we will continue to experience unhealthy forms of stress throughout our lives, that is, stress that gives rise to sinful attitudes and actions. The objective, however, is to reduce the stress, so that it becomes less and less of a problem as we proceed along life's course.

In the meantime, however, how do we handle this unhealthy and unwelcome stress, especially the prolonged stress that missionaries experience so commonly?

The first thing we need to do is to identify what is happening. Stress produces a whole gamut of emotions—a sense of abandonment by God, a sense of failure, anger, frustration, fear, apathy, depression—alone or in combination. Missionaries—being, as we know, very spiritual—don't like to own up to any of these emotions. But in their initial stages, these emotions are as natural as getting hungry or tired when we are deprived of food or sleep. The cause of these emotions needs to be understood and dealt with. If we fail to deal with the cause, these emotions will damage not only our spiritual well-being but our mental and physical well-being as well.

Once we have identified the problem, the next thing to do is take it straight to God. Sometimes God doesn't seem very close when we're under stress. How can he be when we're griping at him? But he's not far away. He understands, and he wants to be told what's eating us, just as an earthly father wants to know what's eating his child.

The reason God seems distant is that the emotion we are experiencing is leading us into a sinful attitude. Emotions are not themselves sins, but they do arise in the "old man." Therefore, emotions, especially negative (stress-related) emotions, if left to themselves, will lead naturally to sin. Negative emotions, therefore, are never neutral; they always tend one way.

For example, feeling abandoned is not a sin, but to cease believing in God's goodness is. Being angry is not a sin, but expressing the anger in ways hurtful to others or storing it up as resentment is a sin. These negative emotions well up of themselves, just as thoughts pop into our minds unbidden. To be angry is no more a sin than to be attracted to a member of the opposite sex. It's what we do with these emotions and thoughts that makes the difference as to whether we sin or not. The choice and the responsibility are ours.

One problem with stress is that it is cumulative; emotions pile up. We might be able to handle one at a time without sin, but when they gang up on us, we go under. If we're already under stress, and some new provocation comes along, we'll react to it with double force.

Under stress our natural tendencies are exaggerated. If we are naturally prone to be aggressive or confrontational when challenged, under stress we may find ourselves blowing up. Or if we have a natural tendency to withdraw when threatened, under stress we may isolate ourselves from the very people who could help us. If we have a natural tendency to irritability, under stress even trivial things will become intolerable. If we are naturally sensitive to criticism, under stress even imagined criticism will convince us we are failures.

It sounds grim, but don't be discouraged. It is very useful to be able to see our natural tendencies in their exaggerated form. This can lead us, with God's help, to change in constructive ways. Failure is not a word in God's vocabulary. He uses our failures to teach us and train us to be better disciples.

We have looked now at the initial two things we must do when we first experience stress and the negative emotions arising therefrom: one, identify the problem; and two, take it to God. We must do these two things without delay, because as the negative emotions build up and accumulate, they become harder and harder to deal with.

Now, after these first two steps, what else can we do to get these negative emotions out into the open, and either eliminated or transformed into positive emotions? The suggestions that follow are not presented in any order of importance, and not all may be applicable in any given case.

If you haven't done so at the very outset of the stress, as we mentioned in the beginning of this chapter, check to see if the provocation can be removed or modified. Maybe more rest or a vacation is needed. Maybe a change of assignment is needed, with either more responsibility or less, depending on whether you're suffering from boredom or overload. Maybe you need a new roommate.

Next, examine yourself with the aid of Scripture and the Holy Spirit. Have you set realistic goals for yourself? Are the priorities you have set God's priorities? What is behind the negative emotion you are experiencing? Has it already led to a sinful attitude? Are you trying to create a false self-image? Are there old unresolved conflicts at the root of the present stress? Is there an area of disobedience, of jealousy, of lack of faith?

If we discover a sinful attitude, we must confess it. That is the only way to remove it and to gain control over the negative emotions that have led to it. Confession opens the way to repentance, to receiving forgiveness, to forgiving others, to restoration of relationships, and finally, to the elimination of the stress itself.

At some point it may be helpful to talk with a trusted friend or family member or counselor. The only rule in so doing is that you must not speak negatively of a third party who is not present: that is slander.

There's one thing left, without which we cannot gain final victory over the stress we are experiencing, and without which we will not fully learn what God is trying to teach us through the stressful experience. That one thing is this: we must will to offer God our thanksgiving and praise.

Now this last thing isn't just a formality, a mantra. There's a very practical psychological reason for doing this, apart from the fact that God has commanded us to do it. When we praise and thank God from our heart for the stress we are experiencing, we are acknowledging to him and to ourselves that he knows best what is good for us.

I agree that we often start out thanking God through gritted teeth; our heart isn't fully in it. But no matter; start anyway. For just as confession of sin leads invariably to cleansing and healing, so does praising and thanking God lead invariably to the outpouring of blessing, of joy, of contentment. It is a spiritual principle.

Notice that word contentment; it didn't slip in by accident. Paul wrote to Timothy that "godliness with contentment is great gain" (1 Ti 6:6). The very act of praising and thanking God produces in us a spirit of contentment. God knows what he is doing. "...in all things"—stress included—"God works for the good of those who love him, who have been called according to his purpose" (Ro 8:28). We can be content with that.

It may be that God will allow a stress to continue until the point comes when we can truly thank him for it, until we can *accept* it as coming from his hand for our good. Amy Carmichael used to say: "In acceptance lieth peace." Peace is the opposite of stress.

The Psalmist wrote: "[God] chose our inheritance for us" (Ps 47:4). Charles Spurgeon, in commenting on this verse, wrote: "Had any other condition been better for you than the one in which you find yourself, divine love would have placed you there."

Unconscious defense mechanisms

We have said earlier that we are responsible for our reactions and for our attitudes. We also said that all our reactions and attitudes are colored by our perceptions. And we suggested that at the beginning of any stressful experience we check to see that our perceptions are accurate. We are ultimately responsible for them too.

But there is a fly in the ointment—or, as we might say in Nepal, there is a stone in the rice. Things aren't as they appear. Some of our perceptions we are conscious of, and these we can alter or control. But other perceptions derive from the subconscious; we are not aware of them and hence cannot control them. These are the perceptions that result from unconscious defense mechanisms that exist in all people. They are normal mechanisms, and at times helpful. But usually they end up causing harm, because they distort reality. They hide from us the real cause of our problem, and hence prevent us from dealing with it.

The more we are aware of these defense mechanisms, the more we can correct for the distortions they produce. Here is a place where an experienced friend or counselor can give us insight into why we see things the way we do, and why we react the way we do. We are all aware of these mechanisms in others; but when it comes to ourselves we have blinders on.

Below are some of the more common defense mechanisms.

1. Denial. "Who, me? I'm not experiencing stress. I'm not upset." Or angry, or depressed, or whatever.

A positive variant of the denial mechanism goes this way: "I love the Nepalis and their country." Or, "I love my project director." But my actions and attitudes prove otherwise.

2. Displacement. I may be angry with myself or with another person; in either case the anger is making me uncomfortable or guilty. So I displace my anger onto the weather, or a tree, or a dog. That's all right initially; but if I should start kicking every dog in sight, then I'd better quickly ask why. Because my problem is not with dogs but with my project director, or my spouse, or my roommate—or myself. Kicking dogs will bring no lasting solutions to these problems.

3. Projection. "She is angry with me." But it happens not to be true. Instead, it's I who am angry with her. I can't accept the hostility in myself, so I project it on to her. This has the added advantage that I then can go around criticizing her for being an angry person—which, of course, satisfies my original anger! I'm getting back at her.

This is why Paul was psychologically astute when he wrote to the Romans that "you who pass judgment do the same things" (Ro 2:1). That anger I "see" in the other person is in me. My "seeing," my perception, is false.

4. Rationalization. "I don't help the natives because they'll take advantage of me," or, "because they'll become rice-Christians."

Rationalization substitutes an acceptable motive for an unacceptable one. We are uncomfortable with the unacceptable motive; it's not Christian. So we find or invent a reason that is plausible and valid. The only hitch is: it's not our real reason. We are again deceiving ourselves and others.

What are the real reasons I don't want to help the natives? I don't want to give the necessary time or money. I don't want to get involved; I don't want to have to make a sacrifice.

The danger in rationalization is that it hides from view our true, sinful motive, and prevents us from confessing it to God and receiving a new motive pleasing to him.

All of these mechanisms we've mentioned so far function by means of false perceptions, through which we deceive ourselves. This is why none of us can be confident our motives are pure. And if we can't even sort out our own motives, what makes us think we're entitled to judge other people's motives!

There are additional defense mechanisms—compensation, withdrawal, and others—but the problem with them all is that they divert us from getting at the real cause of our unhappiness. And although they are called "defense" mechanisms, they don't really defend us. Instead, they get us deeper into trouble. They cover over the painful emotions we are experiencing. So the emotions go underground, and begin to eat away at us, or they cause guilt (because we know something is wrong somewhere), or they erupt inexplicably in inappropriate and destructive ways.

As we said earlier, we need to get our emotions out into the open. This is painful, but it is the only road to overcoming stress. If we don't, we are headed for a nervous breakdown, or fatigue, depression, or even physical illness.

Burnout

Some months ago, *The Rising Nepal*'s "quote of the day" said: "It's better to burn out than to rust out."

Henry Martyn, the great missionary to India in the early 1800s, said upon his arrival on the field: "Now let me burn out for Christ."

And my wife Cynthia, when asked by a friend what kept her from "burning out," replied, "I am strengthened daily; I am in God's will; I have the Holy Spirit. Why should I burn out?"

What were these three esteemed authorities talking about? What is burnout?

A young missionary woman assigned to a rural area gave out and gave out year after year. She couldn't say "no." She felt obliged to help all comers. She assisted people in need, comforted the sorrowing, taught students, and acted as village doctor, counselor, and peacemaker. She was loved and trusted. She stayed up late to prepare Bible lessons, and got up before dawn to pray. And the Sabbath was the busiest day of all: Sunday school, a long church service, and many visitors. Among the missionaries she had few friends.

After some years she began to have trouble sleeping. She lost her appetite; her weight fell. A doctor advised her to get some more rest, to take up a hobby, to do something for pleasure, and to have at least one day in seven when she did no work.

But she wouldn't listen. Surely a servant of Christ should be able to give of oneself unstintingly. The doctor's advice was unspiritual. Do something for pleasure?

Eventually her health broke down altogether, and she had to leave the field. Then she had no ministry whatever. Much better to have paced herself, to have followed Scripture and rested one day a week, or one hour in seven, or one week in seven. But she wanted to show her love for Christ, her love for the people, her own spirituality. And indeed she succeeded; her witness was powerful and fruitful. But it came to an untimely end. What, then, went wrong?

Burnout, of course; that's the title of this section. Indeed, this seems to be as pure a case of burnout as one could ask for.

But as we shall see, this wasn't a "pure case" of burnout at all. In fact, there has never been a pure case of burnout. We like the term because it has a heroic ring to it, as in Henry Martyn's usage. Who wants to leave the field because of exhaustion, depression, a nervous breakdown, interpersonal conflict, or spiritual defeat? Much better to leave with the diagnosis of "burnout," and be carried home with head held high.

Well, it's all right to use the term "burnout," I suppose, as long as one realizes it doesn't really mean anything. It is not a diagnosis. It is a loose descriptive phrase that can signify any number of specific problems—physical, emotional, or spiritual. But by using the term, we may prevent someone from finding out the real cause of his problem, and we may lose the chance to prevent the same problem from arising in others. Therefore, I urge that we do away with the term "burnout" altogether.

What happened to the young missionary we described above? By her own admission later on, she realized that what had been driving her was not the Holy Spirit alone, but spiritual pride as well. She was trying to be an Amy Carmichael. Her self-image had been very important to her. Thus it wasn't the doctor who had been "unspiritual"; it had been she.

There is another reason why burnout is a bad term. If there are no problems, Christians do not burn out. As Cynthia rightly told her friend, "I am in God's will; I have the Holy Spirit. Why should I burn out?" But the term "burnout" suggests a candle running down. The Christian life is not a candle running down! A modern parable is told of the lighthouse keeper who gave all his oil away because he couldn't say "no." But does the Holy Spirit limit the amount of oil he gives us? In fact, just the opposite; if we don't expend it, use it, share it, the inflow of spiritual power into our lives will soon dry up.

Am I saying we shouldn't pace ourselves? Not at all. Pacing ourselves ought to come naturally; it's largely a matter of common sense (which the Lord gave us). We rest when we're tired, eat when we're hungry.

There's room for wide individual variation in the matter of pacing ourselves. Some people need more rest, some less. Gregarious people need more social diversion, contemplatives less. Some people thrive on work and seldom need a break; other need a slower pace and more frequent breaks. And we need to respect each other's differences without name-calling.

With the guidance of the Holy Spirit, the advice of family and friends, and with frequent self-examination, each one of us should choose the pace that is most suitable for us. The pace may vary at different stages of our life.

In choosing our pace, more of us err on the side of too slow a pace than too fast a one. A greater danger than "burnout" is self-indulgence. And the older we get, the greater a problem self-indulgence becomes.

One way *not* to pace ourselves is to allot God a certain number of hours each day and keep the rest for ourselves. God wants all twenty-four hours. "I'll burn out," you say. No, not if you give him all twenty-four. It's when people struggle to keep those few precious hours for themselves that stress levels rise and "burnout" begins. We need to trust God with our entire day. He's not a tyrant. He won't let us burn out.

Paul said, "...offer your bodies as living sacrifices" (Ro 12:1). And he meant twenty-four hours a day. And in verse 2 he says, "Then you will be able to test and approve what God's will is—his good, pleasing and perfect will."

When we have given everything to God—skill, time, even our bodies—we will know his will. We will know how to pace ourselves day by day. At the end of the workday we won't say, "Now, I've had enough for today." We'll let God decide when we've had enough, and what we should be doing next. It's called walking in God's will, and it is the only way we'll know if we're going at the right pace.

Helen Roseveare tells of one period during her service in Africa when she had been under particular pressure. Then in the midst of the pressure came one particularly bad day: up in the early hours to treat an emergency, all day at the hospital, administrative problems in the evening. Finally she dragged herself home at 11 P.M. She shut out all the front lights, and pulled down the shades in the kitchen so no one would think she was there. She was planning to have a bowl of soup and plop into bed. Then came a knock at the front door. Helen sat still in the kitchen. She wasn't on call, so it couldn't be from the hospital. She waited, thinking the knocker would quickly realize there was no one at home and go away.

But the knocking continued. "Can't that person tell there's no one here?" Helen thought to herself. Then finally she asked softly, "Is that knock from you, Lord?"

Without waiting for the answer, she went on: "You know I can't do another thing tonight. And if I had to, I'd have no energy left over for tomorrow. But I have three operations scheduled tomorrow, and a full day's work besides. I can't answer that knock."

The knocking continued. And Helen went to the door.

It was a young male member of the hospital staff who had professed faith some time before, but had recently backslidden. He came in and poured out his heart to Helen. They talked for over two hours. They shared the soup Helen had heated. In the end, Helen helped lead the young man to repentance, restoration, and a deep renewal of his commitment to Christ.

Helen was finally in bed at two. She was up at five, and all that day, she said, she had never felt so full of energy.

The balanced life

"It's better to burn out than to rust out." I would heartily agree. But we have a third and vastly superior choice: the middle road, the balanced life.

Satan wants to get us off balance. If he can get us off to one extreme or the other, he can accomplish two things at once: first, he can make us unfruitful; and second, he can get us fighting among ourselves over whose extreme is better. Satan loves to polarize us, in both doctrine and behavior. The Holy Spirit, on the other hand, brings unity, harmony, and balance.

It's appropriate to talk about balance in a chapter on stress. Think of the tightrope walker: when do you suppose his stress level goes up? And it's the same for us. Come to think of it, being a missionary is quite often like walking a tightrope.

We've already seen one possible area of imbalance: between too fast a pace and too slow. Another closely related area is the matter of grace and legalism, or freedom and discipline. The legalist is always feeling obligated to do more and more and more. He feels he needs to prove to God that he is obedient, that he is worthy, that he is sacrificing himself. But that is the wrong motive for obeying and sacrificing; that's merely an attempt to justify oneself. If that is the motive, one's activity cannot be sustained for long; it will lead to physical and spiritual depletion. The only self-sustaining motive is love.

On the other hand, too much freedom and too little discipline leads to laziness, carelessness, and a failure to fully utilize the gifts God has given us. It's hard to know which of these two extremes is worse.

Another area of polarization is between work and worship. This is another one of those false dichotomies; it is quite possible to worship God through one's work—if the work is motivated by love for him. Here we see the Mary and Martha syndrome. Many missionaries function best by keeping busy. Others need to spend more time walking along the rice paddies singing and meditating. Here's a case where the "balance point" may be different from one individual to the next. Indeed, in all these examples, what is "balanced" for me may not be for you. The point is, each of us must find our own balance.

Remember that the Lord didn't rebuke Martha for being too busy; he rebuked her because of her anxiety and her complaining spirit. And neither will he rebuke us for working harder, going faster, and keeping busier than our fellow missionaries. But when we fast-and-busy types get off our balance points, we become anxious, frantic, hassled, and exhausted. Then it's time for a walk in the rice paddies.

There are many other places where we can lose our balance and end up on one extreme or another. A new worker comes out to the field and sees older missionaries living in comfortable houses, and says: "That's not right; I'm going to live like the nationals." And if it's a poor country, he may end up living at a level of poverty he can't maintain. He's gone to an extreme—and all the worse for having criticized his fellow missionaries for their "comfortable houses."

We could go on. Some of us are too enthusiastic; others are too cautious. Some of us are too independent; others are too dependent. Some leaders suffocate people under the guise of "shepherding" them; others fail to lead with a strong enough hand. How can we chart our way through these extremes and keep a balanced course?

The answer is the same as it's always been: Walk closely with Christ. Keep communicating with him, keep reading his word, keep in fellowship with his servants. There is no shortcut to knowing God's will, day by day and hour by hour.

Before we do anything else, we need to know God's will. Without it, we can't keep a balanced course for one hour. Knowing God's will is the most important work a missionary (or any other Christian) can do.

Fatigue

One of the commonest problems on the mission field is fatigue. Here we are not talking about ordinary physical tiredness, which can be cured by rest. Rather we are referring to the chronic fatigue that results from underlying stress and its associated negative emotions.

A heavy workload alone does not cause the kind of fatigue we're talking about here. The cause will always be some unhappiness in the work: boredom, pressure, aggravations, uncertainty—as in, "Will thirty patients come to the hospital today, or three hundred?" It is these "unhappy factors," not the work itself, which produce the stress, which in turn produces the fatigue.

The uncertainty factor in the work is a major cause of chronic fatigue on the mission field, simply because uncertainty is a fact of life in missions. When we don't have control over our day, we get anxious. We know we're supposed to have given God control, but being imperfect creatures, we don't always do so. Serves us right, then, if we get anxious. This anxiety can affect everyone from the wife whose husband is always bringing home unexpected guests to the hospital staff who are always being swamped with new admissions from the doctor.

It is incumbent upon leaders to be sensitive to the amount of work they are giving to those under them, and to do everything possible to make the work predictable. The worker, in turn, needs to communicate with the leader when things are getting rough, not just endure, or grumble behind the leader's back. There is nothing unchristian about telling your leader that you're overworked. Also, the worker needs to understand that the leader often has little control over the work himself. How, for example, does a doctor control the number of patients he admits?

In many cases, then, the workload and its unpredictability can't be controlled; things remain as they are. But the very fact that the problem is out in the open and all sides are working in good faith to ameliorate it is often sufficient in itself to dispel the anxiety and stress. And when that happens, the fatigue goes too.

Since stress is the main cause of chronic fatigue, anything that produces stress will produce fatigue as well. Indeed, fatigue is one of the earliest signs of underlying stress; it is a signal that something is not balanced in our life. As a signal, fatigue is helpful. It should lead us at once to take stock, to examine ourselves to find the source of the stress. If we don't do so, the fatigue will increase and eventually incapacitate us.

In addition to work-related stress, there are a couple of other causes of stress that especially lead to missionary fatigue. One is the "drop in the bucket" syndrome. "The need is so vast that my contribution won't make any difference. What use is it?" Yes, the need is so vast that we can get fatigued just thinking about it. But as to what use our tiny contribution is, the answer is clear: it's of eternal use. Every cup of water given in Jesus' name counts in God's sight.

There are physical causes of stress-related fatigue on the mission field: heat, sleepless nights from bedbugs or barking dogs, various illnesses. You ask: What does stress have to do with these? Don't these things cause fatigue directly? Yes, they do, but that is not our focus here. I believe the anxiety associated with such physical factors is a greater source of chronic fatigue than the physical disturbance itself. I have found, for instance, that worrying about whether I am going to get enough sleep tires me as much as the actual loss of sleep. The anxiety or stress associated with a chronic illness like amebiasis can be as fatiguing as the disease itself. It is this chronic anxiety or stress-produced fatigue rather than purely physical fatigue that causes the real long-range problems among missionaries.

Finally, there is a type of fatigue commonly affecting missionaries that is related less to stress than to negligence and lack of good sense. Sometimes missionaries think they are above the physiological and psychological laws God has established. So they run themselves down, eat poorly, take unnecessary health risks, and then they're surprised when they get fatigued or sick.

Eating proper food, taking proper rest, heeding the advice of doctors, counselors, and friends are all part of our duty as Christians. Otherwise, we are not exercising faith; we are merely tempting God.

And if the fatigue does not respond to practical common-sense measures, then look beneath the surface. Look for the cause of the stress that will always be there. Is there a sinful attitude? Deal with whatever the Holy Spirit shows you at any given time. We are not responsible for unconscious problems. But as we work on what is conscious, the submerged part will gradually rise to view. Only in more serious cases will the subconscious cause so much trouble that trained counselors will be needed to get at the problem's root.

When a person becomes a missionary, he or she is accepting a greater load of work than falls on most people at home. Busyness is an inescapable fact of missionary life. Therefore, it is well for every missionary to recall the words of Paul Tournier: "The yield of our life does not depend so much on the number of things we do, but more on the quality of self-giving that we put to each thing." It doesn't really matter how many patients we treat, how many classes we teach, or how many sermons we preach. What matters is: Was God in those activities? Were they done by his direction, in his way, and through his Spirit? If not, the end will be fruitlessness and fatigue.

Let us remember also, it is God who has given us these works to do.

He sends each patient, each student. He creates each opportunity for service. He invites us to minister with him. Each thing we do is eternally worthwhile because it is his work. He will not give us more to do than we are able. His "yoke is easy" and his "burden is light" (Mt 11:30). "I will give you rest," he said (Mt 11:28). This promise alone should go a long way to alleviating our fatigue.

Discouragement and depression

Jesus never promised us lives without discouragement. Temporary discouragement is as natural as physical fatigue. The mission field holds more that its share of setbacks, and each step backward is a source of discouragement. And discouragement, like other negative emotions, is cumulative. Sometimes the backward steps seem to come all at once. Some young believers you are discipling are slipping backwards. You help an impoverished family get on its feet and the husband turns around and robs you. You encounter obstacles in the work. There are staff conflicts. Throw in an illness, some bad news from home, and if by this time you're not feeling discouraged there's something wrong with you.

And what makes it all the worse is when you look over at your colleague and he or she is sailing along without a problem on the horizon. Which brings us to rule number one: If you want to double your discouragement, the foolproof method is to compare yourself with others.

Well then, you say, "I'll compare myself with someone who's doing worse than I am; that will encourage me." Good luck. First of all, you'll end up the kind of person who is always rejoicing in his brother's failure. Second, you'll get no incentive to improve your own situation. That's one of the reasons so many Christians lead mediocre lives: they are comparing themselves to mediocre people. "He's not bearing much fruit, so I can't be that bad." There is only one person we should be comparing ourselves with, and that is Jesus. He has set the highest standard we can follow, and what's more, he gives us daily encouragement to reach it.

Most discouragements we just "get over"; we move on. But some discouragements come from our being thrust into a situation we weren't suited for; we are temperamentally mismatched with our assignment. We don't have the gifts necessary, or our gifts aren't being used. Call this job dissatisfaction, if you will; job dissatisfaction is a major cause of discouragement on the mission field. Nevertheless, it can be a valuable experience, through which God develops some undeveloped part of our character. When God has done his work, then he'll move us on.

Some people are more prone to discouragement than others. They have a habit of putting themselves down. This is not humility; this is more self-pity, self-absorption. Don't be like the missionary who started every prayer by saying, "I am a worm and no man." He only stopped after his colleagues began thanking God they weren't worms.

Let us remember who we are. We are disciples, priests, friends of the King of kings. No matter what we feel, that's who we are. Simply remembering who we are will help us act like it.

Some people are prone to mood swings. We sometimes brush them off as being "emotionally unstable," but that is unfair—unless, of course, the mood swings are extreme and unpredictable. Mood swings are normal, and can be used constructively. When we are "up," we should use every opportunity for useful, creative work and for reaching out. At the same time, we should control the talkativeness, self-assertiveness, and restless energy that are characteristic of these "up" times. When we are "down," on the other hand, we should use the time for recuperation, self-examination, study, and doing helpful things for others. During that time we need to resist any tendency to self-pity, grumbling, or laziness.

The line leading from discouragement to depression is a continuous one. Depression is an overreaction or unduly prolonged reaction to some adversity or loss. Discouragement is a natural response; depression is an exaggerated one.

The kind of depression we are speaking of here is not a mental illness, but it needs to be taken seriously all the same. If neglected, it can lead on into a depressive psychosis, where the person loses insight, loses touch with reality, and resorts to destructive behavior. In such cases, psychiatric care will be needed. But in the early stages, depression can be overcome by the individual himself, often with the help of a wise counselor or friend.

The common early-stage depression that is seen among missionaries is almost always rooted in stress. Indeed, most of the things we have said about chronic fatigue apply also to depression; they are closely related problems and, in fact, usually occur together. Depression is the more serious and more disabling of the two.

If stress is behind most missionary depression, then behind the stress will be a sinful attitude. Most depression is at root spiritual. It is often said: "Don't ask what is behind the depression; ask who is behind it." Because more often than not it will arise from an interpersonal conflict and the sinful attitudes that accompany it. We often attribute our depression to surface causes, and that's easy to do because there is so much around to depress us! But always we need to look deeper into ourselves for the real cause.

Probably the commonest sinful attitudes at the root of depression are bitterness and resentment. These attitudes we suppress, because as Christians we know they are wrong. It is said: At the bottom of depression we find resentment; at the bottom of resentment we find resentment against God. Many people don't pull out of their depression until they have recognized and confessed their resentment against God.

Once we have exposed and confessed our sinful attitudes, we can become free of them through God's forgiveness and cleansing. Then whatever surface problems there are can be dealt with easily.

This is not to say that rooting out sinful attitudes is easy. It's a lifelong struggle. But it is there that we need to focus our attention if we want healing—not on the climate, or the Nepali government, or disagreeable Mr. X, the project director.

There is a positive side to depression: see it as the discipline of God, for that is what it is. The writer to the Hebrews says to those being disciplined: "Therefore, strengthen your feeble arms and weak knees!" (Heb 12:12). If anything characterizes depression it is "feeble arms and weak knees." In other words, accept the discipline; repent and be restored.

There are two additional factors which aggravate depression: one is loneliness, which will be discussed in Chapter Eighteen; and the other is guilt.

Guilt is of two kinds: subjective and objective—that is, feeling guilty and being guilty. These two kinds often occur together, but they require different therapy.

Objective or true guilt can only be healed when atonement has been made for our sin. While we can atone for some sins by paying the consequences, ultimately only Christ can atone for our deepest sins, which are against God. We are cast on his mercy. But the biblical promise is sure: "If we confess our sins, he is faithful and just and will forgive us our sins and purify us from all unrighteousness" (1 Jn 1:9). And when our objective guilt is removed, any subjective guilt will disappear as well.

Subjective guilt existing by itself is not uncommon. Some people have a tendency to blame themselves for everything that goes wrong, even when they are not in the least responsible. The roots of this complex often go back to childhood, when the person may have suffered frequent and unfair criticism from parents and others, and has come to assume as a result that he or she is the cause of every problem. Such guilt or inferiority complexes are not easy to eradicate, but they can usually be alleviated by sober self-assessment, together with the help of a friend or counselor.

There is a particular combination of subjective and objective guilt that needs special mention. A person may feel guilty for some trivial or non-existent sin, whereas in reality he is guilty of a deeper and more serious sin. Such misplaced guilt serves as a cover for one's real sin. By focusing only on the trivial or imagined sin, one can avoid dealing with the real sin. Only when the real sin is exposed and confessed can the individual be free from both his real and imagined guilt.

Past emotional hurts

There is a category of emotional problems for which the sufferer is not, in the first instance, responsible: namely, childhood emotional trauma. It is sometimes easier to accept earthquakes, floods, and pestilence than it is to accept the injuries children receive at the hands of adults. Be that as it may, there are quite a few fine Christians who come out to the mission field carrying with them the scars of childhood trauma.

Missionaries, because they are on the front line of spiritual warfare, are often tempted to see demons lurking everywhere, especially in cases of emotional disturbance. Demon possession and oppression do exist, but they are not nearly as common as ordinary psychological disorders. And in the case of Christians, many believe that true demon possession is impossible. We must be very cautious about labeling anything demon-possession. The gift of discernment is necessary, and two or more mature Christians should agree on the matter before any action is taken. Because if we are wrong, we shall end up doing harm to the person with the problem.

Even if we don't see a demon as the cause of some abnormal behavior, we may come up with another equally erroneous explanation, especially in the case of fellow believers, whether missionaries or nationals. If we see a Christian brother or sister with some hang-up, some persistent emotional problem such as depression, poor self-esteem, or irrational fear, we tend to apply a standard formula: "You need to have faith; you need to pray more; you need to get right with God." And we simply add an extra burden of pain and guilt on someone who is already hurting by implying that if they were better Christians they wouldn't be having this problem. Instead, we need to recognize that many very good Christians, including our national brothers and sisters, may have had deep hurts in their past that affect their behavior years later. Simply becoming a Christian does not immediately heal these hurts. And even when they are healed, a tender scar remains. Let us not reopen these wounds by our insensitive judgments.

Thus when we see a missionary or national colleague with an emotional disorder, we are not entitled to attribute it to "spiritual failure." It may be so; it may even be so in most cases. (Who of us, after all, is a one-hundred-percent spiritual success?) But there will be some remaining whose weakness of faith, inordinate fear, inability to reach out will be due not to some sinful attitude but rather to a crippling and distorting childhood scar.

Childhood trauma is either suppressed, transferred, or resolved. When it is suppressed, one's emotional development is arrested or distorted, and one is left to face adult life with an enormous emotional handicap.

When the childhood trauma is transferred, the effects of the trauma are not so crippling, but they condemn the individual to keep fighting childhood battles throughout adult life. The problem arises in mild form whenever adults work together: "We don't 'hit it off'; I don't like his type; he turns me off." But its severer manifestations are exceedingly harmful to the unity and proper functioning of the missionary team. There may be a fellow missionary you instinctively dislike, or distrust, or are jealous of, or are afraid of. Why? Because he reminds you of someone from your past. And until the past has been brought into the open and dealt with, the present conflict cannot be resolved.

What do you do? First, try to look objectively at that person who is provoking these negative reactions in you. Who does he remind you of from the past? It is not helpful to delve into our subconscious; the stuff that's there is usually best left alone. But ask the Holy Spirit to help bring to mind any recollection that may be helpful in solving your present problem. Trust him to do so. At the same time, try to understand what makes your unpleasant colleague tick; put yourself in his shoes. Pray for a forgiving spirit—and then forgive him.

Even when we've done all this, we may continue to experience one or more negative emotions. But that is all right; we cannot be completely free of negative emotions. However, we must not let them cripple us or lead us into sinful attitudes.

The third outcome of childhood trauma is resolution. But that doesn't mean all residual effect of the trauma is obliterated. Nothing in our past experience is obliterated; everything leaves some effect. In the case of "resolved" childhood trauma, the main residual effect is a tendency to overprotection and overreaction. "I'll never let my children go to that boarding school"—and so you keep them at home under inappropriate circumstances and the children suffer. We must not allow our own past childhood traumas to lead us to make unwise and unbalanced decisions about the present.

So even resolved childhood trauma leaves its scar. The scar will produce a mild but noticeable contraction of the personality and an increased sensitivity in the area of the past pain. Thus when we meet up with such people, we need to make allowance for their past and help to protect their sensitive areas.

Finally, we should remember that all emotional pains and hurts, whether they have arisen in childhood or not, have their positive side. They send us a message, just as physical pain does. Even as we try to ease the pain and heal the hurt, we must not lose sight of the message the pain and hurt are sending, for the message will be from God. We mustn't deny we are hurting, for then we will be denying God the opportunity to communicate with us through the hurt.

There will always be a spiritual component to every emotional problem, simply because we are both emotional and spiritual beings. And if we are honest, there will be some element of sin at least aggravating if not causing the problem. Unfortunately, in our desire to be gentle with the hurting Christian we tend to slide around the sin. But that's the exact message of the pain: through the pain and hurt, God wants to call our attention to our sin. When sin is at the root of the problem, one minute of confession is worth a hundred hours of therapy.

Most of the pain and hurt we experience builds our character and draws us closer to God. But the wounds can be deep. Even if we have escaped them in childhood, they will catch up with us on the mission field. And Christians need to be patient and tender toward those who are suffering from these wounds. It is not the time for unfeeling lectures and admonitions, much less for judgment. The body of Christ must learn to nurse its wounded.

Body life

As much as any other Christians, missionaries need some kind of body life, some opportunity for mutual caring and sharing. It is good when the circle of fellowship can include national believers; certainly this is an ideal worth striving for. But in the early stages of a missionary's career, he or she will draw most support from fellow missionaries.

Cynthia and I will always remember a young couple from our early years in Nepal who exemplified more than anyone we know the body life that knits a Christian team together. These folks came from a small-town background; they didn't have a bunch of high-powered degrees; they didn't have a leadership position. They were quiet and unassuming. Yet they did more to draw our team close together than anyone else. How? By doing nice things for people. By being ready to help—at any time. Of course, I may be prejudiced in their favor. I met this couple on my initial trip out to the mission hospital where Cynthia and I were later assigned. On the evening before I was to return to Kathmandu, they invited me to supper. Marilyn made me a dozen brownies for the trail next day, and told me to eat no more than one that night on my way back to the room where I was sleeping. Well, I have never tasted such good brownies. I ate every last one on the twenty-minute walk to my room that night. I made up in brownies what I lacked in the ninth fruit of the Spirit.

In order for body life to exist, there must be unreserved acceptance of one another, and absolutely no spirit of criticism or judgment. The instant one senses that anything he might share or confess may later be used against him, he will clam up, and for him "body life" comes to an end. Body life begins with John 13:34. "As I have loved you...." Jesus' love was unconditional, and so must ours be.

It is unscriptural for missionaries to work alone. From Genesis 1:18 to Ecclesiastes 4:9-12 on down through the New Testament, God's pattern is for us to work in teams, and the reason is obvious: we were made to need the support of our fellows. True, Paul says that God will meet all our needs (Php 4:19), but he usually does so through fellow believers.

When only two or three members are on a team, they may not be able to fully support one another. Their temperaments and experiences may not match. In such cases, the members need to retreat periodically to a larger group for additional support.

Within any team or fellowship, we each need at least one or two specially trusted friends to whom we can open our hearts. It is within this smaller group that James 5:16 can more readily become a reality. When we are able to confess our sins to each other, then we know that we are functioning as a body should. And the purpose of confessing sins to one another? "...so that you may be healed."

There are two rules to observe when we share with our trusted friend: one, don't run off at the mouth; and two, don't speak one negative word about an absent third party—or else you will be answering to God for that word. And there is a companion rule for the trusted friend: don't listen to that negative word (if it should be spoken), or you will be participating in the speaker's slander.

Even trained and officially designated counselors must be scrupulously careful about listening to slander. The Bible gives us no license to speak negatively about someone to a counselor any more than to anyone else. The counselor must immediately point out that the negative talk is not only wrong, but it is not going to help solve the problem. The counselor must encourage the counselee to approach directly the other party in the conflict. The counselor can also offer to act as a face-to-face mediator—if both sides agree.

Most large missions have full-time counselors these days. But during a recent period one mission in Nepal had no one to fill the post of counselor. So a dozen mature missionaries were asked to become "listening ears" for troubled missionaries until a regular counselor could be appointed. Listening ears! It's not about spiders, dogs, and flies that those "listening ears" will be hearing; it will be about third parties. Talking negatively about others is bad enough; we must take great pains not to institutionalize it!

Counseling

Counselors have provided inestimable aid to hurting and troubled missionaries over the years, and we need to be grateful for them. Indeed, it were better to call for them earlier rather that later, when problems become full-blown and are harder to deal with.

The first line of approach to any person with a personality disorder or mental problem is to see if the person is living out of line with God's commands as revealed in Scripture. Because this is the root problem of the great majority of people suffering from psychological disturbances. And it is the same for missionaries on the field who run into emotional and mental difficulties. As we have said before: don't blame external factors; the problem lies within, usually in the form of one or more sinful attitudes.

Books and articles continue to be written about missionary stress and missionary casualties with very little reference to sinful attitudes being the major cause of the problems. Yes, we can call these people wounded, but the wound has come because Satan found a chink in their armor.

In dealing with one burdened with a psychological problem, however, we must not automatically assume that the cause is disobedience to God. As mentioned earlier, there are some mental problems which are not directly due to sinful attitudes, such as damaged emotions from childhood and outright mental illness. But generally one should start with the commonest things first. When you see a patient with a cold, you don't immediately think he has lung cancer—though he may, in fact, have it.

The counselor's approach will always be gentle. Even in cases of outright sin, Paul admonished us to "restore" the person "gently" (Gal 6:1); all the more so in situations where the sin is hidden, or only one of several factors. The counselor will seek to avoid adding unnecessary guilt to an already burdened mind. However, if disobedience to God is the underlying problem, then guilt will already be present. It will not be a question of adding guilt, but rather of bringing it into the open where it can be dealt with by confession, repentance, and restoration.

Psychological counseling should never be divorced from spiritual counseling. The Christian counselor is not neutral; he is directive. He uses God's word to influence the behavior of the counselee. The counselee is always responsible for both his behavior and underlying attitudes, and he must be led to make the necessary changes to get his life back in line with God's commands.

It is much more constructive to focus initially on changing behavior, rather than on changing attitudes. True, we know from Matthew 5 that Jesus placed great importance on attitudes; he taught that a sinful attitude is just as much a sin as sinful behavior. But here we are talking about changing both sinful attitudes and behavior, and it is best to start with the behavior.

First of all, behavior can be changed more readily than attitudes. Attitudes are linked with our emotions and thus with our autonomic nervous system, which is not directly under our control. But behavior is always under our control.

Second, if we change our behavior, we will find that our attitude will change as well. Behavior determines attitude just as much as attitude determines behavior. This is the secret of praising God in adversity. If we will simply will to praise him and then do it, our anxiety, fear, and depression will diminish and even disappear. If you are feeling resentful against someone, don't start off by trying to change the feeling. Rather, go and show love to that person and pray for him, and your resentment will begin to melt away.

"But," you say, "I just can't bring myself to go to that person. I just can't praise God. He hasn't given me the grace, the strength." But the truth is that if we will but step out in faith and obedience, then God will provide the necessary grace and strength to do his will. We sit around waiting for God to act, but God is waiting for us to act.

Secular counselors drag out counseling interminably, and sadly the motive for many is money. But even Christian counselors take unnecessarily long letting their patients ventilate and waiting for them to think of solutions on their own. First of all, ventilation is little more than scratching an itch. Second, there is no evidence that solutions arrived at by the patient himself are any more likely to be heeded than the ones offered by the counselor.

The point is: if you have an abscess, you don't sit around thinking about it; you drain it. And you drain it all at once; you don't let the pus ooze out. Yes, I know, I'm a surgeon and not a psychiatrist; but there's a lot of people out there in the counseling profession who will agree with this.

Most people who come to a counselor will have, as part of their reason for coming, an interpersonal relationship problem with somebody else. As we have said earlier, the counselor must encourage a face-to-face resolution of the conflict. He can even offer to meet together with the two parties. But often the other party will not agree or not be available. In that case, the relationship problem can be discussed with the counselee, but only insofar as the counselee's own failings and sins are concerned. The other person's failings and sins are off-limits. Even if the third party is a non-Christian it makes no difference; the command not to slander applies to non-believers also.

In the case of a problem between a husband and wife, it has become customary for counselors to interview both partners separately before a joint interview. I cannot agree with this practice. The counselor looks at separate interviews from the point of view of a therapist, but in so doing he may inadvertently be driving an additional wedge between husband and wife. Sure, the husband and wife are separate individuals and each will need to be allowed to speak; the counselor can ensure that. But not behind one another's back. Occasionally there may be some special reason for conducting separate interviews, but in that case both partners must agree in advance without pressure.

It is understood that what is disclosed to a counselor will remain utterly confidential. (There are certain well-defined exceptions to this, as in cases of potential suicide or where there is danger to others.) If written notes have been taken, they remain equally the property of counselor and counselee. Only with the counselee's unpressured assent can these notes or reports be made available to the counselee's administrator.

There has been an unfortunate tendency in mission organizations to use the counseling profession almost as an arm of the administration. Busy administrators are called upon to deal with personnel problems, but don't have the time to get to the bottom of things. So they suggest the counselor look into the matter. However, this is a misuse of counselors. The counselor is to help the counselee, not to help the administration sort out its personnel problems. Aside from the routine psychological interviews of missionary candidates, the administration should not even ask for the counselor's report; this in itself puts pressure on the counselee to agree. Unless these injunctions are carefully adhered to, it becomes possible to use counseling as a means of intimidation.

In practice, many missionaries benefit from open give-and-take cooperation between themselves, their administrator, and the counselor. But this kind of approach must be at the initiation of the missionary. It should not be standard procedure.

Administrators aren't meant to be therapists, but they do have a responsibility to find out what is troubling those under them; they are shepherds, not just administrators. They can't put their people's problems off onto counselors. They need to take the time to sort things out as best they can, and then come to their own decision as to what needs to be done. Don't envy your administrators these tasks: pray for them!

Dropping out

The term "dropping out," as used here, means an unanticipated early departure from the mission field. A person may have come out planning to spend two or three terms on the field, but leaves after one. Dropping out means that something untoward has happened to change one's plans.

Many people come out to the field intending to stay "as long as the Lord leads them to stay." It is difficult to apply the term "dropping out" to this large group, because when they decide to leave for whatever reason they will say they were following God's leading. In many cases this will be so, but in some cases it will not be. It is easy to deceive oneself here. Many missionaries today come out with the idea of "seeing how things go." If they go well, they stay. If things don't go well, they leave. It is a little like choosing a career, or a company to work for. This approach isn't, in itself, wrong. What's wrong is that the individual keeps the control of his life in his own hands. "If I think things are working out, I'll decide to stay; if not, I'll choose to leave." Where is God in this? There would not be a worldwide church today if the early missionaries had gone out with such an attitude. If a person is not totally sold out to God, he or she shouldn't come to the field for even one year.

I hasten to make it clear that I'm not talking here of the very short-term workers, especially the students, who do legitimately come out to "test the waters." These people are seeking God's will. Their main purpose for coming is not the ministry they accomplish, though that's important; the main purpose is to allow God to work in their lives. Let these short-termers keep coming! Many of them will turn into long-termers, and the rest of them will fire up their churches back home.

Here follows a number of common reasons why missionaries drop out: health reasons, needs of aged parents at home; needs of the children, job dissatisfaction, inability to adapt with resulting emotional stress, discouragement because of lack of spiritual fruit, disagreement with mission policy and leadership decisions, concern for professional advancement, desire for the life at home, the wife's unhappiness after her children are grown, psychological disorders—all this adds up to twenty-five percent of the total. What's missing? That old bane, interpersonal conflict with fellow missionaries and one's leaders. Many writers on this subject state that this is the major reason behind seventy-five percent of missionary dropouts.

There are a few other reasons: people get married; they are asked to work in the home office; or they transfer to a new mission field. These moves don't leave problems and disappointments in their wake; they do not constitute "dropping out," so they are not our concern here.

People rarely drop out for only one reason; they might have five or six reasons. It is impossible to assign each reason an exact percentage of the total reason for dropping out.

Notice that the first three reasons in the list above—those relating to health, aged parents, and children—are "acceptable" reasons for dropping out, while all the rest are "unacceptable" to varying degrees, that is, unacceptable to the missionary himself or to the home constituency. Naturally one feels better about dropping out if at least one of the reasons is in the "acceptable" category. Indeed, the unacceptable reasons are often not even stated by the missionary. That is why it's very hard to come up with accurate figures as to why people leave the mission field.

It would be most helpful if one could screen out in advance those who were going to drop out early, and save them the trouble of going to the mission field in the first place. It is often these very people who cause the greatest problems among their fellow workers. But there is no such screening test. At best, mission agencies can detect special risk factors, such as: inflexibility, dogmatism, unwillingness to submit to authority, poor communication skills, and uncertainty in the call and motivation of the wife. Any of these factors, if present, indicates there is a real risk that the missionary will not make a good adaptation to the mission field and hence will be more likely to drop out.

In determining what is an "acceptable" reason for leaving the field, there is only one question to ask: Is it acceptable to God? Sometimes even our "acceptable" reasons are not acceptable to him. And to complicate things further, he may be telling us to leave the field, but we're not listening. This confusion arises most commonly when the needs of our children and the needs of our elderly parents (reasons two and three in the list above) conflict with the needs of the work. Where does our first duty lie? What is God's will in such cases?

The parallel passages in Matthew 10:37 and Luke 14:26 clearly state that we are to put Christ first, ahead of any family member. But they do not speak of putting some specific "work" first. Christ's "work" is to obey him always. If our parents or children need us, then that becomes our "first work"—even if it means putting aside our mission work for a greater or lesser period.

The New Testament has stern words for those who neglect their God-given responsibilities to their parents and children (1 Ti 5:8). We can never say: "I can't go home because I have a 'higher call.'" That is similar to the "Corban" argument of the Pharisees, which they used as an excuse not to provide for their parents. Jesus had no kind words to say about that (Mk 7:11-13).

In almost every missionary's career, the thought of dropping out has come at some time or other. What do we do when we begin to feel like calling it quits?

Our first response must be to turn to God. We must assume that we are to stick it out, unless he clearly directs us otherwise. Are we faltering in our commitment to him? If so, confess it and pray for grace and strength.

Why do we have the desire to drop out? Have we been "wounded" in the spiritual conflict that missionary life entails? Yes, we may have been. But these wounds have been allowed by God; as we saw in an earlier chapter, they are God's discipline. They are God's loving acts designed to purge us of our self-life. These disciplines show us those areas where we have not truly died to self.

But missionaries, like others, prefer to avoid such disciplines. Our self-life resists. We choose, instead, to turn back from a life of self-denial. We decide that missionary life wasn't God's will for us after all.

It is the discomfort and irritation caused by our imperfect fellow missionaries that is hardest for us to accept as God's discipline. Yet we need to see them as instruments in God's hands to perfect us. God's discipline is a sign of his favor toward us, not his anger. He is leading us onward, not signaling us to turn back. The greatest tragedy in dropping out is that we forfeit the chance to learn obedience through the discipline God sends us. Even Christ had to learn obedience through "what he suffered," and it is through his suffering that he was "made perfect" (Heb 5:8-9). How much more do we, then, need to learn obedience on our way to perfection!

Why are we thinking to drop out? Is it because we have forsaken our "first love"? (Rev 2:4). People speak of "losing their first love," but we don't lose it—we forsake it. What is this "first love"? It's not the first flush of love we experienced when we came to Christ. It's not some spiritual "high" we experienced in the beginning. No, our first love is manifested by our obedience to Christ. "First love" means surrendering our will to Christ. We did that when we first accepted him as Lord, and we need to keep on doing it every day of our lives.

Let us turn for a moment now to those who do drop out—whether in accordance with God's will or not. If the decision to leave the field was indeed directed by God, they should have relatively little difficulty adjusting to a new situation back home. They will have confidence that they have made the right and necessary choice and that God will bless their obedience. Those, on the other hand, who have left the field with a sense of defeat or failure or guilt will have a greater problem making the transition and getting started again in a fruitful ministry.

The situation facing missionaries who have left the field is not properly the subject of this book. A very good chapter on their problems can be found in Marjory Foyle's book *Overcoming Missionary Stress*. However, let us just close this chapter with a few observations concerning those missionaries who must begin again in their home country.

They face immediate practical problems on arrival at home, such as housing, finances, and the need for friends. They will experience reverse culture shock. They will feel professionally inadequate. They will suddenly become "nobodies," whereas on the mission field they were "somebodies" with a useful and important job.

They may feel personally discouraged, even depressed. Here is where their local church is absolutely crucial in aiding their recovery and restoration. This is one of the many reasons why a missionary's links to a local church must be close and enduring.

But regardless of the reason the missionary is now home, God is ready to use it for good. It is a well-worn saying, but nonetheless of great comfort to returning missionaries, that God is a God of new beginnings. He plans to place that missionary in a new ministry, which could well end up being just as valuable as any ministry on the field could have been. Don't call "dropping out" a defeat; call it redeployment. What a wealth of experience that missionary has; what a resource he or she will be to the church at home!

If you are one who has left the field, keep these positive things in mind. No matter how deep your sense of failure, distress, discouragement is, God will help you overcome it. You have been blessed "with every spiritual blessing in Christ" (Eph 1:3). God has placed "all things" under Christ's feet (Eph 1:22)—including your failure, your discouragement, even your disobedience. And if you are feeling like a "nobody" that nobody needs and nobody knows, just remember that it is "nobodies" that God especially chooses to glorify himself. You will be a blessing—"poor, yet making many rich; having nothing, and yet possessing everything" (2 Co 6:10).

17

Prayer and the Holy Spirit

This chapter is only five percent of the book, but it contains ninety-five percent of the secret of being a missionary whom God can use.

Dr. Dennis Kinlaw, president of Asbury College, describes meeting a young man who at the age of twenty had quit his university studies, sold his possessions, and bought a one-way ticket to Latin America to serve as a missionary among a primitive tribe of Indians. His family had opposed his going; he had gone out with no financial backing whatever. He had now been working with those Indians for over ten years.

Dr. Kinlaw asked him, "Why did you have to go then? Why could you not have waited until you had finished your training and secured some support?"

The young man replied, "I had found an intimacy with Jesus that I was afraid I would lose if I did not do what he wanted me to do."

That young man carried with him to the mission field the luster of Jesus, and that luster came from his intimacy with him. What a tragedy when a missionary's light grows dim. The people are left in darkness. "If then the light within you is darkness, how great is that darkness!" (Mt 6:23).

Intimacy with Jesus, as with any loved one, must be nurtured. This is all the more true for missionaries out on the field, where there are fewer

331

props, fewer supports, fewer opportunites for fellowship, where the church may be small and weak, and the language hard to understand. Our support must come from our intimacy with Jesus. We must cherish that intimacy above all other earthly blessings. We must spend time, much time, with Jesus.

Our constant temptation as missionaries is to let our ministry take priority over our personal relationship with Jesus. Our main safeguard against this tendency is to maintain frequent times of communion with him through prayer and meditation and the study of his word. If we want the inflow of Jesus' life and light and power in our lives, we must know him intimately and fellowship with him daily.

One of the commonest spiritual problems missionaries face is a sense of "dryness." The presence of Jesus, the joy, the spontaneity of worship they once knew is lost. The fire of the Spirit is bought but embers. No wonder they talk of "burnout."

What is the answer? The same as always: turn back to Jesus. Take time out and spend it with him. Regain the freshness and wonder of his presence, and the dryness, dimness, and discouragement will be replaced with a new strength and vitality and joy.

We don't seek intimacy with Jesus for what it will do for our ministry. We seek it for Jesus' sake alone, for the pure delight of fellowship with him. Jesus is more to be desired than all his gifts.

Our spirituality grows out of our intimacy with Christ. Many people regard spirituality as something ethereal, a state of "being" as opposed to "doing." They are the ones who say, "What you are is more important than what you do." But Jesus would not have agreed with that. He told us to go and bear fruit. Yes, we must first be a tree, but a tree that bears no fruit is a useless tree; it "will be cut down and thrown into the fire" (Mt 3:10).

True spirituality is very practical. It is not just time spent in prayer and meditation—though that is a very important part of it. It is not the exercise of supernatural gifts—prophecy, tongues, healings—though these gifts are often manifested in Spirit-filled people. Rather, spirituality is walking in the light, loving and forgiving our brother. The greatest challenge to our spirituality comes when we need to forgive our fellow missionary, our team leader, our spouse.

Sounds familiar? That's right. It's just the same with folks back home. Missionaries are no different.

Lack of spirituality lies at the root of all our problems. If we were emptied of self, cleansed of sin, and had appropriated the fullness of the Holy Spirit through faith and obedience, we would be at perfect peace.

When missionaries lose their peace and joy, it is for spiritual reasons. God has work to do on us.

Our spirituality is determined by the extent to which the Holy Spirit fills our lives. All believers are indwelt by the Spirit, but not all are filled. To be filled we need to give the Spirit total control. Total surrender of our will is the one key to the infilling of the Spirit and hence to spirituality.

Our spirituality, like our faith, is both tested and deepened by trial. When trial comes—and it always comes where we're most vulnerable— do we give thanks? Can we say with Thomas á Kempis: "Blessed be thy name, O Lord, forever; for that it is thy will that this temptation and tribulation should come upon me...." Speaking of á Kempis, every missionary should be encouraged to read *Imitation of Christ* before leaving for the field. It's more important than any book on missions.

Prayer

Samuel said to the Lord, "Speak, for your servant is listening" (1 Sa 3:10).

We say to the Lord, "Listen, for your servant is speaking."

The first thing in prayer is to wait upon the Lord. Then as he reveals his will to us, we will know better how to pray.

As we wait on God, we bring our thoughts, our mind, into conformity with the mind of Christ. We begin to see his will more clearly. We can't automatically assume we're doing God's will simply because we are missionaries. We need to learn afresh his will for us day by day.

We too often spend all our prayer energy asking God to help us in our work. Our prayers are self-centered. Our prayer energy should be spent mainly in getting to know God, in listening to his will and submitting ourselves in obedience to it. The attitude of submission is crucial; we won't find out what his will is until we have agreed in advance to submit to it, whatever it might be.

The more intimately we know God, the more clearly we shall be able to see his purpose in the circumstances that come into our lives and the lives of others. This is the key to aligning our will with his will, to aligning our prayers with his purpose. That's when our prayers will really become effective. God waits for us to pray for his purpose, and he uses circumstances to prod us into doing so.

Sometimes we experience periods when we can't get through to God. Occasionally God does withdraw himself for reasons hard to understand, but far more frequently the reason lies with us. We may be self-absorbed, focused on our problems, our plans, rather than on God. We may have grown indifferent to the spiritual and physical need around us. We may be cherishing sin in our hearts (Ps 66:18). We may not have forgiven someone completely. We may be grumbling at circumstances instead of thanking God for them. We may have a critical spirit. Any known but un-confessed sin will hinder our prayers. And finally, we may not have sub-mitted our will fully to God's will. We may not long for God's will above all else. Any of these reasons will destroy our intimacy with God and block our prayers.

Andrew Murray asked, "What is the reason why many thousands of Christian workers in the world have not a greater influence? Nothing save this—the prayerlessness of their service.... It is nothing but the sin of prayerlessness which is the cause of the lack of a powerful spiritual life."

When Jesus looked out at the mission field, the first thing he instructed his disciples to do was to pray. "Ask the Lord of the harvest...." (Mt 9:38). Workers are necessary, their work is necessary, but before any-thing else comes prayer.

Most people may not be called to cross-cultural ministry, but they are certainly called to pray. Some people have been praying for Cynthia and me daily for many years. That they should do so is for us a deep source of inspiration and encouragement. But it is more than that; their role has been every bit as vital as ours in the overall fruitfulness of our work in Nepal.

Prayer is not a magic formula. Some missionaries with great prayer support have fallen ill and left the field, or suffered major setbacks and discouragements. Yet we surely must say that prayer is essential to fruit-fulness; it is essential to power. We can beam radio waves into closed countries, but it takes prayer to open hearts to receive the message. We can witness to non-believers, but it takes prayer to carry the word to their hearts. We can cooperate with other Christians, but it takes prayer to mold us together in unity. We could go on. Prayer is essential to the suc-cess of everything we do. Let our prayers be large; our God is not small.

For our first twelve years in Nepal, Cynthia and I lived high on a mountain two thousand feet above a valley. Little streams trickled down the mountain slopes past our house and down into the valley. And each year when the monsoon rains began, those little streams turned to rushing torrents which swept down to flood the parched fields in the valley be-low.

Our little church of a couple dozen believers stood near the top of this same mountain—surrounded by a million non-Christians, whose thatch-roofed villages spread out below us as far as the eye could see. Little trickling streams weren't going to change that; it would take rivers. But that was the problem: we had been praying only for streams—and getting them. We'd been, in a sense, wasting our time, because God wanted to give us rivers instead.

So we began to experience an inward urgency to pray that the full power of the risen Lord let loose on that first Pentecost would be let loose on our mountain to turn our streams into rivers. Jesus said, "He who believes in me, as the Scripture has said, 'Out of his heart shall flow rivers of living water'" (Jn 7:38, RSV). Why pray for streams when the world needs rivers?

When Jesus spoke of "rivers of living water," he was speaking of the outflow of the Holy Spirit from our individual lives. To be born of the Spirit is the beginning; that is the inflow of the Spirit. To be filled with the Spirit is the mark of maturity; it is to have sufficient grace for our own needs. But to be overflowing with the Spirit is the culmination of the Spirit's work in us; it is to have overflowing grace for others. This overflowing grace is essential for ministry. Let it be the daily prayer of every missionary that out of his or her heart the Spirit might overflow, not in trickles but in torrents, to bring water to the parched and thirsty land. The world needs rivers. Why pray for something less?

Prayer is missionary work. Paul the missionary wrote to the Corinthians: "On him we have set our hope that he will continue to deliver us, as you help us by your prayers" (2 Co 1:10-11). In a mysterious way prayer releases the activity of the Holy Spirit. The Holy Spirit waits for our prayers. Prayer itself has no power, but it acts as an ignition switch by which we can tap the power of the Spirit. Whether the need is for workers, for finances, or for fruit, the Holy Spirit will provide them in response to our prayers.

For over thirty years missionaries working in northern India along the Nepal border prayed for an opening into the land of Nepal. Not only did the missionaries pray, but many other Christians from around the world also prayed that Nepal would open. Included among them was the mother of one of the missionaries working near the Nepal border. She was an Australian, and had been praying for Nepal for twenty years. Finally, when Nepal opened its borders to the outside world in the early 1950s, her son, along with several dozen other missionaries, entered Nepal. At that time there was not one Nepali Christian in the land. It was illegal for a Nepali to change his religion from Hinduism, the state religion.

The mother of the missionary kept praying, along with thousands of others from many lands. Gradually the church was established and began to grow. The Australian woman's son went on to become the director of the largest mission organization in Nepal. And when she died in 1990, after fifty years of praying daily for Nepal, the church had grown to more than one hundred thousand believers—and that under intense persecution from both the government and society at large. God knows, but that lone woman in Australia is possibly the greatest missionary Nepal has ever had. And she never set foot in the country.

The Holy Spirit and mission

The disciples had fished all night and caught nothing. They were experts at fishing. Then a man standing on the shore told them to let their net down on the other side of the boat. Who was this guy telling them where to put their net? What difference was that going to make? The boat wasn't more than a dozen feet wide.

The difference was that the guy on the shore happened to be Jesus. The difference was: "He said...." (Jn 21:6). What drew those fish into the net? It wasn't the maneuver of the disciples, not the currents, not the slant of the sun. It was Jesus.

Missionaries don't build the church; only Christ builds the church. Missionaries don't "turn the church" over to nationals, thus making it the nationals' church. It is Christ's church, from beginning to end. Missionaries are helpers, supporters, trainers—partners with nationals, co-sharers in Christ's work of building his church. The growth of the church does not depend on the missionary's care and oversight; it depends on the Holy Spirit indwelling the believers in each locality.

This is not to say that missionaries working in difficult fields are not being led and empowered by the Holy Spirit. Jesus knew well that some people would not be receptive. He told his disciples not to stay with people who did not welcome them or listen to their message (Mt 10:14).

But the sole mover, sole motivator, sole converter in all mission work is the Holy Spirit. The Acts of the Apostles could equally well be titled "The Acts of the Holy Spirit." And the Holy Spirit is still writing the book of Acts today.

It is of immense importance that our acts, our work as missionaries be impelled and directed by the Spirit; otherwise, no lasting fruit will result. On the other hand, we are much too prone to make judgments about whether someone's work was done "in the flesh" or "in the Spirit." The only way to tell is by looking at the fruit of one's work, but sometimes that is slow to manifest itself.

Indeed, it is not a matter of all "flesh" or all "Spirit." There is flesh in everything we do, simply because none of us is as yet a perfectly spiritual being. The point is that as we consecrate our flesh, our bodies, to God, the Holy Spirit transforms and empowers us to do his work. Flesh itself bears no fruit. Flesh consecrated to God and empowered by the Spirit does bear fruit.

Take some missionary, by nature shy and inarticulate, and ask him to give a message. He prepares long and diligently and in the end delivers a passable message. Did he speak "in the flesh"?

Or take your mission organization. The board deliberates for hours, even days, over policy questions and finally comes up with plans. Did they work "in the flesh" that it took them so much time and effort?

The answer is "no." Whether people are working in the flesh or Spirit is determined by their inner attitudes and motives, on their inward dependence on the Holy Spirit and their desire for God's glory, not by the amount of sweat and labor expended.

We do not "use" the Spirit; the Spirit uses us. The Spirit's power is not something under our control; rather we are under the Spirit's control. It is not our working that counts; it is the Spirit working through us that accomplishes God's work.

If mission work does not depend primarily on missionaries but on the Spirit, even less does it depend on money and methods. We use money and we employ methods, but we don't depend on them. The introduction of business and managerial disciplines to missions has been beneficial overall. But we always tend to rely too much on these disciplines. They are not the last word; they are merely tools that may be helpful in determining what the Spirit is saying.

Take the matter of selecting missionaries. We have batteries of interviews, references, psychological tests, and these are all important and useful. But many fruitful missionaries would possibly have failed these tests, including Amy Carmichael, Gladys Aylward, Hudson Taylor—and even the apostle Paul himself. Paul was, after all, quite dogmatic and opinionated; probably not a good team player.

Let us use helps, but ultimately we must rely only on the leading and confirmation of the Holy Spirit. We spend almost all our meetings discussing at length who to accept, where to send them, what projects to open, but we spend very little time in prayer and in seeking the Spirit's direction in these matters. Prayer is more important than our procedures; it puts us in touch with the Spirit. And the Spirit's guidance is more important than all our human disciplines put together.

I well recall four days of meetings at which we were to develop the mission's long-range health plans. We were scheduled to start each day with twenty minutes of prayer and devotions. On the first day of business we got bogged down in disputes over what percent of worms we were going to eradicate over the next five years from the intestines of the people served by our hospitals, and other similar matters. On the second day after devotions, as we got down to business, it was quickly apparent that no one's head had cleared overnight. So we took another hour out to bring all our plans and disputations to the Lord and seek his will. After that, the business at hand fell quickly into place, and we finished the meetings a day early, and in complete unity of mind and spirit.

It's not that we have to set a fixed time and format of prayer at our meetings; that would turn it into another form of legalism. What is necessary is the constant awareness of all participants that the meeting is really being chaired by the Holy Spirit and that all must look to him in every decision.

We need the Holy Spirit's guidance not only to make the right decisions; we need his empowering in order to carry out the decisions we make. Before his ascension, Jesus very clearly told his disciples to wait until they were "clothed with power from on high" (Lk 24:49). We are powerless to accomplish spiritual work without the Holy Spirit's power. And he won't empower us until he has filled us, and rules in us. When the Holy Spirit rules in our individual lives and in our committees, mission agencies, and churches, then we can expect him to manifest his power through us, through our skills, our knowledge, and our methods, to bring forth fruit glorifying to God.

Very simply, all true mission work begins and ends with the Holy Spirit. We are merely instruments in his hands. Our call to service is from the Spirit; our choice of ministry is the Spirit's; and all our fruit is of the Spirit. If you forget everything else about being a missionary, at least remember this.

I could draw upon many, many illustrations—just from Nepal alone—of the Spirit's marvelous working in our midst, and even then I'm sure I don't know a tenth of a percent of the total. I'll share but one story, and that's about a dentist who has done as much to provide the Nepali church with literature as anyone I know. Though a dentist by profession, his special gifts are in computers and desktop publishing. He was called in to help a group of translators publish the Scriptures they had been working on. But try as he might, he could not get a visa to stay in Nepal. It wasn't as though Nepal had too many dentists; there were only fifteen dentists in the entire country at the time—one dentist for a million people! He went day after day to the Home Ministry in Kathmandu and tried to see the Home Minister, but he could not see him. Finally the Assistant Minister became irritated with his visits and told him that he was not to come back; the visa would not be issued. He would have to leave Nepal within the week.

That same evening a Nepali dentist, an acquaintance, called the missionary dentist and asked him to come over and help him on a difficult case. He went over and gave his assistance, which proved crucial to the successful outcome of the case. When the session was over and the patient was about to leave, the Nepali dentist introduced the patient to the missionary.

"This is Hem Raj Adhikari," he said. "He is the Home Minister of Nepal."

The next day the missionary received a two-year resident visa to stay in Nepal—twice the length of stay that other foreigners received. And his work for the church of Nepal has continued ever since.

Spiritual warfare

As missionaries, we go out to fight poverty, injustice, disease, and ignorance. Satan is quite happy when all of our energy is consumed in these struggles, because these struggles are not the main one; these are but "flesh-and-blood" struggles. The main struggle is against "spiritual forces of evil in the heavenly realms" (Eph 6:12). That is the battle which Satan would like to distract us from fighting.

One of the ways we engage Satan in battle is through the exercise of power in so-called "power encounters." In the New Testament the preaching of the apostles was usually accompanied by a demonstration of spiritual power, such as healing miracles or the casting out of demons. In Nepal and in many other resistant lands, the demonstration of such spiritual power has played a prominent role in the establishment and subsequent growth of the church.

Signs and wonders, then, are a manifestation of spiritual power. While the importance of signs and wonders is sometimes overstated, they nonetheless have a real place in the warfare against Satan. For those who question whether signs and wonders are for the church today, two things can be said. First, we are seeing them on the mission field. Second, when Jesus, in the Great Commission, commanded the apostles to make disciples of all nations, he said that they were to teach those new disciples "to obey everything I have commanded you" (Mt 28:20). That would include Jesus' previous commands to the Twelve to heal the sick, to drive out demons, and even to raise the dead (Mt 10:8).

Power encounters don't have to be flashy and dramatic; these are uncommon. The usual power encounters are low-key events. Their effect is often cumulative. In most of the mission hospitals in Nepal there is a spiritual power present that causes more people to recover from a given illness than could have been expected statistically for people with that illness. And simple witnessing and silent prayer are "power encounters" in their own right, and can be just as powerful tools against Satan as miracles are. Let us keep signs and miracles in perspective, neither giving them too high a place or too low.

The commonest "signs and wonders" seen in Nepal are those related to healing the sick. Patients first go to the witch doctor. When the witch doctor has exhausted his remedies and the patient's resources, a group of "illegal" Christians may be called in to pray for the patient, and recovery takes place.

A second common group of signs and wonders relates to exorcisms. Exorcism is the most direct type of engagement with Satan's forces. In exorcising demons, Christians should work in teams, at least one should have the gift of discernment, and all on the team should have on the armor of God. The details of exorcism are well-covered in other books and needn't detain us here. Exorcism depends for its final success on the released person's acceptance of Christ as Lord. All aspects of the person's former religious practice must be renounced, or else the same demon or other demons will return.

The battle against the spirit world goes forward on a much broader scale than just that involving afflicted individuals. Buildings, villages, cities, entire countries can be bound by spirits of unbelief, indifference, fear. Many Christians today have been called out to pray on a global scale against these territorial spirits. In numerous places their prayers have led to rapid church growth after years of stagnation. Many attribute the dramatic fall of atheistic communism to just such prayers. Missionaries, of all people, should be in the vanguard of this prayer warfare.

As we said regarding signs and wonders, these broader "territorial" power encounters also need to be kept in perspective. Power encounter alone is not evangelism. It is an adjunct, albeit an important one, to bringing people to Christ. But ultimately people must encounter Christ himself if they are to be saved. In evangelistic meetings, if there is too great an emphasis placed on the display of power and not enough placed on an encounter with the living Christ, then the faith of those who make decisions for Christ is likely to be very shallow, if it is real at all. The greatest "power encounter" of all occurs when an individual transfers his allegiance from Satan to Christ; any other type of power encounter must be kept subordinate to that.

Missionaries ask: Should we expect dramatic signs and wonders, dramatic answers to prayer as a routine accompaniment of our missionary work?

I'll let the experience of Amy Carmichael give a possible answer to that question. Though she spent virtually her entire adult life in India, she started out as a missionary to Japan, and was there for several years until she suffered a nervous breakdown and had to leave. Early during her time in Japan she went to a village where the Lord had intimated to her that she would win one person to Christ. And one person did turn to Christ that day—in spite of the fact that Amy hardly knew the language.

Some time later she went back to that village. This time the Lord had told her she would win two new persons to Christ. And that day two more people from that village accepted Christ.

Again some months later she returned. This time the Lord had told her it would be four new believers. And this also came to pass.

Near the end of her stay in Japan, she visited that village one last time, and the number eight was given to her. Surely it was ridiculous to think she could win eight souls in one day in a village that generally had been resistant to the gospel. But in a most extraordinary manner, she led eight people to Christ that day.

In all her subsequent years in India, nothing of a similar nature ever occurred again.

Fruit we can expect. But signs and wonders are God's sovereign actions, which occur not according to our demand or expectation but according to his will and purpose. Our faith must not rest on these outward manifestations of God's power, but on the inward fact of our relationship to Christ.

We said that power encounter is not evangelism; by itself it has no power to save. The power to save is in the word of God. "I am not ashamed of the gospel," says Paul, "because it is the power of God for the salvation of everyone who believes" (Ro 1:16). "For the message of the cross is foolishness to those who are perishing, but to us who are being saved it is the power of God" (1 Co 1:18). In all power encounters, the Holy Spirit's main weapon is not signs and wonders and dramatic answers to prayer; it is the word of God, the "sword of the Spirit" (Eph 6:17).

What caliber missionary?

The single ultimate purpose of the missionary enterprise is to reconcile men and women to God and to bring them into his kingdom. An older generation of Christians called it "soul-winning," and they spoke of the need to have a "passion for souls." That may sound funny to our modern ears, but if you can think of a more apt phrase you are welcome to use it.

I don't write easily on this subject, because a passion for souls is something I have personally felt lacking in my own life. And my prayers to receive it have been wanting in fervor and consistency, largely because I've feared I might receive my request. And then that would lead to complications, to new demands, new priorities. I have found it easier to face people with a surgeon's scalpel than with the word of God. I am tempted to say that soul-winning is "not my gift," but I know I can't get away with that. Maybe it's not my gift, but it is my duty.

A missionary with no passion whatever for winning souls is a contradiction in terms. Oh, how we need this passion! It must be at the top of our prayer requests each day. This passion is a sign of the outflow of the Spirit from our lives. We need more than just filling; we need overflow. Can we say with Paul: "My dear children, for whom I am again in the pains of childbirth until Christ is formed in you"? (Gal 4:19). "Pains of childbirth"! That's where our passion will lead—and that is why we shrink from it. A passion for souls will mean expenditure of time and energy; it will mean interrupted schedules; it will mean sacrifice and pain. But one thing it will never mean is "burnout." If our passion is from the Holy Spirit, our fire will not burn out.

What caliber missionary is Christ looking for? One overflowing with the Spirit, one with a passion for souls. And also one armed for spiritual battle. The spiritual struggles are fierce on the mission field; Satan has more tricks, more weapons, more darts, more allies out here than he does at home. We need to be fully armed (Eph 6:13-17).

As we battle with Satan, both in our individual lives and on a broader field, we can remember two things: first, Christ has broken Satan's ultimate power; and second, we have all the resources to fight the battle that Christ himself had. He is sitting on the throne, and so are we. He has been raised up, and so have we (Eph 2:6). As we do battle, let us remember that we are above, and Satan is below.

A cousin of mine, John Magee, left college at the age of nineteen to join the RAF at the very outset of World War Two. He wrote the well-known poem "High Flight," quoted by President Reagan when the Challenger Space Shuttle blew up. He wrote home shortly before his death in a mid-air collision that the secret of shooting down the enemy's aircraft was to get higher than they were and then attack them from above. The pilots slept by their planes, so that when the warning of an enemy attack sounded, they wouldn't lose one second getting into the air and gaining that crucial altitude. It's a little different for us: we're already there.

Hardly an RAF pilot survived those early years of the war; one knew before joining up that it would mean giving one's life. And yet they joined—even an American, whose country had not yet entered the war.

We Christians are too calculating today. We calculate how much risk we're willing to take, how much sacrifice we're willing to make. We seem to forget that the highest and most glorious privilege in the world is to have the chance to suffer for Christ. When we consider going to some dangerous and hostile area, our friends call us mad. Our parents accuse us of not loving them. But Jesus said to his disciples, "I am sending you out like sheep among wolves" (Mt 10:16).

Throughout history, the greatest advances of the gospel have come through suffering and sacrifice. That is God's preferred way—starting with his own Son. And today many around the world have severely suffered and are suffering for Christ. Those who would join the ranks of the missionary endeavor must likewise be willing to suffer and sacrifice. They must count the cost and be prepared to pay it. God is ultimately the one who will set the price of their service. Let their calculating spirit be replaced with a sacrificing spirit. Lord, send to the mission field such workers.

What caliber missionary? We need missionary "failures." I'm thinking of failures like Hudson Taylor, E. Stanley Jones, Amy Carmichael—and you add your choices to the list. At one point in their careers, they all considered themselves failures—and from the world's view, they were. I believe we have to fail before God can fully use us. We have to fail in order to succeed. "Unless a kernel of wheat falls to the ground and dies, it remains only a single seed. But if it dies, it produces many seeds" (Jn 12:24).

It was out of failure that these people received their passionate love for God and for those to whom they were sent. It was out of failure that they accomplished such extraordinary things for God. And they were ordinary men and women. Today are such men and women out of date?

Read the missionary biographies. As George Verwer of Operation Mobilization says: "We have all measured ourselves so long by the man next to us that we can barely see the standard set by men like Paul." Or by any other of the great missionary figures of the last two centuries.

It is possible to go through all the motions of work and prayer, and to be a good and to some extent fruitful missionary, and yet not be fully consecrated to Christ, not be fully submitted to the Holy Spirit. Yes, it will always be so in this life, but there are stages of spirituality, and we must, above all else, long to reach a yet higher and higher stage. We must earnestly aspire to the fully consecrated life. When Paul spoke of "pressing on," of "straining toward what is ahead" (Php 3:12-14), he was speaking of the fully consecrated life. For it is as our life is fully given to Christ that the fruit of our labors will come in greater and greater abundance.

Let us never be satisfied with our present state. How short we fall! Just reflect: what do we do with our spare minutes? Do we turn instinctively to the things of God? To silent prayer? Yes, we must have rest and recreation; God knows that. But it's the idle, in between minutes I'm speaking of. Have we brought every thought into captivity to Christ? (2 Co 10:5). And we're content?

What caliber missionary? Not one who has "already obtained all this" (Php 3:12); such a person doesn't exist. But rather one whose surpassing desire in life is to be conformed to the image of Christ. All we have said so far leads up to this one supreme standard. All the worthy and essential things we have mentioned—the passion for souls, the spirit of sacrifice, the fruit of the Spirit, the overflowing of the Spirit—all these are included in the one great yearning of our hearts: that we might be like Christ. That is the caliber of missionary we must "strain" to be, "until we...become mature, attaining to the whole measure of the fullness of Christ" (Eph 4:13).

Drawing spiritual support from the churches at home

The home church and other supporting churches are a missionary's spiritual life-line on the field. The field headquarters and the home office of the sending agency provide much essential support, but they are no replacement for one's home churches.

At the same time, the missionary has some responsibility toward his supporting churches. He has the responsibility to keep them informed, to report on successes, failures, and needs, and to thank them for their support. While on the field he does this primarily by means of prayer letters and personal correspondence. These letters should be interesting and inspiring; they should elicit continued prayer and financial support, and keep alive the bonds of fellowship. Especially important is answering those who write inquiring about missions; don't discourage a potential missionary by neglect.

I will not go into the mechanics of keeping in touch with home churches, nor into the details of how to write a missionary prayer letter. For this one can refer to a book entitled *How to Write Missionary Letters*, put out by Media Associates International. But herewith are a few hints, if you do not want all your prayer letters relegated to the "circular file."

You must resort to the form letter, or you will soon cease being a missionary and become a letter writer. The home office of the mission should undertake to send these out. If there is no home office, family or friends or home church should be asked to volunteer—unless, of course, the missionary is based at home.

Try not to start a letter conventionally; that first paragraph has got to be good. Don't say, "I can't write." If you can talk, you can write. And that's the key. Write like you talk. When you finish your masterpiece, read it out loud. If it doesn't sound like you talking, then write it over again.

Be personal; be honest; be yourself. Make your letter "alive." Describe your feelings and reactions. You are the point of contact with your reader. Be vivid, descriptive. Don't write how "wonderful" something was without telling why it was wonderful. And don't take space describing time-dependent events. Your letter about that "wonderful Christmas program" will be doing well if it gets to your supporters by Easter. Avoid sermonizing and moralizing; if you absolutely have to, limit it to one sentence of under twelve words.

If you use photos, be sure they reproduce well. I've seen a lot of photos in missionary prayer letters that would make good toothpaste ads, but nothing else. In general, don't rely on gimmicks; what you write is most important.

Some of your readers will like newsy letters; others will like a story. A useful format to please both is a two-part letter: the first half, a story or experience; the second half, four to five news items for prayer and praise. If your supporters happen to be a married couple, the husband can read the story and his wife can read the news.

If it's the missionary's responsibility to communicate with the home church, what is the home church's responsibility to the missionary— besides sending money and M&M's? The answer is prayer. As we have said before, the prayer work done by the people at home is every bit as important as the mission work done by the people on the field.

What do missionaries need praying for? Some missionaries in Nepal have friends at home who have prayed that they might be able to endure the harsh winter at high altitudes, when in fact the missionaries were stationed in the broiling tropical heat at 1500 feet. I'm sure God is able to translate such prayers, but it would obviously be better if our prayer partners knew our circumstances.

So, what should the home folks pray for? The same kinds of things they pray for each other—except with a cross-cultural twist. They should pray for their missionaries' health, for their facility in language learning, for their ability to adapt to the people and to new ways, for love for people so different from themselves, for protection from the evil forces that surround them, for their children who weren't called to Nepal but landed there anyway, for unity and love in the missionary team, for the national church and for the people of the countries where the missionaries work— all these prayers, and many, many more—prayers for specific needs and projects, for safety in travel, for wisdom and guidance. And above all, they should pray for those things we mentioned a few pages back: that their missionary might be filled to overflowing with the Holy Spirit, that he or she might burn with a passion for souls, that he or she might be conformed to the likeness of Christ.

If those at home knew how often their missionaries were running on "spiritual empty," they'd pray harder. The last thing we need is to be put on pedestals. Every time I hear someone say to me, "My, how dedicated you are," I want to turn around and tell that person, "I wish you'd pray that I'd become as dedicated as you think I am."

You ask: "You mean you want even young and inexperienced Christians to pray for the spiritual health of mature missionary veterans who have been on the field twenty or thirty years?"

You bet I do. Personally, I covet the prayers of a new Christian. I want him or her to pray that I might know the joy and freedom of the Lord in the fresh way a new believer does. I want those struggling with spiritual dryness to add me to their prayers. I want those struggling with temptation to add me to their prayers. I want those who suffer, who know the fellowship of Jesus' suffering and the power of his resurrection to add me to their prayers. I want those whose first love has not dimmed to add me to their prayers. I want people to pray that I might surrender every area of my life to the lordship of Christ; that I might have the mind and the love of Christ; that people might more clearly see Christ in me, including my wife. Everything you pray for yourself, pray for your missionaries too.

Fancy words? Just a rhetorical flourish to extract a few more prayers from the home front? Do I really care about your prayers? Do they make a difference?

Let me tell you a story. It's about a medical missionary serving in a developing country who had just come home on furlough, and who was asked by the pastor of his home church to give a report of his work at one of the church services.

This missionary doctor told the congregation about his work at a rural hospital, and how periodically he had to journey by bicycle two days to a nearby city to get supplies. The journey each way required camping overnight at the halfway point.

On one of these trips he encountered a young man in the city who had just been injured, and so he treated the man's injuries and witnessed to him about Christ. He then journeyed back to his hospital, camping overnight at the halfway point, and arriving the next day without incident.

The missionary doctor continued his story. "Two weeks later I repeated my journey to the city. When I arrived I came across the young man I had treated two weeks earlier. He said to me, 'I know you come to the city regularly to collect money and drugs for your hospital. So, on your last trip, some friends and I planned to follow you back to the camping spot where you spend the night and rob you and kill you. So we followed you, and waited until you were asleep. Then as we were about to attack you, we saw twenty-six armed guards standing around you.'"

The missionary said to the congregation: "When I heard that I laughed. I told the young man that I was absolutely alone at that campsite. But the young man persisted. He said to me, 'No, you were not alone. My five friends also saw the guards. We all counted them, and came up with the same number: twenty-six. It was because of those guards that we were afraid and left you alone.'"

At that moment a man in the congregation jumped to his feet and interrupted the missionary's story. He said to the missionary, "Excuse me, but could you tell me the exact day and time that these men were planning to attack you?"

The missionary took a moment to recollect the date and hour, taking into account the change of time zone, and then told the man standing in the congregation.

The man then said to the missionary, "An hour or so before that attack would have taken place, I was on my way to play golf. But the Lord suddenly put a burden on my heart to pray for you. I didn't know why. The burden was so strong that I returned home, and called some other men in the church to meet together to intercede on your behalf."

Then the man paused, and looking around at the congregation, said, "Will all those men who joined me in prayer that day please stand?"

When they all had risen, there were twenty-six men standing.

18

Singles and Doubles

The more difficult and dangerous the field, the greater the proportion of single women that will be found there. Yes, there will be some single men—especially in the pioneering missions and those missions with a special focus on youth, such as OM and YWAM—but the fact remains: the vast majority of single missionaries are women, and they generally take the hardest assignments. There's a saying on the mission field more true than false: If you've got a man-sized job to get done, find a woman to do it.

On the average around the world, single women make up between twenty and thirty percent of the missionary work force. The rest are married. The few single men who come out don't stay single for long.

Women do all sorts of things on the mission field, largely because they end up in places where there are no men. They are wonderfully capable; indeed, some of them may come to look upon men as useless—or at least unnecessary. All the more frustrating, then, when a female missionary has spent years building up a work or establishing a church, and along comes some young, freshly trained male national quoting one of Paul's more popular verses—"I do not permit a woman to teach or to have authority over a man" (1 Ti 2:12)—and relegates the missionary to teaching Sunday school, if that. In spite of such problems, women have accomplished much on the mission field in teaching, administration, and leadership capacities. That is a historical fact. Surely God wants to use the gifts of all his children, both men and women.

Why are more women going out to the field than men? Are men not answering God's call? Perhaps that is a factor. But another possible reason is this: more women than men are needed on the field. In most of the developing world women do not have equal status with men. They do not have equal educational opportunities. They have less opportunity to hear the gospel. They have less opportunity to grow spiritually in male-dominated Third World churches. Single women missionaries have reached out to these women, started women's schools and colleges, and in general have performed a gigantic service in improving the condition of women worldwide. We have to say that today we still need more women on the field than men.

Yet on many fields the question still rings out: "Where are the men?" The discrepancy between the number of single men and single women offering for service is still too great; the ratio in many missions is five to one. Surely more men than that should be stepping forward! Single men are badly needed in many areas to spearhead the work. Young men of other ideologies and religions are willing. Why not Christians?

And for single men—do I dare say it?—there will likely be an earthly reward for answering God's call to missions: a fine wife. And there will always be those in the missionary community who are happy to help things along—with utmost discretion, of course.

A day's walk from our hospital in Nepal, two young women from Scotland were teaching in a local village school. A three-day journey away, in another part of Nepal, a young missionary engineer from Ireland was developing technology for producing methane gas from manure for use in cooking—one of the ways the mission is trying to reduce firewood consumption and thus spare Nepal's vanishing forests. Among his friends he was known as the "septic-tank man."

We decided to install one of these gas plants at our hospital, and called the Irish engineer to install it. We suggested a time that would be "convenient for the hospital," a time that "happened" to coincide with the Scottish teachers' school holiday. After receiving intimation of interest on the part of one of the teachers, some on our team invited her down to spend her holiday in our project guest house. The engineer duly arrived. The tank for producing the gas seemed to take forever to install. The various members of the team invited the pair "by chance" to the same meals at their homes, so that by the time the week was up they'd had at least fifteen joint invitations—all of which in the end produced the expected engagement announcement. I'm not suggesting that mission match-making efforts are always carried out with such finesse, but our team's performance would have been hard to improve on.

Singleness: pros and cons

All married people were once single, so we are not totally disqualified from addressing this subject. But never having been a single missionary, I will limit my remarks here to a few observations, and refer the reader for further coverage to Jeannie Lockerbie's book *By Ones and By Twos*, and also to the chapter entitled "Stress and Singleness" in Marjory Foyle's book *Overcoming Missionary Stress*.

A single woman coming out to the mission field for career service must have settled in her heart that she has likely been called to a life of singleness. I say "likely," since I know of many older single missionary women who have gone on to become happily married; but the odds are against it. For most, this is a major sacrifice. But this truth remains: there is not a sacrifice we make for Jesus' sake that he will not honor and in the end reward us for.

That doesn't mean that the longing and the loneliness is any less real for the person who willingly makes that sacrifice. Just because a single person is in Christ and is filled with the Spirit doesn't mean that he or she no longer desires to be married and to have the companionship of a spouse. Neither does it mean that natural biologic urges are erased. The longing, the empty place is still there. But in the experience of most singles, it gradually gets more and more crowded out with spiritual blessings as life goes on.

The furlough is a particularly difficult time for singles. As years pass, singles especially have a decreasing circle of friends at home. Parents die; other contacts are not close; common interests are few. Most of the single's friendships are on the field, with both nationals and fellow missionaries.

The difficulties of singleness must not be glossed over; especially when combined with some other problem or disappointment, the unhappiness of being single can be very hard to bear. If singleness is not inwardly accepted, spiritual growth will be slowed or arrested. Depression may occur, and force one to leave the field.

One young missionary woman served one term in Nepal and said she wouldn't come back without a frying pan and a husband. Well, she did come back—with the frying pan but not with the husband. But she never seemed happy, and returned home for good after that term was up. Maybe a husband would have made the difference.

The main disadvantages of being single on the mission field are four, the first of which is that you usually don't get to choose your roommate. Incompatible roommates are a great problem for single missionaries.

The second disadvantage is that as a single you're more likely to be uprooted and moved from post to post. It's much easier to move a single person than a whole family, and so singles find themselves discriminated against in this regard.

Third, singleness in most Third World cultures is not accepted as a normal state. Single missionaries get questioned repeatedly about their age, about why they aren't married, about what "went wrong." True, the people soon accept the missionary's single status—until, of course, the missionary moves to a new location, at which point the questions start all over again. In Muslim countries, being a single woman is especially difficult; before deciding to go to a Muslim field, consult with another single who has already been there.

The fourth and greatest disadvantage of being a single missionary is loneliness. The main diversion becomes one's work. Coming home to a roommate is not the same as coming home to a spouse. We all need at least one close and caring companion, who is at the same time compatible. On the mission field, however, it's not always possible to match every single with a suitable roommate. Administrators do their best, but there are limited personnel to choose from; plus there are furloughs, sicknesses, and necessary transfers, all of which the administration has little control over.

Practical but partial solutions to loneliness exist: hobbies, books, providing hospitality, and making friends with other missionaries and nationals. Avoid self-pity; practice praise and thanksgiving. Use the gift of singleness to bring joy and comfort and companionship to others. And look ahead: you are part of a growing family that will become more and more enriching and fulfilling as the years go by—a foretaste of the heavenly family we have been promised.

Don't think, "If only I was married my loneliness would end." Marriage is not a cure for everyone. Some get married because of loneliness and end up more lonely than before. That is the most painful loneliness of all. Ultimately the only lasting solution for loneliness is to draw close to Jesus and to find a deep level of companionship with him.

Indeed, there is a wonderfully positive side to singleness. Evelyn Mumaw has written: "The fact that Jesus himself found it preferable to live and do his work as a single person is significant. Marriage was not a requirement for perfection of personhood or fulfillment of the highest purpose in his life. It is the privilege of the single adult to identify with him in his singleness."

In addition to this great privilege, there are other advantages of single-ness. First, singles have more free time; they are free of family re-sponsibilities, free of the preoccupations that are an inevitable part of family life. They have more time to learn the language. Second, singles are able, on average, to get closer to the nationals. Nationals feel more free to drop in on them; the single person can devote more time to cul-tivating relationships with nationals. Singles can adopt a life style closer to that of the nationals, which will aid in relationship building. Third, sin-gles are more flexible. Their flexibility can be taken advantage of, as we have seen, but when it is necessary to move or to change plans, it is much easier for the single missionary. Fourth, singles are cheaper to sup-port (because of no children)—plus they do more work! They are a bar-gain when you come to measure cost-effectiveness.

Finally, for the single missionary there are spiritual rewards in abun-dance. Singles are often the most competent, stable, fruitful, Spirit-filled missionaries on the field. If someone fears that kind of life, then let that person not volunteer for missionary service.

A few single women are tempted to feel spiritually superior to married couples. One single woman told me that she was "married to Jesus," and in the context of the conversation her implication was that she was closer to Jesus than I. She may well have been, but it was not solely because she was single. Furthermore, she made my wife Cynthia feel second-class. Cynthia had made a poor choice by comparison!

Single women can also be quite critical of their married sisters for not doing as much "mission work" as they should. The single may think—and, sadly, sometimes say—"What did those wives come to the field for? They're not doing any more than if they had stayed at home." Let sin-gles, as well as guilty wives, remember: Caring for one's family is just as much "mission work" as any other kind of work. It is a God-given prior-ity for married couples.

Singles should ordinarily not plan to live alone, certainly not for pro-longed periods. There will be exceptions, of course, but for most people a roommate is the best solution. Two together usually works out better than three, despite Ecclesiastes, because of the tendency for two to grow closer together and leave the third one out.

Now what about this business of a roommate being a "solution"? For many singles, the roommate is anything but! I remember two missionary women who were roommates for a spell, and they were as opposite a pair of people as I could ever imagine. One was full of fun, bubbling over with energy—irrepressible is the word—and the other was quiet, gentle, meditative. You get the picture. They both loved the Lord and loved each other, but they were temperamentally incapable of meeting each other's need for companionship. As the irrepressible one said, "We drive each other bananas without doing anything."

One would think that if God put two single missionaries together in one house, he'd know what he was doing. How come he put these two together? Answer: so they could both grow in grace. There is absolutely nothing on earth better designed to spur us on to maturity than an incompatible roommate. "We didn't choose each other," you say. That's right; God did.

However, God doesn't choose a difficult roommate for us in perpetuity. If two people still aren't able, after a reasonable period, to support each other emotionally and spiritually, then they need to find new roommates, or change projects if necessary. Certainly they should not be forced to live together because of the "needs of the work"; the work will end up suffering anyway, because of their unhappiness.

There is no reason why two relatively congenial single roommates shouldn't share thoughts and feelings with each other to the same extent married couples do. There are, after all, things that married couples do not or should not share: confidential information about another person, negative information about another person, and various private feelings or past experiences which it would not be useful to share. Even in marriage, each partner has the right to a little private compartment which the other respects; so with singles. But all the same, the more deeply two singles can share their lives together, the more mutually supportive and rewarding their relationship will be. They need to be assured of each other's unconditional acceptance.

Allowing for the exceptions, nationals do not provide the same close friendship and companionship to a single missionary that a fellow missionary does. But as the years pass, the missionary has greater opportunity to develop national friendships on a deeper and deeper level. And a few missionaries find, in the end, that they get along better with nationals than with their missionary colleagues.

A single person should almost never plan to live with a married couple except, if necessary, for a short period of time. Unless they are able to maintain separate housekeeping, the privacy of both the single and the couple will be impinged upon. The single only rarely becomes fully part of the family.

However, warm and supportive relationships between families and singles are mutually beneficial. The initiative must come from the couple here, or else the single will feel like he or she is intruding. And couples, don't reach out to singles because you think they'll make good baby sitters! Never ask singles to help with the children except in instances of real need. Then you will usually find that the offer of help has already been made.

Singles who enjoy children, on the other hand, can make a wonderful contribution to missionary families. Let them share themselves. They offer not only short-term blessings to the family as a whole, but they are able to add to the children's lives for a lifetime. Don't feel uncomfortable being called "Aunt" or "Uncle," or "big sister" or "big brother," as the Nepali custom is. Missionary children need aunts and uncles on the field—and "aunts" and "uncles" need children.

Our two boys had a favorite "aunt," though they called her just by her first name, which she preferred. She played games with them, challenged them to sword battles (they were reading King Arthur at the time), played soccer with them, and even volunteered to be the catcher in softball—until one day I pitched a super-duper fastball that my son missed cold but which caught Aunt Shelagh dead on the upper lip, after which her enthusiasm for catching noticeably diminished.

Today our boys, who are grown up, will travel a hundred miles out of their way to see their favorite aunt. She was a significant reason why they enjoyed growing up in Nepal. And it wasn't just the fun—though there was a lot of that. She shared with them her own insights, experience, knowledge. She enriched their lives. And she enriched their parents' lives too. Let singles not underestimate the blessings they bring when they share themselves.

There are two cautions to observe; the devil is always trying to mess up a good thing. A mother can sometimes be overprotective and insecure in regard to her children, and thus when their favorite aunt comes along, the mother may feel anxious or threatened. The single should be sensitive about this, and never do anything that would "show up" the mother or undermine her authority. On the other hand, mothers should be sensitive to the single person too. They should never think, much less say, something like, "Oh, you wouldn't know; you don't have children of your own." Such a thought is wrong on two counts. First, the single may know a great deal about children and family life. Didn't she grow up in a family? Perhaps she has had training and experience in dealing with children. Second, such a thought is hurtful. It may be that the single person deeply desired to have children of her own—or still does. This may have been the greatest sacrifice she made in becoming a missionary. To rub this sensitive area is nothing short of cruel.

The second caution concerns the relationship between the single woman and the married man. Missionaries are human too, in case you hadn't noticed by now. In the work place a husband has to work with single women, and that relationship must not become too close. Even when the relationship is completely innocent and pure, the wife may have feelings of jealousy or hostility toward the single person. It's not enough for the husband to say, "There's nothing to worry about." He, too, must do nothing to fan his wife's misgivings. Yes, missionaries are saints, like those at home, but....

A few singles will choose to room with a national. That has often been successful and has led to a fruitful ministry for both. There are risks: the national may incite the envy of other nationals; the missionary may find that other missionaries become distant. But, in spite of the risks, a national and missionary rooming together is a powerful testimony to the way Christ unites believers of every race and nation.

Missionary marriages

The pros and cons of being married on the mission field are the mirror image of the pros and cons of being single. Except that there are two additional advantages to marriage. The first is that in any reasonably happy marriage, each partner is emotionally and psychologically strengthened and enhanced by the relationship—more so than in the average relationship between singles. In marriage, one plus one equals more than two—and I'm not referring to children. And if the individual is enhanced by marriage, his or her ministry and usefulness will be enhanced as well.

The second advantage has to do with the witness of a Christian marriage: the deep mutual tenderness between husband and wife, the respect for womanhood, the discipline of children with love and firmness, the order and harmony. The witness of God's ideal for marriage is especially important in societies where women are demeaned and children go undisciplined. In popular Hinduism, for example, the wife is basically a form of property; she serves the function of a garden in which the husband plants his seed. And she has about as many rights as a garden. There is little concept of partnership in Hindu marriages. Men value their sons more than their wives. National believers in such countries need to see the ideal of Christian marriage worked out in missionary family life.

The apostle Paul seemed to imply that marriage would diminish the ministry of each partner as they look out for each other's and their children's interests. But on the mission field, aside from the mother with young children, this has not been the general experience. A couple can minister not only to singles of each sex but also to other couples and families. Husband and wife support each other in their individual ministries.

Even when they are caring for each other and their children, a couple demonstrates a strong outgoing testimony of how God intended the family to be. There is no need to over-spiritualize singleness and look down on marriage. God is pleased to use both states equally.

Young children themselves are no barrier to ministry for the mother; indeed, they create opportunities for ministry, which the mother can build on as the children grow older. Children are a universal topic of interest and conversation. And the children themselves know no cultural walls. Our boys, some Norwegian girls, and various Nepali children all used to play together, blending their three languages together as if they were one. Even a single sentence might have a Norwegian subject, a Nepali verb, and an English object; no problem. Children are bridge-builders.

Although being a missionary is a more stressful occupation than most, and these stresses are reflected in missionary marriages, still being a married missionary couple is a grand adventure. Because of their unusual circumstances, husband and wife generally have more opportunities to pull together, to support one another—in short, to be a team. This feeling of constituting a little team is tremendously strengthening for a marriage. Each partner shares the same vision for the work; each contributes his or her part to the whole. Even if the wife is largely at home with small children, the sense of equal partnership need not be lost. The wife is always a partner in the work, a true missionary in her own right. Two working together in this way is an added testimony to the beauty and fruitfulness of a Christian marriage.

Some of our happiest times as a couple were when Cynthia and I were the only doctors at our little mission hospital; then there was no mistaking that we were a team. Other couples report similar experiences. One doctor couple we know split up the medical duties and homemaking duties half and half, and for them, that worked very well. But let me emphasize again that it is not necessary to be physically working in the same place to experience this sense of being a team. Let a young wife not bewail the time she must spend at home "away from the work." As if being at home wasn't work!

If a smoothly functioning missionary marriage is a powerful testimony, a poorly functioning marriage is a powerfully poor testimony. The nationals will be quick to notice disharmony, quarreling, bad moods, lack of mutual submission; and even if they don't notice, the cook surely will, and the cook won't leave anyone in the dark!

Speaking of cooks, Dr. Marjory Foyle writes of a missionary couple who communicated with each other for two solid years only by means of their cook. Hard to say if that was better than nothing. Dr. Foyle's point, of course, is that missionary couples need to work on communicating with each other just like any other couple. That takes both time and practice.

Both husband and wife must be individually called to the mission field. It is not enough for the wife to say, "I'm called to go where my husband goes." The wife also must receive a deep assurance that God is calling her to ministry in that particular field. Otherwise, when the going gets tough, she will begin to feel like she has been dragged into something she didn't choose. Furthermore, unless the wife is also called, she will use her lack of call as an excuse to retire into her home and avoid opportunities for outside ministry. Then, once the kids are older, she will have no ministry at all. Generally, if a wife does not have her own call to missions, the couple should not go. During candidate interviews, husband and wife should always be interviewed together—never the husband alone—and the wife's own call needs to be fully affirmed at that time.

I was called specifically to Nepal when I was in high school. My wife Cynthia had also been called to missions in high school, but not to a particular country. We met over a cadaver in medical school—we were lab partners in Anatomy—and very quickly discovered we were both studying medicine in order to become medical missionaries. In such a romantic setting marriage was inevitable, but Cynthia still needed God's assurance that she, too, was meant to go to Nepal and not somewhere else. And, as mentioned earlier, God graciously spoke to her through Psalm 67 in the Living Bible, which tells of our being sent "around the world" so people from "remotest lands" will worship God. Since Nepal was "around the world" and was as remote a place as Cynthia could imagine, she felt that God, through his word, was commissioning her to go to that remote land. And as things turned out, her call to Nepal became every bit as strong as mine.

"The husband's work comes first" is a statement that should be retired from active duty. Even if the husband has the main assignment and his wife has opted for a homemaking and support role, it is still "our work," not the husband's work alone. Husband and wife are equal partners, even when their roles are different; and, as equal partners, they both contribute equally to the missionary endeavor.

The husband must take extra pains to insure that his wife not only be an equal partner but feel like one too. Let him help out at home as much as his work permits. Let husband and wife take turns going to evening meetings. Let the wife be encouraged to use all her gifts and training, as her time allows. Let both husband and wife strive to make their partnership a daily reality.

Mission agencies have different policies on the role of wives, and a couple should look very closely at those policies before joining a mission. Some missions expect to assign the wife as a full-time missionary worker; other missions go to the opposite extreme and prefer not to assign the wife at all. Most mission agencies today lie somewhere in between, and allow the couple to have the major say in what role the wife will play.

Four types of role are available to the wife: first, homemaker; second, assistant or supporter; third, actual colleague or teammate in the work itself; and fourth, a parallel worker doing her own work. A wife will move from one role to another as the kids grow older or her own interests change. Cynthia has moved progressively from role one to role four over the years, and many other wives have done the same. Even husbands will change roles along with their wives. Nowadays wives are sometimes getting the main mission assignment, and the husband is either in the support role or has some independent project to work on. There is only one rule in this business of choosing roles for husband and wife: let the wife have equal say as to her role. And if for some reason the mission you're looking at has some other rules on this matter, be sure you're happy with them before signing up.

Mission agencies today are observing a growing number of candidates who believe that the wife's role should be limited to that of homemaker. This is held by some to be the biblical model of the ideal family. That's fine, as long as the view is not held intolerantly and the "ideal family" is not turned into an idol. The danger comes when young couples come out to the field convinced they are the only ones who are right and that everyone else with a different view is wrong. Such an attitude is extremely disruptive and harmful to the work on the field.

The key issue here is that the wife reach her full God-given potential and that she be convinced she is in God's will, whatever her role may be. The qualifications and training of wives should be given as much attention as that of the husbands. As much concern should be given the wife's role fulfillment as that of her husband. Husband and wife are partners, and they will each function maximally when they are treated as partners.

There are extra costs to a marriage when couples decide to become missionaries. All the ordinary stresses of marriage may be amplified on the field, especially in the early years of adjustment to a strange culture. This is why it is unwise to send newlyweds out as new missionaries; let them have at least three to six months to adjust to each other before sending them to the battlefield.

Some marital stresses that are especially problematic on the field are those which come when partners have unrealistic expectations of each other; they are always disappointing one another. In other cases, one partner may be seeking affection missed in childhood—more than the spouse can give. One partner may be overdependent and need constant reassurance and support, so much so that the other partner is drained emotionally. Sometimes the dependent spouse looks outside the marriage for support; let single missionaries beware the danger of filling this need!

One spouse may be immature in other ways, and lack self-confidence, or be unduly sensitive to criticism. The slightest look from the other partner is like a dagger. "My husband is always 'angry,' or 'displeased,'" which may or may not be accurate. "I'm not angry," says he. "I'm only raising my voice." The problems in marriage are as varied as the pleasures. And both are intensified on the mission field.

There are other costs. The couple may end up in a country where the wife's role is strictly limited by the culture of that country, as in Muslim lands where the wife is expected to stay at home. In some societies husbands and wives shouldn't touch each other in public—not even in their own homes if the cook is around. In other countries husband and wife don't walk together; the husband walks in front carrying his spear—or, as in Nepal, his transistor radio. We talk about setting an example in our marriages of the respect due to wives, but it is not always culturally acceptable to show that respect in the way we would like. All these things put extra strain on a marriage.

Another cost to a marriage is the lack of privacy one experiences on the field. Partitions to rooms are paper thin, or made of bamboo slats. And there is no lack of peeking eyes.

However, by far the greatest costs of being a married missionary revolve around the children and the sometimes necessary separations that missionary families must endure. This subject will be dealt with later on.

Balancing work and family

Providing for the needs of one's family is a sacred obligation. It comes before one's mission work. Older generations of missionaries, thinking they were obeying Christ's words in Matthew 10:37 and Luke 14:26, put their work before their families with often tragic consequences. They sincerely believed that if they took care of God's work, God would take care of their wives and children; but it did not always happen that way. In committing themselves to their mission work, they set aside not only their marriage vow to love and cherish their wife but also many other passages of Scripture which clearly state our responsibility to our families. The missionary who neglects his family is no better than the businessman who neglects his family. What good is it to gain a church and lose a home, or to win the heathen and lose your children? God never expects us to fulfill one responsibility by neglecting another.

In the passages in Matthew and Luke referred to above, Jesus is talking about our allegiance to him, not to his work. We put him above all else, over our wife and children. But after him comes our wife, and then our children. Only after that comes his work.

For what, after all, is his "work" but to obey him in everything. Loving and cherishing one's wife is work—joyous work, to be sure, but work nonetheless—requiring time, effort, and concentration. And I don't need to say that raising children is work—Christ's work. Paul says that if we don't manage our own families properly, we aren't qualified to take responsibility in his church (1 Ti 3:5).

Note that the word "balancing" is used in the title of this section. It is quite as easy to go overboard in the opposite direction and make an "idol" of one's family. An idol is anything we put before Christ. It is possible to be too protective of our family time. It is possible to become too inward-looking, to stop giving out, to stop sharing one's home. A Christian home is Christ-centered, not self-centered. Use your home for ministry and it will be blessed.

The balance we strike is going to vary from day to day depending on circumstances. It will also vary with the type of work we do and with the needs of our family at any given period. At times we must give the work priority. At other times the family needs extra attention. Usually things work out. If we neglect the children one afternoon, we'll get time off the next. God will always enable us to fulfill all the obligations he lays upon us. If we find it is simply impossible to do everything we think God is asking us to do, then there's something in there that he's not asking of us! There never need be an ongoing conflict between work and family. If there is, we're not reading God's will aright.

One beautiful solution that often works out is to combine family and ministry together. Take the children when you go out visiting and witnessing. Invite nationals in and have the children share in the evening. We used to have members of the hospital staff in twice a week for singing, folk dancing, or showing slides. Our boys loved it. Make the children a part of your ministry, and that's what they'll remember most—not the cookies you stayed home to bake. Mothers, don't stop baking cookies! I'm only saying that the children will remember the times of shared ministry more.

Remember, too, our children belong to God; we must not keep them for ourselves. The parents who out of fear or a skewed theology overprotect their children are not only doing the children a disservice but are also dishonoring God.

Following the balanced and common-sense principles outlined here would be easy if it weren't for all the inconvenient exceptions, the daily dilemmas that confront the missionary family. Let us say it's your afternoon off, and you have just settled down to read to the kids from your favorite book, *The Merry Adventures of Robin Hood*. A former hospital employee whom you haven't seen in a while brings a friend of his around to see you. The friend is probably looking for a job; it's going to be at least a fifteen-to-twenty-minute visit, and you already had one such visitor half an hour before. So after a couple minutes of greetings, you come right to the point: "I can't talk now; this is my special time with my kids. Please come back and see me this evening."

"We're leaving today; this is our only time to see you."

"I'm very sorry; I just can't take the time to talk now."

From the visitors' viewpoint I'm obviously lying. Of course I can take the time. I'm not doing anything important. Nepali fathers don't read to their kids. What a silly thing to use as an excuse.

In the present case, great offense was taken, resulting in a bitter letter from the former hospital employee. I wrote back apologizing, and received a halfway mollified response. But damage was done. And such dilemmas come on you again and again.

Then come the unusual situations, the exceptions to the rule. We may be called to temporarily set aside certain of our family obligations—not for the work's sake, but for Jesus' sake. These times will be rare, and they require an absolutely clear understanding of God's will. Both husband and wife must be in agreement, as well as any older children; there must be confirmation that the exception to God's usual pattern is indeed his will for this present time. Otherwise, beware!

It is critical to understand that husband and wife are equally guided by the Holy Spirit. Woe to the husband who thinks "headship" means that he has an exclusive line to the Spirit. When disagreement between husband and wife occurs, that is not the time for the husband to assert his headship. Rather, it is the time for both husband and wife to pray and wait on God. Only in a continuing impasse should the wife defer to her husband. Long before that, the husband should have listened to his wife and in nine times out of ten settled for at least a compromise.

So in the balancing of work and family obligations, we come, as always, to our daily walk with God, our discerning of his will day by day and hour by hour. If we as husbands and wives and parents truly desire his will above all else, then we will be able to rest in him and trust that he will guide us. We will be able to let him plan our days, instead of struggling to do it ourselves and missing his full blessing. We will not be distracted or upset by the unfair criticism of others that we're spending "too much time" with our families. And we will have the assurance that, as long as our hearts are pure and free of selfishness, God will unerringly lead us on the path that will honor our commitments to both work and family, and at the same time bring him the greatest glory.

Wives

There are still home supporters who expect wives to have a "full-time missionary job"; they want two missionaries for the price of one, not one missionary for the price of two! What they need to realize is that just being a wife and mother in a foreign culture is already one-and-a-half full-time jobs—running the home, raising the kids, providing hospitality, helping national women and children, witnessing for the Christian family in a non-Christian society. I say to the supporters back home: You're already getting more that your money's worth.

For the mother with young children, there is no question where her primary duty lies. Her main "mission work" is her children and her husband. As the children grow older, the mother can add more and more outside activities. Yet "family work" and "mission work" never need be compartmentalized; everything the missionary mother does is done unto the Lord.

Should the missionary mother be doing something more in the way of extra-family ministry than she'd be doing if she had stayed in her home country? I will venture the answer "no." After all, the home-side mother should also be engaged in extra-family ministry to some extent, the same as the missionary mother. The only thing different between the missionary mother and her home-country counterpart is that the missionary mother lives and ministers in a cross-cultural setting.

Generally, the missionary mother should be encouraged to have at least one ministry outside the home. This gets her out of the house, gives her a break, and gives her practice in using the language—which she must learn no matter how busy she is. But the outside ministry has long-range benefits as well as short-range. As the children get older and need Mom less, she needs to step more and more into outside activities and find a fruitful ministry in her own right. Many mature, valuable couples have left the mission field in their prime, because as their kids got older the mother no longer had a satisfying role to play.

Missionary wives and mothers are at times going to feel themselves pulled in different directions, and they will have to make practical decisions about how to balance a career and family. If the missionary wife has a crucial skill that the mission needs, she should consider sending her children to school earlier than she might have otherwise. If the missionary wife strongly desires to have a ministry in addition to homemaking, this should be arranged for her, but she should not take on so much she has insufficient time and energy for her family. There must be much give-and-take between the individual family and the mission administration. Always in coming to a decision, the long-range welfare of the children should be the most important consideration of both mother and mission.

Mothers (and dads too), let no outside pressures of work prevent you from treasuring each day in the lives of your children. They will never be that old again. Many are the missionaries whose main regret in later years is that they did not spend enough time with their children when they were small. Mothers, don't be jealous of your husband who is immersed in "the work" all day, while you seemingly accomplish nothing. You have a high calling, a calling to be relished, to be rejoiced in. Will your children have fond and happy memories of their childhood and family life? You are responsible to see that they do. The quality of life you provide them will be the single greatest human factor in determining whether your children follow in your footsteps. Missionary kids are usually turned off or turned on by missionary life; they are seldom neutral.

Those mothers who do involve themselves heavily in mission activities outside the home should refrain from judging those who don't. Each mother, each child, each family is different. Let us not forget our freedom in Christ to seek God's will for ourselves and for our family. We do not need to be governed by the expectations of others—even of senior missionaries.

Some wives who have no specific training or profession ask: "What can I do in the way of ministry outside the home?" One answer I can give is that you have an almost limitless ministry aiding, befriending, and loving national women, and sharing the gospel with them. In most countries where missionaries work, the lot of women, and especially married women, is terrible. They are uneducated, illiterate, unloved, overworked, undernourished, often despised, and even abused. In some societies they are one step above a man's animals. They work from before dawn to after dark, cooking, sweeping, washing, taking care of four, six, eight children and all of their husband's needs—while the husband is often off in the bazaar playing cards, drinking, and socializing with his friends. There are so many ways these women can be ministered to: literacy, non-formal education, teaching of skills such as knitting. To give such women help and hope and the Good News is one of the greatest ministries—indeed, one the greatest privileges and joys—any missionary can have.

One of the major problems that a missionary wife encounters is the difficulty in finding time for daily prayer and Bible study. The early morning is still the best for most people, but even that is no sure thing on the mission field. Visiting hours start at dawn here, and that's when the kids start too. And Mom may still be exhausted from the previous evening's dinner party.

No one denies the need to have regular periods of quiet, of meditation, worship, prayer, and Bible study; but let us not turn our quiet times into a law. God looks at the heart. He understands the interruptions, the demands, the fatigue. The quiet time is not magic; if we miss it one day we can make it up the next. And no one said a quiet time couldn't be interrupted. One of the chief characteristics of missionary life is interruptions, and we need to accept them as from God—even when they occur during our quiet time.

In fact, it is possible to have many quiet times with the Lord each day. It's an important habit to develop. We can redeem otherwise wasted time. Who said you can't pray walking down a mountain or riding on a bus (provided you're not sick)? And we don't have to be alone either, as some interpret "your room" in Matthew 6:6. We may not find private places everywhere in the overpopulated Third World. But we can commune with God alone in our hearts. Sarah Wesley, the mother of John and his sixteen siblings, used to put a paper bag over her head when she prayed, and that was her "room."

Before leaving this section on wives, I want to quote a paragraph from Joyce Tuggy's book *The Missionary Wife and Her Work*. She writes: "There is a statement to which some may perhaps take exception, but which women should very seriously examine. It is the conviction that missionary women are at the root of the great bulk of missionary personnel problems."

No man would have dared write such a thing—and I've taken my life in my hands even to quote it. But the experience of Cynthia and myself over a period of twenty-four years in Nepal would tend to support this statement. There are four possible explanations for this observation. The first is that women on the mission field outnumber men, sometimes two to one. The second explanation for the statement, written in 1966, is that women have suffered from the benighted policies of male-dominated missions. A third explanation is that women bear the greatest brunt of culture shock and the trials of adaptation. And a fourth explanation applies to single women, some of whom, especially early in their missionary careers, have not yet been fully able to accept their singleness.

Why do I include this quotation here? Simply to counterbalance the opposite charge, which I have heard more than once, that most missionary personnel problems are caused by insensitive, autocratic men!

Let's put the guns away! One thing is certain: We all have enough sins and shortcomings of our own to worry about without pointing fingers at others. Not only that, if we could just get the finger-pointing to stop, eighty percent of missionary personnel problems would disappear overnight.

It's one of those days

Being a missionary wife and mother is the most difficult mission work there is. Right from the start, the young mother is the one hit hardest by this new, strange culture. Naturally: she's the one who has to cope with the day-to-day running of the household under adverse conditions. Let us never underestimate her problems. If you want to know who the real missionary heroes are, just take a peek inside the home of a young missionary mother.

Problems are cumulative. There is no way to adequately describe what living in the Third World is actually like for a young mother unless we follow her through an ordinary day. So I have chosen a day from the life of my wife, as recorded in a letter home (what follows is an abridged version), a day that took place back in 1972 when our older son Tommy was six and our younger son Christopher was three; we had been in Nepal two years.

This particular day had begun early for Cynthia. She had been aroused at 5:00 by a commotion in the boys' room. A dispute had arisen over a pet frog that Tommy was holding, tightly squeezed, in his fist.

"That's my frog."

"No, it's not. You have your own frogs, Chris. Go play with them."

"I don't know where they are."

Christopher didn't know where his frogs were because he had let them out of their box the evening before; he wanted Tommy's. But before the frog in question was pulled to pieces, Cynthia appeared on the scene. With the frog rescued and the dispute settled, the day began.

The first order of business was to light the wood cooking stove. Cynthia had enough difficulty in the rainy season getting paper to burn, let alone wood. To begin with, it was still dark. Then she found a large, pot-bellied spider with a three-inch leg span sitting on the handle of the burner. This she killed without flinching.

Cynthia put on her poncho and groped her way through the early morning mist to the outdoor woodshed, raking down with her face three new spider webs in the ten-foot journey. It was raining. It had rained most of the night. It would rain much of the day.

The wood was damp, as it had been for two months. Firewood was not available during the rains, so you were supposed to stock up in the dry season—which Cynthia thought she had done. But now her supply was almost gone, and there were still two months of monsoon rains to go. The main problem was that Cynthia's stove consumed enormous amounts of wood. The heat didn't circulate properly, and most of it went up the chimney. It took a roaring blaze to get the oven hot enough to cook anything, and then whatever it was would get cooked on one side and not on the other.

Cynthia felt around and selected the least wet wood. The next step was getting it to burn. No, the next step was getting the matches to burn. The matches were made in Nepal; match manufacturing was at the time one of the country's prize industries. But however prized the industry might have been, it didn't always produce prize matches—though, I must say in fairness, no country's matches would have done well in those monsoon rains.

This particular morning Cynthia was fortunate and got the third match to light. But then she dropped it. She had better luck on the sixth match, and soon she had the paper in the burner blazing merrily. Tenderly she began placing bark shavings and wisps of straw into the flame, then little twigs, then slightly bigger twigs. They began to smoke, then glow—but the paper was burning out. There wasn't much time left—would it catch? Yes, there was hope; some of the twigs were beginning to burn. However, at that moment Cynthia thought she heard water pouring out of the bathroom sink onto the floor; but she didn't dare leave the fire. Yes, it was water. Christopher was bathing two of his frogs. By this time, because of the slope of the bathroom floor, the water would be running into the living room. If only she could get the fire to catch. Suddenly she heard a loud thud, followed by even louder screaming. One of the frogs had escaped, and in an effort to recapture it, Christopher had slipped off his stool onto the cement floor. Tommy appeared in the kitchen to say that blood was coming from Christopher's mouth. The fire was in a precarious state; it needed blowing. Cynthia had a special bamboo tube just for that purpose. After spending a moment to locate it—it had rolled under the stove—she gingerly placed the end of the tube into the burner, drew her breath, and blew the remains of the fire up the chimney. At the same time, clouds of soot and ashes billowed out of the other portals of the stove into the kitchen.

While Cynthia was attending to Christopher, she heard someone coughing outside the kitchen door. This was the Nepali method of knocking, and whoever it was had already coughed himself hoarse by the time Cynthia got there, since he hadn't been heard over Christopher's screaming. It was the *nashpatti* man, who had come to sell *nashpattis,* a variety of pear. We'd been eating *nashpattis* every meal for three weeks; it was *nashpatti* season. But as no other fruit was available, Cynthia purchased some more. And she didn't want to discourage people from coming: there were no markets in our area, so whatever shopping we did depended on who coughed at our door.

Tommy by this time had gotten hungry for breakfast, and said he wanted some French toast. But Cynthia had no eggs. She hadn't had any eggs for the past two weeks, because somehow the last egg shipment from Kathmandu hadn't arrived; eggs weren't available locally. Cynthia offered Tommy some *nashpatti* sauce, which was not well received. He settled in the end for "multi-mix," a homemade mixture of coarsely ground millet, corn, and soybeans. What it lacked in taste it made up for in nourishment, according to Cynthia. But I had trouble believing her: nothing could have made up for that taste.

Today Cynthia had the usual odd jobs to do, and then she needed to check on the gardener, which took a lot of her time. For one thing, she placed great importance on feeding her children nutritious food, and where we lived that meant having her own garden. For another thing, our gardener's performance tended to be erratic, and unless closely watched, he often undid in a few minutes what had taken him hours and days to accomplish. Just the previous week, for example, while weeding the beet patch, he had "weeded" fully two thirds of the beets. This had agitated Cynthia greatly, because she liked beets; but remembering her position, she had smiled weakly and sent him off to do something else.

The rest of Cynthia's morning passed uneventfully. The children played happily in the rain, collecting millipedes, slugs, land crabs, and more frogs. Cynthia had always been a little uneasy about the boys' zoological pursuits. Two days earlier Christopher had brought in a four-inch-long centipede to show her. Fortunately, he wasn't bitten. However, she made sure he knew never to pick one up again. Millipedes he could play with, she offered by way of consolation; at least they were harmless, and besides, they were more abundant. But somehow, not nearly so interesting.

Just before lunch the week's supply of eggs arrived from Kathmandu, so now the boys would be able to have scrambled eggs, a great favorite. In they marched, covered with mud, bringing with them their recently collected specimens of animal life. Baths were in order, but much to Cynthia's dismay, there was no water. It was the middle of the monsoon rains; there was water running down the hillside, washing away topsoil and causing small landslides; water was cascading down footpaths, transforming them into muddy streams; there was water everywhere. Except in the faucets. For one of a half-dozen frequently recurring reasons, the tanks were empty. Christopher didn't want a bath anyway.

Cynthia always liked the scrambled eggs cooked at the last minute. I had just gotten home from the hospital, so we all sat down to eat. Our cook had finally gotten the wood stove going and was heating the skillet. We heard an egg crack—there was a loud gasp, a howl rather, and the cook was out the door. Cynthia ran to the kitchen to see what had happened, but she needn't have bothered. Within two seconds all of us knew. The egg was rotten, utterly rotten. And so were all the rest. Indeed, the eggs that had come were the missing ones from the previous week—and now they had come with a vengeance.

As soon as the lunch of bread and *nashpatti* jam was over, the boys got up to go outside, hoping mother would forget to give them their respective medicines for intestinal parasites. No such luck. Tommy was taking his for giardia; Christopher was taking his for amoeba. Last month it was the other way around. The amoeba medicine, Flagyl, was particularly bitter, and it was no simple task coaxing Christopher to take it. Today Cynthia tried mashing it up in *nashpatti* jam.

Cynthia had much to do between lunch and supper time. We had invited two Nepali families for supper, which we tried to do at least twice a week. It had finally stopped raining, so the cook (who was also the housekeeper) could take the clothes she had washed some days before out to the line to dry. There was bread to be baked. Most of the house needed cleaning again. An ill child was expected, whose father, a district official, had heard there was a pediatrician at our hospital. The boys would need baths, and Cynthia would have to wash her hair—that is, if the water came back on.

The bread was now ready to go into the oven. The cook had made a good fire, possibly a little hot for bread—but who could be sure. Then Cynthia discovered that the milk for making the evening's dessert had spoiled, so she sent the cook out to borrow some from a neighbor.

Then as luck would have it, it began to rain again, and the clothes were still on the line. The clothes hadn't dried in three days. The boys had hardly any dry clothes left, and the napkins for supper were out there too. The bread needed checking, but the rain was coming on fast and Cynthia hadn't a moment to lose. She knew she'd find no room to hang things inside the house if they got wet now; damp clothes already filled the bathroom and kitchen and the back of every chair.

Cynthia gathered the clothes and returned to the house to find the kitchen filled with the smoke of burning bread. Yes, it was too far gone to salvage. There was no time for lectures about the fire being too hot. Cynthia set the cook to making the pudding for dessert, and turned her attention to getting the kids cleaned up and the house tidied.

Somehow the guests were late, and the water came back on. It was a rare day when everything went wrong. The baths were taken, the house cleaned, the food cooked. There's no time left to tell about the several thousand ants that came out of the wall into the house just as the guests arrived; or the raspberry-flavored chocolate pudding that the cook concocted. There was no tea for supper because the hot water had been used to fight ants, and we were out of kerosene, and Cynthia wasn't about to light the wood stove.

At 9:30 the hospital generator was turned off, and the lights went out. The guests left, having had a good time singing and playing games.

The house was a mess. Nine children had eaten on the floor; the adults had eaten at the table. There was food everywhere. Many varieties of insect life were gathering. Already the legions of ants that had escaped the extermination proceedings earlier were regrouping for the feast. But by 10:30, the house had somehow been cleared of at least the gross debris, and it was time for bed. Then Cynthia suddenly remembered that tomorrow was mail day. She needed to write a few important letters and get them into the mailbag, or it would be another week before they got sent. So by the light of the kerosene lamp, she began to write, and as the cockroaches, moths, and great buzzing beetles gathered about the lamp, she thought of the poor frogs who hadn't been fed all day. So she fetched them and set them on the dining-room table around the lamp; and as she wrote they fed heartily on the insects that had been attracted to the light. The frogs had never had it so good. Cynthia, I could tell, was fond of frogs. They ate bugs.

Well, just change a few details, and this is a story any missionary mother could tell. If you want to know where the real action is, just spend a day with a missionary wife.

19

Missionary Children

The difficulty of raising and educating children on the mission field is the commonest reason given for a couple deciding against being missionaries.

This is a great pity, because the reason is based on a misconception. I'd far rather raise my children on the mission field than in the USA or some other Western country. My reason is simple: I am convinced that children raised on the mission field have a greater likelihood of turning out to be fruitful disciples of Jesus Christ. Furthermore, it has been shown over and over that missionary children have no higher incidence of serious problems than children raised at home by Christian parents.

And you ask: Do the kids feel the same way? Yes, they do. In a survey by Sprinkle in 1976, a large group of missionary children were asked: "If you could do it all again, would you choose to be an MK (missionary kid)?" Ninety-five percent of them said, "Yes"; five percent said, "Not sure." To the question, "Would you be willing to raise your own children on the foreign mission field?" ninety percent said, "Yes."

More often than not, when a young couple says they don't feel they should go to the mission field "because of the children," they are using the children as an excuse not to go. In other words, it's a false reason.

Many others are taken up by the home-schooling movement and feel that sending children away for their education is wrong. This is being taught with such dogmatism today that many couples are refusing even to consider missions for fear they won't be able to keep their kids at home. In the first place, this fear is unjustified, as we shall see later. In the second place, when a movement (such as the home-schooling movement) leads people to turn aside from God's call to missions, it is very clearly going too far. Satan loves it when Christians carry good things too far.

There is only one question that young couples need to ask when confronting the choice of being missionaries or not: What is God's will? For there is only one safe and proper place to raise children, and that is the place where God has put the parents. If a couple is refusing to consider missions out of consideration for the children, they not only have an utter misunderstanding of the facts but also an utter misunderstanding of God's ways and purposes.

Many people think that missionary children are in some way deprived—deprived of necessary things like Sesame Street, Batman, video games, tennis, good food, ice cream. Many missionary parents themselves worry lest their children suffer some sort of adverse reaction and end up hating everything connected with mission work. No doubt that has happened, but it's almost always due to another kind of deprivation—deprivation of parental attention. Let me quickly insert here that sending children away to school does not preclude giving them adequate attention, as long as their separation from parents is made up for when they're home for the holidays.

Far from being deprived, most missionary children gain much more than they give up. Their education is usually better than the education they would get in their home countries—home schooling included—and often markedly better. Their teachers are more likely to be people with initiative and gumption; their classmates will be international, with interesting and varied backgrounds. They are exposed to different cultures and have a chance to learn firsthand how people outside the West actually live. They have the chance to escape the narrowness and insularity so typical of young people who have no exposure to other lands. Missionary children in Nepal trek through the Himalayas in the fifth grade, and tour India in the sixth. They're hardly losers.

One of the great advantages of most Third World mission fields is the absence of television; your kid learns to read, and enjoy it. In rural areas there are all kinds of experiences and adventures to be enjoyed, not to mention a profusion of wildlife—bugs, butterflies, birds, flying squirrels, baby leopards. And where in the world but the mission field could you have a monkey for a pet? Then again, who would want one?

Children on the mission field learn to take initiative, to be resourceful, to be adaptable. They learn a healthy kind of independence that speeds along their personality development. After those first five or so crucial years, during which the child's self-image and self-confidence are established through parental love and affirmation, the time comes to get out from mother's shadow and begin to explore the world outside. The mission field is a wonderful exploring ground, and yields rich dividends in learning and experience.

One of the side benefits of being an MK (I will bow to convention and use this term; the MK's themselves use it) is the opportunity to participate in the ministry of the parents. That doesn't mean dragging the child along on every outing or trip, but rather it means making the child feel a part of the family team. This may not be practical to a great extent, but in small ways it will be, and it will broaden the child's life and plant the idea that one day such a ministry may become his also.

We need to talk to our children about our calling, our ministry. We should ask for their prayers from an early age. We should let them know they are an important asset in our ministry, as indeed they are. Not only are children bridge-builders, but they also gain for their parents increased respect from the people. Never should a child be considered an interference or a hindrance to the work; don't even think it, for the child will detect it instantly. And if he detects it repeatedly, you will have lost him to missions, and perhaps to yourself as well.

In total, then, the advantages of raising children on the mission field distinctly outweigh the disadvantages. But what about the disadvantages? Let's look at them.

First are the frustrations and inconveniences of transportation and communication. Our son missed getting a college scholarship because of poor communication facilities—and almost missed getting enrolled in college for the same reason.

Second, MK's face a definitely increased risk of getting a serious illness on the mission field. My guess is that it's about double that of kids at home; I've not seen figures. But that is still very small—probably under five percent. Most mission stations today have ready access to good medical care. The risk for our children is but little higher than the risk for ourselves, and that's not very much. Our predecessors in missions took fifty to a hundred times the risk we take today.

Third, a minority of MK's have problems in adapting to their own culture when they return home for high school or college. These problems are real, and involve such things as social adjustment, loneliness, a feeling of not belonging. But there are ways of minimizing these problems, which we shall look at later.

Fourth, and most serious in the opinion of many, are the separations that missionary life entails if parents choose or are obliged to send their children away to school. We need to say right off that mission agencies have become much more flexible on this issue, and that most missionaries today have the choice of whether to send their kids away to school or keep them at home. Thus the matter of separation can be discussed openly between mission, parent, and child, and the best solution worked out for all concerned.

Practical thoughts for missionary parents

Our children are assets to our ministry as long as they are well-behaved. Sadly, if you go to a church service in Nepal, the worst-behaved children sometimes turn out to be those belonging to missionaries. Of course, the little dears are cute, and the Nepalis egg them on. But I was embarrassed recently to sit in a service in which the three-year-old daughter of a missionary couple spent the entire time migrating back and forth between the male and female sides of the church, here and there stepping on someone, or getting lost, or chatting amiably with a new acquaintance; and though Mom and Dad listened attentively to the service throughout, few others did—including myself.

The proper disciplining of our children is one of the most valuable things that we, as Christian families, can show the nationals, especially national believers. So when we allow our children to misbehave, it is not only setting a bad example, but it is also a lost opportunity to demonstrate loving but firm and consistent discipline.

Parents should come to the mission field prepared. They should have read some good books on child rearing and child development. If they are going to be in a rural area where there is no doctor, they need to have access to the book *Where There Is No Doctor* and other suitable health literature. Missions have medical advisors and all kinds of health policies; there will always be someone who can tell the missionary what to do when a health problem arises.

The first five to six years are the most important in a child's life. This is when the child's personality is formed and the child develops confidence and an ability to trust and relate to others. Don't blow it, Mom and Dad. Especially Dad—don't wait until your child can play football before you begin to relate to him!

Those early years set the foundation for the remainder of a child's mental, emotional, and spiritual development. Make those years count. If you fail there, you and the child will be in for a rough haul. If you succeed there, the child will be able to handle many bumps and bruises thereafter, and instead of succumbing to them he will grow and mature through them. Therefore, work on creating a truly loving and happy home. This is as important on the mission field as anywhere else.

One of the first rites of passage that a new missionary mother undergoes is the entrusting of her precious baby or toddler to an *aaya*, or national nanny. Well, my advice is: don't merely sit back and trust God. Make sure you know what this woman is doing with your child! She needs to be supervised. Your instructions are absolutely contrary to most everything she's done all her life—and she probably didn't even understand your instructions. Even if she understood, she may not follow them.

These nannies will spoil your children rotten; that's the custom in many Third World countries. Discipline doesn't begin until the child reaches seven or eight. So, before you know it, your nice little boy or girl is soon beginning to act like the prince or princess of England. Be on your watch! And never let your child boss around the household help.

Every family needs to set its own policy on how long a time to leave a child with an *aaya*. A child under two should not be left for more than two hours. Over age three, children can go half days in a nursery school setting. There are exceptions, but this is the general range.

Mothers especially may feel guilty about sending their children away to school. While the child is still at home, they compensate for the guilt by tying the child closely to themselves. This is only natural. But it prevents the child from learning self-reliance, and makes the eventual departure from home more traumatic. One of the biggest favors a mother can do her child is to give the child some leeway, to allow the child to make decisions, and to give the child increasing independence. Many MK's have written years later how grateful they were that their parents had done just that, and how much easier it had been for them because of it.

On a related subject, don't discourage your children from mixing with the national children. First of all, it will be interpreted by the nationals as racism, though they may not call it that. It's akin to the old mission policy forbidding members to marry nationals, which in spite of all the practical reasons given, is at root a manifestation of racism—something that no mission wants any part of.

Secondly, when you limit your children's contact with nationals, you impair your own witness as a Christian family and lose the benefit your children can bring to your ministry. Let them sleep overnight with their national friends. Sure they may bring home some creepy-crawlies in their clothes or scalps, but they'll have a wonderful time.

One important point: speak your own language in your home. The kids will learn the national language from their friends. But their own language they will learn only from you.

Parents ain't perfect. They make mistakes. An occasional mistake won't hurt a child if it is confessed and covered by love. Children are very forgiving. Even a zinger of a mistake won't hurt; Jesus will make it right. He will erase the effect of the mistake.

If parents quarrel in front of the children, let them make up in front of the children. Children need to see that a quarrel is normal, and they need to see how you make up. Furthermore, make sure the children know that the quarrel wasn't caused by them. Children tend to internalize everything and blame themselves when things go wrong.

Children are quick to pick up their parent's attitudes. If the parents are wringing their hands over little Johnny going off to school, be sure that little Johnny will be wringing his little hands as well. If the parents show on their faces that little Johnny is deprived in some way, little Johnny is going to feel deprived. And if the parents are having trouble adjusting to the host country, little Johnny will be having trouble too.

Are the parents feeling negative about the country, about the people? Johnny will too—but he won't know why. If you see this kind of negative attitude in your child, you'll know where it's coming from. You'll need to search your own attitudes. You'll need to start focusing on the bright points of the country you're working in—every country has some. Zoos, parks, seacoasts, boat trips, and if you're lucky enough to live in Nepal, the most spectacular scenery in the world. But more important than all this is developing a love for the people. If that's missing, you and your child will never feel at home in the country.

Parents should be in agreement on issues pertaining to the children. Don't let your kids play one parent off against the other. Don't give something your spouse refused to give. Don't use the father at work as a threat: "When Daddy comes home you're going to get it." That's not fair to Daddy.

Don't let the sun set on your anger. All pains must end that same day. Each morning is then truly a new day for the child. Painful events have been canceled.

If parents have a sense of security in their marriage and are able to trust in God's provision for their needs, and if they are able to communicate their love for each other and for their children consistently, and if they have the deep conviction that God is guiding the family, then their children will be protected from emotional harm. If the parents' attitude is positive, then their children will be able to face new experiences as adventures rather than as threats. Pass on positive attitudes! Love is not inherited; children love because they have been loved.

Your adolescent children will demand special wisdom of you—which presumably you have gained during the first dozen years of their lives. Adolescents need a wide margin, but they do need limits. Widen the limits as they grow.

Adolescents test everything, including their belief in all the principles their parents taught them. This is normal and necessary. Don't condemn them. Be relaxed. Get earplugs for the hard rock. Read a book on adolescence. Take a walk. It will pass.

What do you do if your adolescent child doesn't want to go to the mission field, either on your first time out, or on your second, third, or fourth time out? You talk it over; find out the reasons. If it's the first time out, consider a preliminary visit. Talk about your calling, your own feelings. Usually agreement will follow. But if your adolescent child remains steadfastly opposed to going, it may be wisest not to go.

But there is an opposing consideration. As parents, we want to protect our children from pain. And yet God-given pain is absolutely necessary to our children's growth, especially their spiritual growth. To refuse missionary service simply to protect our children from pain is a tragic error, both for us and for our children.

We Christians are always taking things into our own hands. We need to take more seriously the New Testament teaching about offering our bodies to God, about leaving all, including our children (Mt 19:29). God isn't asking us to abandon our children; he is asking us to obey him—just as he asked Abraham to obey him when he told him to sacrifice Isaac.

Do we really seek God's will for our children? Would we obey God if he led us to a decision which conflicted with our previous understanding? Do we really trust God with our children? With ourselves?

In the end, it is God alone who shields our children, and even with all our wisdom and experience we must not lessen our dependence on him. God cares for our children more than we do.

Education of missionary children

No subject relating to missionaries elicits stronger emotion than the subject of educating missionary children. My main plea throughout this section will be that we put away dogmatism, that we keep an open mind, that we stop being sure we "know what's right for our kids in every circumstance"—not to mention what's right for other people's kids. What's right for one family isn't right for the next family. What's right for the first child in a family isn't necessarily right for the second. What's right one year in a child's life isn't necessarily right the next year. And to those who protest, "But Scripture says..." I simply reply that nowhere in Scripture are we told how to educate our children in academic subjects. To be dogmatic in this matter is to go beyond Scripture.

Gone are the days when missions set fixed policies stipulating that all children should be sent away to school at age six. All the more pity, then, that young parents, having just been freed from one set of fixed policies should now be coming out to the field bringing with them a new set of rules of their own.

Missionary parents have three basic choices in the education of their children: one, home schooling; two, boarding; and three, day school, of which there are many varieties. All three of these options are good. One option will be better for one child one time, and another option will be better for another. Each child, each family, each work situation is going to differ, and it is an unwise parent who comes to the mission field thinking there is only one way to educate a child—or, what's worse, tries to impose that view on others.

Vastly more important than the method of education in children's upbringing is the relationship between Mom and Dad. If that is bad, no kind of education is going to make up for it—least of all, keeping the child at home!

One thing that often gets lost in the debate is the need to talk to our children about these choices. For younger children we must make the major decisions, but we still should ask them about their feelings. That will give us the chance to allay their apprehensions, correct misunderstandings, and help them see that what we're doing is best for them. Children over twelve should have an increasing say in the choice of their education.

Let's take a closer look now at the different choices before us.

One choice that is seldom suitable is the educating of one's children in national schools. There are exceptions, especially for missionaries living in major cities of Europe or Latin America, but as a general policy, it is not recommended. The standards, even if high, don't usually match those of the home country. The child will absorb the cultural values of the host country. This becomes even more of a problem in high school during the difficult period of teenage adjustment, and will exacerbate the problems of eventual reentry to the home country for college.

A very popular option, where possible, is keeping the children at home but sending them to a nearby day school or some form of tutorial program. There are high-quality international schools in almost every capital city of the world. These are expensive (scholarship help is sometimes available), and they tend to draw the student into the "ghetto" of the foreign community; but they provide excellent education.

Missions often run tutorial programs in the larger cities. Here students can study at their own pace using correspondence courses of their choice, and at the same time have the benefit of trained teachers to assist them and the facilities for science, drama, music, art, and sports. In addition, these programs provide the opportunity for normal social interaction with other children, which is an essential part of the educational process.

In more isolated areas, small clusters of missionary families have set up their own tutorial programs, and have invited a Christian teacher to come out and teach the little group of students. Many Christian teachers, some young, some retired, have made an enormous contribution to missions by coming out to run small tutorial programs for MK's, thus enabling their parents to stay at their jobs.

Space does not permit a description of other variations of the tutorial group concept. Wycliffe Bible Translators, with its specialized needs, has developed a Field Education System, which is well spoken of. And there are others.

We want to turn now to the two remaining major options, home schooling and boarding. First, home schooling.

Home schooling is an excellent option as long as the following conditions are met: first, the mother must be able to teach; second, she must feel it is her calling to do so as a missionary mother; third, the child must relate well to the mother in a student-teacher setting; fourth, there must be nearby playmates of one's own culture; and fifth, there must be the possibility of joint activities with other missionary children. If one or more of these conditions is absent, home schooling should not be pursued, for to do so would be detrimental to the intellectual and social development of the child.

I would estimate that in no more than a third of mission situations would all five conditions be present. Even if the first three were present, you still have no control over the latter two. Suppose you're in a mission community, and the other families have decided to send their kids away to school. Your child is going to be left alone, while his friends go off—a most unhappy situation.

We have known of several instances in Nepal—and other fields report a similar experience—where a young couple has persisted with home schooling even when things weren't working out, and has eventually left the field because of emotional stress in the mother, the child, or both.

But let's look again at the mission situation in which all five conditions for home schooling are more or less met. Is this still the best option for a particular child? We must remember why the home-schooling movement started: it started because of widespread dissatisfaction with the educational system in the West—most egregiously represented by the U.S. public school system. But what has worked well in suburban America isn't necessarily going to work well on every mission field. What the proponents of home schooling have failed to take into account is that there is a world of difference between suburban Los Angeles and a rural mission outpost in the hills of Nepal.

Not only that, suburban Los Angeles may offer no alternative between public school and home schooling, but on the mission field there are almost always other alternatives. Is it in the best interest of the child to deprive him of a school experience, when good Christian schools are available?

There's another question that missionary mothers need to answer: Is it the best use of your gifts to be spending five to ten or more years on the mission field primarily in schooling your children? Is this really how God wants to use you as a missionary?

Mothers in particular need to look very closely at their motive for keeping their children at home. Is it selfish? Is it possessiveness? The child that you once dedicated to the Lord, can you now not trust to the Lord? It is very easy to use the rhetoric of the home-schooling advocates as an excuse to keep the kids at home with you—not for their sake, but for your own.

I have spent some time on the home-schooling question because, to be frank, the strong pronouncements of the leaders of this movement have been deterring young couples from answering God's call to missions. Even if the couple has gone to the field, they have often had increased problems trying to adhere to a home-schooling program.

One of the main texts that home-schooling proponents use to justify their strong stance is Deuteronomy 6:6-7: "These commandments that I give you today are to be upon your hearts. Impress them on your children. Talk about them when you sit at home and when you walk along the road, when you lie down and when you get up." First of all, these verses refer to the teaching of the law, of moral and spiritual truth, not academic subjects. Second, the words suggest that we are not to teach by words only but also by our daily lives—by our sitting, our walking, our getting up and lying down. And verses 8 and 9 spell it out even more clearly.

You reply: How are you going to obey this verse when you send your kids away to school?

The answer: First, missionary children are at home until at least age six and usually older. Those first six years, as we said earlier, are far and away the most crucial years in a child's development. Second, children who are in boarding are with their parents an average of three to four months out of the year, and as much quality time can be fitted into those few months as takes place during a whole year with the child at home. It's quality time that counts, not the number of hours. One month of close and happy fellowship is better than a year of strained communication. Third, there are letters. Don't downplay the power of a letter.

Thus, missionaries who send their children away to school are not disobeying Scripture; rather they are demonstrating obedience to Scripture, which Deuteronomy 6:6-7 enjoins. The missionary doesn't pack up and go home and renounce his calling the moment he can't educate his children at home.

But neither does he send his children away to school to get them out of his hair. He sends them away to school because in almost all cases it's the best thing for the children. Otherwise, he would have chosen another alternative.

The final option to discuss, then, is the mission boarding school. And the first thing to say is that the great majority of them today are exceptionally fine educational institutions. The teachers have a high level of competence and dedication. Students who attend them get consistently way-above-average marks when they return to their home country. They are more mature, self-reliant, and broad-minded than other home-side students. The longer the time in boarding school, the more pronounced the benefits. The great majority—the usual figure cited is ninety-five percent—have an overall happy experience at boarding school. Those who stay at home don't do any better than that.

So why all the hand-wringing when little Johnny goes off to boarding school? Who is the hand-wringing for? These kids are the lucky ones. And to keep a child from going who wants to go, whose friends have all gone off, is just about as selfish a thing as a parent can do. Our older son's comment to his mother on graduating from Woodstock School in India was: "Thank you, Mom, for not keeping us at home for your sake, but letting us go away to school for our sake." He also announced that he would encourage his own kids to go to Woodstock—even if they were living in the States when the time came. That's not a bad recommendation!

The parents' attitude has a lot to do with whether or not the child has a positive experience at boarding school; possibly it's the single biggest factor. Emphasize the positive. Resist anxious thoughts. The child who has been secure at home will be secure at boarding school. And re-member: if it doesn't work out after several months, you can review the matter. A single three-to-four month period of unhappiness is not going to emotionally harm your child.

But we do need to look at the downside of boarding school. Those highly competent and dedicated teachers do not totally replace Mom and Dad, especially in the earlier years. There is homesickness and lone-liness; and though it's helpful to know that others are experiencing it too, it does not eliminate the pain of separation. The worst thing is to feel that you're the only one with these sad feelings, that somehow you are differ-ent. These are real traumas. Don't brush them off; don't try to talk the child out of it. These traumas need to be met with loving support and un-derstanding. They are worse the younger the child, which is why most missionary couples try not to send their kids away until they are at least nine or ten, and older if possible. We do not want to cover over the fact that there is a small minority of students who have problems, and that these problems will require a change of course on the part of the parents.

Again, let us keep perspective. Though separations are painful, they can also, if handled rightly, be growing experiences. Remember, too, that boarding school produces no greater percentage of unhappy children than a home environment does; the only difference is a different set of prob-lems.

And back to the young couples at home who are wondering if the problems of educating their children on the mission field are too great to face, I'll simply repeat what I said before: no matter what combination of educational methods you choose, children raised and educated on the mission field are more likely to turn out to be fruitful disciples of Jesus Christ than those who grow up in their home countries.

If boarding school is to work, there is one key requirement: When the kids are home for holiday, parents must give them absolute priority over the work. When this is done, it makes up for most of the pain of separa-tion. It has been the experience of many parents, ourselves included, that they have spent more quality time with their children on their school hol-idays than they would have spent had the kids been home all year. It's only reasonable. That tree house that you never have time to build—always next week, next month—well, it gets built if the kids are only home for that one-or-two-month holiday.

Two of the most pleasant months of my life were spent at Woodstock School, seven thousand feet above the plains of North India. One month was spent at our older son Tom's graduation, and the second was spent at our younger son Chris's graduation four years later.

It is the second visit I remember most vividly. We arrived from Nepal after dark, and the next morning we went out to look at the view from the mountainside on which the school was located. There were quite a few other people, most of them recently arrived parents, standing in front of the big guest house and looking down the hillside. Five hundred feet below us was the hostel for the older boys, with its prominent red tin roof jutting out from the mountain slope. But something new had attracted the attention of all these visitors: a huge, yellow smiley face had been painted on the hostel roof overnight. It had been done with great care; the face was a perfect circle, and there were other neatly executed embellishments. Obviously the work of an artist.

Soon the word spread through the crowd that the head of maintenance, an Indian, was highly incensed that one of his roofs should have been desecrated in this way—and in violation of school rules to boot. Then we heard that a meeting of the high uppy-ups was being held to determine what disciplinary action should be taken. Would the perpetrator of this deed be allowed to graduate? Would he be expelled? It's a wonder how a bunch of parents with nothing better to do can stand around for an hour and speculate on such stuff. Finally someone thought to ask: "Anyone know who did it?"

Somebody said, "A guy named Chris Hale, they say."

"Oh," I said, involuntarily.

A few people turned to me. "You know him?"

"Yeah, sort of."

"Well, it sounds bad, doesn't it? Poor guy. I wonder how his parents are going to feel."

"I'd be tickled pink if it was my son," I said.

And within two minutes that entire crowd of thirty or so missionary parents were all agreeing among themselves that that smiley face was indeed a great idea, something to cheer up everyone on the hillside—all except for the Indian maintenance supervisor.

The next we heard was that the school administration had decided to reprimand the culprits (another student was involved—plus a teacher, who had provided the paint!) and to have the smiley face painted over the following day. Hot on the heels of that news came word that the senior class would refuse to attend their graduation if the face were painted over. A new meeting of the administration was called; and I'm not sure what all was worked out, but I do know that we continued to be cheered by that smiley face for the next four weeks, and then it was time to leave.

Chris and I had a great time wandering over that mountainside while he showed me all his favorite haunts. One of the more popular student diversions was to hop an open truck to somewhere, and then hope to hop another one back. So one day he showed me the ropes. As we were bouncing along outward bound, I asked, "Is this legal?"

"With you along it won't be so bad," Chris said.

I decided not to ask any more questions.

On the return we had the misfortune of choosing a coal truck, and by the time we had gotten back to Woodstock we looked like two tar babies. We jumped off the truck and bumped plunk into the headmaster crossing the street to his house. I have always felt it was a mark of singular grace on his part that he pretended not to recognize us. But he was probably thinking to himself: "Thank goodness he doesn't have any more sons to send to Woodstock!"

While we're at it, let me give a plug here for the teachers of missionary children. Theirs is a most high calling. They fill one of the greatest needs on the mission field. What they do is just as much "true missionary work" as anything else. We other missionaries couldn't stay on the field without them; we need their support. And they, in turn, need the support of churches and people back home. "Please keep such teachers coming," is the plea of missionary families from around the world.

English is the language of international missions. Missionaries whose mother tongue is not English have special problems when it comes to educating their children, especially during the high-school years. In Nepal we have had Finnish schools, Norwegian schools, and Dutch schools, which have served their respective families well, but only up to the high-school level. Then most of these families have had to return to their home countries—a great loss to the field.

However, no one I know would recommend sending a child back to the home country alone for high school. It's one thing to be at a mission boarding school, where the culture is the same and the child is surrounded by like-minded peers and supportive and understanding teachers. But reentering the home culture involves a major cultural change, which is added onto all the other changes going on in the adolescent's body and emotions. It is most risky to let a child face that alone—certainly during the first year back in the home country. If living arrangements are ideal and the child has strong support from other family members, and if the child wholeheartedly agrees, it is reasonable for parents to consider a return to the field after that first high school year; but not otherwise.

Once their children are out of high school, however, many missionary parents then return full time to the field. With today's relatively inexpensive air fares, missionaries now have a mobility that a generation ago would have been unthinkable. God, together with missionary leaders—who today are more concerned than ever about the welfare of missionary children—will guide each family in the wisest course for all concerned.

With few exceptions, children should return home for college. I have never yet heard of an MK deprived of a good college education because his or her parents were missionaries. Yes, the student may have to economize; he may have to skimp. But then, so have the thousands of other students who have made it through college on a shoestring, who have worked their way through—and are the better for it.

Missionary children, like any others, need to learn that they are not the center of the universe. There are greater goals, greater needs in the world than their education, their happiness, their convenience. Self-indulgence and self-centeredness make a sure recipe for a lifetime of unhappiness. Let us, as parents, not fear to let our college-age children learn to fend a bit for themselves.

A final thought about the missionary child's exposure to other faiths. Most mission teachers believe, and I would agree, that school curriculums should include host-culture studies, including the study of the host religion. To shelter children from all contrary beliefs is, in the end, detrimental to a child's faith. To teach only one set of beliefs is not education; it's indoctrination. It is a major cause of many children rebelling against their parents' faith during college years.

Bringing up children to faith in Christ is primarily the responsibility of their parents, and only secondarily that of their teachers. Teachers, for their part, need to teach students to critically evaluate their own as well as other cultures. Students need to learn that Christianity is true not because they were told it is, but because they can see it is. They need to be challenged by other beliefs; otherwise, their faith will end up a weak faith. Christian schools are an excellent place for our children to be exposed in a controlled and incremental manner to the outside world in which they are eventually going to have to take their place.

Being an MK

Our discussion of missionary children so far has been "relentlessly upbeat," and the suspicion may surface that objectivity has been thrown to the winds. In particular, one will ask, "Where are all the casualties, the MK disaster cases we've been hearing about for years? Are you hiding them under a big smiley face?"

No, I don't want to hide the problems, and we're going to look at them now. But first, a statement. The "disasters" are but a fraction of what they were a generation ago. The missionary movement has made enormous advances in the care of families in the past twenty to thirty years. The MK "disaster rate" is no higher than that for children raised in the home country—and my hunch is that it is lower. And the same can be said for the lesser problems and struggles that all children face. The bottom line is that even setting aside the matter of obeying God's will, a missionary couple is subjecting their children to no greater risk of unhappiness and emotional difficulty than if they had stayed at home. Keeping this in mind, let us look at the problems.

The problems center on two main areas: one, the lingering trauma of family separation; and two, the loss of belonging, the loss of identity.

MK's experience more separation than their Christian counterparts at home. Yes, missionary parents do all in their power to make it a learning, growing, maturing experience for the child. They understand, they reassure, they love. They talk to their child about the separation, which helps to bring out hidden, unexpressed fear and anger. And the people at the other end who will take charge of the child do the same. But in spite of all this, in at least five and possibly ten percent of cases, deep hurts will be experienced by the child which will affect their future lives, unless they can be brought out into the open and dealt with.

It is often hard to tell how much a child has suffered; frequently the child himself will repress the painful experience. His very independence and maturity, which his parents are so proud of, may sometimes be a cover for deep hurts within. On the outside he looks tough and able to cope; inside, he is crying for help.

Especially in younger children, separations can breed insecurity. Their pillars, Mom and Dad, are suddenly taken from them. Who can they count on? Who can they trust? And indeed, one of the more frequent manifestations of unhealed childhood trauma is the grown-up child's inability to make close and trusting relationships. Even the times the family is together are tinged with pain: another separation will inevitably follow. The pain of parting takes the joy from all reunions.

One of the saddest results of separation in early childhood is the inability of some children in later years to draw close to their parents. They may laugh and joke, they may visit frequently, but they avoid closeness. They don't want to get hurt again. They put up walls to protect them from any recurrence of pain. And those walls constrict their lives, constrict their choices. They affect their marriages; they can't be relaxed with their spouse. "Will he or she go away like my parents did?" This insecurity can cause grown-up children to react in harmful and inappropriate ways. They become overpossessive, jealous—or distant and suspicious.

And when it comes to raising their own children, they overcompensate. "I'll never allow a separation to occur." So they tie their children to them, with equally bad results. Because of these protective instincts, their judgment is distorted, they overreact, and they pass on to their children new woes. It is in this way that our own past hurts come back to haunt us—and haunt our children, and their children.

There is much help available for troubled MK's—counseling, seminars, retreats. The mission community is ready to provide all possible support and assistance, in addition to that provided by the MK's own family. Virtually all MK's come through in the end, though for a few it can be a tough road for a number of years.

The second major problem area for MK's is a diminished "sense of belonging." Who am I? This lack of clear identity becomes a problem when the older MK reenters his own culture. It is bound up with the adaptation the MK must make when he returns to the home country. He must find his place; he must fit back in.

As with any transition there is a sense of loss, loss of one's old identity and place. There is also increased stress, which may even result in some atypical behavior. But almost always the crisis passes, and the MK is the stronger and better for his experience.

Reentry problems are real; even well-adjusted MK's coming home for high school or college don't always find it easy. Dave Pollock and others have contributed much to our awareness of these problems. There are now reentry seminars available for returning MK's, which have been of great benefit to many.

I'm sure that that first month or two in college is pretty hard to take. Our older son Tom wasn't troubled by the size of the student body jumping from four hundred to twelve thousand, the size of Cornell at the time. He was troubled by the ignorance and insularity of his classmates.

They were friendly enough. "Hi! Where ya from?"

"Nepal."

"Hey, that's great! I used to know a girl from Naples" (a small town not far from Cornell).

"No, Nepal."

"Oh, Italy. What do you do over there?"

"No, Nepal. You know, Mount Everest."

"Oh. That must have been really cool. Well, I gotta be going now. See you around."

If the MK in one in ten times is able to elicit any interest in the world beyond Nintendo, the Redskins, and the Grateful Dead, the encounter might continue something like this.

"Ah, Nepal. Then you must live in a thatched hut."

It's very important for the MK to give the proper answer at this point.

"Absolutely. And we have foot-long lizards that live in the roof. Sometimes they fall down into the soup, but we eat the soup anyway, and the lizards too if we're hungry."

There is too much worry about our "not having our own country" or "our own place." God calls us to be pilgrims, wanderers. The security we need to be giving our children is not the security of place and country, but the security of being in God's family forever.

True, we the parents didn't have to give up our childhood security, our culture, our home base, our "sense of belonging." We can't quite understand what it's like—unless we were once MK's ourselves. But an MK does belong—to a worldwide culture of international Christians. MK's have deep wide-ranging friendships, with none of the superficiality so common in student friendships back home. MK's are going to be in the forefront of the worldwide church; they have the cross-cultural experience and the spiritual depth to play a major role in completing the task of world evangelization.

So, for the average MK, let us not be overly concerned with this question of "reentry." Reentry into what? I hope not back into secular, insular America! MK's are already in the worldwide Christian community. In a larger sense, they don't need to reenter anything.

MK's are multicultural. They bring to reality the truth of Galatians 3:28 and Colossians 3:11. These verses aren't just for heaven. Those in the worldwide community of believers can begin to live these verses here on earth. All the concerns we have about "preserving our culture," avoiding interracial marriages, "putting America first," are all—to put it bluntly—sub-Christian. Indeed, they dishonor Christ.

So, what does the final balance sheet show? Advantage, MK's. On all of these points they beat out their home-side counterparts: resourcefulness, creativity, self-reliance, cultural broadness, maturity, ability to cope with the unexpected, ability to build lasting relationships, scholastic achievement, accessibility to the job market, and fellowship in the international Christian community. And, if it's important to you, a much higher percentage of missionary children end up in *Who's Who* than any other professional category.

And you're thinking to deprive your child of all this?

20

Furlough

After living for five years in the foothills of Nepal fifteen miles from the nearest road, we went home to the USA for our first furlough. We got some special inexpensive deal for missionaries that routed us through Bangkok and Iceland.

Part of the deal was a two-night stay in Bangkok in a modern hotel with elevators, something our boys had never seen. They never seemed to tire of riding up and down the elevators, running along corridors, and exploring every floor. On the final day, an hour before we were to leave for the airport, we got an emergency call in our room from the hotel manager saying our younger son had just run through a glass door and had been rushed to a hospital—bleeding profusely, he added for emphasis.

Hurrying through the lobby to get a taxi, I noticed the shattered glass door. It would have been hard to pass a newborn baby through that jagged and irregular opening, let alone a six-year-old. My surgeon's mind calculated he must have lacerated half a dozen major nerves and arteries. Great way to begin one's first furlough!

When I got to the hospital, Chris was lying peacefully on a table and a little Thai nurse was sewing up his dozen superficial lacerations. She did as quick and slick a job as I have ever seen—a lot better than I'd have done it. Chris didn't make a peep. And we made our plane—though not without paying for the glass door.

I asked Chris why he had run through the door.

"I never saw it," he said.

Reasonable. He'd never seen a glass door before. We didn't have them at our mission station in Nepal.

Reverse culture shock—that's the first thing missionaries and their kids bump into when they go on furlough.

The second installment occurred two days later in Iceland, where we spent the night in a hotel that cost as much for one night as we paid our cook in a whole year.

And then home. Home to endless miles of concrete highways, walls, bridges, buildings. Home to supermarkets with endless shelves stacked with endless choices. Home to wall-to-wall carpeting, elegant tiled bathrooms, electronic kitchens. Home to dogs and cats eating pure meat products—enriched, no less, with vitamins and minerals. Home to the affluent West, whose affluence the missionary may have never really seen before. And you wonder why your missionary looks "out of it"?

We found the same mechanisms at work in reverse culture shock that were present when we first arrived on the field: we're leaving one world and entering a new one; things familiar are being replaced by things that have become almost unfamiliar since we've seen them last. A missionary can get quite badly "out of sync" with his own country in just a few years.

The Vietnam POW's were arriving home about that time. I remembered what I had read in *Time* magazine about the reverse culture shock they were experiencing, and now found it helpful in dealing with my own culture shock. That's one more advantage in reading a weekly newsmagazine or an equivalent: it keeps you in touch. You don't need to be backward in conversation. You don't need to ask: "Who is Madonna?" An out-of-touch missionary could give a very wrong answer to that question.

Time magazine doesn't orient you to everything that has happened at home. A couple of years ago I was on the highway and had to use a pay phone for a long-distance call. I had over three dollars in change, mostly dimes and nickels. I read the instructions on the phone and dialed my number. A sweet-sounding operator told me to deposit $2.85. I told her I'd be happy to do so, and began counting out my dimes and nickels.

"Please deposit $2.85," the operator said again.

"Yes, ma'am, I'm just counting out my money."

"Please deposit $2.85."

"Yes, I'm going to. I've got nothing but nickels and dimes here."

"Please deposit $2.85."

Was the woman deaf? By that time I'd lost count, and a third of my coins had slid off onto the floor.

"I told you, I was..."

"Please deposit $2.85."

Ah, so that was it. A recorded voice. Funny—I could have sworn she'd been getting more impatient!

Missionaries on furlough sometimes feel as if they had just awakened from a long sleep. At the beginning of our fourth furlough I went to our local library to take out a book. The young woman behind the desk told me I needed to become a library member, and to please show her my driver's license for identification. I pulled it out and gave it to her.

"What's this?" she said.

"My driver's license."

"I've never seen one like this." She took it over to the head librarian.

A few minutes later she returned and said, "This expired twelve years ago."

"Goodness, what have I been keeping that for?" I poked into my wallet again. "Ah, here it is."

"That looks more like it," she said. But she must have been on to me, because a moment later she said, "Wait a minute. This expired seven years ago."

The head librarian came over at this point eying me suspiciously. I pulled out all the dozens of papers that had accumulated in my wallet, and at last found my unexpired license. I explained that I was a missionary to Nepal, but that only seemed to increase their suspicions. I got my book in the end and walked out, thankful at least that I'd gotten myself sorted out with a librarian instead of a traffic cop.

Traffic—cars—you've got to learn to drive again. But before that, you have to learn how to get in and out of a car. Cynthia drove her mother's new car downtown on our last furlough, parked, and then couldn't get out of the car. The key wouldn't turn; the doors and windows wouldn't open. After five minutes she began to panic. No further details of this episode have been divulged to the writer, but I have a wonderful picture in my mind of this Phi Beta Kappa medical doctor waving frantically at passers-by, and finally some gruff old codger coming up and yelling through the window, "Try puttin' it in 'Park,' lady."

Missionaries on furlough find they've lost some of their shopping sense. I'm not sure I had much to begin with, but whatever I had I quickly lost once I got to Nepal. I was needing a toenail clipper—my old one had broken—and I had searched all over Kathmandu for a year with no luck. Then came a furlough.

On the way home we stopped in Seoul, Korea. We were taken by a friend to the observation floor on top of the tallest building in Asia. The place was packed, and the line to go down the single elevator was two or three hundred people long. The line extended—not by accident—along a row of shopping counters, and the sales clerks were doing a brisk business with their imprisoned patrons.

Half an hour later we had gotten in sight of the elevator when something on the counter caught my eye: a toenail clipper, just the kind I'd been looking for. It was silly to wait till I got to America to buy one; all such things were imported from Asia anyway. Why not get it right here, where it would be cheaper. Cynthia looked dubious. Then the line began to move. I hastily paid my three dollars and, quite pleased with myself, carried off my prize.

On the elevator I took another look at my purchase. It was encased in plastic with a cardboard back. I turned it over and read, "Made in Danbury, Connecticut."

Ten minutes later we walked past a little shop and what do you know, they were selling toenail clippers, $1.50, made in Taiwan. They had a curved cutting edge, which the Connecticut clippers didn't, so I bought one.

Twenty minutes later, we stopped for a coke at a little corner store. I stepped up to pay my money, and there next to the cash register was a box full of toenail clippers, fifty cents each, made in Korea. I bought two of them: I was going to get my money's worth somewhere. I would have bought more—"They'll make good house gifts," I said—but Cynthia restrained me.

I'm sure most missionaries on furlough manage better than I do, but some of us feel a little bit like returning Vietnam POW's—or Laotian refugees. Be patient, folks at home, and try not to raise your eyebrows too often.

Practical matters

Each mission has its own advice and procedures regarding the furlough time. Here we will merely look at some matters of more common interest.

Furloughs need to be well planned. The first one to four months—depending on the length of the furlough and the missionary's needs—should be set aside for real rest, reunion with family members, and reentry into the home church. During this period the missionary can also prepare various presentations he or she will be giving at other churches during the latter stages of the furlough. If further training is being taken, that obviously will have been planned well in advance.

The first issue to be faced is where to live. This will usually depend on where the missionary's family members live, where most of his or her supporting churches are located, and whether or not the missionary is going to do further study during furlough. Fortunate is the missionary who has five to fifteen supporting churches in relatively close proximity, and an apartment to live in. Some missions and home churches are able to provide such an apartment. Living with family members can work if enough space is available, but the potential for strain and stress is obviously greater than when the missionary lives independently.

Since furloughs involve so much disruption, dislocation, expense, and general inconvenience, not to mention the loss to the work on the field, why have them? Roman Catholic missionaries don't go on furlough; why should Protestants?

The overall benefit of furlough far outweighs the disadvantages. First, if living arrangements are suitable and the missionary doesn't have family and supporting churches scattered in every corner of the continent, furlough can be a time of physical, mental, and spiritual refreshment and renewal. This is needed for sound health reasons. Life on the mission field is definitely more stressful than at home, the spiritual warfare more intense, and the soldiers and supplies fewer. Sure, God is strengthening and supplying missionaries daily, but he has provided furloughs to give them a longer time of rest and restoration. Most missionaries need it.

The second benefit of furlough is that it allows the missionary to renew contact with family and church at home. Links are strengthened. Prayer and financial support is supplemented. Needs of the field are made known.

Third, the missionary is an extremely important resource in the recruitment of new workers. More missionary recruits are influenced by missionaries on furlough than by pastors, teachers, or anyone else.

Fourth, the necessary speaking on deputation is itself valuable in the missionary's life in terms of producing confidence in speaking and in leadership. It also produces new and lasting friendships wherever the missionary goes.

Fifth, the missionaries' children are reintroduced to their homeland—or in many cases introduced for the first time. This helps to minimize the feeling among some MK's that they are people "without a country."

Sixth, furlough gives the opportunity for further training, refresher courses, and advanced degrees. Especially it is a chance for the missionary wife to get further education. If the missionary is a professional person, the matter of "keeping up" is an important one, and many missionary candidates are rightly concerned about it. Yes, you should plan to keep up, so all that training doesn't become obsolete and go to waste. Another practical reason for keeping up is that you may have to leave the field sooner than you planned, and you will need to be able to step back into your profession in your home country.

So, by the end of the furlough the missionary is all rested up and ready to return. That's how it should be. But, as often as not, by the end of the furlough the missionary is so tired out that he or she can't wait to get back to the field to rest up! Don't call furlough a rest; call it a change. Don't even call it a "furlough," which implies lack of activity; let's instead call it "home assignment"—as many missions are now doing.

Asking for finances is a source of discomfort for most missionaries. Each mission has its own policy for raising support. Some do not make needs known; some make needs known but ask for no money; and some ask for money. These three broad approaches are all correct in appropriate circumstances; after all, it's the Holy Spirit who prompts the giver in any case.

Those who advocate not even making needs known feel it is a test of faith to tell God alone and then let him provide. Indeed, it is a great privilege to live by faith in this way, and if one is led of the Holy Spirit to do so, fine. But it is not the leading of most. It requires no less faith to raise support by stating needs and asking for money; God is the provider, and we are all equally dependent on him. God usually chooses ordinary means to provide for his workers; in Samaria, Jesus sent his disciples to town to buy some food. God resorts to extraordinary means for our provision only when ordinary means are not at hand.

Missionaries need to follow their own mission's policy on this matter. But I, for one, can't see anything wrong with being straightforward. If someone asks about your financial needs, the Spirit is prompting that person to ask. Not to answer is not only rude; it borders on tempting God.

Some missions and missionaries have qualms about accepting donations from non-Christians. "God's work is to be done by God's people," they say, and they refer to Ezra in the Old Testament who refused to accept non-Jewish gifts. But all gifts are from God; all the money and resources in the world are his. As General Booth of the Salvation Army once said, when asked whether he accepted "tainted" money: "I will accept any kind of money—even the devil's. I'll wash it in the blood of Christ and use it for the glory of God."

Raising finances need not be irksome. We're not asking for ourselves; we're asking on behalf of God and for his work. Our own personal worthiness has nothing to do with it. If we are doing God's will and doing his work, we can feel free to ask God's people to help. And the experience of having to depend on others is good for our pride. We are cast upon God and his people. To walk in such dependency is spiritually healthy.

Our independent, self-sufficient, Protestant work-ethic mentality rebels at this dependence. But the Bible clearly states that full-time workers should receive their living expenses. Accept support and gifts graciously and thankfully as from the Lord—and don't fail to thank the "instruments," the people he has used to provide the support, especially when they have given sacrificially.

Speaking to inspire

Furlough isn't all "getting"; that's the lesser part of the purpose. The greater part is giving, especially to churches at home. So, what do missionaries have to give? Plenty.

No one better than the missionary can bring the missionary vision to the home church. No one better than the missionary can inspire young people to a life of sacrifice and dedication to Jesus. No one better than the missionary can expand the people's outlook, broaden their thinking, and stimulate them to become part of the world church. The missionary represents in person that wider world, the field ready for harvest; he or she is the contact point. The missionary is uniquely able to bless, to edify, to inspire the home church. If you come across a church that has grown cold to missions, it may well be they haven't had a "live missionary" by in a long time. And remember, most people considering mission work finally offer for service as the result of a face-to-face appeal from a missionary. Don't let such an opportunity go to waste; don't let such an obligation go unmet.

Obligation, yes. The home church has sent you out. Now you're back, just as Paul and Barnabas came back from their first missionary journey. And just as they "reported" to the Antioch church, so you need to report to your home church; you are accountable to them. But don't give them just a dry, factual report; make it speak to the hearts of the listeners. It's God's work you are reporting, and that is never dry.

Some missionaries dread deputation and especially the public speaking associated with it. They feel self-conscious. But self-consciousness is just another form of self-centeredness; let the missionary pray to be delivered from it.

Some missionaries lack confidence in speaking and in presenting missions. If they could but see the potential for effective ministry in even the most ordinary missionary, their lack of confidence could be replaced by the godly confidence that God can use them at home as much as he has used them on the field.

Maybe you are a missionary mechanic, a secretary, a printer. "I have no dramatic stories to tell," you say. Well, you may have no dramatic stories to tell of your own particular work, but you are part of a team that is doing dramatic work; tell about that.

You say, "I'm just an ordinary person." But all those ordinary people in the home churches will more easily relate to you than to the big-name guy with the flashy presentation. You can give as much information as he can; you can challenge and inspire as well as he can; your personal testimony is as powerful as his. Don't be intimidated because you're "ordinary"; in the end, you may get a greater response from your audience than the big name. It's not the performance that counts; it is the response. And the response depends on the Holy Spirit. The Spirit's persuasion, not human persuasion, is the key. Remember Paul at Corinth (1 Co 2:1-5).

Some missionaries are naturally more gifted in deputation than others; they may enjoy it, and be challenged and stimulated by it. Well, let those missionaries do as much deputation as they have opportunity for. But other missionaries who find it difficult should not be forced to do more than absolutely necessary.

For those who do find it difficult, let them remember that none of us found it "easy" at first. But one gets better at it with experience. A few practical tips can turn anyone into a passable speaker—we're not looking for orators. So let us do everything we can in the beginning to encourage the timid and diffident person to set out, to give it a try. Only if it continues to be too much of an ordeal is the person then justified in backing off and finding a non-public-speaking role for the furlough time.

Another major rule for missionaries on deputation: Be honest. Tell it as it is, good and bad. But try not to leave your listeners with a negative impression; emphasize the positive—at least at the end. If you have nothing at all positive to say, don't go on deputation.

But deputation isn't a confessional either. You don't have to spill the beans about everything. Withholding items that are unedifying or critical of others is not being dishonest; you'll have enough negative to say without saying it all.

Remember, too, as you are delivering that honest, "things-as-they-are" presentation, some national from your country may be in the audience. Won't you be red-faced when he comes up to you afterward and says, "You were a little hard on my country, don't you think." That's if he comes up to you at all. Having been stung several times myself, I now assume that anywhere I speak there'll be a Nepali in the audience.

Two things missionary speakers should avoid: sermonizing, and sending people on guilt trips. Generally, church people prefer their own pastors to give the sermons, and the missionaries to talk about missions. The two categories overlap slightly, but don't wander too far into the sermon-giving side. And don't hound people. Just present Jesus, and what he has been doing through you. If they will respond to him, then he will kindle the missions flame within them without your having to poke the embers.

Sometimes, though, someone asks you to "poke the embers." Resist. I remember speaking to a group of doctors in a well-appointed hotel in a U.S. city. U.S. doctors aren't exactly middle-class, and the banquet they had put on for the occasion was quite elegant by Nepali standards. After Cynthia and I had finished our presentation and were answering questions, a man stood up and asked, "What special word do you have for American Christians?"

I suspected by the intensity of his tone that he wanted us to lambast the lifestyle of these comfortable physicians and call down prophetic denunciations upon their heads. (It turned out he wasn't a doctor; I can't recall how he got there.)

Well, if that was his desire, we disappointed him. Were we now to denounce the very people who had just fed us a delicious dinner? That would be graceless, to say the least. But we did have a word to say—the same word we'd say to any group of Christians, Americans or Nepalis. We reminded them of Jesus' words: "If anyone would come after me, he must deny himself and take up his cross and follow me" (Mk 8:34). That's a "special word" for Christians of any country.

Don't get caught criticizing your own country. All societies are equally materialistic and equally under God's judgment. Jesus' word is the same to all men, and that word we must always be ready to share.

Deputation talks are like letters: think them through, prepare them carefully, practice their delivery. Be vivid and dramatic as you describe your country and what God is doing there. Your listeners will want to know what your own role is in that work. Don't hesitate to tell people what you have been learning and how God has been working in your life. Just avoid cliches. And in your prayer, pray not only for the people of the country where you work, but also for the members of the congregation you are talking to, that their missionary vision might be sharpened and

that young people in particular might hear God's call to mission and respond.

Here are a few simple tips that I've picked up from various places and
found useful.

Make eye contact with anyone whose eyes are open. But not for more
than a few seconds; you need to move around from person to person.

Speak to that one person you're looking at. Remember that the audience is made up of single individuals; it's one to one. You're not out-
numbered. No need to feel intimidated.

Avoid repetition. You're allowed to repeat your main point once.
Avoid repetition.

Don't tell people what you're going to tell them, and don't tell them
what you've told them. Let them figure it out for themselves. Your job is
to tell them, period.

Don't jingle coins in your pocket while you speak; you're a missionary, not a banker.

Don't go over your time limit; that's an absolute rule. But expect your
time allotment to be reduced without warning. Know in advance how to
turn your thirty-minute talk into a ten-minute one. I was invited to speak
once at a college assembly, and was told I had the last twenty-five minutes of the period, which ended promptly at noon. The proceedings went
on and on. 11:35 came and went. 11:40...11:45...11:50. I could keep
track: a huge clock faced the podium from the balcony. All that time I
was busy throwing out one paragraph after another. If I had known in advance, I'd have just given my eight-minute speech. But don't ever complain; you're the guest.

Incidentally, be sure you know what they want you to speak about, no
matter how many minutes you have!

Be focused. Decide what you want to cover. Develop two or three
main points and make them memorable. Don't ramble. And those "Minute for Missions" time slots they give you in the church service are the
worst of all. You don't need focus for those; you need a reverse tele-
scope.

Remember that people are interested in you. Don't be afraid to use the
word "I," unless you're married.

You will create interest more by your enthusiasm than by your content. It's nice to have both, though.

Finally, don't comment about something not being right, such as the
microphone, the lights, or whatever. Carry on as if you weren't fazed in
the least—unless the building is on fire.

Slides: every slide must be good in its own right. Never apologize for bad slides; just don't show them. And try your very best not to show group pictures. If you absolutely must show a group picture, at least spare the audience the biographies. Take no more than a minute a slide, and usually less. Some people show a rapid succession of slides to give a kaleidoscopic image, which is a useful style of presentation when the slides themselves aren't very interesting.

I've shown my Nepal slides over four hundred times—sometimes forty slides, sometimes eighty, depending on how much time I have. Now I know what Broadway actors have to go through to keep every performance fresh and alive as if it was the first time you did it. And, of course, that's precisely the point: It's always the first time for that particular audience. And if you think of your audience and not your presentation, you will respond to them, warm to them, and they to you, and it will be like new.

I personally advise against using a taped commentary for your slides. You might as well pass out sleeping pills—unless, of course, your slides happen to be shockingly lewd or gory. Or unless they're of the Himalayas. I've always been thankful to God that he sent us to a photogenic country like Nepal, and not to some place where if you've seen one scene you've seen them all.

One of the most important parts of a missionary's presentation is the time at the end for questions and answers. Announce it beforehand, so people will be thinking of questions. Don't give ten-minute answers, even to complicated questions. No one else will get a turn. Break up complex questions; answer one part at a time. Keep your answers simple. If you don't know the answer, say so. You're not a politician who has to know everything. Don't let one person hog the questioning. Towards the end, when you see two hands still up, say that there's time for just two more questions; that way you don't end with a long silence, which tends to be anticlimactic.

It's marvelous all the things that can go wrong during deputation. I won't even mention car trouble, getting lost, driving fifty miles in the wrong direction on Interstates. That happens to everyone. The most fun is the slide show. There you can experience exploding bulbs, shattering lenses, sticking slides, collapsing screens, and projectors being tipped over by racing children. You may be delayed by blizzards and hurricanes. You may fall asleep at the wheel and collide with a truck—and still make your meeting. You may set out on a twelve-day, twenty-city speaking tour with laryngitis, and end the tour with the same laryngitis. You may even go somewhere and there's no audience. Sounds like a list of Paul's woes from 2 Corinthians.

The main thing to remember about things going wrong is not to be dismayed. When things go wrong, look for God's special blessing. Expect him to work in unusual ways. He may use your weakness, your mistake, even that blankety-blank projector bulb to do his work in that particular meeting. God does not rely on our smooth presentation, our projectors, our gadgets and gimmicks. All he needs is our presence and our obedience, and he could get along without those if he had to. I've reached the point where I can actually be grateful when something goes wrong, because over and over I've seen God especially bless those meetings.

A few more practical thoughts. Setting up a display table is a good idea. You'll need a few curios, but don't overdo it. You can show your butterfly collection, but leave the spiders, scorpions, and medical specimens back on the field.

Have gifts handy to give to your hosts as you travel. The best we've found are batiks, made by Christian leprosy patients in Nepal. They are light, unbreakable, and their origin tells a story of hardship and suffering overcome by faith.

If you're into national costumes, that's okay. But go easy on dressing your kids up in the national outfit. They'll get the idea they are part of a sideshow.

However, if your children want to participate in deputation in various ways, encourage them. One MK, when asked what he wanted to be when he grew up, answered, "A missionary on furlough." For him, it seemed like a perpetual feast. Generally conferences can be fun for the children, and there's time to be together as a family. But dragging them around to churches is not desirable.

During our second furlough, our family took a driving trip around the USA, combining deputation with showing our boys their country. We visited museums, factories, parks, friends, and churches. Most weeks we spoke in a church somewhere. Toward the end of the trip we were in a church where I had just given The Talk for the umpteenth time. The boys had found an empty Sunday-school classroom in the basement, and had gone there to look at books while Cynthia and I visited with the people above. When it was time to leave, I went to find the boys. As I was passing a room I heard the older boy's voice, accompanied by some raucous laughter. Tommy was standing at a little podium giving my Talk word for word—"Behind the magnificent facade of Nepal's towering mountains, cascading waterfalls, seventy-foot-tall rhododendron trees and picturesque villages lies..."—while Christopher, pretending to be the audience, was almost rolling off his seat howling with laughter. I changed my talk the next week, and after that trip we stopped taking the boys along to churches.

MK's occasionally have a rough time during furlough, especially during the adolescent years. They are socially out of it. They may feel second-class; they don't have all the things other kids do. And they may blame you, the parents, for their distress. "Why did we have to be missionaries?"

Missionary parents should not feel guilty about this. Don't lament, "Our kids weren't called to be missionaries; why should they have to go through this?" Of course they were called. If you were called, they were called. And if you can refrain from perpetually beating your breast, you can help your kids deal with these reentry stresses, and grow and mature through them. And don't be upset if your children blame you; children need someone to blame, and parents are ready at hand. Then as children grow, they learn to identify the real causes of their problems and begin to deal with them appropriately. It's the kids that haven't learned to do this that end up out on the mission field years later blaming their field director for everything that goes wrong.

Goals and evaluation

Furlough is a time for assessment, for sitting back and taking stock of what has passed and what lies ahead. For example, a missionary should never make a decision to resign from the mission just before furlough. First let him come home and evaluate his situation, talk it over with the home council, family and friends. We gain perspective after a few months at home, and things begin to look different.

Before furlough, the missionary and the field leadership should have had clear communication about any problem that might have arisen during that term of service. Most missions conduct a pre-furlough interview for that purpose. Then when the missionary arrives home, the same clear communication is needed with the home staff.

If problems have developed, these need to be worked through. If the problems are physical, a medical evaluation is needed. A medical check-up on furlough is routine for missionaries over fifty.

If emotional or psychological problems have surfaced, these too need to be worked out. In such cases, counseling can be extremely helpful, at times crucial, in getting someone through a difficult period. It should be made available. Naturally, the missionary should desire counseling, not just agree to it under pressure; otherwise it will be of little benefit. If a person is reluctant to see a counselor for whatever reason, that reluctance should be respected. Never should counseling be forced on a person with the implicit judgment, "If you refuse, that proves there is something wrong with you." Acceptance of counseling should never be made a condition for return to the field. Just as there should be no stigma attached to accepting counseling, neither should there be any stigma attached to refusing it. The mission, of course, has the right not to send people back to the field, but not on the grounds that they declined counseling. There will usually be other grounds.

When all that is said, we must again affirm that counseling can be of great value if carried out under the proper circumstances. It would ordinarily be unwise for a missionary to refuse to avail himself of this professional help. But if he does, let him search his motive and make sure that the reason is not pride.

In an effort to stay ahead of possible problems and keep in close touch with their missionaries, most missions have resorted to the annual self-evaluation form. These forms seek to ascertain to what extent the missionary has achieved his goals of the previous year, what his goals are for the coming year, and any problems, failures, or successes that have occurred along the way. Generally such forms are helpful both to the missionary and the mission; but their limitations should be recognized.

First of all, filling the forms out should be voluntary, not compulsory. Some people don't like forms, can't express themselves easily on forms. Some would prefer to write an essay rather than answer prefabricated questions. One missionary I know disliked forms so much that he filled in every blank space with "N/A" (not applicable), and dutifully returned the form to headquarters.

Second, serious problems will rarely be picked up on these routine forms. People usually prefer to talk these matters over personally and privately.

Third, forms asking one to set out goals and objectives and expecting an evaluation of how far such objectives have been met are not equally applicable to everyone, and must be constructed in very general terms. For example, a doctor in a hospital can state his goals and objectives in two sentences, while someone spearheading a community health program might need two pages. Some fields are cut and dry; others are open-ended. New projects need more planning; projects about to conclude need less. Things that haven't begun can't be evaluated. Let the missionary not hesitate to write "N/A," instead of concocting a bunch of stuff just to fill up the blank spaces.

The home churches have begun to get in the act also. They are paying out good money to support these characters on the field, and they want to make sure they're getting a return on their investment.

Just recently we received a several-page evaluation form from one of our supporting churches. Cynthia spent six hours filling it out—she's conscientious about such things. Then we got a similar form from another church. What are missionaries to do when they have ten or fifteen supporting churches, or more? If a form can be filled out in fifteen minutes, fine; if not, it is too long.

Of much greater concern is the whole concept of the home church evaluating the performance of their missionaries. The home constituency has a right to know what is going on, and it is the missionary's duty to keep his supporters informed; but evaluation is another matter. And at the risk of raising hackles, I'll state here clearly that people without field experience are not qualified to evaluate the performance of missionaries. Furthermore, that field experience should have been in the general area where the missionary under evaluation is working. Neither can a one-month jaunt out to the field on a work project count as "field experience"; such folks can get a very mistaken notion of the real conditions on the field. As a practical matter, then, the only people really competent to evaluate a missionary are the missionary's own field leaders.

It is a mistake to think that by getting a form filled out by a missionary the home church is going to understand the difficulty of the field, the spiritual resistance of the people, the appropriateness of the missionary's approach, the amount of spiritual fruit borne. These things can't be measured in numbers. Maybe a missionary's main job is to remove stones from the soil; then later one will come to reap the harvest. Who's to evaluate the "success" of each one. "Success" for a missionary, or any Christian, is measured by obedience to God's leading day by day—and that is something the home church simply can't evaluate.

The home church may ask: Is our missionary really needed on that field? It might be that according to standards of the business world the missionary isn't cost-effective or isn't "producing enough"; but supposing he was called of God to be there? Supposing the fruit he's producing isn't yet visible? It is hard enough for field leaders to evaluate these questions without the home church thinking it can do so too.

If a church is looking for a "return on investment" from its missionary giving, I think it would be better for that church to go into business and leave missions to others. Who is the investor here? It is God. And he gives the increase, not the missionaries. Much more is involved in producing spiritual fruit than only the missionary's performance.

There is a danger in missionaries becoming too "result oriented." Missions is not a joyless burden, with a taskmaster, God, keeping a score card of "our results." Rather, missionaries and their supporting churches need to feel the joy of missions, and sense the tremendous privilege of being partners together with God as he brings the increase.

The home churches are the stewards of God's resources; they send out the workers. They need to be assured that their workers are working, that their objectives are being pursued. They need to have an idea whether they should continue to support a particular work, a particular missionary. So let them ask the missionary and the mission agency hard questions. But let them not expect the answers to come in business-world terms. The mission field does not lend itself to that kind of analysis.

Furthermore, let the home churches not worry that there are a whole lot of lazy, inefficient missionaries out there eating up their scarce funds. That is not the case. "Bad" missionaries don't stay on the field long; they leave within a couple of years. The demands of the field are very high. We missionaries are much tougher on ourselves than the home churches could ever be. If our observation of mission work in Nepal counts for anything, I'd say that the home churches have been getting their money's worth from their investment!

If a home church has undertaken to send out and support a missionary, it has undertaken a responsibility which it should not relinquish lightly. One of the hardest things any missionary can experience is to come home on furlough and find that his or her home church has lost interest, has not been praying, has no time to give.

Missionary and home church share a mutual responsibility to one another. Let the furloughing missionaries give of themselves to the home church as time and energy permits. Attend the services and prayer meetings. Motivate the youth. Teach Sunday school. And be available to visit members in their homes to share yourself and your work.

Let the home church members, on their part, befriend the missionary, welcome him back. Invite him over to watch the ball game. Let him put his feet up. We've had home church friends do all sorts of wonderful things for us, and we are deeply grateful. I remember one elderly couple who spent eight hours with us in the Chicago Museum of Science and Industry, showing our kids the wonders of submarines, coal mines, and accelerators. And it's possible the one who enjoyed it most was myself.

A final caution for missionaries: Don't be critical of the home church. It is not your place to be critical under any circumstances. The home church people may have a whole pile of concerns they care about deeply and that are important in God's sight. Just because they don't fit in with your own concerns is not reason for you to judge or criticize them.

Likewise, do not criticize your field leadership while you are home on furlough—or any time else, for that matter. God is listening.

You will have undergone many changes during your term on the field. You will see your home church, your home country with new eyes, with a new perspective. You may feel out of touch, unable to fit back in easily; you may have other uncomfortable feelings. But you have something new to offer your church, your community. You have the chance to enrich and challenge them, just as you have been enriched and challenged by your experience on the field. Don't lose that chance.

Finally, people ask about missionaries in retirement. Do they have a place to live, or do they have to stay in Old Folks' Homes? Do they have to live on cabbage and leeks, or can they get three decent meals a day? I am amazed at how often people ask us what kind of pension we get, and will we be able to survive or not.

I'm sometimes tempted to tell them that I fully anticipate a slow death by starvation and loneliness but I'm so dedicated to the Lord I'm ready to face it; it's just another cost of being a missionary. So far I've resisted the temptation. I tell them the straight truth: I've never heard of a retired missionary whose basic needs were unmet, and who in time of sickness or other difficulty was not fully surrounded by the love and support of family, mission, and church.

But even if it weren't so, I'd still be a missionary.

Afterword

What, finally, can we say of the missionary life? How can we sum it up?

First, missionary life draws us into the multicultural richness of the human race. It is a foretaste of heaven, a foretaste of John's vision when he saw "a great multitude that no one could count, from every nation, tribe, people and language" (Rev 7:9).

Second, missionary life is army life. But it's not just any old army; it's the Lord's army. And it's not just any old job; it's a front-line job. This is the army foretold by Ezekiel in the valley of the dry bones. "Then he said to me, 'Prophesy to the breath...and say to it, "...Come from the four winds, O breath, and breathe into these slain, that they might live"'" So I prophesied as he commanded me, and breath entered them; they came to life and stood up on their feet—a vast army" (Eze 37:9-10). Not a club, not a society, but an army!

Third, missionary life is a life that makes a difference, a life that counts, a life that leaves a legacy. The missionary has gone where he or she was needed most, where the workers are few, where part of the harvest would have been lost if the missionary had not gone. Because the missionary went, one more "people," one more "tribe" will stand before the throne of God. And God will say, "Well done, good and faithful servant!" (Mt 25:21).

Fourth, missionary life is a life of adventure and challenge. It is never

405

boring. It is living the book of Acts all over again. It is extraordinary how vivid and real the book of Acts becomes when you're on the mission field. What a privilege it is to be able to relive those first-century days now in the twentieth century.

Fifth, missionary life is a life of abundance of riches. Missionaries have friends all over the world, a huge family of national believers and fellow missionaries. We have homes open to us everywhere, brothers, sisters, children in profusion. It's just as Jesus said: "...no one who has left home or brothers or sisters or mother or father or children or fields for me and the gospel will fail to receive a hundred times as much in the present age" (Mk 10:29-30). God has spread a feast before Christians; why should we go away hungry?

But Jesus adds a couple of other words to that saying. He says we shall receive "homes, brothers, sisters, mothers, children and fields—and with them, persecutions" (Mk 10:30).

Persecutions, another side of missionary life. Jesus never said it would be easy. He didn't say, "Receive me." He said, "Follow me." Follow him where? To the cross. To the "fellowship of sharing in his sufferings" (Php 3:10), which Paul counted such a privilege. Christ's sufferings? Not just his pain, but his suffering for the sin of the world, his suffering because of the lukewarmness of believers, the suffering that is involved in dying to self. Can we thank God for the privilege of suffering in this way? It is part of the missionary life.

Part of our suffering as missionaries comes from the failures, the defeats, the discouragement. Your friends back home think you're a bit "off." The nationals may not appreciate you. Colleagues may speak against you. You are misunderstood. And then you wonder why you became a missionary. That's when you are ready to learn humility.

Paul wrote to the Corinthians: "For it seems to me that God has put us apostles on display at the end of the procession, like men condemned to die in the arena. We have been made a spectacle to the whole universe.... We are fools for Christ.... Up to this moment we have become the scum of the earth, the refuse of the world" (1 Co 4:9-10,13).

Missionaries stand in the tradition of the apostle Paul. He was a nobody, buffeted by Satan, deserted by all his friends; even his stumbling new churches were constantly going astray. A sad spectacle.

But it proved a deep truth of God: God has chosen the humble, the nobodies, to do his work. "God chose the foolish things of the world...the weak things...the lowly things...the despised things...so that no one may boast before him" (1 Co 1:27-29).

The weak, the lowly, the foolish—that's us. That's a description of missionaries. Today the church of Christ is growing in almost every country of the world, and God has used such missionaries to bring it about.

Some thoughts for churches at home

The church is for the lost, not for the saved. Andrew Murray says, "The church exists only for extending the kingdom of God...every member must be trained to take part in it."

A church has many ministries but only one mission, the mission of witness, of evangelism, of disciple-making, both at home and abroad—"in Jerusalem...and to the ends of the earth" (Ac 1:8). Many churches have a separate department for missions and evangelism. There are good reasons for this, but it can lead to a wrong conception of the church. "Missions and evangelism" is not one department among equals. Every other department of the church exists to further the church's missions-and-evangelism outreach. Even the disciple-making function of the church serves the purpose of making new disciples, who will in turn make other new disciples. The church is always to be reaching out, reaching out—like a light into the darkness. The church which has ceased reaching out and has lost its missionary vision is a dying church.

Likewise, the worship of the church must be in the context of the church's mission. Worship without a commitment to mission turns inward and ceases to please God. The church's mission is central to all of its activities, including worship. All the functions of the church—worship, education, nurture, fellowship—subserve its primary purpose, which is to be a light. It is this which glorifies God.

Missions, then, is not the responsibility of mission societies and missionaries; it is the responsibility of the church, every church. A spiritually healthy church is going to be a missionary-sending church. Indeed, the spiritual health of any church is not measured by the number of people it attracts, but rather by the number of people it sends out. And let the churches send their best people. No church ever suffered because it sent out its best and most qualified people to work in a more needy area; indeed, such churches will be blessed. We gain by giving; it's true of churches too.

Some thoughts for Christians at home

C. Peter Wagner said, "Once you ask Jesus Christ to take control of your life, involvement in world mission is no longer optional."

The average evangelical Christian is not personally concerned that two billion people are out there who have not heard the gospel and that there are too few workers to reach them. Yes, he may be aware of the problem, but he's not aware that he is part of the problem. The problem of reaching the unreached is every Christian's concern. Every Christian is called to be involved.

To reach the unreached, the whole church must be mobilized; the laity is the key. It's been the key since the first missionary outreach of the church in Acts 8. "On that day a great persecution broke out against the church at Jerusalem, and all except the apostles were scattered throughout Judea and Samaria.... Those who had been scattered preached the word wherever they went" (Ac 8:1,4). Those who were scattered were the laity.

As we said earlier in this book, the Great Commission has been explicitly given to every believer. Jesus told the disciples to "go and make disciples of all nations...teaching them to obey everything I have commanded you" (Mt 28:19-20). That "everything" includes the Great Commission itself! No believer can escape it.

Every believer has a role. He may be a hand or a foot, a sender or a goer; but his role is crucial. Our reward will depend not on our role but on our obedience, on how much we emptied ourselves and allowed the Holy Spirit to fill us and use us.

How do you determine your role? God doesn't write it in the sky. He has given you gifts—that's one way. Then he's given you leadings; you've heard a speaker, or read a book. And third, he has shown you the need. Ask yourself: Where is the greatest need? There are relative needs everywhere; I'm talking about the greatest needs. If you are a preacher, where is the greatest need? If you are an engineer or agriculturalist, where is the greatest need? If you are a doctor, where is the greatest need—not America surely! If you are a young Christian seeking God's direction for your life, where is the greatest need?

The greatest need today is establishing churches and discipling believers among the two billion unreached people of the world. Christians need to heed the admonition: "If you're not clearly called to stay within your own culture, you should assume God wants you to move into a culture that is as yet unreached, or which does not have its own self-multiplying church." I can't believe it's God's will that most young Christians should spend all of their lives in the conventional pursuit of their professions. God wants to send people where they're needed most. It's only common sense, and God has common sense too.

"But what difference am I going to make?" you ask. "The need is so great. How are you going to reach two billion people?"

"One at a time," as the World Vision ad says.

The story is told of an old man who was throwing into the ocean tiny sea creatures that had been washed up on the beach overnight. Someone asked him, "Old man, why are you doing that? This beach stretches for a hundred miles. There are thousands of these creatures all along this shore. What difference are you making to the rest of them by throwing these few back into the ocean?"

The old man said, "I can't say about the rest of them. But for these few I throw back, it is the difference between life and death."

It may be that you've not been called specifically to the mission field. But you have been "called" in the most basic sense, called to offer your body as a living sacrifice to God. Have you done that? Do not rest until you do. And when you do, the Spirit will begin to lead you into new ministries of prayer, of service, of giving, of going. There are not two kinds of Christians—disciples and non-disciples. We are all called to be lifetime disciples, whether we stay at home or go abroad, whether we are missionaries, pastors, bankers, or businessmen.

This call to be a disciple of Jesus is our chief calling, whatever our specific employment might be. And as disciples, what are we called to do? To go and bear fruit. Jesus said to his disciples, "I chose you and appointed you to go and bear fruit—fruit that would last" (Jn 15:16). Jesus is not referring to the "fruit" of the Holy Spirit here; one doesn't have to "go" in order to bear the fruit of the Spirit. By fruit here, Jesus is referring to new believers. "This is to my Father's glory, that you bear much fruit, showing yourselves to be my disciples" (Jn 15:8).

Why is it that out of all the millions of Christians in the world such a small percentage are actually sharing God's word with their non-Christian neighbors? The answer is simply: disobedience. We are unwilling to do what Jesus told us to do. Our love for Jesus is lukewarm.

"If you love me, you will obey what I command" (Jn 14:15).

We have been redeemed by Christ in order that we might follow him, witness to him, and obey him. He has empowered us through the Holy Spirit; he has filled us with his love. All that remains is for us to obey. "If you love me, you will obey what I command." The key to the evangelization of the world lies in that one verse.

The only way to increase missionary zeal in the church is to increase each individual Christian's love for Christ—to deepen, to revive each one's spiritual life. Correct doctrine won't do it; there's many a doctrinally correct church that has no missionary zeal. No, it's a matter of personal revival. With revival, missionary zeal will come of itself. As Christians more and more passionately desire the presence and power of Christ in their lives, they shall more and more want to pass those blessings on to others.

Why has our love for Jesus grown lukewarm? The answer is the same as always: sin. The sins of lack of faith, of not being filled with the Spirit, of attachment to the world, of absorption with self, of narrow interests and wrong attitudes. These and all the other ordinary sins of omission and commission are the reason why our love has grown lukewarm.

Jesus has the final word for us. "I know your deeds, your hard work and your perseverance. I know that you cannot tolerate wicked men, that you have tested those who claim to be apostles but are not, and have found them false. You have persevered and have endured hardships for my name, and have not grown weary.

"Yet I hold this against you: You have forsaken your first love. Remember the height from which you have fallen! Repent and do the things you did at first. If you do not repent, I will come to you and remove your lampstand from its place" (Rev 2:2-5).

Oh friends, may we let this word sink deeply into our hearts. "Repent." This is where it begins—and always has. Without our repentance and a returning to our first love, there will be no revival, and the unreached people of the world will not be reached.

As we look at the accomplishments and advances of the missionary movement, we have much to thank and praise God for. And we must not neglect to do so. But the other side is this: how much more could have been done, should have been done? When we think of this our sense of satisfaction fades. Instead, contrition and repentance fill our hearts. How greatly we have held back the work of Christ by our lack of prayer, lack of faith, lack of obedience, lack of love. Oh Lord, forgive us, revive us, and set us aflame once more.

Bibliography

Adams, Jay. *Competent to Counsel*. Grand Rapids: Zondervan, 1970.

Allen, Roland. *Missionary Methods: St. Paul's or Ours?* Grand Rapids: Eerdmans, 1962.

Almquist, Arden. *Missionary, Come Back*. New York: World, 1970.

Augsberger, David. *Caring Enough to Hear*. Ventura, CA: Regal, 1982.

Beals, Paul. *A People for His Name*. Pasadena: William Carey Library, 1985.

Borthwick, Paul. *How To Be a World-Class Christian*. Wheaton, IL: Victor Books, 1991.

Cable, Mildred and French, Francesca. *Ambassadors for Christ*. Chicago: Moody, 1935.

Carlson, Dwight. *Run and Not Be Weary*. Old Tappan, NJ: Revell, 1974.

—— . *Overcoming Hurts and Anger*. Irvine, CA: Harvest House, 1981.

Clark, Dennis E. *The Third World and Mission*. Waco: Word, 1971.

Coggins, Wade. *So That's What Missions Is All About*. Chicago: Moody, 1975.

Collins, Marjorie A. *Manual for Today's Missionary*. Pasadena: William Carey Library, 1986.

—— . *Who Cares About the Missionary?* Chicago: Moody, 1974.

Conn, Harvey. *Reaching the Unreached*. Phillipsburg, NJ: Presbyterian and Reformed, 1984.

Cook, Harold R. *Missionary Life and Work*. Chicago: Moody, 1959.

Danielson, Edward. *Missionary Kid—MK*. Pasadena: William Carey Library, 1984.

Douglas, J. D., ed. *Let the Earth Hear His Voice*. Minneapolis: World Wide Publications, 1975.

Drewery, Mary. *William Carey: A Biography*. Grand Rapids:Zondervan, 1979.

Duewel, Wesley L. *Ablaze for God*. Grand Rapids: Zondervan, 1989.

—— . *Touch the World Through Prayer*. Grand Rapids: Zondervan, 1986.

Echerd, P. and Arathoon, A., eds. *Planning for MK Nurture*. Pasadena: William Carey Library, 1989.

—— . *Understanding and Nurturing the Missionary Family*. Pasadena: William Carey Library, 1989.

Fenton, Horace L. *Myths About Missions*. Downers Grove, IL: Inter-Varsity Press, 1973.

Fernando, Ajith. *The Christian's Attitude Toward World Religions.* Wheaton, IL: Tyndale House, 1987.

Fouke, Ruth. *Coping with Crises.* London: Hodder and Stoughton, 1968.

Foyle, Marjory. *Overcoming Missionary Stress.* Wheaton, IL: Evangelical Mission Information Service, 1987.

Gallagher, Neil. *Don't Go Overseas Until You've Read This Book.* Minneapolis: Bethany Fellowship, 1977.

Garrison, V. David. *The Nonresidential Missionary.* Monrovia, CA: MARC, 1990.

Griffiths, Michael M. *Give Up Your Small Ambitions.* Chicago: Moody, 1970.

Hale, Thomas. *Don't Let the Goats Eat the Loquat Trees.* Grand Rapids: Zondervan, 1986.

——— . *Living Stones of the Himalayas.* Grand Rapids: Zondervan, 1993.

——— . *On the Far Side of Liglig Mountain.* Grand Rapids: Zondervan, 1989.

Hesselgrave, David J. *Communicating Christ Cross-Culturally,* 2nd ed. Grand Rapids: Zondervan, 1991.

——— . *Today's Choices for Tomorrow's Mission.* Grand Rapids: Zondervan, 1988.

Hiebert, P. and Hiebert, F. *Case Studies in Missions.* Grand Rapids: Baker, 1987.

Houghton, A. T. *Preparing to Be a Missionary.* London: InterVarsity Christian Fellowship, 1956.

Houghton, Frank. *Amy Carmichael of Dohnavur.* London: SPCK, 1953.

Howard, David. *Student Power in World Mission.* Downers Grove, IL: InterVarsity Press, 1979.

Jones, E. Stanley. *The Christ of the Indian Road*. New York: Abingdon, 1925.

Kane, J. Herbert. *Life and Work on the Mission Field*. Grand Rapids: Baker, 1980.

———. *The Making of a Missionary*. Grand Rapids: Baker, 1975.

———. *Understanding Christian Missions*. Grand Rapids: Baker, 1974.

———. *Wanted: World Christians*. Grand Rapids: Baker, 1986.

Kenney, Betty Jo. *The Missionary Family*. Pasadena: William Carey Library, 1984.

Kyle, John E., ed. *The Unfinished Task*. Ventura, CA: Regal, 1984.

Leas, Speed. *Leadership and Conflict*. New York: Abingdon, 1982.

Lindell, Jonathan. *Nepal and the Gospel of God*. Kathmandu: United Mission to Nepal, 1979.

Lingenfelter, S. and Mayers, M. *Ministering Cross-Culturally*. Grand Rapids: Baker, 1986.

Lockerbie, Jeannie. *By Ones and By Twos*. Pasadena: William Carey Library, 1985.

Mathews, Arthur. *Born for Battle*. Singapore: OMF Books, 1978.

McGavran, Donald. *Momentous Decisions in Missions Today*. Grand Rapids: Baker, 1984.

Mickelson, Alvera. *How to Write Missionary Letters*. Wheaton, IL: Evangelical Literature Overseas, n.d.

Miller, Basil. *Praying Hyde*. Grand Rapids: Zondervan, 1943.

Miller, Edgar. *Nine Years in Nepal*. (Privately published).

Murray, Andrew. *Key to the Missionary Problem*. Fort Washington, PA: Christian Literature Crusade, 1979.

Narramore, Clyde. *The Psychology of Counseling*. Grand Rapids: Zondervan, 1960.

Neill, Stephen. *A History of Christian Missions*. New York: Penguin, 1964.

——. *Christian Faith and Other Faiths*. Downers Grove, IL: InterVarsity Press, 1984.

Nelson, Martin, ed. *Readings in Third World Missions*. Pasadena: William Carey Library, 1976.

Nida, Eugene A. *Customs and Cultures*. Pasadena: William Carey Library, 1975.

——. *Message and Mission*. New York: Harper and Row, 1960.

O'Donnell, K. and O'Donnell, M. L., eds. *Helping Missionaries Grow*. Pasadena: William Carey Library, 1988.

Palmer, Donald. *Managing Conflict Creatively*. Pasadena: William Carey Library, 1991.

Reed, Lyman. *Preparing Missionaries for Intercultural Communication*. Pasadena: William Carey Library, 1985.

Richardson, Don. *Eternity in Their Hearts*. Ventura, CA: Regal, 1981.

Samuel, V. and Sugden, C. *Evangelism and the Poor*. Bangalore, India: Partnership in Mission, 1983.

Seamonds, David A. *Healing for Damaged Emotions*. Wheaton, IL: Victor Books, 1981.

——. *Healing of Memories*. Wheaton, IL: Victor Books, 1985.

Sider, Ronald J. *Rich Christians in an Age of Hunger*. Downers Grove, IL: InterVarsity Press, 1977.

Soltau, T. Stanley. *Facing the Field.* Grand Rapids: Baker, 1959.

Stacy, Vivienne. *Christ Supreme Over Satan.* Lahore, Pakistan: Masihi Isha'at Khana, 1986.

Stafford, Tim. *The Friendship Gap.* Downers Grove, IL: Intervarsity Press, 1984.

Stott, John R. W. *Christian Mission in the Modern World.* Downers Grove, IL: Intervarsity Press, 1975.

Tournier, Paul., ed. *Fatigue in Modern Society.* Atlanta: John Knox Press, 1965.

Troutman, Charles. *Everything You Want to Know About the Mission Field.* Downers Grove, IL: Intervarsity Press, 1976.

Tucker, Ruth. *From Jerusalem to Iryan Jaya.* Grand Rapids: Zondervan, 1983.

Tuggy, Joy. *The Missionary Wife and Her Work.* Chicago: Moody, 1966.

Van Reken, Ruth. *Letters I Never Wrote.* Oakbrook, IL: Darwill Press, 1985.

Verwer, George. *No Turning Back.* Wheaton, IL: Tyndale House, 1987.

Wagner, C. Peter. *Frontiers in Missionary Strategy.* Chicago: Moody, 1971.

——— . *On the Crest of the Wave.* Ventura, CA: Regal, 1983.

——— . *Warfare Prayer.* Ventura, CA: Regal, 1992.

Wakatama, Pius. *Independence for the Third World Church.* Downers Grove, IL: Intervarsity Press, 1976.

Ward, Ted. *Living Overseas.* New York: Free Press, 1984.

Weber, James. *Let's Quit Kidding Ourselves About Missions.* Chicago: Moody, 1979.

Williamson, Mabel. *Have We No Rights?* Chicago: Moody, 1957.

Wilson, J. Christy. *Today's Tentmakers*. Wheaton, IL: Tyndale House, 1979.

Winter, R. and Hawthorne, S., eds. *Perspectives on the World Christian Movement*. Pasadena: William Carey Library, 1981.

Yohannan, K. P. *The Coming Revolution in World Missions*. Carol Stream, IL: Creation House, 1989.

Index of Subjects